P9-EKE-121

CALGARY PUBLIC LIBRARY

SEP   2016

MY APPEAL TO THE WORLD

TIBET HOUSE AND
AMERICAN INSTITUTE OF BUDDHIST STUDIES
PUBLICATIONS

The Adamantine Songs (Vajragīti), by Saraha, trans. Lara Braitstein (2014)

Dolgyal Shugden: A History, The Dolgyal Shugden Research Society (2014)

A Drop from the Marvelous Ocean of History, Lelung Tulku Rinpoche XI; trans. Tenzin Dorjee (2013)

The Dalai Lama and the King Demon: Tracking a Triple Murder Mystery Through the Mists of Time, Raimondo Bultrini (2013)

Great Treatise on the Stages of Mantra (Sngags rim chen mo) Chapters XI–XII: (The Creation Stage), by Tsong Khapa Losang Drakpa; trans. Thomas F. Yarnall (2013)

Scholastic Sanskrit: A Handbook for Students, Gary A. Tubb and Emery R. Boose (2007, rev. 2013)

A Catalogue of the Comparative Kangyur (bka' 'gyur dpe bsdur ma), Paul G. Hackett (2012)

Maitreya's Distinguishing the Middle from the Extremes (Madhyāntavibhāga): Along with Vasubandhu's Commentary (Madhyāntavibhāga-bhāṣya), by Maitreya, Vasubandhu; trans. Mario D'Amato (2012)

Cakrasamvara Tantra (Tibetan and Sanskrit Editions), trans. and ed. David Gray (2012)

Ratnakīrti's Proof of Momentariness by Positive Correlation (Kṣaṇabhaṅgasiddhi Anvayātmikā), trans. Joel Feldman and Stephen Phillips (2011)

Consciousness, Knowledge, and Ignorance: Prakāśātman's Pañcapādikāvivaraṇa, "Elucidation of Five Parts," Section on Inquiry (Jijñāsādhikaraṇa), First Part (Prathama Varṇaka), trans. Bina Gupta (2011)

The Range of the Bodhisattva, A Mahayana Sutra (Byang Chub Sems Dpa'i Spyod Yul): The Teachings of the Nirgrantha Satyaka, trans. Lozang Jamspal (2010)

The Range of the Bodhisattva, A Mahayana Sutra (Ārya-bodhisattva-gocara): The Teachings of the Nirgrantha Satyaka, Critical Tibetan Edition, Lozang Jamspal (2010)

Brilliant Illumination of the Lamp of the Five Stages (Rim lnga rab tu gsal ba'i sgron me): Practical Instructions in the King of Tantras, The Glorious Esoteric Community, by Tsong Khapa Losang Drakpa; trans. Robert A. F. Thurman (2010)

The Kālacakra Tantra: The Chapter on Sādhanā Together with the Vimalaprabhā Commentary, trans. Vesna A. Wallace (2010)

A Shrine for Tibet: The Alice S. Kandell Collection, Marylin M. Rhie and Robert A. F. Thurman (2010)

Vanishing Tibet, Danny Conant and Catherine Steinmann, ed. Thomas F. Yarnall (2008)

Kālacakra and the Tibetan Calendar, Edward Henning (2007)

The Cakrasamvara Tantra: The Discourse of Śrī Heruka (Śrīherukābhidhāna), trans. David B. Gray (2007)

Āryadeva's Lamp That Integrates the Practices (Caryāmelāpakapradīpa): The Gradual Path of Vajrayāna Buddhism According to the Esoteric Noble Tradition, trans. Christian K. Wedemeyer (2007)

Nāgārjuna's Reason Sixty (Yuktiṣaṣṭikā): With Candrakīrti's Commentary (Yuktiṣaṣṭikāvṛtti), trans. Joseph Loizzo (2007)

A Catalogue of the Sanskrit Manuscripts at Columbia University, David Pingree (2007)

Visions of Tibet: Outer, Inner, Secret, Brian Kistler (2006)

The Kālacakratantra: The Chapter on the Individual Together with the Vimalaprabhā, trans. Vesna A. Wallace (2004)

The Universal Vehicle Discourse Literature (Mahāyānasūtrālaṁkāra): Together with Its Commentary (Bhāṣya), by Maitreyanātha/Āryāsaṅga and Vasubandhu; trans. Lozang Jamspal, ed. Robert A.F. Thurman (2004)

Epistemology of Perception: Gaṅgeśa's Tattvacintāmaṇi, Jewel of Reflection on the Truth (About Epistemology); The Perception Chapter (Pratyakṣa Khaṇḍa), trans. Stephen H. Phillips and N. S. Ramanuja Tatacarya (2004)

Wisdom and Compassion: The Sacred Art of Tibet, Marylin M. Rhie and Robert A. F. Thurman (2000)

The Tibetan Wheel of Existence, Jacqueline Dunnington, ed. Thomas F. Yarnall and Robert A. F. Thurman (2000)

Worlds of Transformation: Tibetan Art of Wisdom and Compassion, Marylin M. Rhie and Robert A. F. Thurman (1999)

Mandala: The Architecture of Enlightenment, Denise Patry Leidy and Robert A. F. Thurman (1997)

My Appeal to the World

In Quest of
Truth and Justice
on Behalf of the
Tibetan People,
1961–2011....

◄┼◆┼►

H. H. the Dalai Lama XIV

Presented by
Sofia Stril-Rever

Translated from the French by
Sebastian Houssiaux

Tibet House US • New York

Published by:

Tibet House US
22 West 15th Street
New York, NY 10011
http://www.tibethouse.us

Distributed by:

Hay House, Inc.
www.hayhouse.com

Copyright © 2015 by Tibet House US
All rights reserved.

No portion of this work may be reproduced in any form or by any means,
electronic or mechanical, including photography, recording, or by any
information storage and retrieval system or technologies
now known or later developed, without
written permission from the publisher.

Library of Congress Cataloging-in-Publication Data
Bstan-'dzin-rgya-mtsho, Dalai Lama XIV, 1935– author.
[Appel au monde. English]
My appeal to the world : in quest of truth and justice on behalf of the
Tibetan people, 1961–2011.... / Presented by Sofia Stril-Rever.
pages   cm
Includes bibliographical references and index.
ISBN 978-0-9670115-6-1 (hardback : alk. paper)
1. Tibet Autonomous Region (China)—Politics and goverment. 2. Tibet
Autonomous Region (China)—History. 3. Tibetans—Social conditions.
4. Peace-building—China—Tibet Autonomous Region. I. Title.
DS786.B75713   2015
951'.505—dc23
2014034290

BOOK DESIGN: William Meyers
COVER DESIGN: Milenda Nan Ok Lee
COVER IMAGE: © 2014 Olivier Adam

Printed in the United States of America on acid-free paper.

22 21 20 19 18 17 16 15 14 13   5 4 3 2 1

CONTENTS

PART 2. THE MIDDLE PATH, OR THE CHALLENGE OF PEACE, 1980–1990

4. Tibet-China Dialogue, 1980–1985
113

March 10, 1982

March 10, 1983

March 10, 1984

March 10, 1985

5. Tibet, Sanctuary of World Peace?
1986–1990
139

March 10, 1986

March 10, 1987

March 10, 1988

PART 3. CULTURAL GENOCIDE IN TIBET: THE HEADLONG RUSH, 1991–2010

The Dalai Lama on October 28, 1960 at his home in Dharamsala,
North India. *(AP Photo)*

FOREWORD

Robert Thurman

A S PRESIDENT OF Tibet House US, I am deeply honored to present
here to the English-speaking world His Holiness the Dalai Lama's
fifty-year-long, sustained, emergency appeal to the world community for
help, on behalf of his beloved people of Tibet, skillfully arranged and powerfully elucidated by Sofia Stril-Rever, originally published in French, and
ably translated by Sebastian Houssiaux.

The brave people of Tibet have been undergoing extreme suffering for
sixty-five years, since the invasion that began in 1949, at the hands of the
Communist—"dictatorship of the proletariat"—government of the People's Republic of China (PRC). The nation of Tibet—known to its inhabitants as "Böd Khawajen," Böd, the Land of Snows—have lived on their
three-mile-high plateau, "the roof of the world," in relative peace since the
ninth century. At that time, under the civilizing influence of Buddhism,
they lost their own thousand-year-old imperial Chögyal dynasty. From the
time of the Mongol conquest of Eurasia in the thirteenth century, a mainly
demilitarized Tibet, inspired and ruled by a succession of enlightened lama
teachers, played a major role in keeping the peace in Central Asia, among
Turkic, Mongol, Chinese, Manchu, Indian, Nepalese, Russian, and British empires. In the twentieth century, the Great Thirteenth Dalai Lama,
under somewhat ambivalent British tutelage and protection, brought Tibet

into the era of nation-states by declaring independence in 1913, creating a national anthem, flag, postal service, coinage, and a small defense force. He also tried unsuccessfully to present Tibet's credentials to the League of Nations. It is said that he passed away prematurely in 1933, in anticipation of the Communist Chinese invasion and occupation, in order to be of age to help his people when the tragic event was predicted to occur.

His successor, the Great Fourteenth Dalai Lama—the author of the half-century-long "Appeal" of the present work—faced in 1950 the invasion of the Chinese People's Liberation Army, the immediate loss of his inherited token defense force, a treaty imposed under duress for the euphemistically named "Liberation of Tibet," and a gradually intensifying occupation of his entire country. His calls for help to the Indian government, which had inherited the protector role of the British Raj; the U.S. government; and the United Nations went mostly unanswered. Both Dalai Lamas failed to find influential supporters for Tibet in the community of nations, since the major powers were all engaged in some form of campaign to win favor with either Nationalist or Communist China, both of which have falsely but continuously claimed a primordial ownership of Tibet. These false claims have been uncritically accepted by the world's nations, in spite of having absolutely no basis whatsoever in historical fact. China's greed for the treasures of Tibet—it is called Xizang ("Western Treasury") in Chinese—and the world powers' greed for the imagined treasures of China have caused the suffering that Tibet has experienced over the last sixty-five years.

Tibetans still face genocide today, not only the overt cultural genocide evident to the casual observer but also an actual genocide as a distinct people whom the Chinese leadership wishes to extirpate root and branch, both by outright extermination and by systematic assimilation, much as the Western colonial powers virtually extirpated the Native Americans, the Australian aborigines, and many other peoples. It is nothing personal, in a way; it is simply a policy imperative for successful colonialist expansion in a new world order where colonialism is supposedly out of fashion and unacceptable. The original native owners of an occupied land must be removed in one way or another, to avoid the danger of their eventually reclaiming their land and country.

In this dire situation, which resembles the plight of a number of peoples in "minority" or "unrepresented" nations around the world, His Holiness the Great Fourteenth Dalai Lama has never given up seeking the (de facto if not necessarily de jure) freedom of his people and the restoration of their livelihood and culture in their homeland, and has steadfastly refrained from calling for violent intervention, even when his own brothers—against his will—engaged in a guerrilla resistance campaign in the 1960s in association with the American CIA. Despite the agony of the loss of over a million of his compatriots, the continuing decimation of his monastic brothers and sisters, the suppression of their culture, the destruction of thousands of sacred monuments and institutions, and the devastation of large swathes of territory by clear-cutting deforestation, desertification of vast pasturelands, pollution and obstruction of rivers, and destruction of fragile high-altitude ecosystems by destructive mining practices, he still patiently repeats his calls for dialogue, for reconciliation, for reasonable negotiation with the PRC leaders. Against the emotional inclinations of his people, he still wishes sincerely to be a truly autonomous part of an actual Chinese federation under the existing Chinese constitution.

I have heard people say that he is well-intentioned but hopelessly naïve in expecting a positive response from leaders who daily show themselves to be unrelenting in their dictatorship over their own people and unswerving in their campaign of local colonialism and mercantilist expansion over the economies of the other nations of the world. "He has tried nonviolence for half a century, and what has been the result?" Such are the critical challenges from numerous quarters. But my question to them is, "How about the Afghanis, who have been fighting foreigners and each other for more than half a century? How well are they doing? And what about the Middle East? What has violence accomplished there? How secure indeed are the temporary winners of those conflicts? And what are their future prospects?"

His Holiness the Dalai Lama tends not to respond to the challenges with such specifics, but he himself has expressed his view of the world beyond Tibet and China and India and has proclaimed in no uncertain terms, in numerous public forums, that the twenty-first century cannot be a century of war and violence like the twentieth. Dialogue and reconciliation of conflict are the only options with any chance of success, according to his vision of the modern, interconnected, technologically empowered world.

The present work deeply moves me, because in it we can trace the evolution of not only a spiritual leader of global significance and impact but also, and just as importantly for the world, a truly great statesman, who dares to respond to hatred and violence with love and patience. He never gives up his conviction of the basic human goodness lodged somewhere deep down, even within people who are acting to all intents and purposes as deadly enemies. He does not lose sight of that, he reaches out to it, and he steadfastly performs his "act of truth," bearing witness to the inevitable freedom of his people and all people, even those trapped in the momentum of enmity. He is today the living icon of the *satyagraha,* the "enacting of truth," that Mahatma Gandhi, Martin Luther King Jr., and so many less well-known others, especially the heroic women of our world, so powerfully exemplify. And he must prevail, for all our sakes.

Year after year, decade after decade, he cries out the truth in these appeals to the world on behalf of his people. He speaks fifty times, each year on the day of March 10th, when his people were massacred on the streets of Lhasa and throughout Tibet, as they rallied for their freedom from the foreign occupation; they fought and died in his defense, during his miraculous escape into the larger world to tell their story, to make known the truth of Tibet and the Tibetans. Persistently and patiently he made these appeals from exile, even when the powers that be turned their backs on him and stubbornly held on to their denial of the suffering he pointed out to them.

Perhaps they couldn't understand that he was not speaking out of hatred of the Chinese aggressors, he was never demanding a war of liberation. He was only asking for courage in facing up to the truth, in speaking that truth to the power of the Chinese governing elite, requiring of them a basic human honesty and decency as the price for their gaining their people's rightful place as a great nation in the modern world. World leaders and businessmen and diplomats have become perhaps accustomed to the "truth" not being a matter of objective facts of history, not a matter of assessing the justice and injustice of the situation, but rather as coming only from the barrel of a gun, as a bargaining chip in a game of profit and power.

Even today, after so much futile waste and destruction during this last half century—Vietnam, Afghanistan, the Middle East, the "war on drugs," and the current "war on terror"—they seem not to understand that the Dalai Lama is being not naïve and idealistic but practical and realistic in his call for dialogue under any intensity of provocation.

In this context I am extremely grateful to Sofia Stril-Rever for her passionate and lucid work of bringing to our attention His Holiness the Dalai Lama's *My Appeal to the World*, both in her original French and in this English translation. It has the greatest relevance still today, and will endure in its importance as we, the world's people of the twenty-first Common Era century, finally are empowered to realize our true potential in a climate of peace, sustainability, and the spiritual priority of the real happiness that comes from truth, wisdom, justice, compassion, ethics, and love.

Robert A. F. Thurman, Ari Genyen Tenzin Chötrak
President, Tibet House US
Ganden Dekyi Ling
July 31, 2014 C.E., *Tibetan Royal Wood Horse Year, 2141*
Druk pay Tseshi, Dharma Chakra Day

ACKNOWLEDGMENTS

I could not present this book other than by associating it with all those who have accompanied my writing work, starting with the one who has guided and inspired it, His Holiness the Dalai Lama, an encounter with whom transformed my life in 1992; His Holiness Sakya Trinzin, Choegye Trinzin Rinpoche, Samdhong Rinpoche, Kirti Tsenshab Rinpoche, Jhado Rinpoche, Dagri Rinpoche, Pema Wangyal Rinpoche, Geshe Drakpa Gelek, Phakyab Rinpoche, and Dr Nida Chenagtsang, my masters of wisdom; the Venerable Palden Gyatso, Tenzin Choedrak and Ani Pachen, former prisoners of conscience who have taught me the power of forgiveness; the Venerable Lobsang Dhongak, from Kirti Monastery; Tashi Wangdi, former representative of the Dalai Lama at the European Union; Tenzin Tsepag, translator of the Dalai Lama; Tsering Woeser, poet, under house arrest in Beijing, whose writings are an inspiration; Tenzin Tsundue, poet, whose life is an exemplary struggle for freedom; Harry Wu and Wei Jingsheng, Chinese dissidents, role models for resistance; Robert Badinter, friend of the Dalai Lama, of justice and life; Elsa Rosenberger, my French Publisher at Le Seuil, Robert A. F. Thurman, editor of the American version of this book, and Sebastian Houssiaux, its translator from French into English; Senator Jean-François

ACKNOWLEDGMENTS

Humbert, President of the Tibet Senate Group, Louis de Broissia, Honorary President of the Group, and Vincent Poux, Executive Secretary; Vincent Metten, from the International Campaign for Tibet in Brussels; Matthieu Ricard, Yahne Le Toumelin, and all my friends on the Dharma path; and Choesang Dolkar and Khoa Nguyen, my loved ones on this life journey.

TRANSLATOR'S NOTE

The Dalai Lama's speeches of March 10, since the first one given in 1961 until that of 2011, are herein presented in the form of condensed extracts. Every year, the Tibetan leader gave an assessment of the situation, subsuming information already given previously. The complete reproduction of the speeches in a linear and chronological presentation thus contained a risk of repetition. We have also taken the liberty of editing them to improve the fluidity and continuity of the reading.

A choice of extracts from the original French edition is available on the website dedicated to this book, www.appelaumondedudalailama .com, and accompanied by additional information, maps, photos, and archival documents. An English compilation of all of the March 10 speeches is online on the Dalai Lama's official website: www .dalailama.com/messages/tibet/10th-march-archive. The Dalai Lama's Nobel Lecture is at www.dalailama.com/messages/acceptance-speeches/ nobel-peace-prize/nobel-lecture.

MY APPEAL TO THE WORLD

The Dalai Lama in 1967, in the garden of his exile residence, Dharamsala, North India. *(AP Photo)*

INTRODUCTION

———+———

In the Name of Humanity

THE "LIVING BUDDHA" AND THE FERVOR
OF THE INDIAN CROWDS

That morning of April 24, 1959, a dense crowd assembled at the entrance of Mussoorie,[1] along the winding road that descends toward Delhi. At the foot of the Himalayas shearing the sky, hundred-year-old oak trees still overshadow this old haven of refreshment for the British Raj officers. Wealthy Indian families had transformed their lodges and cottages into hotels, of which the Savoy, a gothic-style building, was the most illustrious, visited by an international clientele. A few steps away, a new chapter in the world's history was beginning, with a host who was far from ordinary. Sovereign of the last buddhocracy of our times, invaded by the People's Republic of China (PRC), the Dalai Lama had taken refuge in Birla House, a spacious manor made available by an industrialist who had once financed Mahatma Gandhi's campaigns.

India is a country where speculative philosophies have met for millennia, to question the human soul. Still today, it is not uncommon in India to come across women and men who have abandoned the ways of the world to devote themselves to the interior quest: ascetics "dressed in space," or *sadhus*, who inhabit naked the glacial solitudes of the mountains; wise men, or *muni*, who travel the pilgrimage routes toward the sacred sites and bless the crowds on their way; yogis teaching meditation in their ashrams; and Brahmins who perform the dawn and dusk rituals. Deeply turned toward the spiritual realities, the Indian people welcomed the 23-year-old Dalai Lama with an immense fervor, as the "living Buddha" returned among them in his native country, 2,500 years after his crossing into nirvana.

As soon as the temporal and spiritual leader of Tibet, fleeing Lhasa occupied by the Chinese army, had crossed the border of the northeastern territories[2] on March 31, 1959, the news of his presence spread from village to village. All rushed to greet him, loaded with offerings of flowers, incense, and food. In his memoirs, the religious leader evokes his emotion facing the effusions of this ocean of humanity. On several occasions, the train that was transporting him was obliged to stop because the rails had been invaded by the crowds: "Hundreds or even thousands of people rushed to welcome me with shouts of *Dalai Lama Ki Jai! Dalai Lama Zindabad!*[3] In three large cities[4] on my journey, I had to leave the train car and take part in impromptu meetings with immense crowds. The whole journey seemed like an extraordinary dream."[5]

Since his settling down in Mussoorie, the effervescence had kept growing, and the most extravagant rumors spread. The Indian journalist Mayank Chhaya remembers having heard, as a child, stories that evoked the magical power of the exiled sovereign. It was said that he had mastered perfectly the tantric rituals of the Diamond Vehicle,[6] and because the sacred mountain of the god Shiva, called Kailash, stood at the center of his kingdom, he was attributed a psychic third eye, of divine essence. A single blink of this divine eye was said to be enough to trigger a destructive force capable of instantaneously annihilating the Chinese armies. Many people awaited this moment of apocalypse. Three years later, in October 1962, when the Sino-Indian border conflict burst out, similar fantasies reappeared. Some do not hesitate to affirm that the Dalai Lama had revenge to take on Mao Zedong. He would not fail to follow the exhortations of the Indian Prime Minister, Pandit Jawaharlal Nehru, if he asked him to use his devastating wrath to destroy the People's Liberation Army (PLA).[7]

In the working-class neighborhoods of Mussoorie, itinerant sellers offered everywhere pictures of the Lama from the "roof of the world," with the background of the Potala crowned by a rainbow. Hanging up his portrait at home offered protection against harmful spirits and bad fortune. In fact, the inhabitants of the small town never missed a single opportunity to see the Dalai Lama. Two months after his arrival, he began giving a public speech every Thursday at the Savoy, seated under a hastily improvised canopy in the hotel garden. Many believed that merely having been in his presence would forever close the gates to unfortunate rebirths and give access to the supernal kingdoms of existence.

In 1959, the supreme leader of Tibet met the world, and the world met him. Yet it was a failed meeting. The journalists relegated the illegal occupation of his country by China to the background, in favor of news reports that privileged the exotic and the sensational. The fantasy was fed by religious confusion without foundation, in spite of the denials from the Dalai Lama, who always fought against this type of superstition. For example, in its edition of April 28, 1959, the French magazine *Paris-Match* exalted the "Tibetan Joan of Arc" who is said to have miraculously guided the young lama beyond the highest peaks on earth. The magazine compared him to a magician who knew how to engage the protection of good spirits. The matter of Tibet's future was, however, becoming urgent. It was a political matter, but myth and incredulity obscured its extent.

THE ENCOUNTER OF MODERN INDIA WITH THE TIBET OF ALWAYS

That day, April 24, 1959, is of singular importance. The charismatic Indian Prime Minister, who had fought for independence beside Gandhi, went to Mussoorie to officially meet the Dalai Lama. It was their first meeting since the exiled sovereign had obtained political asylum in India.

Nehru saluted the crowd that greeted him with wild applause. In the front row, children screamed at the top of their lungs *Chacha Nehru*

Zindabad![8] while throwing garlands of flowers in his way. Accompanied by Subimal Dutt, his Estate Secretary for Foreign Affairs, he stood at the back of his Dodge with curved fins, driving at a slow pace. His aide-de-camp and bodyguards were seated in a second car. Horses waited for them at the foot of the stony and steep slope that leads to Birla House. Nehru pranced ahead of his escort on a white horse, and at his arrival, the Tibetan leader appeared on the front steps accompanied by Phala, his loyal chamberlain. The aged monk, whose shoulders were starting to round, had organized his escape from Lhasa and now assisted him in important meetings. In front of journalists and photographers from across the world, grouped together behind a security rope, Nehru advanced to encounter the Dalai Lama. The Indian Prime Minister adhered to Tibetan protocol by exchanging with him the *katha*, "scarf of bliss," made of white silk, offered as a gesture of welcome. However, the Indian statesman did not bend forward to receive the traditional scarf around his neck, and the Dalai Lama simply placed it in his hands.[9]

These were the preliminaries of a meeting that would last four hours. The two men smiled and gave each other a lengthy handshake in front of the press. They each wore clothes representative of their history. While the Dalai Lama was plainly wrapped in the saffron and crimson robe of the religious of the roof of the world, Nehru wore military clothes, the *achkan,* a dark jacket with a tangerine collar, and the *churidar,* light trousers tight around his calves. He was wearing the white cap with a wide headband that the Mahatma had transformed into a rallying symbol among the pro-independence movement.[10] In the person of Nehru was modern India, democratic and liberated from British domination, which welcomed the leader of the Tibetan buddhocracy, driven out by Maoist China. Religious Tibet, cut off for centuries in its splendid isolation, had changed dramatically without transition into the twentieth century, under the communist authority.

The two men were forty-six years apart in age. There were also cultural and philosophical divergences. Nehru, in his sixties, had been toughened through his fierce struggle against colonialism. As he was educated in the United Kingdom and was well accustomed to all the subtleties of British culture and politics, he stated with humor that he was the last British statesman in India. Having been imprisoned several times, he had risked his life for his country, which he had run since 1948. As for the Dalai Lama, he had received a religious education and very advanced training in the sciences of meditation. He confessed that he knew little about the contemporary world. Under the protection of the 1,400-year-old fortification of the Potala, his improvised tutor for "secular sciences" was the Austrian explorer Heinrich Harrer, who arrived in Lhasa in 1946. For five years he fed the young Dalai Lama's curiosity in history, geography, sciences, and technical know-how. Even though Nehru and the Tibetan leader shared common values, inherited from Buddhist India, their visions of the world would prove largely incompatible. The condescension of the political man was not unknown to the religious one: "Nehru thought of me as a young person who needed to be scolded from time to time."[11] In fact, the Indian Prime Minister confided to the representative of the British crown in Delhi that he felt "great sympathy for the Tibetans," and added that "they were rather difficult people to help, for they were so ignorant of the modern world and its ways! The Dalai Lama was probably the best of them, and a charming, intelligent, and good young man by any standard, but even he was naïve and incalculable."[12]

It was inevitable that their personalities would clash. The disagreement broke out on April 24, 1959. "Until the last day, in Lhasa, I wanted to preserve peace," declared the Tibetan leader, adding that, above all, he wanted to avoid a bloodbath. His comments triggered Nehru's fury. The Dalai Lama remembers in his memoirs how under the effect of an uncontrolled rage, Nehru's lower lip started to tremble. The experienced statesman set out to give the young sovereign a lesson in politics, claiming that it would be impossible to secure the retreat of the Chinese troops through diplomacy alone. Persuasion was powerless, compared to the strike force Mao Zedong could wield. "Let us face facts," said Nehru. "One cannot bring heaven to the people in India even if I wish it. The whole world cannot bring freedom to Tibet unless the whole fabric of the Chinese state is destroyed. Only a world war, an atomic war, could perhaps make that possible."[13]

THE DALAI LAMA CENSORED BY NEHRU

Several motives of discord underlay this encounter, crucial for Tibet's future. The Dalai Lama had not ceased to accumulate grievances since his arrival in India. As soon as he had crossed the border from the Tibetan village of Tawang,[14] the religious leader had addressed a telegram to Nehru, officially asking him for political asylum. The Indian Ministry of Foreign Affairs had answered by announcing the imminent arrival of P. N. Menon, former consul general of India in Lhasa. The Dalai Lama was happy to find someone in the country refuge whom he already knew, and in a moment of great uncertainty.

Declassified documents from the CIA give us a detailed review of their first discussion.[15] After having confirmed the refugee rights of the sovereign and his entourage, Menon delivered Nehru's message. The prime minister expressed his consternation and assured his sympathy for the Dalai Lama, whom he wanted to meet very soon. He equally expressed his concern for the Tibetan people. Nevertheless, apart from this moral support, he rejected the claim of Tibetan independence and only recognized an internal self-government of the Himalayan kingdom, within the People's Republic of China. This point gave rise to the burning disapproval of the Dalai Lama. Since the invasion of his country on October 7, 1950, he had always followed Nehru's advice. All his efforts were with the goal of obtaining real autonomy for the Tibetans, within the frame of the Seventeen-Point Agreement,[16] signed in Beijing on May 23, 1951. Yet the terms of this one-sided treaty, imposed under duress and then infringed upon by the Chinese, reduced to nothing the small amount of autonomy that had been granted to the Tibetans. In March 1959, the religious leader was forced to flee, as his life was under threat. From this point forward, convinced by the Chinese dishonesty, he said he was determined to denounce the Seventeen-Point Agreement and demand that the territorial integrity of his country be reestablished. He had incidentally prepared a press release on the matter, announcing the formation of his government in exile.

Menon begged the spiritual leader to give up on this declaration, which was contrary to Nehru's explicit recommendations. But the Dalai Lama could no longer accept a simple autonomy for Tibet within the PRC. He went even further by retorting that, if his presence embarrassed the Indian government and Nehru was not willing to support his fight for independence, he preferred to renounce his political asylum. He would look for another host land. Before his decision, Menon sent a telegram to the Minister of Foreign Affairs, who answered that they would accept only a short press release, which should not mention the refutation of the Seventeen-Point Agreement or the creation of a Tibetan government in exile. He suggested a preliminary draft, deliberately written in the third person to weaken its impact. The Dalai Lama, supported by his staff members, protested, demanding that he be able to express himself in the first person. Menon was inflexible.

It has to be said, in conclusion, that after this manipulation by the Indian Ministry of Foreign Affairs and against the will of the Dalai Lama, his first press release might have been modified before being released publicly.[17] For the Tezpur[18] statement of April 18 is in the third person and does not bring up any controversial point. Laconically, it limits itself to explaining the circumstances of the Dalai Lama's escape and specifies that, contrary to Chinese allegations, the sovereign had not been kidnapped by alleged British imperialists or Indian expansionists.

On April 20, Beijing criticized "a coarse document, with lame reasoning, filled with lies and confusion." The authenticity of the text was disputed because of the third-person writing style. Furthermore, the fact that the press release had been made public by the Indian authorities meant that they were implicated.[19] In reality, the escape of the Dalai Lama embarrassed China. It proved that Tibet's peaceful liberation was a fiction, masking the invasion and the military occupation of a sovereign state. The Dalai Lama demanded a right of response to these accusations. Overstepping the Indian prohibition, he wrote a short press release confirming that he was the author of the Tezpur declarations and that he assumed all its terms. He then solicited permission to freely contact the Western chancelleries and the international media, to form a government in exile, and to obtain political asylum for an unlimited number of his compatriots. His railway transfer to Mussoorie was then organized, in preparation for an imminent meeting with Nehru.

THE ISSUES OF DISCUSSIONS BETWEEN NEHRU AND THE DALAI LAMA

The Indian statesman was not ready to modify his major aims of foreign policy or to sacrifice his relations with China for Tibet's cause. He only wanted to ensure the Himalayan kingdom a vague autonomy at an internal level, so devoid of substance that he did not associate it with any legitimacy at an international level. The Dalai Lama reminded Nehru of the historical affiliations of his country with India, the only power able to provide evidence of Tibet's sovereignty. Even though, until the Chinese invasion, Nehru had maintained diplomatic relations with Tibet, he pleaded that if the Tibetans admitted the concept of local self-government under Chinese sovereignty, the Chinese would accept the discussion, and the community of nations would be more prepared to support them. For him, the independence of Tibet was an "impractical aim."[20]

Subimal Dutt, present at this meeting, supported these remarks by resorting to international jurisprudence, a field in which he was an expert. He was also opposed to the Dalai Lama's creating a government in exile. India could not officially recognize it, as the sovereignty of the Tibetan state was not established. Always in the name of the law, the high government official also discouraged the Dalai Lama from appealing to the United Nations to denounce the Chinese repression and slaughter. Since Tibet had had only a de facto independence before becoming an autonomous region under the administration of Beijing, under the terms of the Seventeen-Point Agreement, such an appeal would not be admissible. The

Dalai Lama was therefore not entitled to address himself to the United Nations or to claim the independence of the territories taken from his authority: "Spiritual authority is one thing and his temporal authority is another," concluded the state secretary.[21]

Subimal Dutt confided later in his memoirs that this conversation had a "strange effect on Nehru. For the rest of the day he was in a reflective and reminiscent mood."[22] As for the Dalai Lama, in spite of the rebuffs, "he spoke calmly and showed no trace of bitterness against anybody despite the physical and the mental strain through which he had passed."[23] This encounter on April 24, 1959, the Tibetan leader recalled publicly half a century later, when receiving the medal of the National Foundation for Democracy in Washington in February 2010. He admitted that it had then represented a lesson in democracy and tolerance. At the age of twenty-three, he had apprehended Nehru's anger and desire to retaliate. Nonetheless, if the statesman did not approve of him and said it to him frankly, he had accepted the argument. In front of him, the Dalai Lama assumed the defense of the violated rights of his people. He gave evidence that the Chinese had first violated the integrity of the Tibetan territory, and then violated their commitment to respect its autonomy. Yet Nehru maintained his position. The diplomatic skills of Mao Zedong and of Zhou Enlai had convinced him that China had launched a peaceful modernization of "backward and feudal" Tibet. In this second half of the twentieth century, India intended to play a leading role between the West and the communist bloc. Yet the conflict with Pakistan limited its room for maneuver, which the Chinese had not failed to integrate into their strategy. Three weeks after the encounter with the Dalai Lama, on May 16, 1959, the ambassador of the PRC approached Subimal Dutt to protest the granting of asylum to the Tibetan leader. He warned the state secretary: "You cannot afford to have two fronts, right?" The threat of Chinese military support for Pakistan was taking shape.

At the Lok Sabha,[24] several parliamentarians protested against Nehru's reserved attitude on the Tibetan matter. On several occasions, the socialist leaders gathered together their sympathizers in front of the PRC consulate in Bombay. They felt cheated for having believed in the good faith of the communist party and accepted the idea that the Chinese control of Tibet was purely formal, while their own country continued to play the role of a buffer state at the heart of Asia. On April 22, one thousand demonstrators threw rotten eggs and tomatoes at a portrait of Mao Zedong, provoking rage in Beijing. The Delhi government was ordered to ban all "criminal anti-Chinese activity by the Tibetan traitors supported by the Indian expansionists."[25] Nehru replied in a more sentimental than political way. He asserted "his sympathy towards the Tibetans, based on emotion and humanitarian reasons, as well as a feeling of kinship given the longstanding religious and cultural affiliations."[26] Yet politically, the Prime Minister persisted in giving priority to the Sino-Indian brotherhood, or *Hindi Chini Bhai Bhai*, which would remain on the agenda until the incursion of the PLA into India on October 20, 1962.

The meeting on April 24, 1959, was a precursor for the next half century. Although the people had maintained a fervent reception for the Dalai Lama, the Indian administration and the great Western powers denied him the right to represent a sovereign state. For that matter, to this day, the Tibetan government in exile is not recognized by any state's official government. Deprived of sovereignty due to a legislative imbroglio in the context of the Cold War, the Dalai Lama was, in 1959, the representative of a country that held major geopolitical interest only for China. But his battle had only just begun. He was set to defend the cause of his people against all. Exiled, in refuge, without an army, he was nevertheless not without resources. "Our weapons are courage, justice and truth," he declared on March 10, 1960. This motto of his destiny and that of his people is still relevant today, for the spiritual leader has put it into practice in exemplary nonviolent combat. His moral victories have made him a prominent personality, one of the most listened-to spokesmen for the conscience of the world. From international tribunes, he teaches the crowds about courage, justice, and truth. Neither Indian censorship nor the rejection of Tibet's sovereignty, the absence of official recognition of his government, the disinterest of the large superpowers, and the American exploitation of his cause for anticommunist purposes has had a diminishing effect on his determination.

OBTAIN PEACE OR THE VICTORY OF TRUTH

From 1961, the Dalai Lama made a speech every year commemorating the insurrection of March 10, 1959, when the Lhasa people rose up, making a barrier with their bodies, to protect their sovereign, he was threatened by the army of the Chinese occupation. These short speeches are written with his own hand, and Samdhong Rinpoche, companion from the beginning and former prime minister, explains that the Dalai Lama weighs every word before reaching the final version. Historically, there are no other examples of speeches given across five decades and by the leader of a government in exile to commemorate the resistance of his people. These texts, unique in many ways, testify to a relentless fight to attempt to rectify one of the most flagrant injustices of our times.

I have sometimes found myself in Dharamsala on the morning of March 10, squeezed among the Tibetan crowds. They are serious when they mention the "night of terror," "the tyranny and oppression" of their people in agony. On these anniversary dates, I have felt the charismatic ties between the Dalai Lama and the Tibetans. Their unity around their spiritual leader is a historical fact. Before the Chinese invasion, the kingdom was divided, and some parts of the eastern provinces occasionally contested the central power of Lhasa. Nevertheless, faced with the invader, the country became united around its sovereign. Every March 10, I had the impression that his words carried afar, joining from the other side of the Himalayan barrier the people of Tibet, gathered for the defense of their liberty.

I have also perceived, on March 10, the charismatic ties between the Dalai Lama and humanity. Admittedly, he fights so that justice will be given to his people, but his cause is universal. Since the beginning of exile, he has wanted to call out to the conscience of all nations, despite Nehru's intimidation. Guide of a stateless people, in search of a lost sovereignty, he became no less immediately a spokesman for global peace. On the 10th of March every year, he addresses not only the Tibetans but also each one of us. The tone is confident. At the beginning of his international political life, he was prohibited to say "I." Yet every short speech is marked by a very present subjectivity, which clarifies his words in intimate tones. The Dalai Lama addresses himself, in person, to the person we are. His speeches testify to a moving humanity and a strong and inspiring way of seeing the world. They have often been pronounced in the context of spiritual teachings given after the lunar new year. With the same requirement of lucidity that he demonstrates in showing the subtleties of the science of meditation, he exposes the machinery of a policy that for half a century has been breaking the democratic aspirations of the Tibetan and Chinese people. In its statements, the Buddhist doctrine is put to the test against reality.

"Seek truth from facts." The Dalai Lama did not hesitate in picking up the maxim that Deng Xiaoping chose to mark his accession to supreme power in December 1978. However, at the top of the communist organization, this watchword covers a governmental reality. It adapts to disinformation and a systematic manipulation of public opinion. The dividing line is very clear. In contrast to this, the Dalai Lama and Gandhi do not adapt themselves to compromises with the truth; this is the basis of their nonviolent fight. They defend the principle that acting to the detriment of others turns against oneself, and that victory is not obtained at the cost of the adversary. The Dalai Lama has never tried to make triumph a partisan hatred. He aspires to "win" peace through a fraternal reconciliation, through the Tibetan and Chinese people becoming conscious of the ties of interdependence uniting them. With the weapons of "courage, justice and truth," his engagement is not reduced to an ethnic or identity claim. Since 1959, in fact, he has transcended the Tibet-China opposition by introducing a third plea on behalf of the "community of nations," sometimes the "world" or "humanity." In doing so, he has referred to a superior legitimacy, going beyond the reason of the states. If the slogan "Tibet for the world, the world for Tibet," was imposed in many encounters around him, it is because he dedicated his struggle to humanity.

This work presents the speeches that, year after year, have punctuated the Dalai Lama's political struggle. In the commentary that reproduces the context of the time, I wanted to report the number of paradoxes that arose around the Tibetan matter, reflecting our contradictions. Although we show our support for the universality of human rights and the right of a people to self-determination, we have, however, meanwhile accepted the need to recognize the People's Republic of China within its borders, which currently include Tibet—to the extent that it is not unusual to read in today's media that the Dalai Lama was "born in China." The highest denial of a people's identity, dispossessed of their country in contempt of the eyes of the law! In addition, we show an undeniable cowardice and refrain from mentioning the slightest topic that causes discontent in our bilateral relations with Beijing. Favoring the logic of the market, during the visit of Chinese President Hu Jintao in Paris in November 2010, the media headlined: "The Man Who Is Worth 20 billion Euros," in reference to signed contracts thanks to powerful communication. Yet the journalists might have been as justified in writing: "The Man Who Holds the World Record for Political Prisoners and Capital Executions."[27]

We indulge a dictator's policies because the fear of economic failure overrides our principles. Paradoxically, the Dalai Lama seems to believe more than we do in the force of democracy, and gives us lessons in this regard. On June 7, 2009, in front of ten thousand people, Robert Badinter[28] gave him a vibrant homage for his nonviolent fight, led with the weapons of justice and of truth against the "cultural genocide" committed by the Chinese in Tibet.[29]

Throughout the pages of this book, it is fascinating to let oneself be questioned by the Dalai Lama who, in the light of global current affairs, denounces the injustice inflicted on his people for sixty years. He asks the real questions. How has Tibet, which met the criteria of a sovereign state and signed international treaties, been torn apart and reduced to the status of a province of the People's Republic of China, even though it had proclaimed its independence in 1913? If the government of Lhasa only represented a regional administration up against the central power of Beijing, why then, in 1951, did the communist authorities demand from the Tibetans a signed agreement with all the characteristics of an international treaty? Concerning this, Tibet is unique, as the People's Republic did not need such a document in order to clarify its relations with the other autonomous regions.

Today, even in China itself, intellectuals and lawyers are questioning the policy of the Communist Party in Tibet, as it violates the Constitution and several international conventions on human rights and torture, which have been signed and ratified by Beijing. Despite these texts that engage the Chinese authorities and the global communities, how could we have let Tibet become more than ever a "hell on earth," to go back to the Dalai Lama's expression on March 10, 2009—an "open-air prison," where the worst tortures and the death penalty are applied on a daily basis? What is this impunity from which the Chinese leaders benefit, who were found guilty for genocide and crimes against humanity in a report from 1959 from the International Commission of Jurists?[30]

The twentieth century was the time of decolonization. In 1990, the United Nations inaugurated the International Decade for the Eradication of Colonialism and made a census of the countries that were still under such a regime. Although all the characteristics of colonialism were identified in Tibet, why does this country never appear on the United Nation's list of the countries to be decolonized? Is it not surprising that it also does not appear on the list of "nonautonomous territories" published in 2008, and that China is not cited under the title of "administrating power,"[31] while a report from 1991 recognizes the Tibetans as a people under colonial domination?[32]

My Appeal to the World accompanies the Dalai Lama's quest for justice and truth. In the same way that the needle of a compass always points to the magnetic north, his comments invariably align themselves to a truth, human and universal, which I wanted to be heard by all, including the Chinese, who are more and more numerous. Quoting in this book dissidents such as Harry Wu, Wang Lixiong, and Hu Jia, and also the democrat Wei Jingsheng and the Nobel Prize winner for peace in 2010, Liu Xiaobo, I aimed to inscribe my words within the dialogue initiated by the Tibetan leader with Chinese civil society for several decades. He has always rejected militant antagonism. Throughout my research, I have thus made an effort to discover from within the Chinese vision of the last half century.

The truth that the Dalai Lama defends has its martyrs. Numerous Tibetans and Chinese have sacrificed their lives to this ideal in the infamous jails of a dictatorship. From these places of grief, they cry to us. From the prisons and places of isolation, one can only call out to the world, let one's heart strongly call other hearts. In other times, other places, Elie Wiesel cried like this for justice. In Buchenwald, then age sixteen, he thought that the world did not know about the reality of the Nazi regime. He later found out that the world knew, and had let it happen.

The cries of the just whom the powerful oppress have a singular destiny. They travel in the conscience. I heard them on a day in February 2008, when Palden Gyatso[33] wrapped me in his meditation coat and held me tight against his heart. A speechless, intense, and overwhelming transmission of feelings. Before I even started to draft it, this book was embodied. The work was demanding. Without indulgence. It is painful to go through the whole of this story. The Dalai Lama regrets that it is so little known, still today. He is right. I thought I knew it after so many encounters, shared emotions, and secrets. I thought I knew it all, but I knew nothing. I first tried to keep a distance from the horror of the half century gone by. It seemed foreign. But its humanity pierced through me. In my flesh, it imprinted its bruises, its incandescences, its searing intensity. I am not unscathed. I had to agree to continue to the end of a road that oscillates between extremes: brutal hatred of those who torture, and unconditional love of the victims who forgive them. Cruelty and kindness. Horror and the sublime. Barbarism and goodness. Violence and compassion. How not to be torn apart?

During a discussion with the Dalai Lama on September 29, 2010,[34] this wound reopened when I suddenly saw his face freeze in pain. He mentioned the massacre of citizens by the People's Liberation Army at the beginning of the 1950s, in eastern Tibet. During the aerial bombings, women sheltered their babies in the hollow between their breasts. Several survived by sucking the milk from their mother's corpse. Lifeless bodies that carry on giving life. Love triumphs over death. Reasoning is challenged by such contradictions. Haunted by the cries of pain of Tibet and of the Chinese dissidents, I have experienced the temptation of desperation, anger, and hatred. I then understood why the Dalai Lama continues to advocate hope while affirming that Tibet is dying.[35] In situations of barbarism, is hope not the ultimate refuge for humanity?

I also had to learn not to judge. To overcome apparent oppositions. Accept the unacceptable. Such was the inevitable passage for me. "The executioners are also human beings," the Dalai Lama told me. "We must condemn their acts, but admit their suffering and see them as brothers and sisters."[36] By listening to him talk like this in the name of humanity, *all* of humanity, I understood that his political fight opens a path of conscience, in a world where it is so often human to be inhuman. Such is the message of the Dalai Lama, who invites us to invent new paths of humanity.

Sofia Stril-Rever
Menla Thödöl Ling, November 16, 2010

PART ONE
The Struggle for Independence

1961–1979

*In spite of the fact that we Tibetans have to oppose
Communist China, I can never bring myself to hate her
people. I believe that Tibet will be free only when its people
become strong, and hatred is no strength. It is a weakness.
I do not believe in hatred, but I do believe, as I have always
done, that one day truth and justice will triumph.*

THE DALAI LAMA

At a press conference in Calcutta, India, 1972. *(AP Photo)*

1

GENOCIDE IN TIBET:
THE INTERNATIONAL CONDEMNATION

—◆—

1961–1965

Nehru had deemed it appropriate to geographically isolate the Dalai Lama. Mussoorie, four hours away from Delhi by train, was too accessible. He therefore seized the offer of an Indian family to host the leader of the Tibetans in Dharamsala, in disused buildings where officers of the British Raj used to have their summer quarters. From Delhi, the route toward the small village of Himachal Pradesh[1] was long and hazardous. Landslides often made the winding tracks on steep mountainsides impassable, which complicated the journey. The Dalai Lama was not fooled by the stratagem, but he was not in a position to protest. In April 1960, Dharamsala became the capital of his government in exile.

The morning of March 10, 1961, a small group of Tibetans gathered early in front of his residence. Swarg Ashram, the "Heavenly Abode," was a modest bungalow, discreetly withdrawn in a dense forest of cedars.[2] The human presence was so limited in its surroundings that it was not uncommon to spot leopards, lynxes, or silver foxes jumping out of the thickets. The time of the palaces of Lhasa was over. Inside Swarg Ashram, it was impossible to hang the *thangkas*, those silk banners on which artists represent the buddhas in their pure lands, as the rain seeped through the cracked roof. In the room of the

Dalai Lama, at the foot of the bed, buckets collected the water that dripped at every rainfall. Yet these inconveniences were secondary in this period of intense struggle for independence.

The leader of the Tibetan people briskly advanced onto the porch, escorted by his Indian guards, with long rifles in hand. His interpreter and a group of lamas followed. The challenges had matured him. He had to deal with the influx of thousands of refugees, whom he tirelessly visited in the makeshift camps made available by the Indian government. Among them, he was more than ever *Kundun*, "sublime presence," who gave them the strength to rebuild shattered lives. The words he pronounced transported the listeners toward their relatives, on the other side of the Himalayan barrier.

MARCH 10, 1961[3]

Massacres Under the Guise of "Liberation"

O N THE 10TH of March, 1959, the Tibetan people reasserted their Tibetan independence after suffering almost nine years of foreign domination. Foreign rule, alas, still continues in Tibet, but I am proud to know that the spirit of our people remains uncrushed and unshaken in their resolve to fight on until independence is regained. I know that the struggle, which began a few years ago, is still being waged in Tibet against the invader and the oppressor who masquerades under the name and guise of "liberator." I can confidently assert that the civilized world is, every day, becoming more and more aware of those who, in the name of liberation, are crushing out the freedom of defenseless neighbors.

The world has been made aware of the terrible things happening in Tibet by the two illuminating reports of the International Commission of Jurists.[4] These reports have pointed out that the Chinese have ruthlessly trampled on the elementary human rights of our people, that thousands of our people have been killed for the only reason that they asserted their right to live in the manner they desired to do, following their cultural and religious heritage. The reports have further pointed out that the Chinese have been guilty of genocide by reason of their killing many Tibetans with the intent of destroying the Tibetan religion and by deporting thousands of children to China. The sympathy aroused in the world was evidenced by the fact that the United Nations in their Resolution in 1959[5] appealed for the cessation of practices depriving the Tibetan people of their fundamental human rights and their traditional autonomy. I assert that it is not autonomy but independence of which we have been deprived. Anyway, so far as the Chinese are concerned, the appeal fell on deaf ears. Things have become worse, as is clear from the steady and unceasing flow of refugees from Tibet.

Shortly the question of Tibet will come up for discussion in the plenary session of the UN Assembly. I appeal to the sponsors and to the Assembly to get the Chinese to vacate their aggression and to help restore the independence of Tibet. Any half measures will be of little avail. Our gratitude is due to the federation of Malaysia, Thailand, Ireland, and El Salvador for sponsoring our cause. May I appeal to India, our great neighbor, which has given refuge to thousands of us, also to lend its powerful support to our cause. Recently the United Nations passed a resolution on the declaration of the grant of independence to colonial possessions.[6] Our country, which was till recently independent, has been reduced to the status of a colonial possession. We cannot in any event be denied the right to self-determination.

The world has become very rightly concerned by recent murders in the Congo. I join my voice in condemning these murders, whether in the Congo or in Algeria or elsewhere. I would, however, ask the world not to forget that thousands of Tibetans have been and are being killed for the only reason that they refused to accept foreign domination. The cause of Truth and Justice must prevail, and out of this night of horror and suffering a bright day for Tibet and its people is bound to dawn.

The Internationalization of the Tibetan Cause

The Dalai Lama's battle was fought on two fronts: China and the world. He wanted to obtain independence for his country through negotiation and for this aim, solicited the community of nations. Out of fidelity to the principle of nonviolence of his Buddhist faith, he refused an armed conflict. He therefore decided to call on the UN to obtain the retreat of the troops of the People's Liberation Army (PLA). This internationalization of his struggle, initiated at the beginning of the exile, irritated Nehru, who enjoined the U.S. State Department and the British Foreign Office to limit their contacts with the Tibetan administration. History made him the arbiter, as Great Britain handled its former colony with care. Also, when the Indian prime minister availed himself of the absence of any de jure recognition of Tibet's sovereignty to avoid recognizing the Dalai Lama's government in exile, the United Kingdom and the Commonwealth countries also took this position. The United States followed this example, while still using Tibet as a spearhead in its anticommunist crusade. Nevertheless, Great Britain was the first Western power to conclude international treaties with Tibet, as with a sovereign state. On this basis, it could have advocated the independence of the Himalayan region contested by the Chinese, invoking official documents such as the report of the Viceroy of India, Lord Curzon, who, in January 1903, described the alleged Chinese sovereignty in Tibet as a "constitutional fiction" and a "political force."[7] The British decision not to support him was a first setback for the Dalai Lama.

As Nehru had prohibited him any contact with foreign embassies, he appreciated the support of Jayaprakash Narayan, an Indian parliamentarian, who led the socialists of the Lok Sabha (the lower house of the Indian parliament) into pro-Tibet lobbying and negotiations with Western diplomats. He wanted to obtain the support of their government for a plea for Tibet to the UN. His efforts were without any particular success, but a decisive step forward resulted from the initiative of Purshottam Trikamdaas, advocate of the Delhi Supreme

Court and president of the International Commission of Jurists. On June 5, 1959, Trikamdaas made public his report, *The Question of Tibet and the Rule of Law*, where he had assembled the first testimonies from refugees. In it he denounced the atrocities committed by the Chinese occupiers against civilian populations since 1950 as crimes against humanity, and characterized them as genocide, since they were performed with the objective of eliminating the Tibetans as a religious group.[8]

The Sino-Indian Relationship Advocated by Nehru

Despite the gravity of the facts, Nehru advocated "not to throw oil onto the fire of the Cold War," for fear of Chinese reprisals in Tibet.[9] He tried on several occasions to dissuade the Dalai Lama from appealing to the United Nations. According to him, no country would take the risk of going to war with China, which was supported by the Soviet bloc in the UN. He had especially used pan-Asian idealism as the major axis of his foreign policy. Since his country's declaration of independence on August 15, 1947, the Sino-Indian relationship had become his priority. In 1948, Sardar Panikkar, his ambassador in China, had anticipated the seizure of power by Mao Zedong and the annexation of Tibet, which Zhou Enlai presented as "a sacred duty for the Communists."[10] Panikkar had thus advised Nehru to recognize as soon as possible the independence of the Himalayan kingdom, for fear that its occupation would result in a common border between China and India. He recommended the status quo, in a region where Tibet played a role as a buffer state, guarantor of peace.

Nehru ignored these warnings. He considered the "Lamaist theocracy" backward, weak and powerless, incapable of resisting Chinese aggression. India could not allow itself to open a front against China to defend Tibet. The prime minister thus recommended negotiation, which had also the advantage of differentiating his politics from British expansionism. The British Raj had indeed always considered the high plateau a centerpiece in its strategies in Central Asia, with the aim of opening new trade routes, to counterbalance the growing influence of Tsarist Russia. Counter to this interventionist policy, the new Republic of India favored neutrality and dialogue with the People's Republic of China (PRC). Also, during the invasion of the PLA in October 1950, the Indian government had sent a very moderate message to the Communists, reminding them of their promise to resolve the Tibetan issue through negotiation. However, it refrained from condemning their "peaceful liberation" of Tibet. In 1953, it invited a Chinese delegation to New Delhi for a series of roundtable discussions. These talks led to a pact of nonaggression that established "The Five Principles of Peaceful Coexistence," *Panchsheel* in Hindi. In this document, which he signed in 1954 with Zhou Enlai, Nehru set up against the East–West blocs a third bloc in the world, resulting from a Sino-Indian merger. In the context of decolonization, he wanted to introduce major ethical principles in political life, so that the emancipated nations did not reproduce the abuses of the former colonial regimes. The *Panchsheel* principles of Nehru thus formed the charter of the Nonaligned Movement. Asserting mutual respect for the territorial integrity and the sovereignty of the signatories, it was widely adopted among the countries of the decolonized world.

However, Nehru never applied his doctrine to Tibet. He formally recognized Chinese sovereignty over the Himalayan kingdom, and to preserve the Sino-Indian alliance, accepted a colonial regime, directly opposing his democratic convictions, settled on the doorstep of India. Despite the opposition from the Lok Sabha, he refused to abandon his neutrality, relegating the occupation of Tibet to an internal Chinese matter.

The First Appeal to the World from the Dalai Lama

Against Nehru's recommendations, the Dalai Lama pursued his strategy. On September 9, 1959, with the support of Chanakya Sen, an Indian lawyer who advised him on legal issues, he addressed his first appeal to the world directly to the UN Secretary-General. Basing his appeal on the report of the International Commission of Jurists, he denounced an expansion of Chinese military aggression: "All of Tibet is occupied by the forces of the People's Liberation Army. Myself and my government have repeatedly called for a peaceful and friendly settlement, but it was in vain. Before the crimes against humanity and religion perpetrated against the Tibetan people, I solicit the immediate intervention of the United Nations."

The Tibetan issue was debated at the UN thanks to the support of two countries: Malaysia, destabilized by Maoist rebels, and Ireland, moved to protect a less important country on the international scene. On October 21, 1959, a resolution[11] recognized "the distinctive cultural and religious heritage of the people of Tibet and of the autonomy they have traditionally enjoyed," calling for China to respect its fundamental human rights, as well as its "distinctive cultural and religious life." This resolution represented a moral encouragement for the Dalai Lama. However, although stating major principles, the diplomatic text did not demand the retreat of the Chinese armed forces or the opening of negotiations. It was without effect. Chinese violent acts worsened. Yet the Dalai Lama had linked his political fight to the defense of human rights. Of course, in terms of jurisprudence of the states, the community of nations contested the right of Tibetans to exist as a sovereign people. But they did not have less inalienable human rights than those the religious leader intended to enforce. He therefore addressed himself to the conscience of the world in the name of humanity and justice, so that the Tibetan issue could no longer be seen as an internal Chinese matter. In response, Beijing fulminated against the "interference of the reactionary clique of foreigners."

The Tibetan issue extended to human rights was not unanimously accepted. The United Kingdom, France, and Belgium expressed reservations. They feared provoking China, and especially seeing their ex-colonies follow the Tibetan example, while Algeria and Congo fought for their independence. The vast majority of Western nations thus rejected the call from the Dalai Lama. The Afro-Asian bloc seemed more favorable and the Dalai Lama hoped to join them to his cause.

Formed by recently emancipated countries, would it not be helpful in his fight against the colonial policies of China in Tibet? Would it not support him in his appeal to the UN? In 1961, the game of alliances was opened on the international chessboard, where the Tibetan issue continued to raise paradoxes. First paradox: the Afro-Asian countries responded to Nehru's call and united around his vision, though it was based on a policy of friendship with Communist China. They thus did not mobilize themselves for Tibet. Furthermore, within the UN, Nehru stood in the way of the Dalai Lama. He pleaded for non-intervention, and the great powers listened to him promptly. For if the abuses in Tibet were crimes of genocide, how would the West condemn China on principles that it didn't apply to itself? That was the second paradox.

In that context, Chinese propaganda was gradually creeping into people's minds. Nehru and other nations following him accepted the theory of Chinese sovereignty over Tibet. The Dalai Lama had to constantly remind everyone that he was fighting not for the autonomy of his country but for its independence, sacrificed on behalf of the Sino-Indian relationship, the *Hindi Chini Bhai Bhai*, dear to Nehru. The truth of Tibet's status was held hostage by Anglo-Indian relations, and that played into the hands of China. Despite the isolation and the difficulties, the wave of decolonization in the 1960s seemed nonetheless favorable to the leader of the Tibetans. He was confident and believed in his cause, *true* in terms of history, and *just* from the perspective of human rights. How could the world, which condemned colonialism, allow, without being untrue to itself, Tibet to become a Chinese colony?

MARCH 10, 1962

EVERY DAY THAT passes, more and more refugees are fleeing to the neighboring states to escape from inhuman treatment and persecution. But the spirit of the people has not been and cannot be crushed. Those who cannot escape are there still offering their passive resistance to the unwelcome measures of the authorities in the military occupation of Tibet. The events and circumstances during the last three years which forced me and my people to be exiled from our own country have already aroused the conscience of the civilized world. The sufferings of my people were such that there was no alternative for us but to give at least some indication of their full truth. As a result of these sustained efforts, a resolution was passed in 1961 by the General Assembly of the United Nations. I consider that this resolution is a distinct advance in the furtherance of our cause. It not only expresses grave concern of the world authority at the unfortunate events which are taking place in Tibet but also sets out objectives for the future. It clearly lays down that the fundamental rights and freedoms of the Tibetan people must be restored and recognizes for the first time the right of the people of Tibet to determine and shape their destiny. I am fully conscious of the fact that the passing of the resolution cannot immediately lead to the cessation of the oppressive policies and measures of the conqueror. However, I earnestly hope and pray that the appeal of the United Nations will not go unheeded by the great Chinese people.

The government of China was a party to the declaration made at the historic meeting of Afro-Asian Powers at Bandung which reaffirmed the fundamental principles of the Charter of the United Nations and the Universal Declaration of Human Rights. The government of China has also affirmed that the subjection of peoples to alien domination and exploitation constitutes a denial of fundamental human rights, offends against the Charter of the United Nations and is an impediment to the promotion of world peace and cooperation. If these declarations have any meaning at all, the Chinese government must realize that the measures which have been adopted by its representatives in Tibet constitute total negation of these principles and that there must be an end to the policy of force and intimidation which it is pursuing in Tibet.

The only solution to the Tibetan problem is a peaceful settlement consistent with the fundamental rights and freedoms of the Tibetan people. I, therefore, take this opportunity to appeal to the Chinese people to cease immediately the persecution and oppression of my people. The resolution of the General Assembly of the United Nations also calls upon the member States to take appropriate measures for achieving the purposes of the resolution. I hope, therefore, that even if the appeal to the government of China is ignored, the leading peace-loving nations of the world will not hesitate to mediate on behalf of the poor and unfortunate people of Tibet to regain their freedom.

Nightmare, Agony, Terror

On March 10, 1962, the Tibetan leader expressed himself with the tone of a wounded man, and that of a politician in struggle. Emotions came to the surface with the evocation of the inhuman treatment that an occupying army was inflicting upon his people. Tibetans were henceforth part of the large Chinese whole, and Zhou Enlai imposed on them an enforced solidarity, on behalf of the "brotherhood which must unite all nationalities of the motherland." However, Tibet was unable to satisfy the double requirement of the occupiers: feed the PLA and compensate for the catastrophic effects in China of the "Great Leap Forward."[12] The high plateau faced famine for the first time in its history, when the Chinese authorities confiscated the grain stocks with which the monastery granaries were replete, in anticipation of harsh winters. They had to supply five thousand soldiers stationed in Lhasa and ten thousand others, spread along the strategic routes throughout Tibet. In the absence of supplies coming from China for the troops, stocks were rapidly depleted, and the population's supply was reduced to inadequate portions. It often only received barley or wheat husks or poor-quality grains, normally reserved for the livestock. To compensate for these scarce resources, entire herds of sheep and yaks were requisitioned and slaughtered, but the meat was exported to China. This resulted in a massacre: five thousand Tibetans died of hunger during the winter of 1961,[13] and all those who were able to took the route for exodus.

The persecution increased. It aimed to eradicate the monastic institution, considered the main area of resistance against the Communist ideology. Monasteries, temples, and places of worship were thoroughly looted. The Chinese administration first hurried specialized teams, the inspection committees, to establish a complete inventory of precious and semiprecious stones decorating the statues and the silverware ritual objects. The unsealed jewels were carried away with the precious metals in army trucks. Once stripped of their treasures, the monasteries were demolished with dynamite. Beams and pillars were recovered for the construction of military barracks. "The wild attacks of the invaders" that the Dalai Lama denounced were deliberately programmed, in order to take most of the wealth of religious Tibet. In hundreds of tons, sacred objects made of precious metals were thus collected. Certain items in gold or silver were sold on the international antiques market. Buddha statues made of bronze were melted on-site, close to the looted monasteries, in agricultural mechanical workshops used to build farming implements. Yet most of them were transported by railway to the foundries in Shanghai, Beijing, or Tianjin. A company located on the outskirts of the capital was at the time called "Foundry of Precious Metals," for within a few years it treated 600 tons of ritual artifacts from Tibet.

The physical destruction of the buildings was accompanied by a systematic campaign of desecration of the religious heritage. The stones engraved with *mani*[14] and sacred mantras were used for paving in toilet rooms, and the monasteries in ruins were transformed into barns, pigsties, stables, or slaughterhouses. The texts of scriptures venerated by generations of followers were characterized as "instruments of propaganda par excellence of the feudal ideology."

Orders were given to use them in the most degrading possible ways. The pages of sutras and tantras, calligraphed with gold and silver ink, become shoe soles, toilet paper, or fuel, or were mixed into manure.

A witness of this time remembers the day when, by the thousands, sheets of holy scriptures flew across the autumn sky in Lhasa before dropping down again and littering the ground: "The pages of the sacred books were more abundant on the ground than the tree leaves. They rustled as they were trampled on. I felt guilty of trampling like this on the collections of sutras. What was the alternative? The path was covered with them, I was unable not to stamp on them. It was impossible to avoid them."[15]

The Communist power not only stuck to the symbolic desacralization of the objects of faith. It attacked the monastics. No humiliation, no torture was spared. Soldiers forced monks and nuns to mate in public. They challenged them to perform miracles by throwing them into the air, so that they would demonstrate their powers of levitation, or by throwing them into fire, which they were supposed to be able to cross unharmed. Lamas were undressed in the snow and challenged to prove their capacity of generating *tumo*, the psychic heat that allows trained yogis to survive in meditation in freezing cold caves; others were buried alive or crucified. The population was called to the scene of martyrdom to educate its class consciousness. It had to shout down the religious, whom it traditionally worshipped as "living treasures." Those who refused to cover them with excrement or to admit the powerlessness of faith in turn underwent torture.

In the prisons, guards starved monks and nuns, who had to beg the Buddha for their food. They amputated limbs, challenging them to reconstitute their cut members through prayer. Thousands of nuns were forced into marriage with Chinese soldiers during public lotteries. Those who escaped were subject to sexual slavery and prostitution within the army. A great number of them committed suicide. From an estimated religious population of more than half a million, representing one-tenth of the population, more than one hundred thousand monks, nuns, reincarnated lamas, and yogis were tortured and executed. One-quarter of them defrocked under constraint.[16] These brutal and massive executions were the reason for the UN's denunciation of the genocide committed by the People's Republic of China.

The Second Appeal to the World
from the Dalai Lama

Fleeing the horror, 70,000 people sought asylum in India and in the Himalayan kingdoms of Nepal, Bhutan, and Sikkim. In order to help them, the leader of the Tibetan people relied on international generosity. At the beginning of the exile, the world for the Dalai Lama was not only the community of nations in the political and legal sense; it was also fraternal humanity. During these challenging days, he saw the reality of a world gathered together like a big family. As a human being, he entrusted his pain and his hopes to humanity. However, it was also as a politician that he addressed a message to the heads of state.

The suffering of his people was understood in terms of fundamental liberties being violated. The religious leader also claimed the right of the Tibetans to self-determination, which the UN was supposed to guarantee.[17] In 1961, the International Commission of Jurists once again denounced the crime of genocide, already established in 1959. It further declared that, from 1913 to 1950, Tibet had demonstrated its existence as an independent state de facto, according to the standards of international law. Thus, in 1951, China had illegally invaded and occupied Tibet, under the pretext of liberating it from a feudal form of serfdom. Yet, according to the Commission, such an argument, besides being fictional, could not legitimize the abuses committed. No country is justified in annexing another under the pretext of its having an outdated social system. The alleged Chinese civilizing mission had brought more suffering than benefits to the Tibetans, who were perfectly capable of conducting the necessary reforms by themselves. Thanks to the joint action of Malaysia, Ireland, Thailand, and El Salvador, who had supported the Dalai Lama's call, in December 1961, the UN General Assembly adopted a second resolution on Tibet. Signed by fifty-six member states, it called for the termination of practices depriving the Tibetan people of their fundamental human rights and their right to self-determination.

The People's Republic of China completely ignored this. It felt even less obliged since it was not a member of the UN. In his speech on March 10, 1962, the Dalai Lama expressed the hope that the UN would not limit itself to purely declaratory recommendations. He also called upon the Chinese to immediately cease their crimes against his people. Already, in 1959, in Mussoorie, at his first press conference, he expressed himself on behalf of the bonds of friendship established throughout a millenary history: "We Tibetans, secular and religious, do not maintain any enmity or hatred towards the great Chinese people." Even though he condemned the atrocities of the regime with firmness, he kept a moderate tone, referring to them with decency and restraint, without invective or recrimination—unlike the hateful stereotypes in the Chinese government's news release, which stigmatized the "clique of the reactionary and their lackeys," the "servants of imperialism," or the "dishonorable traitors" of the West. Even if the Dalai Lama expressed himself as a political leader, he also spoke as a human being, the supreme leader of a people who were suffering, to other human beings, the Chinese, also victims of the barbarity of their leaders. Even in his speech, he showed them respect. Without ever abandoning this reserve, he tried to create a space for dialogue in the hope of a peaceful and negotiated solution.

The Bandung Spirit, a Hope for Tibet?

In 1962, the Dalai Lama confronted China with its own contradictions. Its policy reproduced the worst abuses of the colonial regimes that it claimed to be fighting. The Tibetan leader referred in particular to the conference that, in April 1955, brought together the representatives of former colonies in Bandung, Indonesia. The participating nations approved unanimously the Five Principles of Peaceful Coexistence adopted by Nehru and Zhou Enlai. Very appropriately, the Dalai Lama observed that the philosophy of the *Panchsheel* reaffirmed the fundamentals of the Charter of the United Nations and of the Universal Declaration of Human Rights. How could China on one hand subscribe to this doctrine of respect for people, and on the other hand deny the Tibetans respect for their basic human rights?

The paradox was even more flagrant that Zhou Enlai, comrade in arms of Mao Zedong and Prime Minister of the PRC, was the strong man of Bandung. Nehru had given him the lead to counteract the American veto prohibiting the Chinese Communists from sitting at the United Nations. The world greeted in Bandung the vigorous emergence of China in a gathering representing half of humanity, as was happily underlined by Nehru, who intended to compete with the UN Assembly. He stood for the power of the nonaligned and the huge crowd of peoples liberated from the Western yoke. Besides, observers admired the fact that the report of international forces came out modified from Bandung, along with open rebuffs against the United States, the USSR being thrown into the shadows, and the stigmatization of the French colonial system. The Third World was born in Bandung, celebrated with lyricism by the Indonesian President Sukarno, who evoked the "aurora of the decolonized peoples." The Afro-Asian bloc, alternative to the bipolar order of global geopolitics, embarked on a mission of favoring the independence of nations that for a long time had been under foreign domination.

In 1962, as in 1961, the strategy of the Dalai Lama consisted of trying to win the emerging countries to his cause. At the moment when Mao began the sinicization of his country, numerous minorities in the world woke up, claiming their emancipation. Tibet therefore found itself in a favorable ideological context, even if India, who initiated the "Bandung Spirit," denied it through its complicit neutrality with China. However, was the wind of freedom, blowing across Asia despite everything, not a sign of hope for Tibet?

MARCH 10, 1963

China Does Not Hear the Voice of the World

THE PASSIVE RESISTANCE of our people still continues. Vivid accounts of unspeakable misery are still being brought to us in exile. The situation continues to be desperate and hopeless. But those of our unfortunate brothers and sisters who remain in Tibet must not lose their faith in the ultimate victory of truth. I believe and believe firmly that the faith and spirit of my people cannot be broken. I believe and believe firmly that evil cannot last forever. It is my earnest faith and hope that the time will come when our struggle for freedom and independence will bring about the end of this vicious and barbarous rule. This memorable day as on other days, I pray with all earnestness and fervor that the great Avalokiteshvara[18] may grant my beloved people courage and determination to enable them to continue their passive struggle against tyranny and oppression.

The inhuman measures which have been adopted by China's representatives in Tibet constitute a total negation of the principles of humanity and justice which it has more than once publicly accepted and endorsed. Unfortunately, the voice of the people of the world has fallen on deaf ears, and my earnest appeal has evoked no response. We have already seen the dire result of their insensate ambition. Without any rhyme or reason, they defied the basic principles of international justice and poured hordes into Indian territory, carrying death and destruction to the innocent people of the frontier areas of India.[19] Their naked aggression has been condemned by the whole world, including almost all the countries of the communist bloc. I hope and pray that the leaders of China have learned their lesson from this vicious adventure. I hope and pray that they have realized that they cannot with impunity defy the conscience of mankind.

We must all, with unshaken faith, continue to struggle for the not too distant day of regaining the freedom of our country. To build and prepare for the future is one of our primary responsibilities. For this purpose, I have prepared a future Constitution for Tibet which is consistent with the teachings of Lord Buddha and with the rich spiritual and temporal heritage of our history and democracy. This Constitution provides for effective participation by the people and also for securing social and economic justice. I have decided that on

Tibet regaining freedom the Constitution shall immediately come into force but later may be suitably recast on the advice of the elected representatives of the people.

Inexpressible Sufferings, Inhuman Persecutions

A night of terror covered Tibet more than ever on that 10th of March, 1963. We were far from the "roof of the world" that Alexandra David-Neel had described four decades earlier, country of laughter and celebration, of festivities and feasts. Far also from the Tibet that other Westerners had visited in the first half of the twentieth century, such as the British diplomats Charles Bell and Hugh Richardson or the Austrian mountaineer Heinrich Harrer. Its living standards, far higher than those of the rest of Asia, had impressed them. The inhabitants supported themselves thanks to a highly developed agriculture, almost in complete self-sufficiency. Famine was unknown before the Chinese invasion, for the monasteries stored provisions that were fairly distributed in case of a harsh winter. Hugh Richardson, a British diplomat who spent nine years in Lhasa, also appreciated the egalitarian nature of the Tibetan society where a relative abundance prevailed, without any significant difference between rich and poor. However, in 1963, the living conditions continued to deteriorate.

Indigence and famine were the consequences of the intervention by the authorities in production methods and in the distribution of the harvest. Barley was the base of the traditional Tibetan food. They used it to make *tsampa*, roasted barley flour of high nutritional value. This cereal, adapted to the altitude of the high plateau, resists the extreme cold. In their contempt for ancestral customs, the Chinese decided to replace it with wheat. Due to low temperatures, the plants did not make it to maturity and the harvest froze. The meager harvest was allocated in priority to the army, and an aggravated famine ensued, the administration having reserved the totality of the arable land for the cultivation of wheat. The fallow land, once used as pastures for the yak herds, had become plowed fields, so that the livestock perished due to a lack of fodder and the earth was impoverished in the absence of manure. As the Chinese had also prohibited the practice of barter, it was not possible to have exchanges of grains and meat between the farmers and nomads. Tubten Khetsun, survivor from this period, describes in his memoirs a desperate situation: the residue of grease, grain husks, and similar refuse, usually reserved for livestock, became scarce and even considered food for humans; to extend rations, people even consumed tree bark and leaves.[20] In his autobiography, *Fire Under the Snow*, the monk Palden Gyatso remembers that in Drapchi prison in Lhasa, so as not to die of hunger, the detainees boiled the leather of their boots in order to concoct a thick porridge: "Some even devoured grass, which inflated their stomach and made them very ill. I could hardly carry the weight of my own body. That's how one starts to die of hunger. When waking up one morning, I saw that two prisoners had passed away during the night. Soon, we never went to sleep without asking ourselves which one of us would still be alive in the morning."[21] However, the authorities refused to admit the real cause of the deaths. The deaths were natural; the hearts of the detainees had simply stopped beating. . . .

"The poisoned arrow drawn... by a reactionary feudal lord"

A verified and precise document describes the reality of Tibet at this time. It was written by a privileged witness, the Tenth Panchen Lama. This second-highest religious dignitary after the Dalai Lama was president of the committee in charge of installing in Tibet a Communist administration. In 1960, the Chinese had equally appointed him vice-president of the National People's Congress, and in this capacity, he visited several Tibetan areas integrated into the Chinese provinces of Qinghai, Sichuan, and Yunnan between 1960 and 1962.[22] He was supposed to report the progress brought by the socialist administration, but saw only misery, famine, and despair.

The indignation of the twenty-three-year-old lama was so strong that he didn't listen to the precautionary advice from his entourage. He took the risk of telling the truth and demanded from the Chinese leaders the application of urgent measures. In his report written in Mandarin, "The 70,000-Character Petition," he addressed himself in these terms to Zhou Enlai, then prime minister: "You must first ensure that the people will not die of hunger. Yet, in many regions of Tibet, people are starving and the mortality rate is extremely high. This is unacceptable, awful, and serious. Maybe Tibet once lived in a dark age of barbaric feudalism, but there have never been such food shortages since the spread of Buddhism. In Tibetan areas, the masses currently remain in poverty in such a way that the elderly and children starve or are weakened to the point of not being able to resist disease and death. Nothing like this has ever happened in the history of Tibet. Nobody can imagine such terrible famines, not even in a nightmare."[23]

Mao called this document "the poisoned arrow drawn on the Communist Party by a reactionary feudal lord," and refused to change his agricultural policy. In 1963, the Dalai Lama was not aware of the text, transmitted at the highest level of the hierarchy of the Party and secretly communicated abroad only in 1996. It was not until China's policy of opening up, from 1979, that American demographers had access to governmental statistics and confirmed the validity of the Panchen Lama's accusations. In his home province, Amdo, half of the population had died of hunger in 1962.

Chinese Hordes Attack India

The Dalai Lama did not cease to remind the leaders of the People's Republic of China of their duty of humanity toward the Tibetans, and also toward India, since 1962, when a border conflict broke out between China and India. This aggression contradicted the principles of peaceful coexistence, the *Panchsheel* ratified by Zhou Enlai, on whose behalf Nehru had sacrificed the Himalayan kingdom. The Beijing government had assured him of the desire to preserve the borders from then, even if, since the annexation, the Chinese occupiers could claim former Tibetan territories attached by the English to the British Raj. These soothing words were enough to lighten Indian fears. However, the border clashes multiplied after India had granted political asylum to the Dalai Lama. To defuse the conflict, Nehru had invited Zhou Enlai to New Delhi, and then gone in person to Beijing in 1960. In vain; on both sides of the McMahon[24] line, troops continued to position themselves.

On October 20, 1962, the Chinese command launched the offensive and, four days later, the volunteers of the Chinese People's Liberation Army confirmed their incursion of 20 kilometers into Indian territory. The Chinese no longer considered themselves bound by any convention, and henceforth intended to take possession of the southern fringes of Ladakh, of Zanskar, of Spiti, and of Arunachal Pradesh, which had formerly fallen under the authority of Lhasa. With Delhi refusing to surrender, the battles continued until November 22. On this date, the People's Republic proclaimed a unilateral cease-fire that endorsed its breakthrough into the Aksai Chin, in the east of Ladakh, a region it still occupies today.[25] Beijing had successfully demonstrated its strength. Nehru lost all credibility, and this defeat marked the end of his political career. His daughter, Indira Gandhi, confided later to the Dalai Lama that her father was conscious of having his good faith abused. He was the first noncommunist statesman to officially receive Zhou Enlai, whom he introduced into the Afro-Asian scene. Nehru did not recover from this betrayal and died two years later, deeply embittered.

This conflict had repercussions in Tibet, where it led to unprecedented militarization. Monasteries that had not been destroyed were converted into barracks or arsenals. In 1963, Tibet was a bridgehead of the People's Republic of China, threatening Southeast Asia: "He who holds Tibet dominates the Himalayan piedmont; he who dominates the Himalayan piedmont threatens the Indian subcontinent and he who threatens the Indian subcontinent may well have all of South Asia within his reach, and with it all of Asia."[26] The Dalai Lama did not fail to alert the community of nations, unanimous in condemnation of Chinese expansionism. Even the Soviet Union broke away and called back its experts, putting an end to its aid programs. China was isolated on the international scene.

"Democracy, our priority"

Echoing the general indignation, the Dalai Lama continued to exalt justice and truth, while preparing for the future of Tibet. For he wanted to believe in its forthcoming liberation. To guarantee the future of his country, he decided to establish democracy. Already in 1951, he was determined to introduce elected representatives into political, economic, and social life. He had therefore established a committee of fifty members, responsible to reflect on this and propose reforms of the property code. However, the Chinese invasion put an end to this initiative, the occupier imposing its own version of reforms.

From the beginning of the exile, the young sovereign wanted to ensure the democratic functioning of his government. Whereas in other nations democracy was developed under public pressure, in the Tibetan community, the impulse came from the Dalai Lama. Temporal and spiritual leader, he considered that the democratic experience was necessary in order to project himself into the future in a realistic manner, and prepare the Tibet of tomorrow. He immediately set himself to the task and, in January 1960, announced the election of an Assembly. The first twelve deputies in the history of Tibet took oath on September 2, which has since become the "Day of Democracy" in the diaspora.

In 1961, the Dalai Lama undertook to write a draft constitution for the future Tibet, based on democratic principles and proclaiming the separation of powers, the equality of citizens before the law, free elections, and political pluralism. The text, promulgated in 1963, legitimized the People's Assembly and the Kashag,[27] the two main bodies of the administration in exile. Based on the Universal Declaration of Human Rights, this draft constitution laid the foundations of a secular state. Tibetan spiritual values were reflected in a solemn commitment to the service of an ideal of nonviolence and of peace.[28] In order to achieve this democratic transition, the Dalai Lama had included a clause providing for the transfer of his executive power to a Council of Regency, in case of incompetence or if the national assembly, with a majority of two-thirds, considered it necessary for the security of the state. This provision struck the convictions of the refugees. It took all the persuasion of their supreme guide to accept the reforms limiting the traditional scope of his own powers. Tradition and an excessive reverence toward him constituted obstacles to the process he had initiated and made it necessary to teach the ideals of democracy. The Dalai Lama therefore strove to make the community in exile aware of their responsibilities and to ensure its cohesion around strong democratic institutions in these times of great uncertainty. He claimed to develop his political philosophy from the teachings of the Buddha, a current example of which he emphasized: the principles of democracy and human rights guaranteed by the Charter of the United Nations corresponded indeed, according to him, to basic Buddhist values. "Modern democracy is based on the principle that all human beings are essentially equal, that each of us has an equal right to life, liberty, and happiness. Buddhism too recognizes that human beings are entitled to dignity, that all members of the human family have an equal and inalienable right to liberty."[29]

The democratic reforms, along with a secularization of the institutions, were the best possible answer to the Chinese propaganda, which accused the spiritual leader of fomenting the restoration of Lamaist "theocracy" with the complicity of Western imperialists. In reality, within the disapora, he strove to preserve the Tibetan cultural identity while fighting for the freedom of his country. On an international level he tried to strengthen the legitimacy of his government in exile, insisting on his adherence to democratic values. In 1963, the Dalai Lama thought he had every reason to prepare for a free Tibet. The UN had twice condemned the Beijing regime, in 1959 and 1961, and the leader of the Tibetan people demanded that UN resolutions be accompanied by coercive measures. Of course, China had ignored these warnings and even engaged in hostilities that violated its commitments with a brother country. But would it for long still be able to turn a deaf ear and refuse to hear the voice of the peoples of the world—especially since it was no longer credible on the international scene? Abandoned by the USSR, its main ally, would the leadership in Beijing not be forced to finally open the bamboo curtain that was closed on Tibet?

MARCH 10, 1964

The Worst of Colonial Regimes

THE BARBAROUS ATROCITIES, even to the extent of exterminating the race and religious belief of the Tibetans, still continue, and the struggle of the people still goes on. Our way may be a hard and long one, but I believe that truth and faith must ultimately prevail. I have myself also made appeals to the Chinese government to bring an end to the inhuman persecution of the people of Tibet and to agree to a peaceful settlement of the Tibetan problem. I deeply regret to say that these appeals have failed to have the slightest effect on the attitude and policy of Communist China. On the contrary, in order to enlist the opinion of the world in their pretensions, they have come forward with a proposal against imperialism and colonialism. I therefore consider it necessary to point out that the present Chinese regime in Tibet has been described by an eminent statesman as "the worst form of colonialism."

The free nations of the world have rightly condemned the suppression of the colored people in South Africa, but the form of oppression and persecution which the Chinese invaders have adopted against the people of Tibet are a thousand times worse than the system of apartheid. Nowhere in the world, even under colonialism of the worst type, has a government ever used public torture as a political deterrent as the Chinese have and are still doing in Tibet. In this connection, I would like to emphasize the fact that the Tibetans are a distinct people, speaking a language unrelated to Chinese and possessing a religion and culture of their own. Moreover, before the Chinese invasion, the Tibetans had remained free and independent for decades. In the circumstances, I respectfully beg of all progressive and freedom-loving countries of the world not to be misled by the propaganda of the Communist government of China, and, in all fairness and justice, continue to help the unfortunate people of Tibet.

Right of the Tibetan People to Self-Determination

In 1964, the Dalai Lama's strategy lay in the postcolonial movement. The UN supported the peoples struggling for independence. International jurisprudence had validated the characteristics that define a distinct people, and the Tibetans met all of the criteria.[30] They are indeed a distinct ethnic group from the Chinese, with a specific language, religion, and culture. Their sovereignty dates back to the Declaration of Independence in 1913. The Dalai Lama drew on these objective elements to convince the community of nations of the illegality of the Chinese occupation and claim the inalienable right of the Tibetans to self-determination. His line of defense was consistent with the tenor of the UN debates. Since 1959, El Salvador had denounced the occupation of Tibet, and in 1961, New Zealand and Ireland had reminded the UN of its prohibition against subjecting a people to a foreign authority, domination, and exploitation. The Dalai Lama thus called upon China to return to the Tibetans "their fundamental human rights and freedoms including their right to self-determination."[31] His claim was legitimate, and as he prepared to launch a new appeal to the world to put pressure on Beijing, he warned the public against the manipulation of Chinese propaganda.

In flagrant contradiction with his neocolonial dictatorship in Tibet, Mao Zedong had indeed embarked on a campaign of anti-imperialist diatribes against the former colonial powers in Africa. During visits to this continent, from December 1963 to February 1964, Zhou Enlai reformulated the *Panchsheel* of Nehru by adding "Eight Principles of Economic and Technological Aid" so as to lay the foundations of cooperation with African states. The Chinese government granted them considerable financial assistance at a time when China, plunged in the doldrums, still suffered the catastrophic consequences of the "Great Leap Forward." In a coordinated investment strategy, Beijing gave more than $2 billion[32] for large-scale projects such as the construction of a 2,000-kilometer-long railway linking Zambia and Tanzania. With a great reinforcement of propaganda, these spectacular actions increased Chinese influence in Africa, and consequently, on the international stage.[33] In the United States itself, Mao Zedong tried to use the struggle of African Americans from the 1960s in his war against the "paper tigers" of the West. He called for international solidarity and called the communists of the world to free a population victimized by the "evil system of colonialism and imperialism which grew on along with the enslavement of Negroes and the trade in Negroes." The Great Helmsman predicted that "this system will surely come to its end with the thorough emancipation of the black people."[34]

In 1964, the Dalai Lama therefore engaged the peoples of the world. Encouraged by the development of international jurisprudence, he wanted to believe in the possibility of a global consensus in favor of Tibet, especially since public opinion supported the major causes of justice and humanity, denouncing, for example, a social system based on racial segregation in South Africa, condemned by a vote of UN sanctions in 1962. The International Commission of Jurists believed that Tibet suffered the worst colonization in history. Why then, under these conditions, did the community of nations not mobilize itself?

MARCH 10, 1965

The Chinese Nuclear Weapon, Threat to the World

A s the international Commission of Jurists has recently pointed out, "Neither the resolution of the General Assembly nor the call of human conscience has had any effect upon Communist Chinese policy." Yet, it is not only the flagrant breaches of human rights and fundamental freedoms from which the people of Tibet are suffering today. What is still more grave is the fact that the Chinese authorities in Tibet are virtually denying that Tibetans are human beings. Thus the Tibetans are being driven from their lands to make room for Chinese settlers. They are being systematically deprived of their only sources of livelihood. In Chinese calculations, the life of a Tibetan has no value at all. It is true that the Chinese authorities vehemently deny all this. But there exists overwhelming evidence against such denials.

In the first place, thousands of Tibetans have braved the hazards and rigors of a long and troublesome journey and sought refuge in the neighboring states. Surely, if their life had been tolerable at all, they would not have left their hearths and homes for an uncertain future. Secondly, the recent events in Tibet also clearly demonstrate that the declarations of the Chinese authorities are totally unfounded. For instance, the recent public denigration of the Panchen Lama by the Chinese authorities in Peking provides impeachable evidence of the gravity of the situation in Tibet. It should be remembered that the Panchen Lama was born in Chinese-occupied territory and was educated and trained in China. He owed his position to Chinese support. But no Tibetan worth the name could fail to protest against the oppression and tyranny of the Chinese conquerors. Hence it is that the Panchen Lama is now being branded by the Chinese authorities as a stooge of the Imperialists, for it is the invariable practice of the Chinese authorities to condemn anyone who criticizes their measures and policies in the interests of humanity as a puppet of the Imperialist powers, however mild and fair such criticism might be. This being the situation today, it is necessary for us, Tibetans and other peace-loving people alike, to rouse the conscience of the world and to lodge a strong protest against the barbarous and inhuman treatment of the Tibetans by the Chinese conquerors.

I also wish to take this opportunity to emphasize the extreme danger of the present situation. I firmly believe that as long as the Chinese remain in occupation of Tibet, there will always be a threat to the peace and progress of the countries in Asia and Southeast Asia. The gravity of the situation has been aggravated by the recent nuclear test by the government of China. So far, the nuclear powers have shown considerable restraint because they fully realize that the use of nuclear weapons would be disastrous to mankind. Would the Chinese authorities exercise a similar restraint once they are in possession of fully developed nuclear weapons? I fear such a restraint could not be reasonably expected from a government whose insensate and godless ambition knows no bounds.

Awakening the World's Conscience

Head of a martyred people and stateless political leader, the Dalai Lama had only two recourses: public opinion and the UN, the guarantor of international jurisprudence. In 1965 he alerted them to this fact: in the framework of its policy on massive colonization, the Chinese government did not treat the Tibetans as human beings. The settlement of ten million Chinese was indeed supposed to "help" them in the name of the fraternal unity of the motherland. Yet this immigration, actually organized in order to accelerate the disintegration of Tibetan society, had in the first instance resulted in an aggravated famine to the extent that the survival of Tibet was threatened.

The imprisonment of the Panchen Lama indicated the critical nature of the situation. Despite his honorary positions within the Chinese government, the "Great Master scholar"[35] remained faithful to his people. Before ten thousand followers gathered around his residence in Lhasa, he opposed the dictatorship of the Communist Party and glorified the Dalai Lama, his "refuge in this life and in future lives," concluding his speech with a call for the independence of Tibet and a vibrant "Long live the Dalai Lama!" This public support for the exiled leader, coupled with sharp criticism of Chinese policy, was intolerable for Mao and Chou. For seven weeks, from September 18 to November 4, 1964, the Panchen Lama was subject to endless sessions of criticism, before being dismissed from his official duties. Then, in 1964, he was transferred from Lhasa to Beijing, where he remained imprisoned until October 1977, in the political prison Qing Chen, of sinister reputation.

The Dalai Lama was concerned not only for Tibet but also for the world. On October 16, 1964, China experimented with its first thermonuclear bomb. Mao Zedong's statements on the atomic war were in the minds of all, when Khrushchev had promised to give him the secret of the atomic weapon in 1957: "If the worst came to the worst and half of mankind died, the other half would remain, while imperialism would be razed to the ground, and the whole world would become socialist: in a number of years there would be 2.7 billion people again and definitely more."[36] This provoking cynicism showed a total lack of respect for human life by the Great Helmsman and his entourage. The Dalai Lama therefore called for a sacred union. He bound together more than ever his cause and that of the world, for China's policy compromised not only the physical but also the moral integrity of humanity. When he alerted his contemporaries, the religious leader formulated an essential solidarity that is true in all contexts of oppression: the denial of humanity not only concerns the group that suffers the loss of its freedom but also affects humanity as a whole: "A man dies within me," says the poet,[37] "every time a man dies somewhere, assassinated by the fear and haste of other men."

On that 10th of March 1965, the Tibetan leader hoped to awaken the conscience of the world. Yet would his voice be heard? It was doubtful, since in January 1964, General de Gaulle had recognized China within its borders, which included Tibet. The French statesman had indeed denounced a liberty-killing dictatorship and marked his reservations: "There is nothing in this decision that shows the slightest approval for the political system that currently dominates China." However, by establishing official relations with Beijing, France intended to "recognize the world as it is." The general added, not without lyricism, that governments which were still reluctant would make the right decision in following France's example: "It may be, in the fast-changing world, that by multiplying the relations between peoples, we serve the cause of men. It is possible that in this way, all souls, wherever they are on earth, meet a little less late at the rendezvous that France gave to the universe, now one hundred and seventy five years ago, that of freedom, equality, and fraternity."[38]

These words indicated the ambiguity of the great powers. The masters of Beijing were the worthy inheritors of Sun Zi.[39] Mao Zedong referenced the name of this experienced strategist, who in the sixth century B.C.E. taught how to use the loopholes of the enemy and win a war without engaging in battle. The skill is to neutralize the opponent, bringing him down through his own internal contradictions. The modern mandarins knew how to play with skill, nourished by the bad faith of Western democracies that denied themselves by flattering the Maoist dictatorship. French diplomacy would soon be followed by other states that also claimed to uphold human rights, but tolerated seeing them violated. Might is right, political pragmatism trumps humanism, and the reason of state trumps conscience. Would the community of nations that recognized the occupation of Tibet also overlook its corollary, the genocide of the Tibetans? Would it overlook the condemnation of this people to a programmed death?

2

THE WORLD KNOWS AND LETS IT HAPPEN?

———+———

1966–1972

MARCH 10, 1966

Tibet Dismantled

IT IS NOW seven years since that historic day when the people of Tibet rose in spontaneous revolt against the tyranny and oppression of the Chinese Communist military occupation. The Chinese Communists, however, continue to camouflage their imperial policies behind empty slogans and impressive façades. Last year, for example, they have fully utilized the full force of their vast propaganda machinery to publicize the inauguration of Tibet as an Autonomous Region. This charade cannot, however, hide the fact that the so-called Autonomous Region of Tibet comprises only a part of Tibet and that other regions are carved into separate parts following the old imperial policy of "divide and rule." Nor can it be denied that one-third of the members of the Council of the Autonomous Region of Tibet are Chinese and the Tibetan members are recruited mostly from what the Chinese themselves call the "feudal landlord class." Moreover, all key posts are in the hands of the Chinese and the Tibetan members exist only as a rubber-stamping apparatus.

The Rhetoric of the "Peaceful Liberation"

In 1966, the Dalai Lama situated the tragedy of Tibet in the context of the Chinese law on minorities and denounced the propaganda focused on liberation and progress. The military occupation of his country was indeed accompanied by an ideological war, intended to make the historical sovereignty of the Tibetan state devoid of substance. The "peaceful liberation" of the Himalayan kingdom and its annexation to the motherland were justified by the theory of a hundred years of national humiliation, from the defeat of the Middle Kingdom in the first Opium War in 1842 until the occupation by and the surrender of Japan in 1945. This period resulted in a victim complex that exacerbated the denunciation of the imperialists, accused of all evils. Using this trauma and maintaining its memory, the Nationalists and Communists said that they were on a supreme mission, like the heavenly mandate of the emperors of the past. They fought to avenge the people for the injustices suffered, first emancipating them from the Manchu emperors, then from the colonial powers, and then from the occupying Japanese. This revolutionary rhetoric of the charismatic leaders, from Sun Yat-sen to Chiang Kai-shek and Mao Zedong, was also used to justify the military aggression against Tibet. The argument of "liberation" was just a fiction, a weapon of ideological warfare, for no foreign state had ever controlled the roof of the world. Based on the theory of a plot by the Western powers, this intentional lie was fed by the fantasy of victimization of China. It did, however, prove to be effective.

"Never forget national humiliation!" This slogan reappeared like a leitmotiv in Chinese politics, where patriotism itself was a political agenda. Based on the popular indignation, on October 1, 1949, Mao Zedong proclaimed the birth of the People's Republic in Beijing. From the terrace of Heavenly Peace, he promised to the applause of a cheering crowd, "Our nation will never again be liable to any insult or humiliation. Together we stood up against injustice." It might seem paradoxical to try to assert one's leadership through systematic reminders of setbacks and humiliations. Yet the Great Helmsman exalted the recov-

ered Chinese identity by vilifying the foreign expansionists. Furthermore, he put back on the agenda the political program of his predecessors, aiming to unite the five fellow peoples. Among them, the Chinese
(called "Han" to appear to be an ethnic group) at the center formed
the majority ethnic group, allied to the four other groups that Sun Yat-
sen[40] associated in 1912 with the foundation of the Republic of China:
Manchus, Mongols, Uighurs,[41] and Tibetans.

The concept of "five peoples gathered" glorified the unity of the
motherland, and in this vein of nationalistic claims against "capitalist and imperialist hyenas," Mao advocated the reconquest of Chinese
territory, which had been "sliced like a melon," according to a cliché
of the time. He said he wanted to reconquer, in addition to Tibet,
Hong Kong, Macao, Taiwan, the Spratly Islands in the South China
Sea, and the Diaoyutai Islands off the coast of Japan. The invasion
of Tibet was thus transformed into liberation through well-developed
propaganda: "Since the victory of the great revolution of the Chinese
people, the imperialists and their lackeys have become even more fran-
tic than mad dogs. They have hastily fabricated the so-called Tibetan
'independence' and conducted various 'anticommunist' plots to try
to cut the Tibetans off from their motherland and make them their
slaves."[42] Still today, such arguments fill the official documents distributed in the West by the embassies of the People's Republic of China.[43]

New Call to the United Nations

In his third appeal to the UN, in 1965, the Dalai Lama had stigmatized the violations of the rights and freedoms of Tibet's people and
the cruel reality of a colonization enterprise concealed behind speeches
of liberation. The resolution adopted in 1965 by the UN[44] was signed
by new countries: the Philippines, Nicaragua, Malta, and most importantly the United States and India. The new Prime Minister of the
Union of India, Lal Bahadur Shastri,[45] seemed to finally abandon
Nehru's neutrality and hear the call of the Tibetan leader. However,
this third resolution only confirmed the previous ones, without provid-

ing for any sanctions or an agenda for talks. It did not involve a legal obligation, especially as China was not yet a member of the UN.[46] The Tibetan people's right to self-determination, however, was reaffirmed, and the report of the Secretary-General of the UN denounced their submission to colonial domination. China, however, persisted in ignoring it. Was the world not speaking with a double-tongued discourse? The nations spoke their conscience through the UN resolutions while contradicting themselves through their governments, who admitted Chinese sovereignty over Tibet. How to demand from China that it give back something already given to her? How to take away with one hand something that had been handed over with the other?

Therefore, with impunity from 1965, the Chinese government took pride in having introduced reforms in Tibet that "made the earth tremble." Six years after the flight of the Dalai Lama, the political and social system of the old buddhocracy had been replaced by a Chinese-style participatory democracy, with elections at the village level and administrative groupings imposed without regard to the area's history and popular aspirations. On September 1, 1965, the territory was dismantled. Beijing announced with great reinforcement of slogans the formal establishment of the Tibet Autonomous Region of more than one million square kilometers, or one-third of historical Tibet.[47]

The concept of an autonomous region was not new. Regional autonomy is indeed a right, registered in the Chinese Constitution of September 1954, that is applied to settlements where minorities represent large groups. Article 3 recognizes the Chinese state as a unitary and multinational whole, in which "discrimination against and oppression of any nationality are prohibited. The people of all nationalities have the freedom to use and develop their own spoken and written languages, and to preserve or reform their own ways and customs." In 1965, there already existed four autonomous regions in the People's Republic of China: Inner Mongolia, formed in 1947, even before the Communist takeover; Xinjiang, populated by Uighurs, founded in 1955; and Guangxi Zhuang and Ningxia, which from 1958 regrouped the Huis. The founding of the Tibet Autonomous

Region had required more time and effort. It had been necessary to overcome significant logistical obstacles and subdue the popular resistance before being able to establish a Communist administration.

The Constitution provided that the autonomous regions would form inalienable parts of the People's Republic of China. However, the only autonomous thing about them was the name. Despite the presidency conferred upon a Tibetan,[48] decision-making power remained in the hands of the regional Chinese Communist Party, whose first secretary had always been Han. The Tibetan in the hierarchy was overruled by a Chinese official who held the real power. From September 1, 1965, China thus achieved the administrative annexation of Tibet with complete impunity. The Dalai Lama urged all those who believed in human values to support the struggle of his people for independence. Accepting the occupation of Tibet left the field open to a power that despised the rule of law, at the risk of escalation throughout Asia. However, at the time of the balance of terror, how to convince the world that the choice of commitment would be more beneficial in the long term than that of cowardice and bad faith? How could the leader of the Tibetans make the language of responsibility and nonviolence be heard? In exile, his fate was no longer only to incarnate on earth Avalokiteshvara, the buddha of compassion, like his predecessors in the Potala Palace. He also had to face political, military, and economic power relations. Yet he had neither the power of weapons nor that of money, only the power of his humanism and his compassion. He had engaged in this single combat, of which history offers no other example, since the beginning of the Chinese invasion by calling out to the conscience of the nations. So far, his strategy hadn't obtained anything concrete for Tibet on a political level. It especially highlighted a gap between the grand principles of states and their pragmatism. Would he be able to persuade them that by allowing the rights of his people to be violated, they created the causes of future conflicts of which they might one day become victims? Whereas by matching their actions to their principles and by defending the independence of Tibet, they would be laying foundations of peace for the world?

MARCH 10, 1967

A Graveyard of Civilization

THE SIXTEEN YEARS of Communist Chinese armed occupation of Tibet is one long catalogue of untold miseries and sufferings. Farmers and herdsmen are deprived of the fruits of their labor. Large groups of Tibetans on a meager ration are forced to construct military roads and fortifications for the Chinese. Countless numbers have been victims of "public trials" and "purging sessions" during which all manner of public humiliation and brutalities have been inflicted. The wealth of Tibet, accumulated over the long centuries, has been taken to China. There is a persistent campaign of "Hanization" of the Tibetan population by forcing the use of the Chinese language in place of Tibetan and by changing Tibetan names into Chinese. This is "Tibetan Autonomy" in the Chinese Communist fashion.

Recent developments indicate that the reign of terror of Han Imperialism has, if anything, increased. The persecution of Buddhism and Tibetan culture has reached a new pitch of intensity with the advent of the so-called Cultural Revolution and its by-product, the Red Guard Movement. Monasteries, temples and even private homes have been ransacked and all religious articles found have been destroyed. Among the countless items of images destroyed was one of Avalokiteshvara[49] built in the 7th century. Two severed and mutilated heads of this image have been secretly brought out of Tibet and recently exhibited in the Press in Delhi. This image has not only been deeply venerated throughout the centuries but also constitutes an important and irreplaceable historical monument of the Tibetan people, and its destruction is a great loss and a source of profound sorrow to all Tibetans. The recourse to such barbarous methods by frenzied mobs of immature school children let loose an orgy of senseless vandalism instigated by Mao Zedong under the so-called "Great Proletarian Cultural Revolution." Is this not a clear evidence of the depth to which the Chinese rulers have fallen in their efforts to wipe out all traces of Tibetan culture?

"Create something new by smashing the old": The Great Proletarian Revolution

It was an already wretched country that in 1966 the "Great Proletarian Revolution" swept through on the roof of the world. Launched by Mao to regain power within the Communist Party leadership, this ideological war took a particular turn in Tibet. The creation of the Autonomous Region in 1965 sounded the death knell of the Tibetan buddhocracy. However, the people's adherence to communism was far from secure. The mission of the Cultural Revolution in Tibet was therefore to give birth to a new socialist man, in chaos and pain. The slogan "Transplanting a new brain in place of the old" shows the degree of the change in mentality that the authorities intended in order to eradicate the "feudal" traditions. The historian Tsering Shakya, who analyzed the vocabulary of the time, highlights the appearance of the pejorative term "green brain" to describe the traditionalists who needed to be reeducated. It was convenient to brainwash them to make them "white" or progressive, capable of absorbing intellectual nourishment supplied by Chairman Mao.[50] Curiously, in contemporary Tibet, the term "green brain" has outlived this phase and is still used as an insult.[51]

The ideological content of the Cultural Revolution, in China and Tibet, can be summarized in this phrase: "Create something new by smashing the old." This slogan accompanied the fight against the "Four Olds": old ideas, old culture, old customs, old habits. It legitimized all the destructive excesses against tradition. A new credo turned ignorance into a virtue and a strength. In his "Guidelines on Education," in 1964, Mao decreed that whoever knows less can do more: "Throughout history, very few majors made their name at the imperial examinations." Obsessed by a simplistic anti-intellectual phobia, he added, "Highly educated people are often defeated by the

uneducated." The Great Helmsman, who boasted of being a "graduate of the university of the green forests," advocated new attitudes of
courage and fearlessness: "Let's not be frightened either by famous
people or by eminent scholars." He had as a model the emperor
of the second century B.C.E., Qin Shi Huangdi, who inspired him
with the slogan "Burn the books and bury the scholars!" Mao also
intended to surpass this Chinese Nero who had become his model
fighter against the reactionary forces: "What is Qin Shi Huangdi? He
only buried alive 460 scholars. We have buried alive 46,000."[52] This
verbal escalation dated back to the Antirightist Campaign, which in
the late 1950s resulted in the internment and programmed death of
thousands of intellectuals for counterrevolutionary crimes. It reappeared with the Cultural Revolution, exacerbating terrorism against
the "educated people." Knowledge assimilated into the "Four Olds"
was to be replaced by the "Four News."

In China, the young-old dichotomy covered the opposition between
modernity and tradition, socialism and capitalism. In Tibet, it had
ethnic connotations: "new" meant Chinese; "old" meant "Tibetan."
In the colorful style of the proletarian revolution, it was necessary to
eliminate the "three burdens that weigh on the shoulders of the masses
like mountains: the old feudal government, the aristocracy, and the
monasteries." Religion, opium according to Marx and poison according to Mao, was a rampart against the spread of communist ideology.
The Great Helmsman therefore decreed that the People's Republic
should annihilate the spiritual basis of Tibetan society in the people's
minds. To remove their attachment to traditional culture, the authorities embarked on campaigns of political education. The will to form
a new mentality was marked in February 1966 by the prohibition of
Monlam, the "Great Prayer Festival," which traditionally celebrated
the lunar new year. On this occasion, a huge banner was deployed on
the south façade of the Potala. One could then see from very far away
the face of a radiant Buddha, who from the top of the ancient lamasery contemplated the plains. Crowds gathered for prayers and teachings lasting several days. However, those times were over.

In August 1966, when the Red Guards arrived in Lhasa, they put up posters and distributed pamphlets in the streets, enacting new rules of behavior. Control was widespread. It became reprehensible to wear a traditional wrist rosary (*mala*) of one hundred and eight beads, counting the beads or even imperceptibly moving one's lips, as do the Tibetans who are devoted to the continuous recitation of mantras. To bow to someone or to join hands in reverence was prohibited because it qualified as reactionary. All symbols of religious Tibet were banned: prayer flags, censers, butter lamps, prayer wheels, and reliquaries. It was forbidden to own statues or images of buddhas or pictures of the Dalai Lama, the Panchen Lama, and the great spiritual masters. One no longer had the right to consult the oracles or diviners, victims of persecution. One must no longer prostrate, visit places of pilgrimage, or picnic. The long braids that men knotted with red ribbons, the traditional headdresses of women wearing turquoise, coral, and amber jewelry, and brocaded clothes were banned. Everyone had to wear short hair under a Mao cap and wear the same uniform: a long tunic, buttoned up over straight trousers.

The Red Guards were not satisfied with laying down the rules. They ensured their enforcement. In organized groups, they roamed the cities and scoured the countryside, breaking into houses. Infringements of regulations, labeled feudalism, were henceforth subject to heavy penalties. Tibetans were spied on by the neighborhood committees, basic levels of municipal administration. Their officers, ironically nicknamed "emperors" by the people, conducted a reign of terror by threatening to withhold food rations from households that did not strictly follow their instructions. Promoted to positions of responsibility, the directors of these committees behaved with even more cruelty and venality, especially as they received administrative benefits. Their victims could for that matter only see the social success of these officials hated by all, for example, the general secretary of the Shol district, at the foot of the Potala. Once the guardian of donkeys at Kundeling Monastery, he distinguished himself through excessive brutality during the Cultural Revolution. Never worried, he drove a Toyota equipped with a revolving light and, through his influence, his children opened several restaurants and teahouses in the area under his jurisdiction.[53] It was with men like him that the Maoist revolution spread.

In Lhasa, each home had to display a red flag, and in the streets, loudspeakers shouted out slogans and revolutionary songs. Books were burned in bonfires, considered exorcism. On family altars, the portrait of Mao Zedong replaced that of the Dalai Lama. *The Little Red Book*, translated into Tibetan and distributed in 300,000 copies from June 1967, replaced the volumes of scriptures. In a climate of terror, the people of Lhasa lined up every morning before the Recovery Center where they had to abandon the objects of worship transmitted from generation to generation in their families. Fear of abuse and punishment outweighed the fear caused by the feeling of desecrating a sacred heritage. In the case of a search, those who kept these "olds" might be deprived of food vouchers or worse, treated as "evil geniuses" of the old society. So as not to incur years of reeducation in a labor camp, they complied, against their conscience. "Deep within myself, I was trembling with fear," remembered Juejig, who was then thirty years old. "Whenever I knocked over buddhas, as I trampled on the sutras, as I was walking on shards of statues, I was seized with an indescribable terror."[54] The same witness told us how the Cultural Revolution conditioned the most private acts of everyday life. For example, it was obligatory to use latrines made with slabs crafted from wooden boards that originally bound the collections of sutras.[55] Those who avoided using these were heavily reprimanded.

Intense guilt feelings! Those who had to deny their conscience in this way to survive now fear karmic retribution for their actions. Perhaps they will be reincarnated as monsters? During sky burials,[56] will the vultures still want to feed themselves with their bodies, sullied by so many infamies? To minimize the profanation of their religious treasures, many chose to sink them in the "River of Happiness"[57] whose waters bathe the valley of Lhasa. Muslim Huis, who do not share Buddhist beliefs, dove at night to retrieve these objects and considerably enriched themselves by reselling them to Nepalese merchants.

A certain number of Tibetans managed to escape, taking with them the most precious relics, which they offered to the Dalai Lama. They were displayed in front of Swarg Ashram, his residence in Dharamsala, on tables covered with pure white *kathas*. The exiles came to pray before these remains of their desecrated country. The outline of a smile of a broken Buddha sometimes appeared on these fragments. They illustrated the fate of the roof of the world, the cemetery of a sacred civilization that worshiped the divine in the form of buddhas with many faces, now disfigured, and multiple arms, now dislocated.

The methods used to eradicate religious sentiment and replace it with the cult of the Party were without mercy: torture, interrogation, political education sessions, public trials or *thamzing*. In the Mao- ist language, *thamzing* was literally a "struggle session." It fought the personality of the victim to destroy their judgment and will. It was for this purpose that daily sessions of self-criticism were organized. Head down, under blows, insults, and accusations, one had to admit often imaginary mistakes publicly. Children and parents were forced to criticize each other in turn because class consciousness was sup- posed to replace family ties.

This type of humiliation led to the suicides of individuals psycho- logically destroyed after long *thamzing*. Several high school teachers from Lhasa came to this extremity, throwing themselves from heights, cutting their throats, or slashing their veins. Others chose hanging, and some preserved the memory of a father who, in desperation, pushed his family to drowning. All perished, with the exception of his youngest son, who floated on the water and was rescued.[58]

For those who survived, the slogans of the new ideology remained. One learned to meditate on the weight of Mao's sen- tences: "The earth is the Party, the blue sky is the People. Between the earth and the sky, you have no way to escape." Impossible indeed to evade Maoization. The Great Helmsman replaced the icons of the past. "I did not know whom to invoke, the Buddha or Mao," confessed a Tibetan thirty years later.[59] With great reinforcement of slogans, in a quasi-religious mobilization of public opinion, ideological brainwashing instructed people to "infinitely worship Chairman Mao, infinitely adore him, absolutely trust him, and be absolutely true to him." The Red Guards who roamed the streets of Lhasa, each wearing a scarlet armband with gold letters,[60] chanted into their megaphones the vibrant call to revolution: "To rebel, to rebel again, always rebelling, to create the red world, brand new, of the proletariat!"[61]

Against this flood of fanaticism, the language of law and common sense was powerless. A U.S. diplomat who was then stationed in Hong Kong confided that he felt submerged by the Cultural Revolution, which was like a sea monster. Invisible, immersed in deep water, "each of his shocks created unexpected and catastrophic tsunamis for the people,"[62] causing the death of 60 to 70 million people.[63] The same images came back to survivors interviewed by Tsering Woeser: "Like a waterspout or a storm, the Cultural Revolution broke out suddenly," they said unanimously.[64] All reported a wave of violence and frenzy, unstoppable, which pulled Tibet into its maelstrom, under Communist control. "Our great nation was in delirium for ten years," remembered Penba, a poet who, at the age of twenty-two, was sentenced to reeducation through labor. "It was senseless. No one dared to contradict Chairman Mao. Any criticism, however small, made you an active counterrevolutionary and made you punishable by imprisonment or death. People were no longer regarded as human beings, they were worthless. Chairman Mao was an absolute monarch."[65] And the Chinese Ye Xing-sheng,[66] who was then a high school student in Lhasa, reported that in the turmoil of the Cultural Revolution, "everyone seemed delirious, looking disorientated and distraught, with shifty eyes."[67]

Between the madness that was ravaging his country and the immobility of the community of nations, what could the Dalai Lama still hope for?

MARCH 10, 1968

Children of Free Tibet

O UR PEOPLE LIVING in exile are conscientiously striving to prepare for the day when we can return to a free Tibet. For instance, Tibetan children, whom I look upon as the future foundation of a free and independent Tibet, are being provided with the best possible opportunities of development, of growing mentally and morally into men and women, deeply rooted in their own culture, belief and living habits, as well as acquainted with modern civilization, enriched by the greatest achievements of world culture, and thus becoming sound and creative Tibetan citizens, capable of serving our nation and the whole of mankind. There are 85,000 Tibetans living in exile outside Tibet. Of these, we are in the process of rehabilitating 20,040 in agricultural settlements, animal husbandry, small-scale industries, and handicraft centers in India, Bhutan, Nepal, Sikkim, and Switzerland. This would not have been possible without the generous assistance, both financial and otherwise, in particular of the Indian government, of the governments of the respective countries, and of the voluntary agencies, and I take this opportunity to express my personal gratitude and that of my people to them. There are still 20,000 refugees who are yet to be rehabilitated and it is up to us to work hard to help expand and improve on what has been done so that we may not only contribute to the prosperity of our host country and our benefactors, but also that a truly Tibetan culture may take root and flourish outside Tibet until such time as we are able to return.

Border Crossing

On this March 10, 1968, while the Cultural Revolution destroyed each day a little more of the Tibetan identity, the Dalai Lama looked for reasons to hope. At the heart of the storm, the children were the hope. They represented the future. While the most gifted in Tibet became the targets of sinicization and were indoctrinated at a young age, on the other side of the Himalayas, the defense was being prepared. If Nehru's support had been ambiguous on a political level, from the early years of exile his solidarity was exemplary with regard to the assistance to young refugees. The young Tibetans were arriving in large numbers, with their families deprived of resources. In order to preserve their language and culture, the Indian Ministry of Education set up and funded an independent and specialized educational structure. The future of the children was a top priority in the eyes of the Dalai Lama. He used to greet them with these words: "My children, you represent the hope of a better tomorrow and you must be able to overcome the challenges that await you. You are on the threshold of life, you must become stronger every day, without wasting your precious time. You have to work hard to gain knowledge and fight with the weapons of justice and law."[68] Concurrently with the education of the youngest, from 1960, secondary colleges were grouped under the authority of an autonomous administration. The same year, the Tibetan Ministry of the Interior worked to ensure the adaptation of refugees spread across fifty camps throughout India, in collaboration with the Indian and international authorities.[69] A Ministry of Culture and Religion also undertook to reconstruct the great monasteries and their universities.

The children in exile had stood the test of crossing the Himalayas. This forced march through the highest passes in the world represented the trauma of a voyage without return, the pain of an irreversible break. The link was cut with the country of birth and family, abandoned to a terrible fate. The absence of news over the years became unbearable, to the extent that some would take the risk of returning. They suffered torture and imprisonment when discovered. When the Cultural Revolution broke out, to allow their children to escape, parents made the sacrifice of being separated and entrusted them to smugglers. Before these fleeing children stood barriers of snow and ice, rising up to 7,000 or 8,000 meters. To cross the passes, one had to advance in temperatures of −20 degrees, without the protection of suitable clothing, without food reserves, and at the risk of being brutally intercepted by Chinese patrols. Some died of cold and hunger. Others reached the end of the trip at the cost of incredible efforts. Sometimes limbs had to be amputated, having been frozen. Tenzin Tsundue,[70] poet and freedom fighter, evokes in *Crossing the Border* the suffering of a Tibetan mother:

We were sneaking silently by night and hiding by day. This is how we reached the snowy mountains. We crawled on the side of mountains like monsters, and often came upon the bodies, covered with sheets, of the passersby who had ventured into them. One night, my daughter complained of a burning foot. She fell and got up on her frozen leg. With skin torn and notched with deep cuts that were bleeding, she crouched, quivering with pain. The next day, her two legs were lost. [. . .] After a long time, in exile, I still see her, waving at me with her frozen hands. Every night I light a candle for her, and her brothers join me in prayer.[71]

The Chinese claimed to have brought happiness and prosperity to the Tibetans. If they were happy in their country, why were so many taking the risk of such a journey?

An Extorted Collaboration

Unlike the Dalai Lama, who spoke of young indoctrinated Tibetans in China who were still loyal to their homeland, the Chinese propaganda glorified those who participated with zeal in destroying their cultural heritage, in book burnings and *thamzing* sessions against their own people. For on August 19, 1966, no less than fifty thousand young people gathered in Lhasa to celebrate the Great Proletarian Cultural Revolution. The largest contingent of Red Guards was not imported from China. Tibetans came massively to swell the ranks of the two rival factions of the "revolutionary Rebels" and the "Alliance" fighting for power in Lhasa. According to the Chinese account, the political education campaigns had finally allowed Tibetans to sharpen their class consciousness. Supposedly, they had now realized that the monasteries symbolized the oppression of the clergy and the aristocracy in the old social structure of slavery. So it was with enthusiasm that they destroyed the remains of a hated feudalism. Some scenes, filmed by official agencies of the Chinese government, showed the former "serf" fanatics taking wooden printing blocks engraved with holy scriptures, statues, prayer wheels, lamps, and other objects of worship, which they broke to exorcise the past. Under their blows, the Tibetan buddhocracy was in agony.

Other sources tended to confirm the remarks of the Dalai Lama, assuring that even if indoctrinated, Tibetans remained loyal. Numerous testimonies attest to this, collected from those who, with death in the soul, had to destroy their ancestral heritage. At the risk of their lives, they saved the treasures, which they continued to cherish. To survive, Bomi Rinpoche, for example, had no other choice but to desecrate the tomb of Tsongkhapa, holy man who in the fifteenth century founded the Gelug school of the Dalai Lamas. At Ganden Monastery[72] in the Lhasa Valley, supervised by the Red Guards, he was ordered to retrieve holy relics and throw them into the fire. However, he managed to conceal the most sacred of them and recover a small urn of ashes. Joenyi, a Tibetan employed in the military administration, reported that in Shigatse, inhabitants managed to preserve the mummified bodies of the nine Panchen Lamas. They reappeared as soon as the end of the Cultural Revolution was decreed: "One brought a finger. The next one brought another piece. Thus were collected their remains. I remember going to the Ganden Monastery and there, people told me: 'The wood we used to build our homes comes from the temples. We were ordered to do so. When the policy was changed, we removed the beams and barrels of our buildings to resend them to the temples.'"[73] Many other stories show to what extent the cooperation of the Tibetans was in most cases extorted and less widespread than claimed by the Chinese.

In prisons, Tibetan executioners also committed acts that went against their conscience. Palden Gyatso recalled that in October 1990, when he was sixty years old, and after thirty years of reeducation through labor, he almost died at the hands of Paljor. The prison guard so brutally inserted an electric baton in his mouth that he lost consciousness for several hours. Yet the day of his release, Paljor came and asked him for forgiveness. When he was instructed to give him an electroshock, he had at first refused to do so. Then, under the threat of his superiors, he had executed the task with even more violence because he feared for his life. These testimonies put into perspective the message of the propaganda. Of course, the new social order brought satisfaction to the outcasts of the old Tibet. A resister from Kham described the collaborators who had deliberately joined the ranks of the Chinese: "The authorities had recruited the scum and discontented, whom they used to denounce traditional leaders, lamas, scholars, and all persons of some importance. To collaborators who did the dirty work was given the title of 'diligent' and 'model citizens,' and they were granted special privileges and rewards."[74] The collaboration of Tibetans is thus especially exalted by Chinese historians, who make the former "serfs" speak the stereotyped language of the proletarian revolution. Indeed, some had found opportunities in this time of upheaval. A Hui confided to Tsering Woeser that some of his Tibetan friends had never imagined that they would one day become homeowners or collect such high wages.[75]

Despite these material advantages, many say they are deeply troubled. At a time manipulated by propaganda and under the threat of retaliation, the population now regrets having acted against their principles. The story of a former Red Guard, called Soprano, is unusual. Endowed with a powerful voice, this singer of the revolution was responsible for loudly chanting slogans. Gutted in a shootout, she put back in place her entrails by compressing her stomach with an enameled bowl, and to the surprise of many, survived. After a career as a journalist for *Lhasa Evening*, she now enjoys retirement and is able to make numerous pilgrimages to holy places, thus easing her conscience.[76] Similarly, at the end of the Cultural Revolution, it was found that the most fervent in restoring the places of worship were those who had ransacked them. This attitude puts into perspective the words of officials who, like the present general secretary of the Communist Party in Tibet, Guo Jinlong, are ironic about Western accusations. "The Chinese did not destroy the Tibetan culture, this destruction was the work of Tibetans; height of alienation!"[77] A population forced to deny itself is made guilty of acts imposed by the occupiers. Tubten Khetsun insists throughout his memoirs on the forced participation of "class enemies" who were automatically designated by non-Tibetans to desecrate and dismantle the sacred buildings.[78] If some collaborators with the system distinguished themselves by their zeal, it is undeniable that the Cultural Revolution was managed in Tibet by the Chinese. This resulted in feelings of remorse and intense resentment, the origin of the existing ethnic tensions between Hans and Tibetans.

Before the tragedy of his people, on March 10, 1968, the Dalai Lama called the Tibetans to serve their nation and the world. How did he find the strength not only to want to improve the fate of his people but also to help humanity?

MARCH 10, 1969

Tibet Will Be Reborn from Its Ashes

WITH EACH PASSING year, the anguish and sufferings brought about by man's cruelty to man perpetrated on the roof of the world have increased in magnitude and intensity. The situation is deteriorating at an accelerating pace, spelling out all the characters of a grave crisis. Yet, the one enduring fact is that as the measures of persecution grow in intensity, so has their determination to resist the aggressor. With an unshakeable confidence and strength of mind they are all waiting for the day when their country can be free again.

In the recent period, reports have reached us that the movement of resistance has even spread to the prisons and concentration camps. Indifferent to the wrath and fury of the Chinese guards, Tibetans condemned to prison cells and labor camps keep up their morale by talking among themselves about the facts of Tibet being an independent nation and the armed violations of Tibetan sovereignty by the Chinese Communists. Those of the prisoners who have read about the history of Tibet are asked by other fellow mates to speak to them about the political history of free Tibet. Criticism and dislike of the alien rule are voiced by the prisoners and other enslaved people through songs which soon spread like a wildfire. The suffering people left in Tibet look up to us. To them we are a symbol of their hopes and aspirations in the fulfilment of the cherished goal of national freedom. The Tibetan question was raised several times in the United Nations. Constant efforts are being made to arouse the conscience of the world to the anguish and suffering to which the innocent people of Tibet are being subjected, and to make known the true facts of Tibet.

When the day comes for Tibet to be governed by its own people, it will be for the people to decide as to what form of government they will have. The system of governance by the line of the Dalai Lamas may or may not be there. It is the will of the people that will ultimately determine the future of Tibet. In particular, the opinion of the forward-looking younger generation will be an influential factor. Even if the Chinese leave nothing but ashes in our sacred land, Tibet will rise from these ashes.

The Tibetan Resistance

In 1969, in his review of the first decade of exile, the Dalai Lama expressed all the suffering of his people, subjected to a terror that never ceased to ransack their religious heritage, bastion of the Tibetan identity. There were 2,700 monasteries in the Autonomous Region in 1959. Eighty percent of them had been demolished by

1965, on the eve of the Cultural Revolution.[79] The remaining 20 percent fell in the late 1960s under the blows of 20,000 Red Guards. The Jokhang Temple,[80] holy of holies in Lhasa, was transformed into public latrines and then into a military dormitory. The Norbulingka, the summer residence of the Dalai Lamas, was first thoroughly looted and then served as an arsenal and as barracks. From over 6,000 places of worship throughout Tibet, only the Potala and 12 other buildings were spared at the express request of Zhou Enlai, who was then Prime Minister.[81]

"The cruelty of man to man" appeared in the stories of the new refugees. Attacks against individuals suspected of counterrevolutionary crimes were widespread in the Cultural Revolution. In 1969, cut hands and tongues, rape, and amputations were common practices. Recalling this period, the younger brother of the Dalai Lama, Ngari Rinpoche, reported that in the eyes of the Chinese, Tibetans were worth less than rats.[82] This comparison is terrible when one remembers that the rodents were subjected to systematic extermination campaigns. In a country where every life form was sacred, the popular religiosity respected rats as reincarnations of the vermin that once touched the Buddha's body—to the point of sacrificing for them part of their harvest. However, the Chinese did not accept wasting food in this way. They therefore organized vermin control operations. One of their techniques was to starve fifteen animals in a cage. They ended up devouring each other in battles that the population was forced to watch. The surviving rat was then released, and showing a tenfold aggression, he decimated all rodents in the neighborhood.[83]

At school, children were forced to crush insects and kill birds with a sling. Thubten Ngodup, now abbot of Nechung Monastery in India, remembers his schooling, made painful by the requirement to destroy the "four pests," flies, mosquitoes, rats, and birds, which the Chinese leaders blamed for poor harvests: "to give a political dimension to the massacre, we were told that these animals were comparable to wealthy landowners who ate the harvest, which was fiercely taken from the poor soil by the people. It was therefore necessary to eliminate them both."[84]

The children's lack of enthusiasm led to retaliation against their parents. As the young Thubten Ngodup had rescued dogs because he was terrified to see the Chinese scalding them to eat them, his father had to undergo a session of self-criticism and for a long time confess to crimes he had not committed. These measures were blows to the soul, which troubled daily life as much as the spirit, in the name of war against superstition and faith. Yet if the old beliefs were removed, the Chinese did not hesitate to replace them with new ones. The representations of Avalokiteshvara, who, through the lineage of the Dalai Lamas, rules the Land of Snows, were replaced by images of Mao Zedong. One had to worship the Great Helmsman, and each house was adorned with his portrait, surrounded by a *khata*. On the walls, instead of the sacred syllables of the mantra of compassion, people had to engrave, by way of a new mantra, the slogan *Mao Zedong wansui*, "May Mao Zedong live ten thousand years!"

Tibetan identity was also attacked in its linguistic heritage. The Tibetan language is religious by nature; the alphabet was formed from Sanskrit, in order to translate the Buddhist scriptures in the seventh century.[85] It has an honorific style reserved for dignitaries and spiritual masters. The Red Guards denounced this language as a legacy of the clergy nobility and replaced it with a new proletarian language. The names of places, evocative of ancient deities, were translated into Maoist jargon. For example, the *Norbulingka* or "Jewel Park" became *Mimang Lingka,* "People's Park," in proletarian Tibetan. To try to escape persecution, parents gave their children Communist-inspired names. This is why a generation of young Tibetans are called "Liberation," "Red Flag," or even "Modernity." At the training school for army officers, Tibetans were forced to abandon their family names, part of the Four Olds. And the new names, which were necessarily composed with "Mao" or "Lin,"[86] had a strong patriotic connotation, such as *Mao Weihua,* or "Mao Defender of China."[87]

In the new society, it was forbidden to hope: "*False hope* was one of the new formulas produced by the Communists who frequently made use of it during meetings," remembers Palden Gyatso. This meant that it was vain to hope for Tibet's independence and the return of the Dalai Lama.[88] "Forbidden hope sapped the courage to overcome the inhuman living conditions" and had to be kept as "a fire in the snow" in order to stay human, to survive. In this context, how could the Dalai Lama promise that Tibet would rise again from its ashes?

His confidence was based on the determination of the diaspora. Within the government in exile, the Ministry of Culture and Religion was one of the most important. It gave priority to the transmission of memory through specialized institutions, such as the Tibetan Institute of Performing Arts,[89] a conservatory of singing, dance, and opera whose founding had been decided by the Dalai Lama in August 1959, just months after his escape. The Tibetan identity was therefore maintained among the refugees, who played a strategic role in the struggle for the protection of their secular and religious culture of origin. They gave international exposure to their cause, encouraging the development of a vast network of associations with individuals and NGOs who supported the children's villages[90] and the monasteries re-created in exile. As for freedom, the Dalai Lama engaged his people to fight in order to recover it, without waiting for the world to give it to them. It was up to the Tibetans to lead the struggle for justice and truth. That March 10, 1969, the religious leader called his people to take their destiny in hand. Given the ineffectiveness of the UN resolutions, how would he redefine his strategy?

MARCH 10, 1970

"We fight colonialism, not communism"

THERE IS NO doubt that the Communist Chinese must have been shocked to find mounting opposition from the young Tibetans, many of whom have been educated and indoctrinated by the Chinese themselves in Tibet as well as in China. These are clear indications that all is not well in Tibet; that Tibetans are not contented and satisfied under the rule of alien power; that desperate resistance still continues; and that the spirit of liberty is still strong. It is now nineteen long years since the armed forces of Communist China trampled Tibet under their feet. The Chinese have had all the time required to educate, indoctrinate and produce a new group of Tibetan leaders who would totally support their regime—but this has not happened. They have not been able to produce a single notable, young Tibetan leader. They are still using a few ex-members of the old Tibetan government who are actually considered to be reactionaries according to the Chinese themselves. This is again a clear indication that the Tibetans, young and old, no matter how they are treated or brought up, are not prepared to yield completely to the Communist Chinese rulers. Many of these Tibetans may be ideologically Communist, but they are definitely nationalist Communists. To these Tibetans their nation comes first, ideology second. We are fighting against colonialism and not against Communism.

When the hopes and aspirations of our countrymen, struggling to survive in a vast prison camp, are so strong and persistent, so unfailing and determined, it is not sufficient to dedicate this day only to the memory of those martyrs who laid down their lives for the freedom of Tibet. We must also renew our pledge to hold high the torch of freedom and to continue the struggle so that the sacred cause for which six million Tibetans are still aspiring can be achieved. It is only fitting that we in the free countries shoulder this responsibility as our duty. The world is ever changing. International changes are occurring almost every day of the year. A change in Tibet will definitely come about. The Chinese must realize that the spirit of freedom in the Tibetans is indomitable.

We also remember and remain deeply indebted to those countries, along with India, who have supported us in the United Nations. Finally, while I call upon my people to strengthen their determination and work conscientiously for the freedom of Tibet, I also appeal to all those nations who cherish freedom to give us their firm and strong support in the just cause of Tibet's independence.

"Throwing eggs against a cliff"

In 1970, Tibet was nothing more than a vast concentration camp. Yet the Tibetans resisted, even if the Chinese claimed that this amounted to "throwing eggs against a cliff." The most violent insurrections took place in Nyemo,[91] in the prefecture of Lhasa; in Pelbar, in Chamdo prefecture;[92] and in Biru, in the prefecture of Nakchu.[93] The Nyemo region became emblematic of this resistance. In 1969, a revolt was organized, instigated by former Red Guards from the faction of the "Rebels of Lhasa." They had drawn to their cause the peasants who were infuriated because of the taxes on their crops, called "patriotic cereal" in proletarian jargon. The Rebels promised to abolish such taxes on behalf of the "struggle against reactionary capitalism." In Nyemo, they were joined by a former nun, Trinley Chodron, a medium possessed by the spirit of the goddess Ani Gongmey. This protector deity of the former Tibet once instructed Gesar of Ling, traditional epic hero of the roof of the world. In Trinley Chodron's trances, the goddess spoke through her, urging residents of Nyemo to rebuild their destroyed monasteries. While officially presenting themselves as the district of farmers and livestock farmers, the Rebels, inspired by the medium, took in secret the name "Army of Gods." The historian Tsering Shakya recognized in this movement millenarian tendencies, in reaction to the chaos of the Cultural Revolution. The double name of the supporters of Trinley Chodron denoted the persistence of Tibetan tradition in a modern ideological form. The gods of the past meddled in the issue of class struggle, at a time when the Tibetan soul was torn. A saying of this time was that "the sky fell upon the earth."

Soon the companions of Trinley Chodron also claimed to be possessed by gods of Gesar's entourage. While wearing the armband of

the Red Guards, they performed rituals of fumigation and propitia-
tion that were then banned. However, the goddess Ani Gongmey had
instructed them to restore their religious traditions. Trinley Chodron
thus galvanized her followers by asserting the invincibility of their
battalion, which would destroy the demons of the People's Liberation Army. During the first attack against a barracks in Lhasa, when
a dozen Chinese soldiers were killed, the followers of Trinley Chodron thought they saw a confirmation of their power. Intoxicated
by this success, they gathered eight hundred supporters to attack a
police squadron. This time, the army chased them while they were
trying to retreat. Trinley Chodron was captured and taken to Lhasa
with thirty-four of her comrades for a public execution. The inhabitants were summoned to the path of the trucks to be shown the convicts, who wore their names, marked with a red cross, on a sign hanging from their necks. Soldiers standing behind them were ordered
to keep their heads down and smash them against the handrail of
the truck. Under the impact of these repeated shocks, the torture
victims had broken teeth, cut tongues, and blood dripping from their
mouths. The vehicles drove slowly to impress the people gathered
along their path.

Though exemplary, the revolt of Nyemo was not isolated and is
open to differing interpretations. Some argue that the Lhasa Red
Guards of the Rebel faction tried to use the charisma of Trinley
Chodron to gather a workforce and fight the rival Alliance faction.
Others argue that the authorities provoked such mob demonstrations to better channel the leanings of separatists and then destroy
them. According to the Dalai Lama, these insurrections illustrated
the fierce resistance to the occupation. The Red Terror had not
eradicated the determination of Tibetans to fight to the death. "The
nation comes before ideology," he said, noting that he did not fight
communism, but colonialism. To enter into struggle against communism would have meant to indeed be taking a position in the context
of the Cold War, where the antagonistic blocs clashed. Yet the Dalai
Lama wished to transcend this type of partisan opposition to seek

justice on behalf of his people. However, did the UN, to whom he appealed in 1970, still assume its role of agent of international law?

The Tibetan leader now expressed himself about the past: "We recall the countries that have defended us in the United Nations." The three UN resolutions had been supported by few great powers. No coercive measures against China had helped to enforce them. There was no firm commitment in response to his calls. The world knew and allowed it.

MARCH 10, 1971

Hatred Does Not Cease by Hatred

ON THE 10TH of March 1959, the Tibetan people's uprising in Lhasa was crushed brutally by the Red Chinese Army. So why do we commemorate this day—a day of defeat when thousands of our people died and when Communist China proved her utter ruthlessness and her total disregard for human values? It may sound paradoxical of me to say that we not only dedicate this day to those who died for the cause of Tibet, but that we also celebrate this day as a day of victory. For it was on this day that the failure of the oppressive system of Red China in Tibet became apparent and that the Chinese in their frustration to cover up their deficiencies had to use violence to promulgate what is essentially the reverse of Communist ideals: colonialism. On the other hand, for us it was no defeat. Rather, it was a proof of the Tibetans' courage and their determination never to live under alien rule.

In spite of the fact that we Tibetans have to oppose Communist China, I can never bring myself to hate her people. I believe that Tibet will be free only when its people become strong, and hatred is no strength. It is a weakness. The Lord Buddha was not being religious, in the particular sense of the term, when he said that hatred does not cease by hatred. Rather he was being practical.

Any achievement attained through hatred can neither be lasting nor binding. It would only be inviting trouble sooner or later. And as for my people at this critical period, hatred would just be an extra mental burden. Moreover, how can we hate a race who do not know what they are doing? How can we hate the millions of Chinese whose very minds are regulated by their leaders? And how can we even hate those leaders who have themselves in the past been so persecuted and have suffered so much for their nation and for what they believe to be right? I do not believe in hatred, but I do believe, as I have always done, that one day truth and justice will triumph.

I believe in this even though I know that millions march in the Chinese army. She now even possesses mighty nuclear weapons that make her feared by the most powerful nations of this world. But history is unpredictable. Many great empires whose glory knew no bounds have crumbled and passed away. And although never in her history has China been so powerful as she is today, yet there is a weakness in this colossus. Her very foundations are based on fear. Like primitive beings, each person in China lives perpetually in fear of retribution for the slightest mistake from his new "God." Can such an institution hope to remain? I say no. Eventually China has to give way or break.

Increasing Repression

In 1971, new rebellions were put down in blood. The authorities, having redistributed domains of monasteries and large landowners, now requisitioned them for a forced collectivization that caused anger.[94] The People's Commune system[95] was widespread, imposing an egalitarian social structure on all rural China.

These measures, intended to promote economic recovery, were part of a Party strategy aimed at intensifying the mobilization and indoctrination of the countryside, where endemic revolts such as that of Nyemo were simmering. The People's Commune system strengthened the control of individuals through its paramilitary organization of privacy, replacing the family unit with the communal group. Kitchens and nurseries were shared; dormitories were first imposed but soon abandoned because they were very unpopular. In June 1970, the New China Agency announced the transformation of one-third of villages within the Autonomous Region into communes, and then of two-thirds in 1971. The propaganda claimed that the system had been voted in through "the voluntary participation of all, to the principle of mutual benefit."[96] The People's Communes were presented as the "Golden Bridge" leading to the liberation of "emancipated serfs." One can measure the gap between the Dalai Lama's speech, which echoes the desperate testimonies as reported by refugees, and the glowing reports of the authorities: "A million serfs," they argued, "suffered once the worst of oppressions and exploitations under the feudal system. However, resolved to follow the road of socialism, today they feel a boundless love for Chairman Mao and socialism."[97]

In reality, the introduction of the communes, directly transposed from China to Tibet, caused a severe slump. Regardless of the failure of previous experiences, the government, once again, imposed the production of wheat instead of barley, ignoring the need for fallow land and the fragile ecosystem of the high plateau. The inevitable consequences were an insufficient harvest, depleted soil, and a shortage that was worsened by the large quantities of grain collected by the state. Meager food rations were given to Tibetans, calculated and based on points earned by working, the *karma*, distributed according to the socialist sharing rule, "To each according to his work." The officials received ten per month, worker models eight, the less performing five to seven, and the livestock farmers four. Senior citizens and children under fourteen were allocated only two or three points, so that their families had to feed them on their own quota. With ten *karma*, one received only fifteen kilos of cereal and a pound of butter per month, barely enough to survive.[98] However, the Party considered this a necessary sacrifice for the making of the socialist paradise.

Fear: The Achilles Heel of China or Cunning Tactic?

To these constant lifestyle upheavals was added the impact of strained relations with the Soviet Union. The beginning of the 1970s resembled the eve of battle. On the banks of the Ussuri River, the border between China and the USSR, clashes multiplied. The tension grew along its 4,000 kilometers, where half a million Soviet soldiers faced 800,000 Chinese. A war of words raged. The People's Republic launched into going-to-war diatribes and said it was prepared for armed conflict, even if it had to last 10,000 years! In March 1969, the USSR claimed to have killed 800 PLA soldiers during a bombing. Beijing refuted this. Then, a few weeks later, the British press announced that Moscow planned to destroy the Chinese nuclear site of Lopnor.[99] In September 1969, the Soviet Prime minister, Alexei Kosygin, went to Beijing to offer a nonaggression pact. However, Mao Zedong refused to believe in the Russian promises—a smokescreen, he said, hiding an imminent nuclear attack.

In Beijing, Kosygin discovered with surprise a population constrained to build bomb shelters and radiation shelters. A city was being built under the city, with a network of tunnels, warehouses filled with food, and radio receivers. All the houses and schools were connected to this maze. The Soviet statesman said he was distressed to see students relentlessly drilling tunnels in their schoolyard. For Mao Zedong continued to mobilize the population. In Lhasa and across Tibet, he gave the same watchword: "Dig deep tunnels, made of grain stocks, the enemy will not pass!" The hill of Marpori was excavated under the Potala,[100] while national defense militias were being trained in the event of Soviet aggression. It is not impossible that this fear, orchestrated across the country, was nothing more than a gigantic manipulation. In a world haunted by the specters of Hitler and Stalin, frightened at the idea of seeing the tragedies of Nagasaki and Hiroshima repeated, the Great Helmsman was able to play on the terror of a Third World War. His strategy, which exacerbated the antagonisms of the Cold War, was in fact aimed at rapprochement with the United States, against the Soviet Union. Hence the lack of enthusiasm for the conciliatory approach of Kosygin. Yet the alliance with the United States could only darken even more the future of Tibet.

"Hatred does not cease by hatred"

The speech given on March 10, 1971, is the first one that does not mention the UN. Already in 1970, the Dalai Lama gave the impression of having turned the page. Abandoning his advocacy of the global organization that had failed to compel China to respect the rule of law, the head of the Tibetans chose to advocate human values and ethics. He came back to the fundamental teachings of the Buddha: "Hatred is never appeased by hatred in this world. It is appeased by love. This is an eternal law."[101] Or, "The Conqueror provokes hatred and the loser lies in his misery. He who renounces both, victory and defeat, is happy and peaceful."[102] Or: "The only conquest that brings happiness and peace is the conquest of one's own mind. Even if one conquers a thousand times a thousand men in battle, only he who conquers himself is the best conqueror."[103]

Is victory in the eyes of the world always a victory in terms of the wisdom that transcends the world? In relation to the tragedy of his people, the Dalai Lama expressed a truth that was not subject to the vagaries of history, because it was founded on essential truths, not on issues of power and influence. From this perspective, he celebrated as a triumph the insurrection in 1959, even if it had been carnage for the Tibetans and the Chinese army had demonstrated its overwhelming superiority. However, the use of violence marked the defeat of China, proving that its operating method on the plateau was a colonization enterprise, opposed to its founding values. In 1971, the Dalai Lama denounced the collapse, even within China, of the communist ideal. The People's Republic had a military power that made the earth tremble. However, it was the power only to destroy. Nevertheless, the system of institutionalized fear was about to deliver Mao Zedong the desired fruit: an alliance with the United States. His strategy on the chessboard of nations seemed victorious. After putting Nehru on his knees in 1962, ten years later, he was getting ready to welcome Richard Nixon in Beijing. However, a free man is not afraid to tell the world the truth. A wise man said without hatred that the Chinese army was defeated on March 10, 1959, in Lhasa, by women and men who had only their courage and determination for weapons.

On the political level, the success of Mao assisted by Zhou Enlai was undeniable. But on the human level? The moral level? The victory of the powerful was relative. Nobody knew this better than the Dalai Lama. Stateless, exiled, but if victory was on his side? And if, as Gandhi once said, "one man can defeat an empire"?

MARCH 10, 1972

China at the United Nations

TRUTH AND JUSTICE can never be hidden. In fact they must ultimately prevail and triumph if justice at all exists in this world— and I believe that justice does exist. One recent, encouraging example is the birth of a new nation in Asia—the emergence of Bangladesh. This indeed was a triumph of justice and a triumph of a people's determination. It is another historic landmark in man's never-ending pursuit of the freedom to live as they wish. Although the freedom of Tibet cannot be predicted, changes are bound to come.

Even in the international scene great changes, unexpected a decade ago, have occurred. China, too, is changing and she is compelled to do so. She must break away from her isolation and outmoded ideas, for today, she is a responsible member of the United

Nations and thus capable of doing much for the peace of mankind. We hope that is what she will do, and we also hope that she will one day recognize the true status of Tibet and the indomitable spirit of our people.

The Week That Changed the World

This speech given on March 10 is one of the shortest. The unpredictable evolution of the world that the Dalai Lama spoke of in 1972 fit into the context of the Sino-American engagement. It was a general surprise, for the negotiations between Henry Kissinger and Zhou Enlai were conducted in the utmost secrecy. Declassified CIA archives show that after years of hostility between the two countries, President Nixon, shortly after his inauguration in 1968, reflected on the opportunity to reestablish ties with Beijing: "We must not forget China and take every opportunity to engage in a dialogue with it, as with the USSR."[104] He wanted to take advantage of the latent conflict between the two communist giants to soften the Soviet position.[105]

Through the Pakistani government, an ally of China against India, Henry Kissinger thus suddenly met Zhou Enlai in July 1971. The latter agreed to normalize their relationship under the express condition that the United States abandon their policy of "Two Chinas." Also, during these preliminary talks, about a quarter of the discussion concerned Taiwan. Without explicitly admitting that the island was part of the People's Republic, Kissinger did not recognize its independence either. Zhou Enlai obtained the United States' commitment to withdraw their troops, stationed there since the end of the Vietnam War. On the Chinese side, this rapprochement was also wanted in order to avoid the risk of an open conflict with the USSR; Beijing could now play the card of the United States.[106] "It was not the first time, nor the last, that the clumsy foreign policy of the Kremlin hastened what was feared the most in Moscow," observed Kissinger.[107] He had, for his part, opted for a triangular diplomacy of tacit alliance with the Chinese and of Soviet disinformation. From

1971, he provided his new partners with the latest computers and sensitive information on the movement of Russian troops, transmitted by spy satellites.

The Sino-U.S. contacts led to the visit of President Nixon to Beijing in 1972, but, from October 1971, the People's Republic of China made its entry into the United Nations. It stood in for Taiwan, supported by the United States, England, and France, and also by the Third World countries who had won their independence with the support of Mao Zedong. Since then, the communist state has sat in all UN bodies that had been visited by the ambassadors of Chiang Kaishek since the founding of the UN in 1945, and has become one of the five members of the Security Council.

Although, unlike Taiwan, Tibet's case was not discussed at the Sino-American negotiating table in 1971, the agreements legitimized de facto the Chinese occupation. Yet the Dalai Lama chose an optimistic interpretation. Forced to break its isolation, China would have to adopt the attitude of a responsible nation and could no longer with impunity throw untruths at the face of the world. As a member of the Security Council, it became one of the guarantors of peace for mankind. While firmly denouncing the abuses of the regime, the head of the Tibetans therefore supported this Chinese opening abroad. Leader of a nation gradually fading from the world map, despite the failure of his attempts to gain recognition of the rights denied to his people, he persisted in declaring his faith in the justice of men. Current events gave him the opportunity with the creation of Bangladesh, which illustrated the sometimes unpredictable game of alliances.

Supported by India and the USSR, the East Bengalis had revolted in December 1971 due to the political and economic discrimination of the Karachi government. They were a common front against the military dictatorship of West Pakistan supported by China and the United States. Fighting gave them the victory, followed by the proclamation of the sovereign state of Bangladesh in January 1972. In his talks with Kissinger, Zhou Enlai insisted on fears in China of this common front of India and the USSR that led to the dismantling of Pakistan. However, the Dalai Lama had a different interpretation of these events, which in his opinion represented "the triumph of justice and the determination of a people" fighting against a military junta. In the accession to independence of the Bengalis, he wanted to see a hope for Tibet. The inevitable evolution of the world toward freedom was confirmed once again. China could not counter it, even while it was becoming partners with the United States and an influential member of the UN. In Bangladesh, the voice of justice had pushed back dictatorship. Why would such an evolution not be foreseeable in Tibet?

3

THE WORLD'S CHANGING WINDS

———+———

1973–1979

MARCH 10, 1973

The Independence and Historical Grandeur of Tibet

THIS YEAR MARKS the 2,100th anniversary of the founding of the Tibetan Royal Dynasty by Nyatri Tsenpo. The year also marks the fourteenth anniversary of the Tibetan people's struggle against foreign domination. On this occasion when we remember and commemorate these two glorious anniversaries, I send my greetings to all Tibetans, both in and outside Tibet. I would like to deal briefly with the history of these 2,100 years. The first dynasties saw a succession of twenty-eight kings, in whose reigns Tibet made steady progress in handicrafts and education. In the reign of the twenty-eighth king, Lha Thothori Nyentsen,[108] Buddhism was first planted in Tibet. Then, during the reign of the Three Great Religious Kings,[109] Tibet emerged as a powerful state. Many Buddhist scriptural texts were translated into Tibetan, while religious and civil codes were promulgated and Tibetan social behavior was made decent and civilized. Politically, land was equally distributed to people and in summer and winter people's representatives held regular meetings. All this made the Tibetan social structure then prevailing democratic and modern. The fame of Tibet spread throughout Asia.

However, the forty-first king, Langdarma, suppressed the Buddhist faith, and in his time Buddhism received a severe setback. The two sons of Langdarma made rival claims to the throne of Tibet and western Tibet was divided between them. Consequently, the whole of Tibet was reduced to many petty principalities and the former strength of Tibet, both military and political, greatly decreased. The frontier provinces seceded from Tibet, and religion and policies suffered degeneration and decline.

Subsequently, since the time of Chogyal Phagpa of Sakya, the successive dynastic reigns of Phagmodrupa, Rinpungpa, and Tsangpa made the strength of Tibetan politics firmer and the hold of religion deeper, unlike during the period of Tibetan disintegration. However, the standard they attained never reached that of the one which prevailed during the reigns of the Three Great Religious Kings of Tibet. Moreover, Tibet was internally continually rocked by disunity. In the reign of the Fifth Dalai Lama, the political influence of the Tibetan government grew and the Tibetan people enjoyed happiness and prosperity. However, in 1949 the Chinese Communists invaded Tibet, and since then we all know the extent of happiness which we Tibetan people enjoy.

After being "liberated" from the "three big feudal lords," the Tibetans were made the "masters" of the country. Through such pleasing propaganda the Chinese are publicizing that the progress achieved in Tibet under their rule is unprecedented and all the Tibetan people are happy! The aim of struggle of the Tibetans outside Tibet is the attainment of the happiness of the Tibetan people. If the Tibetans in Tibet are truly happy under Chinese rule then there is no reason for us here in exile to argue otherwise. Because of scarce food, many of the elder Tibetans fall sick and die. Every day most Tibetans live in fear, suffering, and hardship and do not get a moment of rest and relaxation. Even to the young Tibetans, whom the Chinese have reared and educated, they, the Chinese, do not give jobs corresponding to the type of education which the youths have received. Evoking the ideal of "voluntary work," the Chinese drive the Tibetans like a herd of cattle to work in the fields, in road-building and construction. In short, the Tibetans in Tibet are not treated like human beings.

The Greatness of the Tibetan Nation

"Life has lost against death. But memory wins its fight against noth-ingness."[110] These words of Tzvetan Todorov could appear as an epi-graph of this speech of March 10, 1973. Death was omnipresent in the days after the Cultural Revolution. While the community of nations showed no interest in the genocide it had condemned ten years earlier, the Dalai Lama embodied the resistance of his people. On this day of memory, he turned the clock back, toward the origins: back to the point where Tibet's history combined with myth.

The first Tibetan kings belonged to a dynasty of divine essence. Coming down from the sky on a beam of light, the Mu rope, they ruled the men in the valley of Yarlung.[111] Once they fulfilled their mis-sion, they went back up to the celestial heights on their glaring ray, without leaving any remains. However, during an altercation, a minis-ter assassinated the king Drigum Tsenpo. This murder with weapons broke the mythical rope of Mu that linked the sovereign to heaven, and his descendants became mere mortals. Storytellers spread leg-ends of this first dynasty, but without specifying the dates of the reign of the mythical sovereigns.

The historical identity of Tibet was forged with the advent of Songtsen Gampo in the seventh century. The striking events of his reign and those of his successors are reported in the Tibetan *Annals* and confirmed in the chapters of the *Annals* of the Tang dynasty dealing with Tibetan matters.[112] Ancient manuscripts unearthed at Dunhuang, in Gansu, at the end of the Eastern Silk Road, celebrate the power of the Tibetan empire at the time of this conquering king. After having united the various Tibetan chiefdoms, he successfully waged war up to the borders of Mongolia and northern India. In 640, his armies shook upper Asia, and he forced the Chinese emperor to sign a humiliating peace treaty, which included the clause of his marriage with the Chinese Princess Wencheng. Under the influence of his wife, the king adopted the Buddhist religion. At his death, his empire stretched from the source of the Brahmaputra to the plains of Sichuan and of Nepal at the Tsaidam basin.

A century later, Trisong Detsen had to subdue the rebellion of the Bönpos, faithful to ancient native deities. The introduction of Buddhism competed with the first Tibetan religion, Bön, based on shamanism. To resolve the conflict, the king called a debate between their representatives. The Buddhists came out victorious. From then on, their religion spread widely throughout Tibet thanks to the translation of the Sanskrit, Chinese, and Pali Canon, as evidenced by a number of manuscripts dating from this period found in the Thousand Buddha Caves in Dunhuang. Buddhism forged the Tibetan identity in a society which, under the influence of the third great religious king, Tri Ralpachen, "the long-haired," became democratic, according to the Dalai Lama, because it was based on the principles of compassion, equality, and fraternity. This governance system[113] was inspired by the Buddhist faith, considering that the seed of buddha nature is in every individual, from the greatest down to the poorest. "To say that all men are equal in rights and they also have the Buddha nature are two convergent formulations," said the Dalai Lama.[114] And he challenged the confusion of the Chinese propaganda denouncing "feudalism" in the European sense within the traditional Tibetan society. For its institutions differed profoundly from the Western system by virtue of their roots in the Buddhist culture, which establishes the essential equality of all beings.

At that time, the sovereigns of Tang China, of Iran, and of various Turkish and Arab states sent ambassadors to the court of King Tri Ralpachen. His empire boundaries corresponded to the territorial limits of the three provinces of Tibet claimed by the Dalai Lama since its fragmentation by China. In 822, Tri Ralpachen signed a peace treaty with the Chinese Emperor Muzong. This agreement, which normalized the political, military, and commercial relations between Tibet and China, recognized the Tibetan occupation of Gansu. The text engraved in stone laid the foundation for a cordial understanding. Two pillars bearing this inscription are still standing in highly symbolic places: in Lhasa, before the main gate of the Jokhang Temple, and in Xi'an, at the door of the palace of the emperor. They proclaim: "At the borders, smoke and dust [i.e., warfare] shall not appear. There will be no quarrel or armed invasion. Alarming and unfriendly words will not resonate. . . . Tibetans shall be happy at home, and the Chinese in the land of China."[115]

The epic conquest by the Tibetans ended with the murder of Tri Ralpachen in 838. Religious and political rivalries caused a fragmentation of his empire under the reign of Langdarma, who persecuted Buddhism before being assassinated by a monk in 842. Divided by the intrigues of local potentates allied to local religious traditions, the country was unable to defend itself, either against the Chinese, who took over the northern oasis, or against the Turks and the Uighurs, who returned to Turkestan. Thus in the thirteenth century the Mongol troops invaded a fragmented and deeply religious state. From the end of the tenth century, according to historians, there had indeed been a "subsequent diffusion" of Buddhism in Tibet. Indian masters and Kashmiris, glorified with prestige, came to teach in the high country, and new scriptures were translated. From a conquering kingdom, warrior Tibet turned into a Buddhist country. The society adopted its traditional form, which persisted until the twentieth century, with the rise in power of monasteries that, funded by donations from the laity, became major landowners. The succession system of the hierarchs also became widespread in the early thirteenth century with the recognition of the *tulku*, the emanation on earth of a buddha and the reincarnation of his immediate predecessor.[116] However, discord arising from religious rivalries among the various lineages weakened the kingdom. Also, the Tibetans showed a weak resistance against Prince Godan, grandson of Genghis Khan, when he put to fire and the sword the valley of Lhasa in 1240.

The Fiction of Chinese Suzerainty

The Dalai Lama drew lessons from the past. Disunity led to the loss of influence of a nation that had defied the power of the Son of Heaven. The evocation of past grandeur made one forget, in an instant of commemoration, the current abomination and was a reminder of the historical independence of Tibet. The visit of President Nixon to Mao Zedong in 1972 made one forget that this country was not always a province of Beijing, that in history, the Tibetan people were not a national minority among Hans. Certainly, China exercised at certain times a form of supremacy over Tibet, but the latter continued to function as a sovereign state, and no treaty ever formalized the alleged Chinese suzerainty in Tibet.[117] No Chinese dynasty ever governed Tibet. Religious patronage was offered to Tibetan religious rulers by Mongol and Manchu emperors, during long periods when those non-Chinese conquerors harshly dominated China itself.

In order to ensure control of the plateau in the thirteenth century, Prince Godan entrusted to Sakya Pandita[118] temporal power over Tibet, as the Mongols had no wish to govern Tibet. The Sakya investiture marked a milestone in the history of Central Asia. The Mongols, having conquered China, gradually brought China under the authority of the lamas. Spiritual preceptors of the khans, the Tibetan religious became the enlightened masters of the Son of Heaven. The Chinese even begged them to intervene with the Mongol warlords to spare them from their cruel raids. The authority attributed to the lamas, before whom the emperors prostrated themselves in private, is at the origin of a type of relationship between sovereigns, unique in history, called *chöyön* in Tibetan or, literally, "religious master–secular patron." The supreme lama watched over the spiritual destinies of his disciples at the head of the empire of the steppes and the Middle Kingdom. In return, these sovereigns protected the peace and prosperity of

Tibet. They sometimes intervened to restore order, as under the Manchu Qing dynasty, when in 1720 the Chinese army reestablished the
Seventh Dalai Lama on his throne in the Himalayan kingdom, torn
apart by a civil war. Two representatives of the emperor, the *ambans*,
were stationed in Lhasa along with a small garrison of Chinese soldiers. However, their presence remained purely symbolic.

The *chöyön* relationship assured the stability of Central Asia from
the thirteenth century to the early twentieth century. After the fall of
the Manchu dynasty in 1911, the Thirteenth Dalai Lama condemned
this link, saying it had "disappeared like a rainbow in the sky."[119] He
thus got rid of the *ambans* and the Chinese army corps in Lhasa, and
proclaimed the independence of his country in 1913. This declaration
was based on the vacancy of the throne in China and affirmed the
nullity of prior allegiances. However, in modern China, the religious
master–secular patron relationship received a new interpretation.
The nationalists began to translate it into the language of Western
politics, despite the fact that it was completely alien to that context.
They transposed it in terms of sovereignty, thus denying the spiritual
dimension of this institution, specific to the culture of Buddhist Central Asia. Sino-Tibetan history was completely revised to the point of
distorting the spiritual master (*cho*) to lay patron/disciple (*yon*) relationship of Tibetan lamas to Mongol and Manchu emperors, claiming it to have been imperial domination of China over Tibet.

In the twentieth century, Tibet was therefore trapped in this version of history, which the Communists tried to support by engaging
in a meticulous rereading of the past. The protocols of the meeting
of the Fifth Dalai Lama and the Emperor Shunzi in 1652, or of the
Thirteenth Dalai Lama and the Empress Dowager Cixi in 1908, were
scrutinized in great detail to prove that the Tibetan leader was a subordinate of the Son of Heaven. The Marxist-Maoist interpretation
of history, according to which the Middle Kingdom had been a multinational state, accommodated itself to the paradigm of imperial
ideology considering neighboring populations as both "barbarians"
or inferior and "vassal" or subordinate to the Chinese sphere of influ-

ence. The theory of "minority nationalities" and the incorporation of Tibet as "an integral part" of the motherland were therefore consistent with the Chinese ethnocentrism of earlier centuries.

In this respect, the Chinese took advantage of Western ignorance. From the invasion of October 1950, the Dalai Lama deplored the difficulty of having the independence of his country recognized under international law: "Suzerainty is an old and vague term, perfectly inadequate," he observed. "Its use has misled generations of leaders who did not take into account the relationship between the spiritual Dalai Lamas and the Manchu emperors. Many former Eastern concepts cannot be translated literally by a simple Western political term."[120] At the heart of the geopolitical issues of the twentieth century are decolonization and the right of peoples to self-determination; rather than dwelling on the historical sovereignty of the Himalayan kingdom, Tibetans in exile and lawyers prefer to gather more recent evidence of independence, such as the signing of international treaties or the existence of stamps and of a Tibetan currency, the *sang*, bearing the insignia of the Lhasa government since 1913. Thereafter, Tibet was confined in a fatal isolation, for its independence was not subject to international recognition, and in 1972 the United States accepted that Tibet was part of China.

From Nehru to Nixon, the Diplomacy of "Peaceful Coexistence"

From February 21 to 28, 1972, a summit was held in Beijing between President Nixon and Mao Zedong. Both countries formulated the principles of their agreement on the basis of the *Panchsheel*, the treaty of "peaceful coexistence" that once sealed the Sino-Indian agreement. In 1954, Zhou Enlai managed to make Nehru recognize that Tibet was Chinese, and he did the same with the United States in 1972. Once again Tibet was sacrificed in the name of the territorial integrity of the People's Republic and on the principle of noninterference in its internal affairs. As a conclusion to their visit, the Chinese delegation also expressed pride in claiming to observe the principles of international law: "China will never be a superpower and it opposes any political hegemony. It strongly supports the struggle of all oppressed nations to regain their freedom."[121]

Chinese diplomacy was triumphing. These events were celebrated as a victory: "The Chinese liked to say that easterly winds prevailed on westerly winds," says Palden Gyatso.[122] During Party indoctrination sessions, the favorite theme at this time was the gross error of the Tibetans. They had in vain implored the help of the American imperialists, who didn't help them any more than their gods did: "They played us a topical movie on the welcoming ceremony of President Nixon in Beijing," remembered the monk. "The American President had come to Beijing like a dog, with his tail between his legs."[123] However, the Dalai Lama did not yield to discouragement. In 1973 he wanted to believe that the Chinese propaganda would not continue to delude for much longer. After normalizing its relations with the United States and, shortly after, with Japan, should China not comply with the rules of the community of nations, and finally treat the Tibetans as human beings?

MARCH 10, 1974

"One hand is not enough to hide the sun"

EIGHTY-FIVE THOUSAND EXILES are on this side of the mighty Himalayas and six million on the other, but the spirit of March 10 binds us as one proud nation. What is the spirit of March 10? We say it is the cause of Tibet. But what is the cause of Tibet? Is it a struggle against a race, a nation, and an ideology? Or is it an unreasonable struggle waged by a minority in exile for their own interests? It is none of these. The cause of Tibet is the cause of the Tibetan people, it is the struggle of a people to determine their own identity. Until they are satisfied, the struggle for Tibet will continue. I believe in justice and truth, without which there would be no basis for human hope. I also believe in the right of every nation to struggle for its freedom, including Tibet and its neighboring states that have fallen victim to Chinese aggression.

The younger generation see a contradiction between the "socialist paradise" of factories, roads, and airfields and the simultaneous starvation of their countrymen. These imposing monuments of "progress" have no meaning to the common Tibetan. They only serve to highlight the dissatisfaction among the Marxist-educated younger generation of Tibetans. So long as the people of Tibet are in such dire hardships and discontented with their lot, we have a duty to speak and act on their behalf. It is an onerous duty, but one which we will push through with a determination equal to—if not more than—what our brethren are displaying in Tibet.

MARCH 10, 1975

THE ISSUE OF Tibet is deeply linked with the changes in international politics and especially with the progress of the peace process in Asia. As such, we must steer the ship of our struggle according to the shifting directions of the winds of international relations to reach the shore of Tibetan freedom and happiness.

The Chinese aggressors have killed and jailed countless innocent Tibetans. Without caring for the starving people all around them, the Chinese are channeling the productivity of the country into armaments. To cover up their crimes and misdeeds, they are churning out publications splashed with photographs of dance and drama performances and a few factories, which state that the Tibetans in Tibet are enjoying unprecedented happiness. This is done to fool the world public opinion. But a mere palm of the hand cannot hide the sun. Responsible and informed people everywhere in the world know that there can never be happiness in a society which is given the name of "new" and in which there are not even the material basics of adequate food, shelter and clothing. The elderly Tibetans through their own experience know, since they have gone through both societies, where there is greater happiness, in the old or the new society.

"Socialist Paradise"?

In the March 10 speeches of 1974 and 1975, the Dalai Lama made things clear with conciseness and brevity. He and his people were not fighting the Chinese, nor the People's Republic, nor communism. They had resisted for twenty-five years the dictatorship that the Chinese were trying to impose on them in defiance of international jurisprudence. However, the Chinese propaganda disguised reality, with Mao Zedong applying in the field of international relations another great principle of Sun Zi, his strategy mentor: "All warfare is based on deception." He thus favored a "demonstrative" communication, valued in the 1960s and 1970s, that used thematic exhibitions to convey the official ideology. Thus in Lhasa in 1975, a retrospective entitled *Anger of the Serfs* was launched with much publicity. Whole buses and trucks full of students, workers, and peasants of central Tibet came to admire in the capital a hundred life-size clay statues, reproducing the living conditions at the time of the "man-eating feudal system."

The path began with the "dwelling of the feudal lords, hell of misfortune on earth," passed through the "lamaseries of black demons," and ended in a room dedicated to the new society, where "The serfs rise to fight and win their liberation."[124] The government had used great resources for this scenography, sponsoring artists whose Soviet-style socialist realism put art at the service of the revolution. According to the organizers, it was indeed convenient to educate the younger generation of Tibetans so that they would never forget the dark days of the old "theocracy" and remember the goodness of Chairman Mao. The liberated "serfs" had finally entered the socialist paradise, thanks to the sacrifices of the army and the magnanimity of the officials of the People's Republic. This vast propaganda offensive was a travesty of history. During the invasion and military occupation of

Tibet from 1950 to 1959, China had assured Tibetans that it wanted to liberate their country from the imperialists. Only after the flight of the Dalai Lama did it claim to want to liberate the "serfs." However, authenticity was not the main focus of a scene that was also aimed at impressing the foreigners, Communist sympathizers selected for a tour of the roof of the world. The authorities had included in their program the "Potemkin villages,"[125] equipped with model farms, factories, and hospitals. They were received by "former serfs" who pursued a career in the Propaganda Department, narrating their personal stories under the "Lamaist" regime, not without details, one more gruesome than the other, about the abuses that the reactionary lords had made them undergo. These gross confabulations fascinated some journalists, seized by a romantic predilection for Mao Zedong. Showing little critical thinking and supported by dubious statistics, they defended the thesis of a civilizing mission of the Chinese state in the backward and barbaric Tibetan lands.[126] The mixed-race novelist Han Suyin, with a Chinese father and a Belgian mother, went on praising the "socialist paradise" that Tibet had become, freed from the worst stranglehold, that of famine.[127] Such untruth demonstrates the effectiveness of the propaganda. However, in 1974, the writer and Sinologist Simon Leys denounced the authors of these apologetic works, written after trips offered by an official agency in exchange for complacent publications. Historian Patrick French did not hesitate to accuse them of "intellectual prostitution."[128]

On both sides of the Himalayas, words certainly did not have the same meaning. In Tibet, the Chinese denigrated the "hell on earth" of the past. In India, for the refugees, the "hell on earth" was the contemporary dictatorship. In a country suffering from famine, grinding poverty, convictions, and arbitrary executions, the Chinese staging was insulting. Before these brazen attacks, what could the Dalai Lama do but demand justice and truth? Yet who listened to him, since the United States courted China, attracted by its huge economic potential? The religious leader, however, wanted to keep his hope and comfort his own people. Would "the changing winds of the world" not finally rise up to blow on Tibet the breezes of freedom that were so hoped for?

MARCH 10, 1976

Eternally Slaves?

IN THIS TWENTIETH century, the world has witnessed the rise of the sun of equal freedom. People of many nations are enjoying the warmth of freedom which they did not have before. In ancient times, we Tibetans were known for our high degree of civilization and courage in all Asia. Should we always remain slaves of the barbarous, suffering under their cruel domination? The snowland of Tibet is blessed with a bountiful natural wealth and rich natural beauty. Should this country of ours be converted into a war-machinery manufacturing fortress, and the Tibetan people, its rightful owners, reduced to the status of criminals perpetually subjected to oppression and humiliation? By virtue of our secular karma, we Tibetans have been endowed with priceless mineral resources of gold, copper, iron, oil, gas, coal, and lead. Do you wish to allow the barbarous brigands, who have no right whatsoever, to plunder and cart away these resources of ours as they are doing now?

All worldly phenomena are characterized by the inherent nature of arising, developing, and passing away. Does it not behoove us to wrestle with greater vigor and determination for the recovery of our rights, taking advantage of the ripe conditions and the timely opportunities? We should strive with renewed dedication and determination for freeing the Tibetan people from the present plight, and for realizing the ultimate objective of Tibetan national freedom. Banish the sense of timidity, lethargy, and the effort to evade hardships. Cultivate and develop the spirit of complete self-reliance. Volunteer for challenges and hardships. Work with devotion and with pleasure in the sense that it is in your own interest, and above all, in unity with achieving the goal of national freedom of the Tibetan people.

The Sun of Freedom Does Not Shine in Tibet

Pain and oppression in Tibet overshadowed the "sun of freedom" that the Dalai Lama wished for. In 1975, Chinese authorities declared the collectivization process completed. With the imposition of the People's Commune system, monitoring became widespread. The poorest farmers were elevated to the rank of president or foreman, and in exchange for this promotion, had to denounce the feudal or reactionary behavior around them. If they evaded this duty, they ran the risk of retaliation for their families and *thamzing* or torture for themselves. The new system was supposed to guarantee the autonomy of each People's Commune while allowing for solidarity in times of need. Yet despite the mutual assistance, the situation was disastrous. Famine persisted because four-fifths of grain production was requisitioned. The population only benefited from the last fifth and had to provide intensive work under duress. Indeed, the Party set unrealizable production targets, aligned with the performance of model communes, that Chinese executives in Tibet were required to match. Failing to do so despite the relentless work imposed on farmers, they faced a big temptation to falsify figures and further reduce the proportion of the harvest given to the Tibetans in order to inflate the statistics. Whole villages were thus condemned to starvation by bureaucrats anxious to preserve their benefits. Food and other basic necessities were insufficient, but the Party said that Tibet lived in a time of abundance.

In 1975, the government began to exploit the riches of Tibet, whose name in Mandarin is "Western Treasure House" (Xizang). Traditionally, however, the mineral deposits represented less wealth to exploit than the accumulation, generation after generation, of a sum of merit and spiritual qualities materialized in the form of stones and precious metals. In religious Tibet, people made sure to only withdraw small amounts for the making of ritual objects and jewelry, only scratching the surface; underground, the vastness of the natural reserves remained intact. The population therefore refused at first to participate in drilling in mines, seeing it as a profanation. Authorities fought against these beliefs, linked to a survival of the feudal spirit, using a variety of coercive measures. Before their severity, no one dared to object anymore.

The Tibet of Chairman Mao required the revolutionary commitment of all, while propaganda praised the socialist revolution, highlighting the electrification of the Himalayan region. Yet we know today that the initiative was limited to the construction of a single hydroelectric plant, Ngachen, in the region of Lhasa. Contrary to the allegations of propaganda, it was not the work of the PLA but of prisoners from a neighboring detention camp, who, undernourished and in deplorable hygienic conditions, had to provide labor in exhausting amounts—to the point that many died each day, whose bodies the guards threw into a nearby river. Tubten Khetsun, who worked on this construction site, pointed out that the plant only provided power for the Chinese labor units, with the population benefiting from light only ten days per month, apart from the winter and spring, when the water level was at its very lowest: "The houses were connected by cables to receive electricity, but it was only stagecraft."[129] As there was a lack of candles and kerosene, formerly imported from Nepal, the inhabitants were forced to use motor oil for light, thus living in an unhealthy cloud of smoke in their homes. Electrification was only another fiction.[130] Similarly, the bridges, roads, factories, and hospitals, such highly praised emblems of modernity, were intended first for the Chinese and served the cities where they were the majority, the rural population being left out of the progress.

Nevertheless, on the occasion of the ceremonies in Lhasa that marked the tenth anniversary of the Autonomous Region, endless speeches praised the benefits of communism.

Treasures of Wisdom and Compassion

In this context, the leader of the Tibetans strove to redefine the direction of his fight. Already since 1971, when China became a member of the UN, he no longer pleaded his case to the UN. In March 1976, his speech was a cry of pain. Only the Buddhist philosophy still brought reason to hope. Indeed, the religious leader interpreted the changes on the international scene from a spiritual point of view. They illustrate the law of impermanence, a basic teaching based on the observation that people and events do not carry in themselves the cause of their existence. Because of this absence of self, or emptiness, they are of a transitional nature and once emerged, persist for some time before disappearing, when the causes of their emergence cease. We can hear the master of wisdom express himself through these considerations, something unusual in a political speech. Basing his words on faith, which allows one to accept the unavoidability in the upheavals of life, he urged Tibetans to rely on themselves.

Stateless, in the precarious conditions of exile, they should not expect everything from others. They had to offer the world an exceptional spiritual heritage, a heritage of humanity. From the beginning of his exile, the Dalai Lama favored encounters with religious leaders of other traditions and scientists who made the trip to Dharamsala. He personally received visitors from around the world, such as Father Thomas Merton in 1968. These meetings illustrated his willingness to dialogue with the contemporary world. He himself never missed an opportunity to expand his knowledge by asking his guests many questions and keeping informed by reading works of Western philosophy and history. His concern to preserve the Tibetan culture was not limited to an identity-related claim. The stated intention of the Dalai Lama was always to share the achievements of the internal sciences of the mind. This attitude foreshadowed his subsequent exchanges with scholars of the first order in cognitive science, neuroscience, psychology, quantum physics, and astrophysics. These were among his first steps to awaken the conscience of the world.

From the late 1960s in Dharamsala, he supervised the establishment of a program of Tibetan Studies, including courses in language, philosophy, and religion, for Westerners. He designated the teaching lamas and chose the Indian reference texts, accompanied by their

Tibetan commentaries. The most conservative of his community were angry to see their spiritual culture thus brought within the reach of newcomers. Yet their supreme leader persevered and used his influence with the Indian government to renew visas for students enrolled in this program. He wanted to train a generation of scholars and translators, future transmitters of Tibetan culture abroad.[131] In 1973, during his first trip to the West, he was received in Rome by Pope Paul VI and then met the Archbishop of Canterbury and his followers at the Abbey of Sutton, as well as various other religious and secular figures in Switzerland, the Netherlands, Belgium, Ireland, Norway, Sweden, Denmark, West Germany, and Austria.[132] In all the European capitals, the Dalai Lama declared his desire to speak with women and men who deeply reflected on the problems of humanity. There was no proselytizing. On the contrary, his message was rather that everyone should cultivate his original religion and only change after long consideration of his decision. For those who chose to become Buddhists, he recommended developing compassion, cultivating an understanding of the interdependence and universal responsibility that follows from it, and studying reference works such as *Wisdom: The Middle Way Treatise* by Nagarjuna,[133] a classic of Buddhist literature that demonstrates the absence of the inherent existence of the atom as well as of the shortest moment of consciousness.

After their exile, following the example of the Dalai Lama, the Tibetan masters of wisdom began to travel the world. Many felt that from then on, the enlightenment culture would be transmitted far from their country of birth, where generations of meditators had dedicated their lives to it. The first teaching center of Vajrayana in the West was created in North America, in New Jersey, in 1958; then another in Scotland in 1967; and another in Boulder, Colorado, in 1970. By 1976, the results were impressive. Some *geshes*, or "doctors of divinity," were recruited by research institutes specializing in the Far East, such as at the University of Washington, Seattle; University of Wisconsin, Madison; University of Virginia, Charlottesville; at Oxford and Cambridge; and at the Centre National de la recherche scientifique (CNRS) in Paris. They taught more and more students, while taking courses in comparative religion, philosophy, and psychology. The hierarchs of some of the main schools of Tibetan Buddhism settled in France, which became an important relay point in the transmission of Buddhist doctrine. In the mid-1970s, under the inspiration of charismatic lamas, more than three hundred Dharma centers[134] as well as hermitages and monasteries opened their doors in Europe and America. In 1973, the Dalai Lama for the first time ordained novices outside Tibet. Hundreds of others made the trip to Dharamsala to take their vows. Soon the lamas began to recognize in Western children the reincarnations of Tibetan spiritual masters.

In 1976, Buddhism was dying in Tibet but being reborn in the West. With this in mind, the Dalai Lama reminded the Tibetans that if they were poor in material terms, they were not poor in everything. They had brought from the other side of the Himalayas their treasures of wisdom and compassion. In a weak position on the political level, and in the absence of concrete support from the UN, the Dalai Lama, before the Chinese intransigence, mobilized forces of the soul and spirit. While hoping for more favorable developments on the international stage, he suggested the Tibetans invent a new way to participate in the changing world.

MARCH 10, 1977

Indifference Before the Tibetan Tragedy

ACCORDING TO Lhasa Radio[135] broadcasts, between May 1975 and January 1977, 6,660 retired PLA veterans as well as graduate students from different parts of China were transported to Central Tibet to raise families and settle there. Forty-three separate batches were thus mobilized for this scheme on the pretext that they were volunteers who "had come to join the socialist revolution and socialist construction work in Tibet."

Those of our people left behind in Tibet continue to experience a life of poverty and relentless hard labor. To cite an instance of this, according to reports received on the construction of a new dam during the winter at Lhatse, all young and old, male and female inhabitants were summoned to the site of the construction and compelled to work round the clock without any break until the dam had been completed. Even those who developed open wounds on their backs had no alternative but to work without respite. Many became mutilated as a consequence of severe frostbite. From another report on construction work at Taktse, we learn that the inhabitants were forcibly put to labor on agricultural cultivation by day, and with the assistance of kerosene torches were compelled to work on a hydroelectric plant by night.

At a meeting convened to mourn the death of Mao a few months ago, 300 Tibetans were arrested and several were executed on the grounds that the accused showed a lack of genuine sorrow and grief at the meeting. These reports have neither been fabricated nor exaggerated by us, but were broadcast by Radio Lhasa three or four weeks ago. While at present, the campaign against hegemony and colonialism has taken precedence in international affairs, how is it justified to neglect and leave unattended such tragic happenings in Tibet?

The Death of Mao Zedong

1976: the Chinese power lost many of its highest leaders. On January 8, Zhou Enlai died of cancer. Nearly two million people attended his funeral procession. The crowd cried over the man in the shadows, whose diplomatic skills had raised China to the ranks of a great power. A few weeks later, the Day of the Dead, it defied orders of dispersion in order to adorn the monument to the heroes of the people with white crowns in his memory.

On July 6, Marshal Zhu De died in turn. Strategist of the Long March and victor over the Japanese in 1945, he was the founder of the

Red Army and then the commander of the People's Liberation Army. His death was followed closely by those of Deputy Prime Minister Dong Biwu, Deputy Prime Minister Liu Fuchun, and Kang Sheng, a prominent member of the Party's Central Committee. Mao thus lost, one by one, his companions of the first hour of the main strategies of the regime.

On September 9, China was again in mourning. Mao Zedong had died. Aged eighty-two, he suffered from heart failure and a nervous disorder that paralyzed his lungs. For a week, countless ordinary people and thousands of dignitaries flocked from the whole country by bus, each wearing a black piece of fabric. With a white chrysanthemum on the heart as a sign of mourning, groups passed one after the other, day and night, before the coffin. Emotions were intense before the loss of a guide whose portrait schoolchildren greeted every morning in their classroom. Criticized for having encouraged the cult of his personality, Mao had replied that his image of a peasant risen from the ranks galvanized the nation's energy. He had directed it in the "high tide of socialist transformation," "solid as concrete,"[136] made it pass in one generation from the Middle Ages to the nuclear era.

In his speech of March 10, 1977, the Dalai Lama said little about this death. In announcing the news, his eyes filled with tears. He saw the suffering of the deceased statesman responsible for the violent deaths of 50 to 70 million of his compatriots. From the standpoint of karma, Mao was doomed to suffer the worst tortures in one of the eighteen hot, icy, peripheral, or ephemeral hells that the Buddhist scriptures describe. The leader of the Tibetans offered lamps and prayers for him, guiding several rituals for the soul of "a tyrant of which mankind in several centuries, and in China, for several millennia, have produced only one."[137]

In Tibet, these deaths at the top of the state gave hope for the end of communism, especially as on July 28, 1976, the earth had trembled violently in Tangshan, an industrial city in the province of Hebei. This earthquake, one of the deadliest in history, caused nearly three hundred thousand deaths. The Tibetan people wanted to see a promise of change, which seemed to be confirmed by the passing of a comet, accompanied by a "rain of stones," to quote the headlines. Palden Gyatso was surprised that, despite twenty years of repression and indoctrination, the superstitions revived so quickly. The hope for a more lenient period was intense, in proportion with the sufferings endured. It encouraged people to interpret the signs of the sky and earth in the sense hoped for.

The authorities minimized the number of victims of the Tang-shan disaster and after the death of Mao decreed an official period of mourning. Black banners were hung in the city along the streets and at the entrances of official buildings. In a sign of mourning, people wore white paper flowers on their clothes, the windshields of their cars, and the leashes of their dogs. They even suspended them on the tree branches to the point that, Tubten Khetsun remembered, this profusion of white spots could be mistaken for an early snow-fall. Tibetans who did not conspicuously express their despair were suspected of reactionary thoughts and severely punished. Palden Gyatso recounted how, in his prison, prisoners played the comedy of mourning when a guard announced to the sound of funeral music: "'Our dear leader, the most blazing sun of our heart, the great Chairman Mao is dead.' At these words, some prisoners burst into tears, crying loudly. I heard one of them moan: 'Chairman Mao was more benevolent than my own parents.' The experienced actor that I had become stayed silent and looked tearful. On the platform, officials also expressed their grief without restraint."[138]

The Day After the Cultural Revolution

After the death of Mao, the Cultural Revolution officially came to an end by a declaration of the Communist Party after its eleventh Congress. The authorities, in the person of the new President Li Xinnian, designated the "Gang of Four" as the scapegoat responsible for the excesses of this period. This radical Maoist group was accused of having plunged China into chaos. The role of their leader, Jiang Qing, Mao's fourth wife, was particularly stigmatized even though she claimed that she had only been the "watchdog" of the Great Helmsman, biting whenever he gave her the order to. Her trial, broadcast on television, enabled the new masters of the People's Republic to make Mao innocent, repudiating a policy of terror that discredited them abroad. They tried to thus promote the image of a new China, but Western governments were not fooled by this politico-judicial staging.

The deadly madness of the Cultural Revolution had indeed left Tibet, but the country continued to suffer. Working conditions imposed on the population were inhumane. In Thaktse, a commune the Tibetans nicknamed "Red Flag," the watchword was "Imitate Dazhai." In this city of Shanxi province, propaganda claimed that barren lands had been made fertile thanks to the efforts of the people. The local Party leaders encouraged Tibetans to compete with Dazhai, claiming performance that, as we know today, was deliberately over-estimated so as to require extra work.

In these days after the Cultural Revolution, there was also a major problem in the education sector, most schools in Tibet having been destroyed. Thousands of young teachers from Shanghai and other coastal cities were transferred to the high plateau. Education was an important ideological issue, for the authorities wanted to educate the generations stemming from the proletarian revolution. The Dalai Lama denounced the immigration of so-called volunteers, veterans and teachers, who came to participate in the socialist structure. He saw ahead a risk of irreversible assimilation of the Tibetan population, significantly inferior in numbers to the Han. History has proven him right; this demographic submersion has constantly worsened. In the face of this situation, the indifference of the international bodies persisted. The exile community protested publicly against their passivity for the first time in 1977. In Delhi, a group of young Tibetans began a hunger strike in front of the Information Centre of the United Nations, determined to fast until death, to force the UN to implement its resolutions. Their press release dated March 20 demonstrates their desperation: "We are treated like lepers on a political level and our cause is considered as a shameful and contagious disease. Although victims, we are ignored and ostracized, while our oppressors are courted and celebrated by a senseless world. Peaceful people, we have no other recourse than the United Nations to ensure that justice is returned to us. We are not asking for charity. Only the respect of our rights, guaranteed by the three UN resolutions."[139]

While the fight for emancipation from colonial rule was supported throughout the world, the community of nations allowed a dictatorship in Tibet to perpetrate itself. How could they allow this? Why the Tibetan exception?

MARCH 10, 1978

"An unprecedented happiness"?

RECENTLY THE CHINESE have intensified their propaganda about the "unprecedented happiness in Tibet today" through radio broadcasts and pictorial magazines. It is very difficult for the few selected foreign visitors, who are taken on guided tours for a few days and have to listen to explanations through interpreters carefully chosen by the Chinese, to know and tell us the actual welfare and conditions of the Tibetan people.

If Tibetans are really happy and prosperous as never before there is no reason for us to argue otherwise. In that case, the Chinese should allow every interested foreigner to visit Tibet without restricting their movements or meetings with the Tibetan people. Furthermore, the Chinese should allow the Tibetans in Tibet to visit their parents and relatives now in exile. These Tibetans can then study the conditions of those of us in exile living in free countries. Similar opportunity should be given to the Tibetans in exile. Under such an arrangement we can be confident of knowing the true situation inside Tibet. This is morally right and practicable. Instead of doing this, why are the Chinese indulging only in propaganda to woo the Tibetans in exile to return?

MARCH 10, 1979

O F SPECIAL IMPORTANCE is that the over 20,000 Tibetan youths who were provided with both the traditional and modern education, which are like the wings of a bird, are joining the mainstream of modern life. Our religion and culture—considered poison by the Chinese—are not only preserved and their centers firmly established in the Tibetan settlements in India, but are also spreading among peoples of different social strata and races and gaining much interest and respect in the East and the West. Regarding our political situation, we follow the democratic system and tread the path of freedom. And considering that we were forced to leave our land and wander in other people's lands, the fact that we have achieved a lot of success for the benefit of both the society and the individual is worth remembering.

So now, in order to catch up with the rest of the world, to cope with realities and to modernize China, great changes in Chinese politics have taken place recently. And, particularly, since their propaganda failed, the Vice-Premier Deng Xiaoping has been repeatedly making statements like: "seeking truth from facts," "if the masses feel some anger, we must let them express it," "if you have an ugly face, it is no use pretending to be handsome," "we must recognize our shortcomings and mistakes." Unlike the previous Chinese leadership, there now appears to be a desire for honesty, modernization, and leniency.

Socialism with Chinese Characteristics
Under Deng Xiaoping

Tibetans were happy . . . ? Radio Lhasa told the truth . . . ? The Dalai Lama was ironic—but merely repeated a favorite theme of Chinese propaganda. Previously unseen axes of communication indeed appeared with the inauguration of a period of liberalization, marked in 1978 by Deng Xiaoping's accession to power. This supporter of Mao since 1930 was initially acclaimed and then spoken out against and ousted in 1960. His criticism of the regime's economic policy cost him public humiliation sessions and condemnation to forced labor. He was then acquitted in 1975, thanks to Zhou Enlai. They had been classmates at the beginning of the twentieth century in Montargis, France, "Cradle of New China," where hundreds of young intellectuals went to study and work. Through contact with the labor unions, they discovered Marxist ideas and learned about the making of a revolution.[140]

In the late 1970s, Deng was getting ready to exert a decisive influence on the evolution of China, in which he became the great reformer among the Communist mandarins of the post-Mao era. In December 1978, his closing speech at the Eleventh Party Congress was loyal to the Communist rhetoric but defined an unprecedented capitalist orientation of government action. In his speech of March 10, 1979, the Dalai Lama wanted to believe in the new slogans, promising change, especially as they were accompanied by gestures that had been inconceivable a few years before—like the journey of the Chinese leaders to the United States in January 1979. Seven years after Nixon's visit to China, it was the leader of the People's Republic who went to the United States, a country demonized for decades. The page of Maoist anathemas had been turned. During his state visit, Deng Xiaoping lingered in the high places of capitalism: at the NASA space center in Houston, source of American pride since July 20, 1969, when Armstrong stepped on the lunar surface; then at the headquarters of Coca-Cola in Atlanta, and of Boeing in Seattle. The presence of the Chinese leader, photographed with his delegation, accompanied the signing of trade treaties that buried the anti-American taboos. The Chinese market opened to Western companies: Boeing announced the sale of several airplanes and Coca-Cola its plant project in Shanghai.

The Cold War remained nevertheless on the agenda of discussions, Zbigniew Brzezinski[141] negotiating the installation of an electromagnetic spying base on the border of the USSR in exchange for commercial benefits. However, Beijing remained focused on economic and technological development. The new master of the People's Republic considered it necessary to define a socialism with Chinese characteristics. He therefore repeated at every possible opportunity that "socialism does not mean shared poverty" or that "socialism and a market economy are not incompatible." His "Four Modernizations" aimed at boosting the agricultural, industrial, technological, and military sectors, stagnant under Mao, in order to raise China as a great power.

Before the Court of the World

The message sent out by the authorities to the people was clear: "Enrich yourselves!" In China as well as in Tibet, the very unpopular commune system was abandoned. Farmers had greater freedom to cultivate their land and sell their products. To modernize the Himalayan region, the authorities recognized the need for some concessions, cultural and religious. They even agreed to provide financial assistance to rebuild some two hundred monasteries. In another sign of "goodwill," Tibetan political prisoners were released, from November 1978, with a lot of publicity. Gradually the truth filtered out. Horrified, the outside world learned what the conditions of their incarceration had been. In his memoirs, the Dalai Lama remembered his conversations with his former personal physician, Dr. Tenzin Choedrak. As he had been accused of hiding first-class information, the hardship of his detention defies the imagination: "During his twenty years in prison, reports the Dalai Lama, "he almost died several times of hunger. He and his companions were reduced to eating their clothes, and if they happen to find a worm in their thin faces, they washed it and relished it."[142]

The Chinese dissident Wei Jingsheng, writing in March 1979, describes the horror of the concentration camp of Qingchen, where many Tibetans were detained, including the Panchen Lama. "The prisoners must sleep facing their cell door. If they turn whilst sleeping, the guard will wake them up as many times as necessary. A Tibetan began to suffer from one ear, on which he had slept for more than ten years. As it was swollen and infected, he tried to lie on his other ear but was regularly woken up and reprimanded by the guards. To the point that he became mad and tried to strangle them."[143] Phuntsok Wangyal[144] also describes methods of torture designed to break the psychic integrity of inmates: exposure to ultrasound causing unbearable migraines; to continuous intense light, day and night, which annihilates the spatio-temporal bearings; and gradual and prolonged suffocation in straitjackets with inflatable ties. Exhausted, some decided to starve themselves to death. But the prison administration would not tolerate this ultimate act of resistance. After several days of refusing food, the guards tied up the recalcitrants and introduced by force a rubber hose through the nose and esophagus to fill the stomach. This tube feeding caused bleeding, sinus infection, and headaches, from which the dissident Harry Wu says he still suffers, twenty years later. Yet the psychic pain was the most unbearable: the prisoner was deprived of the opportunity to protest against the inhumanity of his internment, even at the cost of his life. The alienation was total.

The release of prisoners certainly revealed the cruelty of the Communist dictatorship but represented a concession for the Tibetans, as did the authorization given to a few to visit their exiled relatives in India. The candidates for the journey were instructed to report to their families on the modernization of their country, to encourage them to return. At that time, the authorities seem even to have thought that the return of the Dalai Lama would serve the more tolerant image that China wanted to give itself. His presence would appease the demands of the population, thereby favoring the stability and growth of the Himalayan region. In 1978, therefore, several official Chinese declarations invited him to visit his homeland. He did not mention these in his speech of March 10, favoring a cautious *wait and see.*

The speech of 1979 showed an assessment. The twenty years gone by had demonstrated the limits of the rights guaranteed by the United Nations. The UN conventions of 1959, 1961, and 1965 had not been followed through. In addition, although the calls of the Dalai Lama to the United Nations had publicly raised the issue of human rights, they had obscured the problem of the legal status of Tibet. Then the resumption of diplomatic relations between the Western powers and the People's Republic of China had ratified its annexation.

Nevertheless, these calls to the UN had connected the cause of Tibet to that of the world. The Sino-Tibetan conflict was not an internal Chinese affair. Before the court of the world, which cause could Tibet plead? Certainly that of conscience, an ally of truth and justice. However, in 1979 the reason of state prevailed. Truth and justice weighed little against the rapprochement of China and the West, which carried huge economic stakes. The fight that led to a moral victory was not yet won. Yet an evolution was taking shape. In 1975, and even more emphatically in 1978 and 1979, the Dalai Lama posed the question of the happiness of the Tibetans. His cause became less political than economic and social. Could his position have accorded with the pragmatic approach of Deng Xiaoping? Was the process of dialogue finally about to begin?

PART TWO

The Middle Path, or
the Challenge of Peace

1980–1990

*The problems we face today, violent conflicts,
destruction of nature, poverty, hunger, and so on,
are human-created problems which can be resolved
through human effort, understanding, and the development
of a sense of brotherhood and sisterhood. We need to
cultivate a universal responsibility for one another
and the planet we share.*

THE DALAI LAMA

At a Kalachakra Initiation ceremony, Madison, Wisconsin, 1981.
(© Sheldan Collins / Corbis)

4

TIBET–CHINA DIALOGUE

———+———

1980–1985

In 1980, religious Tibet was destroyed. However, on the Indian side of the Himalayas, it was rebuilding itself. Not without sometimes-troubling coincidences: while in Lhasa the Red Guards demolished the statue of the thousand-armed buddha of Great Compassion,[1] in Dharamsala sculptors completed the casting of its replica in bronze. These simultaneous acts struck people's minds. Many thought that the soul of the Tibetan statue had migrated to India.

In the early 1960s, the refugees envisaged a short-lived exile. They therefore opted for temporary living conditions. In 1980, they realized that the hardship would be long. Their priority was to ensure the transmission of their culture to the next generation, and they intensified their efforts in the field of education, both secular and religious. On this morning of March 10, 1980, Tibet in exile had the face of hundreds of schoolchildren in uniform, long light-green *chupa*[2] for girls, dark blue trousers and checked shirt for boys. In tight ranks, they silently awaited the arrival of their spiritual guide to commemorate in his presence the sacrifice of their parents who rose up against the occupier in 1959.

Also revived were the inhabitants of Namgyal Monastery, sitting on the esplanade of the temples that they rebuilt with their own hands. Private monastery of the Dalai Lamas, Namgyal had one hundred and seventy-five monks before the Chinese invasion. Only fifty-two survived and managed to escape. Following the Dalai Lama, they regrouped in Dalhousie, north of Dharamsala. During the day, they worked in road construction for a living and to help the elderly. In the evening, the elders transmitted the heart of the spiritual practice to the younger ones. When the Indian government authorized them to settle in Dharamsala in 1968, they inaugurated a bungalow of modest size, used as both temple and home. It was located near the new eyrie residence of the Dalai Lama, on top of a rocky spur overlooking the Kangra valley.

The traditions were rapidly being restored, driven by the faith and hope of a determined community. In 1970, the Dalai Lama was able to give the first Kalachakra initiation outside Tibet. This rite, the most sacred of "the Diamond Vehicle," was celebrated during the third lunar month, and as they once did in the Potala, the monks of Namgyal created the great colored-sand mandala of the Wheel of Time.[3] This ceremony and the return of the traditional celebration gave the refugees the fortitude necessary to withstand the test of exile. "The Chinese were our conquerors, and they had indeed deprived us of our country," remembers Jetsun Pema, sister of the Dalai Lama. "Yet given what we were fulfilling in India, we had the feeling of triumphing over their victory."[4]

On March 10, 1980, two decades after the first speech at Swarg Ashram, the Dalai Lama went up the steps of the new Theckchen Choeling temple,[5] with its large and airy central walkways. From dawn to dusk, the pilgrims turned bronze prayer wheels, praying that the winds would blow afar the blessings of the mantra of compassion in order to relieve the suffering of all beings. Richly dressed on this morning in tribute to their charismatic leader, all bowed along his path while he ascended the tribune. The members of the Kashag, the Governor of Himachal Pradesh, and Indian officials welcomed him, before the speakers secured at the top of the monastery loudly carried his voice, which resounded through the valley.

MARCH 10, 1980

Twenty Years Later . . .

TWENTY-ONE YEARS HAVE unfolded a shocking experience, which has never had any parallel in the history of Tibet. Never has there been so much systematic and extensive destruction of the religious, cultural, social, and educational values of the Tibetan people. The frightening picture of abject poverty, wretched and helpless general conditions, persistent starvation and famine, had not been experienced in Tibet for centuries.

In the past few years, the fluid international political scene has witnessed rapid new developments; the internal situation in China under the present leadership, who are "seeking the truth from facts," is also undergoing changes. We hear of the repeated calls by the Chinese government requesting us to return to our homeland. We also hear that the so-called wave of moderation has begun to creep into China and, to some extent, into Tibet. However, it is still too early to predict the outcome of what may happen in the future. In response to the request by the Chinese government, I have dispatched a fact-finding delegation to visit Tibet through China. It is the first time in nearly twenty-one years that we have established contact with the Chinese government, as well as our beloved countrymen. The present policy of leniency favored by the Chinese in Tibet, I think, has also room for our contribution toward overcoming this educational discrepancy of the youth in Tibet. There are some Tibetan refugees visiting Tibet now. Why don't some of our youth, who have received decent educational opportunities, offer their service to take up teaching posts in Tibet on a temporary basis, in schools there? And I see no reason, given the present situation, the Chinese authorities should put any objection to this.

In conclusion, once more I would like to remind everybody that the core of the Tibetan issue is the welfare and ultimate happiness of six million Tibetans. The limited leniency that the Chinese have introduced is a welcome first step. But we are still nowhere near being satisfied that the Tibetans in Tibet are content. What the future holds in store, only time will tell.

Everything Except Independence

The initiative came from the Chinese. In December 1978, the director of the Xinhua News Agency in Hong Kong made contact with Gyalo Thondup, elder brother of the Dalai Lama, with an eye to a meeting in Beijing. Gyalo Thondup went there in February 1979 and met with several leaders, including Deng Xiaoping. These talks at the summit proved the seriousness of this approach. On the Tibetan side, the reputation of Deng Xiaoping, who was elected "Man of the Year" by the readers of *Time Magazine* in 1980, gave much hope in his commitment to openness and transparency. He also proposed to Gyalo Thondup that representatives of the Dalai Lama come and evaluate the progress achieved in their country. "Seek truth from facts"—the watchword therefore also applied to Tibet. He highlighted the effort to end the bureaucratic excesses that had led to the systematic falsification of the political and economic situation under Mao Zedong. So as not to incur Mao's displeasure, the Party executives had become accustomed to submitting overestimated statements of account and production reports. When traveling in the countryside, officials mobilized crowds of extras to give the show that the Great Helmsman wanted to see. It was only a skillfully orchestrated montage, young farmers with round cheeks reaping abundant harvests while China was starving to death. In Tibet, the official trick had reached such proportions that Chinese leaders could be the victims trapped in the slogan "Seek truth from facts."

Ren Rong, secretary of the Communist Party in Tibet, and the key executives of the Autonomous Region had indeed let themselves be persuaded that the former "emancipated serfs" were now happy under Chinese law. Convinced that modernization had created among the people a sense of gratitude for the Party, they were optimistic:

as soon as his delegates described to him the progress achieved, the Dalai Lama would return to his native country and renounce the need for independence.

For Deng's invitation was subject to a condition: everything could be discussed, except the independence of Tibet. To the Dalai Lama, who had for many years advocated it at the UN, the concession was important. However, since the late 1970s, his priority was the welfare of his people. In addition, during his first trip to the Soviet Union and Mongolia in the summer of 1979, he had suggested that Buddhism and Communism were reconcilable. Already in 1954, he had confided to Mao Zedong that he felt "half Buddhist and half Marxist" because he appreciated the ideal of social justice and sharing. Twenty-five years later, these words could still be understood as an attempt at pacification in order to defuse the conflict with China on the ideological level and facilitate dialogue. However, they were understood otherwise, the Chinese fearing that the religious leader sought to rally against them the support of the Soviet Union, their greatest enemy. This fear may have pushed them to open the talks that the Tibetans hoped to begin as soon as possible.[6]

Persistent Veneration from the Tibetans for the Dalai Lama

A delegation from the government in exile therefore went to Beijing in August 1979, led by Lobsang Samten, one of the four brothers of the Dalai Lama. It had received permission to visit the Autonomous Region as well as Kham and Amdo. The Dharamsala administration interpreted this as a tacit agreement that the Chinese would include in the discussions the whole of historical Tibet, not only the Autonomous Region. However, in reality they only demonstrated goodwill by organizing a general tour of inspection.

After two weeks in Beijing, the Dalai Lama's delegation went to Gansu and entered Tibet through the monastic citadel of Tashikyil—once the largest eastern monastery, its golden roofs and white *stupas*[7] reaching high into the sky. It was now no more than ruins and silent grief in a country emptied of its soul. The members of the delegation were struck by the magnitude of the destruction, beyond anything they had ever imagined.[8] To their desperation was added the sadness of finding the massive presence of settlers, originating from the Chinese coastal cities. They lived in ugly "boom towns," contrasting with the rugged beauty of the landscape. The delegates no longer recognized their homeland.

Another shock awaited them: the reunions with the population. The authorities had announced the delegates' imminent arrival, specifying that it would only be possible to meet them briefly to ask for news of relatives residing in India. However, all were eagerly waiting for them, hoping that the visit heralded better days. Until the last moment, the secret of the delegation's date of arrival and place of stay was well kept, so that the crowd could not receive them in Lhasa. Yet as soon as the news of their presence spread, men and women, children, young and old rushed to meet them. "Since the popular uprising at the gates of the Summer Palace in 1959, there had never been such a spontaneous demonstration," remembered Tubten Khetsun in his memoirs.[9] All regained the gestures banned by thirty years of indoctrination and persecution. Sobbing, with clasped hands, they bowed down and wanted to touch the envoys of their charismatic leader. The police tried to disperse them with blows with their sticks and rifle butts. Yet all was in vain. The crowd grew and refused to leave: "We were trying to convince people that we are ordinary human beings, not reincarnate lamas," remembered Juchen Namgyal. "But they would reply that, as we came on behalf of His Holiness the Dalai Lama, they saw no difference between us and reincarnations."[10] On the passage of their jeep, many rushed to gather with devotion the earth where the wheels of the vehicle had left their mark. They carried it away like a precious substance, which they ate in order to absorb its blessing. Those who managed to approach the delegates tore their clothes as if they were relics and begged them for hair for making amulets.

The security officers and Party executives were astounded by these religious impulses toward "reactionary feudal lords." They expected reactions of hatred or anger. They witnessed overflows of love. It seemed that the Cultural Revolution had slipped the people's minds, leaving intact the faith of long ago to the extent that the police chief of Amdo called the office in Lhasa to warn Ren Rong. Would it not be wise to cancel the visit of the delegation to Lhasa? Ren Rong committed the same error of judgment as his counterparts in the remote valleys of eastern Tibet, convinced that the inhabitants of the capital city had a high level of class consciousness. How could the Lhasans welcome with reverence the envoys of the Dalai Lama, who had exploited them for centuries? Had the "serfs" of yesteryear not become longtime socialists? In Lhasa, the police thus gave the order to the people not to insult or spit in the faces of the former slaveholders.

A fatal error! In the capital city, the emotion and devotion reached a climax. This visit marked the reunion of a people with its spiritual leader in the person of its delegates. Certainly, the red flag of the occupiers was fluttering over the Potala, the palace of a thousand windows, evoking the thousand eyes of the buddha of compassion attentive to the suffering of beings. However, the absent Dalai Lama was not less present in the heart of the Tibetans. Before this unstoppable popular fervor, the army barricaded the members of the delegation in the Jokhang. An iron gate had been erected during the Cultural Revolution to prevent the faithful from entering the holy of holies of religious Tibet and prostrating themselves before the shattered statues of their gods. Under the pressure of the crowd, the bars yielded. In a huge impulse of devotion, all threw themselves to the ground with clasped hands, faces bathed in tears, chanting mantras that thirty years of ideological hype had not erased from their memory. When, on the esplanade of the teachings,[11] the Chinese officials stationed in front of the Jokhang saw the Tibetans wildly applaud each statement by the Dalai Lama's brother, showing him irrepressible devotion, they lost composure. Some cried out: "What was the use of all our efforts for these people for so many years?" Others, furious, stamped their feet, some crying with rage.[12] The disappointment was immense.

To prevent such scenes from occurring outside the capital, at the last minute, the authorities decreed no access to the forced laborers in the fields. They thought they could prohibit farmers from meeting the envoys. Yet they disobeyed in masses. In southern Tibet, as in Lhasa and in the eastern provinces, the popular refutation was flagrant. The regime had lost face.

Back in Beijing, the representatives of the Dalai Lama shared their observations: poverty, lack of food and basic necessities, deplorable hygiene, educational structures virtually absent. The delegates were outraged to meet some of their compatriots who no longer spoke their own language. In his speech of March 10, 1980, the Dalai Lama included this information without mentioning the talks with the Chinese authorities, as they required him to keep them secret. So as not to cause a rupture in the finally initiated dialogue, nothing was leaked. The Dalai Lama chose to conclude cautiously. Without doubt, it was too early to say what this liberalization held for the Tibetans.

MARCH 10, 1981

"Brown sugar before your eyes, sealing wax in your mouth"

UNTIL THE CONDITIONS ripen for all the people in this world to become one great, united fraternal family, each society should have the right to preserve and develop its unique traditional heritage and culture along with modern science and technology. Therefore, at present, one of our principal concerns in the struggle for the rights of the six million people of Tibet should be the vigilant preservation and continuation of all those excellent aspects of our distinct cultural heritage that are of value to our society, without letting them decline.

The Chinese policy toward Tibet in the past has been like the Tibetan proverb, "Before your eyes they show you brown sugar, but in your mouth they give you sealing wax." While outwardly spreading courageous exaggerations which are clear, sweet-sounding, impressive, and seemingly convincing, but which falsify the facts, they in actual practice have only been subjecting the Tibetans to torture and oppression. In the face of that, the Tibetans had justified cause to strive to free themselves from the bondage of their sufferings, because all people have the right to free themselves from their own suffering. If in actual fact the distinctly Tibetan way of life were being kept fully intact and the people were happier now than under the former conditions, then there would be no point to argue.

In recent times the Chinese have realized that their past self-defeating policies of deception, exaggeration, and empty propaganda have been of more harm than benefit and have now adopted a new policy of "seeking truth from facts" and are trying to implement what they preach. Their admission of their past mistakes, without trying to cover them up, is praiseworthy. However, since the thirty-odd years of actual experience the Tibetan people have had under the domination of the Chinese has not been a short time, it is definitely going to take some time to develop confidence and conviction in a new lenient line.

MARCH 10, 1982

TIBETANS WILL HAVE to keep pace with the progressive changes that are occurring in the twentieth-century world and move toward democratic revolution. The old social system will never be resurrected. The teachings of the Buddha, as contained in the Tripitika (The Three Baskets) and Three Higher Trainings, are beneficial to society since they are based on sound reason and actual experience. These we must preserve and promote. However, the livelihood of lamas and monks and the admiration of the monastic establishment must of necessity change with the changing times. Like the fact that all the waters and rivers of different lands and climes have their ultimate meeting point in the ocean, so too the different viewpoints on society, the variety of economic theories, and the means of their attainment, must benefit, and they do certainly benefit, mankind itself. There is no point in indulging in dissension-creating discussions on differing ideologies. The fact that no positive result has accrued from attempting to convert all men of different temperaments and likings into one common ideology and mode of behavior can clearly be seen from the contemporary history of both the East and West. If a few, without caring the least for the basic welfare of people and the larger interest of mankind, continue to give orders, to beat, and to kill, and yet label this atrocious behavior as "revolutionary," they are only fooling themselves. Persons who adopt such behavior are not needed in any society, and they certainly do not belong to the ranks of those thinking human beings who work for the benefit of themselves as well as that of others.

In the last two or three years the situation in Tibet has undergone some slight change. Because of this a number of people, comparing this to past suffering, feel content with the present liberalization and hope that a good result will come about soon. On the other hand, a number of other people feel that the present liberalization policy is a new attempt to fool the Tibetans and that in the end the Tibetan people will not be given equal rights to freedom.

MARCH 10, 1983

A S A RESULT of some changes in the policy in Tibet since 1979, slight improvements in food and working conditions and the usage of the Tibetan language have given the Tibetan people a breathing space. However, these improvements not only did not uniformly cover all towns, villages, and various parts of Tibet, but even in the areas where these improvements are being implemented, they are temporary, corrupted, and inconsistent. Even now the general living conditions have not reached the level that existed before 1959 in spite of various movements initiated to make the poor rich. On top of this, there is a widening gap and increasing difference between Tibetans and Chinese. There also exists a constant feeling of resentment, fear, and suspicion, and the need by one person to show two faces. The deprivation of freedom to express one's views, either by force or by other means, is absolutely anachronistic and a brutal form of oppression. There are bound to be continuous problems of dissatisfaction and unrest in any region where an act of oppression takes place. The people of the world will not only oppose it but will also condemn it. Hence, the six million Tibetan people must have the right to preserve and enhance their cultural identity and religious freedom, the right to determine their own destiny and manage their own affairs.

Hu Yaobang, the Chinese Buddha

The Chinese authorities imposed discretion, and the Dalai Lama did not mention in public the continuing contacts between Beijing and Dharamsala. The visit of the first delegation in 1979 revealed the gap between the beliefs of the political class and the reality on the ground. The failure of the socialist indoctrination of Tibet had become evident. To explore the mechanisms of this dysfunction, authorities brought together, from April 1980, the first Working Forum on Tibet and decided to send an observation mission to the Autonomous Region in May, led by the Party General Secretary in person.

Hu Yaobang could see for himself the "abject misery" denounced by the Dalai Lama. One-third of the rural population suffered from extreme poverty.[13] Facing the distress of the Tibetans, he delivered a contrite speech in Lhasa: "The present situation is anything but idyllic because the standard of living of the people in Tibet is hardly higher. In some areas it has even worsened. The comrades of the Central Committee are very shocked. The Party has given up on the Tibetans. We are deeply scandalized! The sole objective of the Communist

Party is the happiness of the peoples! We have worked for nearly thirty years for this purpose, but the life of the Tibetan people has hardly improved and we are to blame."[14]

Back in Beijing, Hu Yaobang relieved Ren Rong of his duties and proposed radical reforms for the Autonomous Region. These measures should relax taxes, forced labor, and agricultural production quotas. Subsidies were allocated to help those most in need and to restore religious monuments. The Chinese then made public their desire to rebuild Tibet within ten years.[15] Another directive imposed the withdrawal of 80 percent of Chinese executives from the administration of the Autonomous Region. Only health care personnel and a few technicians were maintained, and all were required to speak Tibetan. Tibet also witnessed the overthrow of the slogan of the Cultural Revolution. In 1966, the "Four Olds" had to be attacked, and consequently the heritage of historical Tibet was demolished. In 1981, the traditions were reestablished by authorizing one of the most popular prayer festivals, the Serthang, dedicated to Tsongkhapa. It took place in Ganden, monastic city of more than 4,000 monks. The population was devoted to restoring such places with an enthusiasm that aroused the suspicion of the authorities. Wrongly suspecting the exile government of secretly promoting these works, Party executives tried to dry up the sources of funding. They did not understand that Tibetans were investing their scarce resources in a work of faith. The renovation of Ganden, carried out by 300 followers, was entirely financed by offerings. Intimidation and threats were in vain. The population was trying to exorcize the torments of the Cultural Revolution and spared no efforts.

It was therefore with an intense fervor that on August 18, 1982, a thousand pilgrims gathered at night around the monastery, finally restored. At dawn, to the sound of femur trumpets, drums, and cymbals, a procession formed. Led by the lamas wearing their high yellow hats with a fringed edge, monks carried on their shoulders a rolled-up monumental *thangka*[16] that they prepared to suspend on the main wall. Using a system of ropes and pulleys, they deployed the vast tapestry that flowed smoothly down the wall. It was covered with a golden veil, woven with symbols of enlightenment. An extreme emotion passed through the pilgrims when they could contemplate this image of the Buddha surrounded by celestial beings, touching the earth as his witness. Following tradition, pilgrims threw *khata*s in his direction, thus expressing their wish to see the Dharma flourish for the benefit of all beings.

Admittedly, most of the monastery was still in ruins and under the supervision of unfriendly soldiers stationed nearby. Yet this first religious festival after the Cultural Revolution demonstrated the resistance of the Tibetans: a martyred people whose faith had triumphed again. Grateful to Hu Yaobang for this beginning of liberalization, some called him the "Chinese Buddha." When he was reelected General Secretary of the Party in 1982, the Dalai Lama sent him a congratulatory telegram, expressing the wish to meet him personally. In vain.

The Mission of Jetsun Pema

A few months after the visit of Hu Yaobang, in July 1980, the Dalai Lama instructed Jetsun Pema, his younger sister, to lead a delegation that would assess the condition of the education system in Tibet. She had solid experience, as she had held since 1964 the post of Director of the Tibetan Children's Villages in India, whose study programs she had defined with the Indian Ministry of Education. Her delegation was the third to go to Tibet. It followed shortly after the second one, which departed in May 1980 and had been interrupted. For despite all their precautions, the Chinese had not been able to prevent her from fortuitously meeting foreign journalists in Lhasa. The government was keen to control information. Following this incident, Yang Jingren, right arm of Hu Yaobang, warned that the representatives of the Dalai Lama were not to make any public statement if they wished the policy of openness to continue. Officially, the Chinese attributed the poverty and destruction of Tibet to the devices of the Gang of

Four under the Cultural Revolution, while ensuring that the current regime strove to rectify these past mistakes. The population was again summoned not to express any joy, not to offer *khatas*, and not to prostrate themselves. If some shouted slogans in favor of independence, they suffered the fate of Tsering Lhamo, a Lhasan tortured for proclaiming "Long live free Tibet!" whom all fondly called Rangzen Ama, "Mother Independence."

Jetsun Pema had prepared herself for the worst. The refugees maintained few illusions about the state of their country. She was nevertheless devastated by a pain of her own: a pain most often mute. Every word, every gesture, every encounter was being observed. The surveillance made the drama even more unbearable. The sister of the Dalai Lama decided to keep a journal: "The whole world must know. It also seems essential that the slow agony resulting from this barbarism is clearly perceived by the international community."[17] During her mission, which lasted from June to September 1980, the Chinese constantly showed bad faith. Before the emaciated faces and bodies of the Tibetans, Beijing administrators dared to boast of confirmed progress by presenting rigged statistics. In every town and village, mayors launched into complacent diatribes. "The more important the city, the more lengthy was the speech,"[18] remembered Jetsun Pema. In depopulated areas, as in the Golok region, officials used climate change to "explain" the almost total extermination of this ethnic group. They tried by all means to hide the truth and prohibited as much as possible any contact with the population. Any excuse was good. Did Jetsun Pema lower the car window to talk to passersby? It immediately had to be closed again, as the cold air gave her Chinese guide rheumatism. Sometimes, sudden vehicle failures prevented planned visits. This camouflage revealed an unfortunate reality. At the monastery of Tashikyil, partly rebuilt since the visit of the first delegation, seven scrawny old monks welcomed Jetsun Pema. Despite their presence, the place remained empty, to the extent that Jetsun Pema wondered sadly if they had not taken these walk-on actors from some forced labor camp, just for her visit.[19]

As the Dalai Lama's sister was supposed to evaluate the educational system, she insisted on visiting schools. However, it was the holidays, assured her guide. But school days were long and without interruption during the summer months; it was on the contrary during the cold winter that classes were suspended! In some villages, schools were even improvised. Under a tent, for example, everything was new, the tent itself, but also tables, the white board, children's clothes. Under the carpet, the still green and tender grass revealed the deception. To add insult to injury, a teacher explained the subtleties of grammar to illiterate schoolchildren. The situation became so ridiculous, Jetsun Pema said in her diary, that even Chinese officials accompanying her showed their discomfort.[20] Even though they spoke to her a lot about 430 primary schools, 55 colleges, and 6,000 private schools, she never saw them. When she brought these facts to the Dalai Lama, he reiterated his proposal to send about 50 teachers and create a liaison office in Lhasa, responsible for education. The Chinese government never followed this up.

Even more than the previous one, this mission was a reunion between the Tibetans and their charismatic leader through his delegates. More than seven thousand people gave them letters destined for him. Those who had written them poured out their heart, confiding their sufferings and hopes. So that these letters did not fall into the hands of the Chinese, the members of the delegation placed them in bags that they never left unattended. Hu Yaobang regretted that Tibetans preferred to bring their grievances to the Dalai Lama, a "feudal lord," rather than to the Party executives. However, this showed that the Chinese were ignorant of the persistence of the devotional link between the people of Tibet and their spiritual leader. Jetsun Pema told how, in Lhasa, a crowd of thirty thousand people massed around her. At the foot of the Potala, now a sterile and lifeless museum, the recently installed sewers overflowed with nauseating water. The only electrified areas were inhabited by Chinese. In the streets, the Tibetans marched headlong. The dignity of a people was scorned, its pride crushed. "I assert," wrote Jetsun Pema, "that the majority of Tibetans in Tibet live like animals. Yet . . . I could, throughout the whole of our journey, notice how their determination remained as strong as ever. All these men, all these women said: 'We have a spiritual and temporal leader, the Dalai Lama, and he thinks of us.'"[21]

Tibet and China—Ripe Time to Come to an Agreement?

On March 13, 1981, the leader of the Tibetans wrote a simple letter to Deng Xiaoping. He began by paying tribute to communism, which "seeks the welfare of people in general and in particular of the proletariat," and to Leninism, which advocates equality between nationalities. If such an ideology were implemented, he continued, it could not fail to arouse admiration and to bring happiness to its people. However, decades had shown a decline in the economy and education, sectors that influenced the well-being of the population. There was also physical violence and massive destruction of the Tibetan heritage. After such a tragedy, caused by human activity and not by natural disasters, emergency measures were necessary. In order to decide on these, it was necessary to establish, as a priority, a relationship of mutual understanding between Tibetans and Chinese: "It is time to implement our common wisdom in a spirit of tolerance and openness so that the Tibetan people finally know an authentic happiness."[22]

Deng Xiaoping did not reply, but Hu Yaobang expressed the wish to meet again the elder brother of the Dalai Lama, Gyalo Thondup. Four months later, on July 28, 1981, he gave him a memorandum. This document envisaged the return of the leader of the Tibetans to the motherland to defend the unity of China in a spirit of solidarity between Chinese and Tibetans. The Dalai Lama, elevated to the rank of vice-president of the National People's Congress, would reside in Beijing. The spiritual leader vehemently rejected this proposal, which deflected his request. Under cover of an honorary position, his presence in Beijing would have legitimized the annexation of the high plateau as well as the exploitation of the population and wealth of Tibet.

His call for tolerance and openness was reduced to a discussion of his rank in the Party apparatus and his unconditional acquiescence to the Chinese colonization.

In order to renegotiate his initial claim, the Dalai Lama once again sent emissaries, who arrived in Beijing on April 24, 1982. Based on the terms of the letter to Deng Xiaoping in favor of reconciliation, they agreed not to raise the question of independence. The government in exile made this concession out of humanitarian concern for its people who had remained in Tibet. However, in return, the delegates demanded the unification of the three provinces of historical Tibet. They also requested that their country be given the status proposed by Deng Xiaoping in Taiwan for its reunification with mainland China. The Chinese leader had indeed proposed to leave to the island the choice of its government system and the management of its economy and defense, all the rest being shared. This would allow the Taiwanese to preserve their traditions and spare them from communist indoctrination. If the Beijing regime was willing to grant as much to the Taiwanese, who were Chinese, were the Tibetans not well-founded in demanding yet greater autonomy?

However, the Dalai Lama's delegates ran into a stone wall. Taiwan and Tibet were not comparable. The first had yet to be "liberated," while the second had been liberated thirty-three years before. The discussions lasted more than a month, and the Chinese remained firm, limiting themselves to setting their conditions for the return of the Dalai Lama. In conclusion, they stated that the members of the delegation were not valid interlocutors, for their government in exile had no legitimacy.

Juchen Namgyal remembers having felt like a hostage. He was afraid to break off the dialogue process but could not accept the Chinese tactic of constantly moving the discussion to the person of the Dalai Lama. The delegation returned to Dharamsala without having advanced. The Chinese made it clear that they did not agree to debate on an equal footing. They behaved as absolute masters, inclined to think that economic reforms and a certain tolerance would eventually ease the contestations of the Tibetans in Tibet—which would make the claims of the exiled null and void. The only obstacle: the people in Tibet had expressed unanimous support for their spiritual leader. It would be necessary to take into account his moral legitimacy.

Hu Yaobang: Kept Promises

The effects of Hu Yaobang's reforms were already being felt. Farmers' incomes, which accounted for 90 percent of the income of Tibetan society, had doubled. This spectacular growth was, however, limited to restoring a standard of living equal to that in the period that preceded the "liberation" of the country.[23] It relieved the extreme poverty without providing wealth. The liberalization of social life, on the other hand, constituted a real factor of change, for it allowed a revival of the Tibetan identity. Hu Yaobang had kept his promise, and thousands of Chinese officials were repatriated, replaced by young Tibetans trained in China. Former respected key figures of the population, persecuted and imprisoned because of their social class, were rehabilitated, and an authentic "Tibetanization" of the bureaucracy took place. It was not a transfer of power to local executives, for the all-powerful Party maintained its prerogatives and kept its decision-making bodies in Beijing. It was thus rather an "improvement" or "cleaning" of governance that took place. At least the vise that had imprisoned Tibetan society was loosened, especially as the endless meetings of indoctrination organized by the Communist Party were suspended.

A sign of a revival of Tibetan identity: traditional clothing replaced the Maoist uniform. The *chupa*, pinafore dresses for women, and belted robes for men reappeared. They were worn during the great festivals that once again moved the crowds. Thirty years of proletarian culture were submerged by the strong comeback of customs. In July 1982, the Panchen Lama even obtained permission to return to Tibet, after being under house arrest in Beijing during the three years that followed his release from prison. Considered a patriot reeducated during his detention, he was appointed a vice-president of the National People's Congress in 1980. His trip to Tibet revealed to what extent the people worshiped him. However, his honorary position gave him no power.

In 1983, the country emerged from the Maoist period, the darkest of its history. Happiness, dignity, and freedom were nevertheless far from secured. The Dalai Lama still tried to obtain Chinese concessions and continued to oppose the dictatorship of Beijing with morality and the law. His humanistic considerations were weighty, especially as the grace period of liberal measures promised to be short. By the end of 1983, a revival of controls was already taking shape.

MARCH 10, 1984

Interdependence, Justice, and Happiness

W E CAN SEE that compared to the world's other refugees, our number of 100,000 is small. And although the majority of this number lives in India, amid its teeming millions, instead of scattering and being absorbed like water in sand, we have managed to preserve our identity and cohesiveness by living in groups of thousands. Most Tibetans in India, Nepal, and Bhutan live in agricultural settlements; others make their living in various professions, different handicraft industries and small businesses. There are between two and three thousand Tibetans living in about 30 other countries, earning their living successfully just as the citizens of their country of refuge and succor. As for the young Tibetans, they are taught the themes of our cultural heritage with the Tibetan language as the basis. At the same time, they are given modern education.

However, we in exile, through great efforts, have collected, preserved, and published whatever scriptural texts we could find, and we have also established centers for the study and practice of Buddhism where young monks can study the Sutras and Tantras. As a result, firm foundations have been laid for the continuity and further spread of Buddhism. Moreover, hundreds of new centers have been established throughout the world where previously there was no trace of Buddhism. And today, many educated people the world over are studying and practicing Buddhism. Furthermore, an increasing number of people throughout the world are acknowledging the fact that the Tibetan race, language, traditions, religion, culture, and political and economic systems are completely distinct and separate from those of the Chinese people, and the fact that Tibet was an independent country with a recorded history of more than a thousand years. Consequently, there is a growing number who are supporting and sympathizing with our just cause.

Despite these recent changes, the situation is far from satisfactory. Although much publicity has been made in China about the freedom of religious worship by restoring a few of the destroyed monasteries, obstructions are still placed on those entering the monastic order and those who start to preach, study, and practice the Dharma. Similarly, regarding the Tibetan written language, apart from the general publications of some Tibetan folktales, plays, and stories, it is not used either in the administration of the affairs of the country or in its economic management. This is a clear indication that the administration of Tibet is in the hands of an alien people who do not know the Tibetan language. The so-called freedom of religious worship and national autonomy through impressive slogans is simply empty talk.

MARCH 10, 1985

A S OUR OLD Tibetan saying goes: "If the root has not dried, the tree is not dead"; our situation is not without hope. And, since there have been positive developments to give us cause for hope, it is of utmost importance that we must not lose heart but find the strength and courage to make a firm pledge to persevere in our struggle.

In ancient times, the problems of one country were seemingly of no concern to the other nations and often remained unknown to them. But today, when the world is becoming smaller and more interdependent, events even in a remote region arouse the concern and attention of the rest of the world. This is because what happens in one country affects the overall global situation. China has also realized that it cannot remain isolated from the rest of the world. As a result, they have been compelled to adopt new ideas and policy. So, compared to the conditions of a few years ago, there has been some progress in their fundamental policies. But in order to achieve genuine happiness in any human society, freedom of thought is extremely important. This freedom of thought can only be achieved from mutual trust, mutual understanding, and the absence of fear. On the other hand, if we only pay lip service to noble sentiments but continue to harbor hatred and ill will within our hearts, sooner or later there is bound to be confrontation.

In the case of Tibet and China too, unless we can remove the state of mutual fear and mistrust, unless we can develop a genuine sense of friendship and goodwill—the problem that we face today will continue to exist. So, at this time, I feel the most important thing for us is to keep in close contact, to express our views frankly, and to make sincere efforts to understand each other. And, through eventual improvement in human relationships, I am confident that our problems can be solved to our mutual satisfaction.

Religious Freedom, Empty Words

If in 1984 and 1985, the Dalai Lama rejoiced about the rebirth of Buddhism and its diffusion throughout the world, in Tibet, some Chinese officials were alarmed at the revival of religion and the fervor of the crowds. Not all shared the liberalism of Hu Yaobang, and more and more officials obstructed his reforms. In 1984 the Panchen

Lama openly criticized leftist factions that blocked the implementation of liberal measures decided in Beijing. The Dalai Lama echoed
his views, denouncing a "so-called religious freedom." It was indeed
limited to the *outward* manifestations of religion; Tibetans were once
again allowed to worship in the holy places, recite mantras, turn the
prayer wheels, offer incense and lamps, and hang prayer flags. These
acts were branded as nationalism, and so these practices were once
again hit by prohibitions, which at first targeted the reconstruction of
the monasteries.

Tolerance was short-lived. The immense enthusiasm set off by the
festival of Serthang in Ganden in the fall of 1982 was seen by the government as an alarm. In 1983, it gave the order to stop such works,
deporting offenders. Each monastery had to meet quotas for monks
or nuns, and the age of ordination was postponed to eighteen years,
breaking with the tradition of very young novices. Authorities insisted that the children receive a socialist education before their spiritual
training, and prior consent from local Party officials became necessary in order to be ordained. The course of study in the monastic colleges was reduced to rituals, whereas in essence Buddhism is a training
of the mind in contemplative sciences—not a blind faith, guided by
superstition, ignorance, and idolatry, as was claimed pejoratively by
the Chinese.

In order to control the monasteries, the Party instituted "Democratic Management Committees." Affiliated with local branches of the
Office of Religious Affairs, on which they depended for the payment
of their wages, the members of these committees had to report any
religious persons suspected of anti-Chinese or nationalist sentiments,
approve requests for ordination, and denounce the "nonregistered."
The objective was to form a "contingent of religious [people] supporting the supremacy of the Party and the socialist system."[24] This
new clergy had to, above all, show evidence of class consciousness
and patriotism, and the curriculum of monastic studies henceforth
incorporated an aspect of antireligious policy. The responsibility of
the monasteries was limited to preserving the heritage of worship,

converted into a tourist attraction. To restrict their initiatives, committees diverted the donations of the faithful and supervised the budget allocated to each institution. By the end of 1984, the authorities had thus again taken over religious life. The alleged freedom of belief was confined to the superficial expression of faith, which presented the advantage of creating an illusion. However, under an artificial order, revolt was brewing.

The Modernization of China and the Sinicization of Tibet

Failing to learn from the mistakes of the Maoist era, Chinese leaders persisted in ignoring the frustration of the people and wanted to believe that a significant improvement in the standard of living was gradually defusing the nationalist claims. However, the directives imposed on the Tibetan economy actually contributed to the development of China, not Tibet, according to the old model of relations of the Middle Kingdom with its vassal states, forced to pay high tributes. The economic and political integration of the high country was solely designed to meet the Chinese need for raw materials and natural resources. The Party officials denounced the Tibetans' backward mentality and lack of training as barriers to their entry into a market economy. "The reason for underdevelopment is underdevelopment." The authors of this very popular slogan were Wang Xiaoqiang and Bai Nanfeng, of the Economic Structural Institute of China, established in Beijing in 1980 by Zhao Ziyang.[25] These experts were tasked with analyzing why Tibet did not evolve despite the reforms, why its abundance of natural resources did not engender prosperity.

After investigation, they concluded that "the traditional lifestyle extends the traditional modes of production and maintains the traditional concepts of values that fulfill tradition."[26] The concentration of wealth in the heritage of religious Tibet was in their eyes a guilty waste. The time required for the maintenance of places of worship or the food offerings illustrated the survival of irrational and unproductive behavior. The Democratic Management Committees incidentally had the mission of recovering the ritual butter lamps so their fuel could be used by government bakeries. To definitively solve the backwardness of the Autonomous Region, Wang and Bai recommended a massive immigration of Chinese, which would introduce modern lifestyles and consumerism—a solution justified by the lack of political awareness and education of Tibetans: "After centuries of slavery, they are not trained intellectually. It is therefore necessary that people of other nationalities help in their administration."[27]

Based on these conclusions, the Second Work Forum on Tibet recommended in 1984 a repeal of the decision of the First Forum of 1981, which had restricted the immigration of Chinese settlers. Hu Yaobang could only ratify this new orientation. On behalf of the modernization of Tibet, he also had to approve forty-three ambitious development projects funded by state investments. Yet none of these aimed at raising the living standards of the Tibetans. Instead, all reinforced the Chinese bureaucracy and the expansion of urban areas, intended for new Chinese settlers. As of September 1984, Beijing announced the transfer of five hundred experts and eight thousand workers. The sinicization process was going to the next level. Tibetans were excluded from the decision-making process, although the implementation of this program would radically transform their lives and their environment. There was no shortage of erupting conflicts, such as around the proposed hydroelectric plant on the shores of Lake Yamdrok, southwest of Lhasa. Since time immemorial its waters had been sacred. Yet they would irreversibly be drained by the construction of the recommended drainage tunnel. The Panchen Lama opposed this himself and obtained a postponement of the work. However, in general, the Chinese forced their ideas through. The Tibetans gradually saw themselves dispossessed of their traditional habitat, and faced with the degradation of their natural environment, they became strangers in their homeland. Their fate was taken from them.

Non-negotiable Conditions for the Return of the Dalai Lama

Could Tibet restrain this Chinese-style modernization? In May 1984, the National People's Congress promulgated a law on the autonomy of the regions, granting them broad powers on the economic, fiscal, educational, cultural, and social levels. The right to amend the laws passed by the National Assembly was also recognized, but with the obligation of deferring to the supreme authority of the central government, which restricted the scope of application. In addition, these clauses delegated no power to local decision making. The authority granted to the government of the Autonomous Region of Tibet remained a mere formality. Even if a Tibetan held the position of governor, the secretary of the Communist Party in Lhasa, above him, was a Chinese. The autonomy of the regional government was therefore subordinate to the control of the Chinese Communist Party. In Tibet, as in China, no level of government could offset the single party, source of all authority. This made the Lhasapas say that a clap of thunder did not bring rain. . . .

Another new fact: to exploit the Autonomous Region, the Party leaders felt they no longer needed the support of the Dalai Lama. If, from 1979 to 1982, they had considered him essential to legitimize the annexation of Tibet, they were now inclined to think that it would be easier to do so without him. It was in this context that in 1984, the Dalai Lama made known his wish to visit his country the following year. Authorities declared his visit untimely, on the pretext that the country would be mobilized in 1985 for the celebration of the twentieth anniversary of the Autonomous Region, and that festivities at several sites would make traveling on the roads impracticable. To further discredit the spiritual leader, a statement of the Regional Assembly of the people even accused him of treason.

Nevertheless, in 1985, the Dalai Lama continued to affirm the need for the Tibetans and Chinese to try to understand one another. Refusing to be trapped in antagonism with China, he developed in his speeches a Buddhist theme. While claiming for Tibet the rights guaranteed by international jurisprudence, he also evaluated the situation according to the law of interdependence, which includes an immanent justice, whereby harming others comes down to harming oneself. According to this logic, China could not remain much longer in isolation without the risk of destroying itself. If the Communist Party had managed to escape until now the law of men, it would not escape the law of interdependence. It would one day soon have to recognize that freedom is the condition of happiness in any society and that democracy is the way of the future.

5

TIBET, SANCTUARY OF WORLD PEACE?

——+——

1986–1990

MARCH 10, 1986

Colonization and Demographic Aggression

OVER ONE MILLION were killed and many more had to endure immeasurable mental and physical suffering. Under the pretext that Tibetans are not competent, large numbers of Chinese, mainly under the guise of skilled labor, are being brought into the major towns of central Tibet. Especially in parts of Amdo and Kham, large numbers of Chinese are continually setting up agricultural settlements in the more fertile areas and places where there are better facilities. The native inhabitants, the Tibetans, are being pushed away to remote areas and being forced to live as nomads.

I would also like to add a word of caution about the new Chinese economic policy for Tibet. Apart from liberalizing the economic system in Tibet, since 1980, China has recently invited foreign capital investment in Tibet. This is welcome, if it will lead to an improvement in the standard of living of the common Tibetans. But for the last twenty-seven years there has been a systematic exploitation of Tibet's natural resources. More than anything else, Tibet was made the source of raw material for the economic development of China. If the present trend continues and also if the Chinese hastily and haphazardly plan the economic development of Tibet to meet their overall modernization target without taking into consideration the conditions of the country and the needs of the people, there is the danger that not only economic chaos but also ecological disaster will befall Tibet.

MARCH 10, 1987

DURING THE LAST few years there has been an unprecedented increase of Chinese civilians throughout Tibet. This policy of colonization and demographic aggression poses a great threat of reducing our people to a minority in our own country. This has also rendered the much-publicized Chinese claim of respecting Tibetan identity, religion, culture, and traditions meaningless. Furthermore, this has resulted in Chinese domination of economic and employment opportunities, particularly in the major towns where almost two-thirds of the population are now Chinese. The large-scale Chinese influx is threatening to transform Tibet into a Chinese territory. Thus, while China accuses others of crimes of racial discrimination and injustice, the Chinese themselves continue the worst forms of genocide, racial discrimination, and colonization in the countries under their subjugation.

In any situation of human conflict it is shortsighted to believe that a lasting solution can be found through the use of force. I have always expressed my firm conviction in the wisdom of following a nonviolent path. Force and confrontation can only bring about temporary gains. In the case of Tibet too, Tibetan opposition will continue to exist so long as the hopes and aspirations of our people remain suppressed. I would like to reiterate that the issue of Tibet is not about the power and position of either the Dalai Lama or the future of the Tibetan refugees alone, but rather it is the question of the rights and freedoms of the six million Tibetans. It is a mistake to presume that mere economic concessions and liberalizations can satisfy our people. The issue of Tibet is fundamentally political with international ramifications, and as such, only a political solution can provide a meaningful answer.

Before concluding, I would like to express my solidarity with many of the educated and intelligent young Chinese who are undergoing physical as well as mental suppression. Even the Chinese themselves, who have an ancient civilization, are deprived of individual freedoms. They are living in a state of great anxiety about the present changes and uncertainty of the future. It is my hope that they too will gain the inalienable rights and freedoms that are basic to all human beings.

Demographic Aggression

The Tibetan administration in exile counted the number of victims of the invasion and occupation of their country since 1950. One million two hundred thousand people had lost their lives.[28] One Tibetan in six died in battles, under the blows of repression; or of torture, internment, or famine. This figure was calculated on the basis of information reported by refugees in India and Nepal. Unlike the Nazi regime that counted the number of victims of the Holocaust, the Chinese authorities in Tibet did not register deaths and even dispersed their numbers through prisons and labor camps. Those who find the figure of one million two hundred thousand deaths exaggerated have noted that this corresponds to about twenty deaths per refugee![29] While recognizing the aleatory nature of such information, the Tibetan administration argued that in a predominantly rural and sparsely populated society like that of former Tibet, inhabitants knew exactly what was happening. Moreover, those who contested this figure did not provide evidence to the contrary. Also, the Chinese government admitted a high proportion of Tibetans killed during the "peaceful liberation" of their country.

The revelation of the scale and brutality of this crime, qualified as genocide since 1959, occurred at a time when the People's Republic positioned itself as a major power on an economic and military level. Western nations were therefore reluctant to ask for its counts for fear of losing access to the largest market in the world. The stories of atrocities and human rights abuses in Tibet continued to filter out, but in 1986 and 1987, most nations strove especially to improve their relations with China. Yet the exploitation of Tibetan natural resources was going to cause a new Chinese violation of international law.

Indeed, these years saw the unprecedented amplification of the transfer of Chinese into Tibet. In 1986, sixty thousand workers settled on the high plateau—engineers, experts, and workmen, joined by entrepreneurs eager to take advantage of multiple opportunities. Beijing's new leaders now admitted that the market economy was based on the free movement of persons. They therefore conceded many advantages to traders in the bordering Chinese provinces: permits and special conditions, tax exemptions, and preferential loans. The Chinese officials in Tibet, for their part, received a salary that was three times higher than normal, high allowances, and extended vacation. Their profits allowed them to import consumer goods until then unknown in Tibet. Business was flourishing, and nearly twelve thousand businesses opened between 1985 and 1987. Most were based in the capital and other cities of importance. In Lhasa itself, there were more than fifty thousand Chinese.[30] Two years later, in 1989, they were a hundred thousand, dominating the employment market and intensifying the economic exclusion of Tibetans amid anarchical urban development.

The transfer of civilians by an occupying government into the annexed territories is condemned by the Geneva Convention of 1946. History shows that colonial administrations and totalitarian regimes have used this to strengthen their dictatorship, like Stalin in the former Soviet Union. The policy of the demographic submersion of Tibet had already been envisaged by Mao Zedong who, in 1952, observed:

"Tibet covers a wide area, but its population is widely dispersed. It must increase to more than ten million inhabitants."[31] This reasoning seems to have been shared by all the Chinese leaders, and in 1985, the Embassy of the People's Republic in New Delhi declared that its government intended to repair the economic imbalance and the demographic deficiency of Tibet. The local population was requested to properly welcome sixty thousand workers from Sichuan, who would be followed by three hundred thousand other migrants.[32] Similarly, when he met President Jimmy Carter in June 1987, Deng Xiaoping did not hesitate to say that the Chinese settled in Tibet out of necessity. The important thing was to modernize the country, and in relation to this objective, the question of the nationality of the workers was a detail.[33] On this point too, the great powers therefore agreed to deny international jurisprudence. Their interests lay in the sinicization of the new Himalayan El Dorado.

Economic Chaos, Ecological Disaster

Foreign capital investment in Tibet, encouraged by Communist China, only accelerated an ecological disaster. In 1985, deforestation had already destroyed more than 100,000 hectares of old-growth forests. The arrival of large numbers of Chinese settlers and the exploitation of mineral resources involved the construction of roads leading to the new industrial sites. The alarming remarks of the Dalai Lama on this subject were justified. Yet who listened to him, before the benefits presented by the Chinese boom? Despite his denunciations, the foreign governments, far from being opposed to Beijing's offers, responded favorably, for they benefited from the consequences of this unprecedented growth. The West therefore supported a neocolonial policy whose principle they officially condemned.

For his part, the Panchen Lama openly criticized the economic consequences of the massive transfer of Chinese during the National People's Congress in Beijing in March 1987, as it resulted in uncontrollable inflation. The price of staple foods such as yak meat had been multiplied by nine, and that of butter by five. The population once again suffered from food shortages. In that context, the celebrations of the twentieth anniversary of the founding of the Autonomous Region resembled a provocation. The situation in Lhasa was so tense that the government took exceptional security measures. The police proceeded again to making arrests and ordered the evacuation of tourists.

Yet the authorities made an effort to maintain a liberal façade and tried to win the support of the Panchen Lama. In February 1986, they therefore authorized him to celebrate Mönlam Chenmo[34] in Lhasa, where he blessed a crowd of a hundred thousand faithful, thus giving the official media the opportunity to praise the return of religious freedom. Tolerance, however, was not on the agenda, neither in Tibet nor in China itself, which witnessed a revival of the democratic movement. During the winter of 1986, demonstrations occurred at about a hundred universities. In Shanghai, on December 21, 1986, the students were joined by a cortege of two thousand workers. They marched under banners proclaiming: "Long live the Commune of Paris!" and "If you want to know what freedom is, go ask Wei Jingsheng!" The "father of democracy" inspired the new protesters, who marched on the provincial governments of Hubei and Anhui to cries of "No modernization without democracy!" They demanded the immediate release of Wei, detained and sentenced to fifteen years in prison, since 1978 when he had challenged the single-party dictatorship and called people to fight for the democratization of institutions.

The Dalai Lama expressed officially for the first time on March 10, 1987, his solidarity with the Chinese in their struggle for freedom. His message was aimed particularly at the young people of this umpteenth "Beijing Spring." He wished them to recover the fundamental rights of which they had been deprived, like his people. Were Tibetans and Chinese destined to unite and stand together against the dictatorship?

The True Face of Dictatorship

The last years of the 1980s marked a turning point in the political struggle of the Dalai Lama, for global public opinion began
to mobilize itself for Tibet. The reports of organizations such as
Amnesty International were overwhelming, but the political class
and the media, especially in France, had until then shown great
leniency toward the leaders of the People's Republic. On behalf
of the right to difference, at the height of the Cultural Revolution,
observers had justified the dictatorship of Mao Zedong. *The Little
Red Book*, a collection of simplistic axioms, sold 800 million copies
worldwide, including 300,000 in France. He had led to the creation
of a new political family, the extreme left French students; Maoism
was used as an alternative to Stalinism. The Trotskyists were quick
to denigrate these new converts, called "Mao spontex" because they
had, without any critical thinking, joined the "revolutionary spon-
taneity" advocated by the Great Helmsman. This wave of Mao-
mania had inspired films like *La Chinoise* by Jean-Luc Godard in
1967 and *Les Chinois à Paris* by Jean Yanne in 1974, the song by
Jacques Dutron, "700 millions de Chinois et moi, et moi, et moi,"
and the best-seller by Alain Peyrefitte that incorporated in the title
a phrase attributed to Napoleon, "Quand la Chine s'eveillera, le
monde tremblera."[35]

In the early 1980s, analysts had chosen to describe Deng Xiaoping
as a debonair democrat, since he had restored in his country the right
to enrich oneself, to drink Coca-Cola and fall in love. It seemed to
be the era of the Chinese Miracle, while in the field of fashion Pierre
Cardin launched the Mao collar, and the People's Republic became
the preferred territory for large industrialists selling nuclear power
stations and aircraft. Under the pen of Alain Robbe-Grillet, China
passed for a romantic paradise, where "everything bathed in a mea-
sured kindness, calm, where every young man could gently hug his
wife without interfering with other couples."[36] In the conclusion of
a report, one could read these words, which insinuated doubts about

the totalitarian nature of the regime: "curious dictatorship, which can today be crossed by bus without seeing surge the shadow of a kepi."[37]

With hindsight, the silence of the media on the repression seems like guilt. Without doubt, it is indicative on the one hand of the fascination exerted by Mao on the French intelligentsia, as he agreed with the libertarian movement of May 1968, and on the other hand of the effectiveness of the disinformation campaigns orchestrated by the Chinese government. Its breadth can be appreciated through a newspaper article from January 1986 stating that executions in China with a bullet in the neck are reserved for "murderers, rapists, thieves, crooks, or smugglers," and that the regime no longer physically eliminates its political opponents.[38] In this context of Mao worship, the events in Lhasa made discordant voices heard. To awaken consciences, it was necessary that from fall 1987, men and women, religious and secular, shout to the world their despair; that hundreds of Tibetans be arrested, executed, tortured, and deported; that the media spotlight unveil the death camps that had been hidden behind the scenes in the falsely smiling landscape of China.

Faced with the emotion aroused in the press, the Dalai Lama found it regrettable that only violence could attract the attention of the international community. Would nonviolence be a dead end? He raised the question by noting that the politicians were alarmed by terrorist acts, without giving nonviolent struggle a chance. In September 1987 there was bloodshed in Lhasa. Despite the efforts of the army to censor reports, images circulated. The world witnessed the outburst of shocking violence against unarmed demonstrators. The dictatorship that the Dalai Lama had repeatedly denounced could no longer hide its true face.

June 18, 1987: Resolution of the U.S. Congress

In China, the year 1987 began with the disfavor of Hu Yaobang, who was dismissed by the left wing of the Party with the support of Deng Xiaoping. He was reproached for listening too much to the opinions of Taiwan and the foreign bourgeoisie. The legitimacy of his reforms in Tibet was challenged because they had fostered a resurgence of anti-Chinese nationalism. In addition, the opening of the Himalayan region to journalists and tourists did not go as planned. Foreign observers had noticed less the modernization of a backward country than the destruction of an ancient civilization and the colonial character of the Chinese occupation. At that time, tourists unintentionally became relayers of information on serious violations of human rights. They were out to explore the roof of the world, but the Tibetans stealthily slipped them paper pellets containing the name of political prisoners, asking them to communicate them to the UN or their government.[39] In an atmosphere of pervasive surveillance, these actions raised a corner of the veil covering the horror of concentration camps. The tragedy of Tibet, the cries of alarm launched by the government in exile took direction . . . finally. Humanitarian and human rights organizations began to create lobbies for the Tibetan cause.

The political impact of this mobilization was felt in June 1987, when members of the American Congress retrospectively condemned the invasion of Tibet in 1950 as well as the occupation and subjection of an independent people. The legislators also appreciated the figure put forward by the administration in Dharamsala, which denounced the death of one Tibetan in six as a result of the invasion. They described the demolition of more than six thousand monasteries as the "loss of an irreplaceable national heritage of art and literature, destroyed, stolen or misappropriated from Tibet."[40] The U.S. congressmen were finally alarmed at the statements of the Dalai Lama on the massive transfer of Chinese settlers. They accused the People's Republic of exploiting the resources of the Himalayan region for its exclusive benefit and of detaining a large number of prisoners of conscience. By a resolution adopted on June 18, 1987, the government of the United States demanded that Beijing open the dialogue proposed by the Dalai Lama. Washington intended to condition its arms transfers and trade on respect for human rights.

Congress also voted for an assistance program for refugees and scholarships for young Tibetans.[41]

The Chinese embassy in Washington protested, arguing that this support for Tibetan claims contradicted the foreign policy of the U.S. government, which had, along with the rest of the world, recognized in 1971 the People's Republic including Tibet within its borders. A note invited legislators to admit that their conclusions were based on fabrication and to correct their mistakes.[42] The estimate of over one million people was a "libel" that the office of Chinese propaganda strove to refute by publishing its own statistics. The decline in the number of inhabitants between 1953 and 1964 was part of a "trend of the millennium toward a stagnation of the Tibetan population."[43] The same study strove to emphasize demographic growth since 1964, thanks to the improvement of living standards. Based only on the number of inhabitants of the Autonomous Region, the Chinese authorities intended to demonstrate that the Tibetans hardly exceeded one million people. The figure of one million two hundred thousand victims was therefore exaggerated.[44]

The Beijing government was nevertheless not satisfied with this refutation and launched a relentless counteroffensive during the summer of 1987. Former President Jimmy Carter was a much pampered guest in Lhasa. On June 30, the front page of *China Daily* attributed to him compliments on the modernization of Tibet. A month later, Chancellor Helmut Kohl was in turn invited to the Himalayan capital, and again, Chinese newspapers boasted of his boundless admiration for the transformation of the high country. The journeys of the two statesmen had been carefully coordinated since their parliaments had seized on the Tibetan issue: indeed, not only had Congress passed several resolutions, but also in the Bundestag, the spokesman of the Green Party, Petra Kelly,[45] in 1987 submitted a written question asking her government to clarify its position on the human rights violations in Tibet. This development illustrates the cleavage in the 1980s between the government's position and parliamentary representation. The reason of state and public opinion were opposed.

Also in 1987, the Dalai Lama decided to override the reserve that he had held until then and to interpolate the conscience of nations. In the post–Cold War era, which witnessed a crisis of thought in the world, new problems darkened the future. The issue of human rights and the dignity of the person were forcefully reformulated given the vital degradation of the environment, nuclear proliferation, and the risk of extinction of traditional cultures faced with globalization. Tibet faced all of these threats. There, universal problems arose on a local scale: "In 1987, the Tibetan cause was a paradigm to the point where this country may be regarded as a laboratory where the answers of tomorrow were being experimented with."[46] On these issues, the Dalai Lama would open unprecedented avenues for reflection.

September 21, 1987: The Dalai Lama Before Congress

In September 1987, the Dalai Lama was invited to the United States for a private visit. The Chinese embassy did not fail to protest this invitation, which it considered unfriendly. It insisted even more than usual, requiring the United States to stop any political activity with the leader of the Tibetans. The State Department assured them that no official reception was on the agenda. However, something seemed to indicate that this visit would be different. The Indian government had not confirmed the escort of the diplomat who usually accompanied the Tibetan leader during his travels abroad. As if anticipating what would happen, New Delhi wanted to avoid any involvement— which would tend to prove that the Indian authorities knew the importance of the trip.

Having arrived on American soil on September 19, the Dalai Lama spoke before Congress on September 21. After criticizing the Chinese government for reducing the Tibetan cause to the matter of his return and his personal status, he asserted he was searching for a solution for the well-being of his six million compatriots. Having been unable to discuss it with the leaders of the People's Republic, he requested the intervention of the international community and proposed a peace plan in five points, laying the groundwork for future negotiations.

The first point would transform the whole of Tibet into a sanctuary of peace for the world. This proposal was based on a precedent: in 1975, during his investiture, King Birendra of Nepal had declared his country a "peace zone" with the approval of the Chinese government. Why would Tibet not benefit from the same status, since traditionally it was seen as a buffer state, guarantor of peace between China and India? The second point of the peace plan required the end of Chinese immigration, and the third called for respect for fundamental human rights and democratic freedoms. "The restoration and protection of the environment" of the high plateau, which the Chinese should stop using as the site of production of nuclear weapons and radioactive waste disposal, was the fourth point. This was a factor in the massive deforestation, since the Chinese invasion had caused severe flooding and silting of rivers in neighboring countries. Respect for the Tibetan ecosystem was therefore crucial for a large part of Asia. Finally, with the fifth point, the Dalai Lama called for a discussion on the status of Tibet and the future of relations with China.

He had barely concluded his speech when the members of Congress unanimously stood up to acclaim him, the ovation lasting several minutes. The next day, eight senators signed a letter addressed to the new Secretary General of the Communist Party, Zhao Ziyang, urging him to accept the proposals of the Dalai Lama and to meet him without delay. They were, however, disavowed by the State Department. Its spokesman regretted that the Dalai Lama had abused American hospitality, his political statements not being compatible with his status of religious leader. He invited the senators not to confuse human rights and political demands. The U.S. government therefore refused to endorse the five-point peace plan and recalled that neither the United States nor the United Nations had ever recognized the independence of Tibet.[47]

On the Chinese side, the rejection of the peace plan was irrevocable. Besides, for Beijing, the issue of Tibet did not exist. The five-point plan was nothing but the "endless preaching" of the exiled leader. An official declared that "Tibetans have never experienced in history a degree of democracy and freedom comparable to that which they now enjoy, and that one cannot turn this truth into lies or slander."[48]

September 27, 1987: Lhasa Set Ablaze

Democracy and freedom in Tibet? The denial was not long in coming. Six days later, on September 27, in the streets of Lhasa the repression showed who was lying and who was telling the truth. For the first time, scenes of police violence leaked out. Tibetans were able to capture a videotape by an observer who had filmed the riots. They entrusted the cassette to tourists. Its content went around the world, broadcast by all television stations—excluding Chinese channels, of course.

The images, filmed on the morning of September 27, showed about twenty monks walking in tight ranks from Drepung Monastery,[49] near the capital. They were protesting against the public execution in Lhasa, on the 24th, of two members of an independence movement accused of being criminals. Joined by a crowd of laypeople, at a rapid pace, they first performed the ritual circumambulation in the Barkor,[50] circling the Jokhang and waving the prohibited Tibetan flags. The religious raised their fists, singing at the top of their voices slogans for the independence of their country. In this Tibetan quarter, other people joined their demonstration of courage, and all present noted the spontaneous nature of this event.

It was quickly crushed. Military trucks arrived on the scene and riot police, assisted by the Chinese people, quickly brought the protest to an end. Tourists confessed that they were shocked by the racial hatred and the violence of the Chinese army. Soldiers pursued the rebels all the way into the corridors of the monasteries. They fought with truncheons, trampling those who had collapsed and throwing some off the roofs of buildings. Others were tied up, arms and hands clasped behind their backs, then piled into buses leaving for the prisons of the valley of Lhasa.

When the official press declared that the monks arrested on September 27 had not received any support from their compatriots, these words inflamed the Lhasapas, prompting many more to express their resentment. On October 1, the anniversary of the founding of the People's Republic, monks and nuns gathered again on the Barkor to shout out independence slogans. About sixty were arrested and taken to a nearby police station. The crowd threw stones at the police, and observers were filming the events from the rooftops. Soon, rioters overturned and burned cars and, taking advantage of the confusion, tried to free the detainees. The situation escalated when paramilitary police began to shoot. Several were killed and hundreds injured.

The following days, a large contingent of troops was stationed in Lhasa. This demonstration of force did not stop the unrest. Less than a week later, on October 6, a hundred Drepung monks were attacked while gathered outside the government office of the Autonomous Region, demanding the unconditional liberation of the imprisoned protesters. The repression greatly exceeded that of the previous days: two hundred and fifty soldiers charged. Monks were kidnapped and a certain number of them released at the end of October. The others had to wait until January 1988 and the explicit request of the Panchen Lama, who, through relentless insistence, obtained their release. However, fifteen of them, accused of crimes against the security of the state, were deported. Palden Gyatso reported in his memoirs the arrival of this new generation of prisoners. Much more politicized than their elders, they seemed to forget to be afraid and did not hesitate in challenging their guards, despite the torture and the abomination of detention.[51]

The political success of the Dalai Lama in Washington had certainly set fire to the gunpowder. However, tension had been brewing for several months. In Lhasa, the inhabitants no longer resigned themselves to the renewed terror and degradation of living conditions caused by the mass immigration of Chinese settlers. The authorities, however, denied the real causes of their discontent, preferring to accuse the Dalai Lama of fomenting the unrest.[52]

The Involvement of Westerners

Among the foreigners present in the capital in these days of riots were the American lawyer John Ackerly and his friend, the doctor Blake Kerr. Both had gone to climb the Himalayan peaks. Shocked by the Chinese violence, they abandoned their adventure project and tried to analyze the events they had witnessed. Blake Kerr investigated health problems and revealed to the world the sterilizations, abortions, and forced contraception to which the Tibetan women[53] were subjected. China had, however, ratified the UN Convention on the Elimination of All Forms of Discrimination Against Women in 1980.

Family planning was one of the priorities of China's agenda in Tibet, and it allowed a maximum of two children per couple. Any family who exceeded these quotas was subject to heavy fines and discrimination. An extra child was a "nonperson." Unregistered, it received no food ration cards, schooling, or allowance. If a woman became pregnant again after reaching the authorized quota of births, pressure from the medical teams, or even coercion, pushed her to abortion. If she resisted, she ran the risk of being forcibly sterilized after delivery.

Blake Kerr testified that abortions and sterilizations were performed in conditions that endangered the lives of women in places without anesthesia or medical aftercare. The number of postoperative deaths was unusually high. In Lhasa hospitals, abortions were performed under duress until the ninth month with an injection of Levanor, a chemical substance unknown in the Western countries. These infanticides, part of the strategy to control the Tibetan population, qualified as genocide according to Dr. Kerr, and were contrary to international norms.

Given the seriousness of the facts, John Ackerly decided to go to Dharamsala to inform the Dalai Lama. Deeply concerned about the fate of his compatriots, the Dalai Lama asked many questions and wanted to know if, in such a context, the protesters had resorted to violence, as was claimed by the Chinese press. He was very moved to learn that the monks had seized guns to break them. The weapons had thus been destroyed and not turned against the aggressor, despite all the suffering caused. Like their charismatic guide, the Lhasapas had said no to violence. The foreign observers noted that the protests, peaceful at first, had then turned violent in response to the brutality of the People's Armed Police. Its murderous methods shocked tourists who witnessed the events, pushing them to testify under oath against the false allegations of the Chinese government. Its ambassador indeed declared to the UN in January 1988 that the security forces had not used their weapons, even in response to the alleged shooting by Tibetan rebels. Before this public outcry, Beijing had to revise its version of events.

Back in the United States, John Ackerly joined in the formation of the International Campaign for Tibet, now the primary defensive organization for the Tibetan people. His first initiative was to request a hearing in Congress. The legislators adopted several resolutions condemning the executions of September 24 and the arrests and repression of September 27 and October 1. China responded by accusing the U.S. government of interfering in its internal affairs. Its embassy in Washington deplored what it called the offensive attitude of Congress, which it accused of using the pretext of the rioters, claimed to have been "criminals under common law," to call into question the future of Sino-U.S. relations. Yet the target of all the criticism remained the Dalai Lama, denounced as the leader of the "separatist clique."

Despite dissuasive terror, the Tibetan revolt again erupted in Lhasa in March 1988, during the Great Prayer Festival, the Mönlam Chenmo. This most important festival of religious Tibet had been authorized by the Party officials, who felt they had regained control of the situation. Without doubt they also tried to forget the repression of 1987. On March 5, 1988, twenty-five thousand worshipers thus gathered on the esplanade of the Jokhang, amid the smoke of juniper branches and songs of praise to the Buddha. However, by mid-morning, monks suddenly seized the microphone to shout slogans in favor of independence. In a few moments, the religious ceremony turned into a patriotic demonstration. The faithful threw a shower of stones on the Chinese officials in attendance. The police replied by firing machine guns, and the confrontation continued for sixteen hours. The cruelty of the repression did not manage to muzzle the rebels, who continued to sporadically express themselves, and on December 10, 1988, the fortieth anniversary of the Universal Declaration of Human Rights, there was another day of riots in Lhasa.

MARCH 10, 1988

Nonviolence and Indifference

IN PAST MONTHS at least thirty-two people have died during the unrest in Lhasa and hundreds have been arrested, beaten, and tortured. Throughout Tibet, additional security forces have been brought in, freedom of movement has now been restricted, and Chinese authorities continue to violate the people's fundamental human rights. Today, we also honor the courage of our brethren in Tibet who have taken to the streets to draw attention to their suffering under Chinese colonial rule. The current unrest in Tibet is not an isolated event. There have been numerous demonstrations in our country since the crushing by Chinese troops of the National Uprising in 1959. It is unique only in that it was witnessed by the foreign press and tourists and was, therefore, widely reported.

The struggle of our people is, unlike many, a nonviolent one. This may have made it more difficult to convince the world of the depth of our misery and the earnestness of our resolve. It may even have encouraged governments to ignore our just cause. It is indeed a sad reflection of the state of the world that violence seems to be required for the international community to pay attention. Given the global concern for terrorism and other forms of violence, would it not be in everyone's interest to support the nonviolent pursuit of just causes?

I have always felt that violence breeds violence. It contributes little to the resolution of conflicts. I therefore renew my appeal to all freedom-loving peoples to support our nonviolent struggle for the survival of our national identity, our culture, and our spiritual tradition, and persuade the Chinese government to abandon its oppressive policies. Tibet should be for the six million Tibetans. Its future, including its form of government and social system, should be for Tibetan people themselves to decide. No Tibetan is interested in restoring outdated political and social institutions. As I have said many times, even the continuation of the institution of the Dalai Lama is for the people to decide. Respect for freedom and democracy is essential for the development of modern Tibet and its people.

June 15, 1988: The Strasbourg Proposal

In the European Parliament at Strasbourg, on June 15, 1988, as in Washington in September 1987, the leader of the Tibetans opened his speech by stressing the interdependence of the modern world: "A nation cannot solve its problems alone any longer. For lack of assuming a universal responsibility, our very survival is in danger. That's why I call for the development of understanding, cooperation, and respect between countries in the world." To lay the foundations for lasting peace, the Dalai Lama advocated a "realistic" solution, later to be called "The Strasbourg Proposal" or the policy of the "Middle Way."[58] Containing the elements of the five-point peace plan for Tibet, it asked for the opening of negotiations between Tibetans and Chinese. To renew the dialogue interrupted since the events of 1987, the Dalai Lama offered to waive the sovereignty of his country in foreign affairs and defense, in exchange for a significant autonomy. He suggested that Tibet in its entirety, including the Three Provinces, become "a self-governing democratic political entity, in association with the People's Republic." The new government of Tibet would have the right to decide all internal affairs, while foreign policy would remain in the hands of the Chinese government. As soon as such a statute was accepted by the Chinese authorities, the Tibetans would no longer seek to secede and would agree to remain within the People's Republic of China. The Beijing government should immediately end its human rights violations and its policy of demographic submersion of Tibet. As in Washington in 1987, the Dalai Lama reiterated on June 15, 1988, his willingness to transform his country into a sanctuary of peace for the world.

This new concession of the Dalai Lama in favor of autonomy embarrassed the Chinese. It lifted the obstacle that they had erected against any compromise. One of their diplomats even admitted to Agence France-Presse that there had been a "change of tone"[59] on the Tibetan side. Yet what bothered the leadership in Beijing was less the content of the Strasbourg proposal than its impact on the public, increasingly mobilized in favor of Tibet. Certainly, the English Conservative, Lord Plumb, President of the European Parliament, had deplored the intervention of the Dalai Lama at a time when Brussels was trying to normalize relations with Beijing. But his statement did not prevent either the members of the European Parliament or the press from unanimously recognizing the desire for peace and dialogue of the head of the Tibetans. His attitude aroused immense respect.

To these words that moved the public, the Chinese government responded with stereotypes evoking the "sacred sovereignty of China over Tibet"[60] and accusing the Dalai Lama of seeking, under the guise of autonomy, independence in disguise. The notion of "free association with China" put forward in Strasbourg could only be agreed upon by two independent nations, which was unacceptable to the People's Republic. However, Beijing did not categorically reject the prospect of talks and proposed exchanges for obvious reasons of diplomacy. On September 21, 1988, the embassy of the People's Republic in New Delhi officially declared that its government was in favor of a meeting with the leader of the Tibetans, inviting him to choose the place and date.[61] The Dalai Lama proposed that talks be held in January 1989 in Geneva, a neutral city. Tashi Wangdi, a minister of the government in exile, was approached to lead the Tibetan delegation, supported by the Dutch lawyer Michael van Walt van Praag[62] as legal counsel. After an initial encouraging response, the Chinese government finally replied by asking for new conditions that contradicted its previous offer: the meeting was to take place in Beijing. Delegates appointed by the Dalai Lama were accused of separatism and could therefore not participate, especially Michael van Walt van Praag, whose presence constituted an interference in China's internal affairs. Furthermore, before even beginning the talks, the Dalai Lama had to admit the unity of the motherland.

The hopes raised in Strasbourg thus fell again very quickly. Furthermore, the response caused a controversy among the exiles. Since the early 1970s, the Dalai Lama had considered that unity and coexistence of Tibetan and Chinese peoples took precedence over demands for independence. He therefore set up debates on the subject, seeking the views of the Tibetan National Assembly and the Kashag. Then, before traveling to Strasbourg on June 15, he brought together on June 6 a special conference for four days in Dharamsala with the Tibetan People's Deputies, the Kashag, and experts who approved the content of the Middle Way.[63] However, the idea of a free association of Tibet with China, which came from Michael van Walt van Praag, was open to discussion. Was it necessary that Tibet's relationship with China be similar to that of Bhutan with India, or that of Mongolia with the Soviet Union? Thubten Norbu, the Dalai Lama's eldest brother, even circulated a petition among the exiles requesting the categorical rejection of this proposal.

His concessions on independence had cost the Dalai Lama the opposition of some of his own, the most extreme interpreting it as a betrayal, while the idea of turning Tibet into a demilitarized zone of peace aroused the mistrust of several countries. On the geostrategic level, the demilitarization of the Himalayan region would indeed have

given India supremacy in Southeast Asia and the Indian Ocean—
something that Nepal, Bangladesh, and Pakistan, ally of the United
States, were not willing to accept. The Strasbourg Proposal therefore
weakened the Dalai Lama on the political level. As for the support of
public opinion and the parliaments throughout the world, it did not
lead states to impose sanctions against China. What could the Dalai
Lama therefore expect for his cause, thus marginalized and deprived
of government support?

MARCH 10, 1989

The Struggle of Tibetans Must Remain Nonviolent

I AM DEEPLY SADDENED to learn that there has been further bloodshed in Lhasa. No amount of repression, however brutal and
violent, can silence the voice of freedom and justice. The frequent
peaceful demonstrations which have taken place spontaneously
throughout Tibet over the past years are clear indications of a much
longer problem. Unfortunately, the Chinese leadership still fails to
understand the real situation in Tibet and the extent of dissatisfaction among the Tibetan people. In his last public statement before
his untimely and sad demise, Panchen Rinpoche expressed the people's feelings when he said that the price Tibetans have had to pay
under Chinese rule has been far higher than any benefits they may
have gained.[54]

Ours is a nonviolent struggle, and it must remain so. The killing,
imprisonment, and torture of peaceful demonstrators or persons
who express unsanctioned opinions is morally reprehensible and a
violation of human rights as internationally recognized. The condemnation by the international community of these actions will, we
hope, persuade the Chinese to abandon such methods. The United
Nations General Assembly passed three resolutions condemning
China's human rights abuses in Tibet. At this time, when the United

Nations is increasingly effective in fulfilling its mission in various parts of the world, I call on the international community to urge the implementation of these three resolutions.

I am encouraged by the support we have received for our initiatives to find a peaceful and just solution to the tragic situation of Tibet. In September of 1987 I presented a Five-Point Peace Plan for the restoration of peace and human rights in Tibet. In June 1988, I formulated further thoughts that could serve as a framework for substantive negotiations. The Chinese government has agreed to hold negotiations with us and left the venue and time for such negotiations for me to choose. Although I proposed that the negotiations should start in January in Geneva, the Chinese have, for one reason or another, delayed commencement of the talks. Nevertheless, as the Chinese have, unlike before, become more realistic these days, I remain hopeful that the Chinese leaders will see the wisdom of resolving the issue peacefully, by negotiations. I firmly believe a resolution based on the framework proposed by us will not only benefit both the Tibetan and Chinese peoples, but will also contribute to regional and global peace and stability.

Today important changes are taking place everywhere in the world, which could profoundly affect our future and the future of all humanity and the planet we share. Courageous moves by world leaders have facilitated the peaceful resolution of conflicts. Hopes for peace, for the environment, and for a more humane approach to world problems seem greater than ever before. It is imperative that we Tibetans intensify our modest contribution to these changes through our endeavors both inside and in exile for the advancement of freedom, democracy, and peace.

Martial Law in Lhasa

Between September 1987 and March 1989, no measures of repression succeeded in breaking the courage of Tibetan protesters. On the eve of March 10, 1989, the revolt once again ignited Lhasa. On

March 5, about a hundred monks and nuns gathered on the Barkor to pay tribute to the martyrs of Tibet. Police fired without warning. Under the eyes of Western witnesses, the shooting of machine guns continued late into the night and started again the following day. The exasperated population set fire to about fifty Chinese-owned stores and threw a policeman from the top of the Jokhang, triggering a wave of reprisals. Calm only returned on the evening of March 7.

Three days later, on the 10th, in Dharamsala, the Dalai Lama lamented the bloodbath. He did not exaggerate. This repression had been the deadliest since 1959. The Beijing government only recognized a dozen deaths on the 5th and 6th of March. However, in August 1990, the Chinese journalist Tang Daxian, a refugee in France after the Tiananmen Massacre,[55] made public a report from the military hierarchy, establishing the actual number of victims: 387 Lhasapas and 82 monastics shot dead; 700 wounded, including a large number who died due to lack of treatment; and nearly 3,000 arrests.[56] Hu Jintao,[57] who had just been appointed Party Secretary of Tibet, received full powers to put down the rebellion. Fearing the situation would become uncontrollable, on March 8 he gave orders to expel all foreigners from the capital and established martial law. Extremely severe regulations imposed a curfew, banned gatherings, and ordered the search of private homes likely to shelter "criminals." Nevertheless, protests continued and were brutally put down by the army. The denial of freedom exacerbated the popular resentment and caused a mass exodus.

During the ruthless repression, the Dalai Lama continued to advocate for nonviolence and negotiation. Yet in Beijing he was accused of being the cause of the turmoil and of seeking foreign interference in a crisis that the Republic intended to deal with internally. The events in Lhasa strengthened the position of the Party hard-liners. In order to restart talks and with the strength of the international audience he had acquired, the Dalai Lama thus decided to make a major concession to the Chinese.

NOBEL LECTURE

December 11, 1989

Brothers and sisters, It is an honor and pleasure to be among you today. I am really happy to see so many old friends who have come from different corners of the world, and to make new friends, whom I hope to meet again in the future. When I meet people in different parts of the world, I am always reminded that we are all basically alike: we are all human beings. Maybe we have different clothes, our skin is of a different color, or we speak different languages. That is on the surface. But basically, we are the same human beings. That is what binds us to each other. That is what makes it possible for us to understand each other and to develop friendship and closeness.

Thinking over what I might say today, I decided to share with you some of my thoughts concerning the common problems all of us face as members of the human family. Because we all share this small planet Earth, we have to learn to live in harmony and peace with each other and with nature. That is not just a dream, but a necessity. We are dependent on each other in so many ways that we can no longer live in isolated communities and ignore what is happening outside those communities, and we must share the good fortune that we enjoy. I speak to you as just another human being; as a simple monk. If you find what I say useful, then I hope you will try to practice it.

I also wish to share with you today my feelings concerning the plight and aspirations of the people of Tibet. The Nobel Prize is a prize they well deserve for their courage and unfailing determination during the past forty years of foreign occupation. As a free spokesman for my captive countrymen and -women, I feel it is my duty to speak out on their behalf. I speak not with a feeling of anger or hatred toward those who are responsible for the immense suffering of our people and the destruction of our land, homes, and culture. They too are human beings who struggle to find happiness and deserve our compassion. I speak to inform you of the sad situation in my country today and of the aspirations of my people, because in our struggle for freedom, truth is the only weapon we possess.

The realization that we are all basically the same human beings, who seek happiness and try to avoid suffering, is very helpful in developing a sense of brotherhood and sisterhood; a warm feeling of love and compassion for others. This, in turn, is essential if we are to survive in this ever shrinking world we live in. For if we each selfishly pursue only what we believe to be in our own interest, without caring about the needs of others, we may end up harming not only others but also ourselves. This fact has become very clear during the course of this century. We know that to wage a nuclear war today, for example, would be a form of suicide; or that by polluting the air or the oceans, in order to achieve some short-term benefit, we are destroying the very basis for our survival. As interdependents, therefore, we have no other choice than to develop what I call a sense of universal responsibility.

Today, we are truly a global family. What happens in one part of the world may affect us all. This, of course, is not only true of the negative things that happen, but is equally valid for the positive developments. We not only know what happens elsewhere, thanks to the extraordinary modern communications technology, we are also directly affected by events that occur far away. We feel a sense of sadness when children are starving in eastern Africa. Similarly, we feel a sense of joy when a family is reunited after decades of separation by the Berlin Wall. Our crops and livestock are contaminated and our health and livelihood threatened when a nuclear accident happens miles away in another country. Our own security is enhanced when peace breaks out between warring parties in other continents.

But war or peace; the destruction or the protection of nature; the violation or promotion of human rights and democratic freedoms; poverty or material well-being; the lack of moral and spiritual values or their existence and development; and the breakdown or development of human understanding, are not isolated phenomena that can be analyzed and tackled independently of one another. In fact, they are very much interrelated at all levels and need to be approached with that understanding.

Peace, in the sense of the absence of war, is of little value to someone who is dying of hunger or cold. It will not remove the pain of torture inflicted on a prisoner of conscience. It does not comfort those who have lost their loved ones in floods caused by senseless deforestation in a neighboring country. Peace can only last where human rights are respected, where the people are fed, and where individuals and nations are free. True peace with oneself and with the world around us can only be achieved through the development of mental peace. The other phenomena mentioned above are similarly interrelated. Thus, for example, we see that a clean environment, wealth, or democracy mean little in the face of war, especially nuclear war, and that material development is not sufficient to ensure human happiness.

Material progress is of course important for human advancement. In Tibet, we paid much too little attention to technological and economic development, and today we realize that this was a mistake. At the same time, material development without spiritual development can also cause serious problems. In some countries too much attention is paid to external things and very little importance is given to inner development. I believe both are important and must be developed side by side so as to achieve a good balance between them. Tibetans are always described by foreign visitors as being a happy, jovial people. This is part of our national character, formed by cultural and religious values that stress the importance of mental peace through the generation of love and kindness to all other living sentient beings, both human and animal. Inner peace is the key: if you have inner peace, the external problems do not affect your deep sense of peace and tranquility. In that state of mind you can deal with situations with calmness and reason, while keeping your inner happiness. That is very important. Without this inner peace, no matter how comfortable your life is materially, you may still be worried, disturbed, or unhappy because of circumstances.

Clearly, it is of great importance, therefore, to understand the interrelationship among these and other phenomena, and to approach and attempt to solve problems in a balanced way that takes these different aspects into consideration. Of course it is not easy. But it is of little benefit to try to solve one problem if doing so creates an equally serious new one. So really we have no alternative: we must develop a sense of universal responsibility not only in the geographic sense, but also in respect to the different issues that confront our planet.

Responsibility does not only lie with the leaders of our countries or with those who have been appointed or elected to do a particular job. It lies with each one of us individually. Peace, for example, starts with each one of us. When we have inner peace, we can be at peace with those around us. When our community is in a state of peace, it can share that peace with neighboring communities, and so on. When we feel love and kindness toward others, it not only makes others feel loved and cared for, but it helps us also to develop inner happiness and peace. And there are ways in which we can consciously work to develop feelings of love and kindness. For some of us, the most effective way to do so is through religious practice. For others it may be nonreligious practices. What is important is that we each make a sincere effort to take our responsibility for each other and for the natural environment we live in seriously.

I am very encouraged by the developments that are taking place around us. After the young people of many countries, particularly in northern Europe, have repeatedly called for an end to the dangerous destruction of the environment that was being conducted in the name of economic development, the world's political leaders are now starting to take meaningful steps to address this problem. The report to the United Nations Secretary-General by the World Commission on the Environment and Development (the Brundtland Report) was an important step in educating governments on the urgency of the issue. Serious efforts to bring peace to war-torn zones and to implement the right to self-determination of some people have resulted in the withdrawal of Soviet troops from Afghanistan and the establishment of independent Namibia. Through persistent nonviolent popular efforts dramatic changes, bringing many countries closer to real democracy, have occurred in many places, from Manila in the Philippines to Berlin in East Germany. With the Cold War era apparently drawing to a close, people everywhere live with renewed hope. Sadly, the courageous efforts of the Chinese people to bring similar change to their country was brutally crushed last June. But their efforts too are a source of hope. The military might has not extinguished the desire for freedom and the determination of the Chinese people to achieve it. I particularly admire the fact that these young people who have been taught that "power grows from the barrel of the gun" chose, instead, to use nonviolence as their weapon.

What these positive changes indicate is that reason, courage, determination, and the inextinguishable desire for freedom can ultimately win. In the struggle between forces of war, violence, and oppression on the one hand, and peace, reason, and freedom on the other, the latter are gaining the upper hand. This realization fills us Tibetans with hope that someday we too will once again be free.

The awarding of the Nobel Prize to me, a simple monk from faraway Tibet, here in Norway, also fills us Tibetans with hope. It means, despite the fact that we have not drawn attention to our plight by means of violence, we have not been forgotten. It also means that the values we cherish, in particular our respect for all forms of life and the belief in the power of truth, are today recognized and encouraged. It is also a tribute to my mentor, Mahatma Gandhi, whose example is an inspiration to so many of us. This year's award is an indication that this sense of universal responsibility is developing. I am deeply touched by the sincere concern shown by so many people in this part of the world for the suffering of the people of Tibet. That is a source of hope not only for us Tibetans, but for all oppressed people.

As you know, Tibet has, for forty years, been under foreign occupation. Today, more than a quarter of a million Chinese troops are stationed in Tibet. Some sources estimate the occupation army to be twice this strength. During this time, Tibetans have been deprived of their most basic human rights, including the right to life, movement, speech, worship, only to mention a few. More than one sixth of Tibet's population of six million died as a direct result of the Chinese invasion and occupation. Even before the Cultural Revolution started, many of Tibet's monasteries, temples, and historic buildings were destroyed. Almost everything that remained was destroyed during the Cultural Revolution. I do not wish to dwell on this point, which is well documented. What is important to realize, however, is that despite the limited freedom granted after 1979, to rebuild parts of some monasteries and other such tokens of liberalization, the fundamental human rights of the Tibetan people are still today being systematically violated. In recent months this bad situation has become even worse.

If it were not for our community in exile, so generously sheltered and supported by the government and people of India and helped by organizations and individuals from many parts of the world, our nation would today be little more than a shattered remnant of a people. Our culture, religion, and national identity would have been effectively eliminated. As it is, we have built schools and monasteries in exile and have created democratic institutions to serve our people and preserve the seeds of our civilization. With this experience, we intend to implement full democracy in a future free Tibet. Thus, as we develop our community in exile on modern lines, we also cherish and preserve our own identity and culture and bring hope to millions of our countrymen and -women in Tibet.

The issue of most urgent concern at this time is the massive influx of Chinese settlers into Tibet. Although in the first decades of occupation a considerable number of Chinese were transferred into the eastern parts of Tibet—in the Tibetan provinces of Amdo

(Chinghai) and Kham (most of which has been annexed by neighboring Chinese provinces)—since 1983 an unprecedented number of Chinese have been encouraged by their government to migrate to all parts of Tibet, including central and western Tibet (which the People's Republic of China refers to as the so-called Tibet Autonomous Region). Tibetans are rapidly being reduced to an insignificant minority in their own country. This development, which threatens the very survival of the Tibetan nation, its culture and spiritual heritage, can still be stopped and reversed. But this must be done now, before it is too late.

The new cycle of protest and violent repression, which started in Tibet in September of 1987 and culminated in the imposition of martial law in the capital, Lhasa, in March of this year, was in large part a reaction to this tremendous Chinese influx. Information reaching us in exile indicates that the protest marches and other peaceful forms of protest are continuing in Lhasa and a number of other places in Tibet, despite the severe punishment and inhumane treatment given to Tibetans detained for expressing their grievances. The number of Tibetans killed by security forces during the protest in March and of those who died in detention afterward is not known but is believed to be more than two hundred. Thousands have been detained or arrested and imprisoned, and torture is commonplace.

It was against the background of this worsening situation and in order to prevent further bloodshed that I proposed what is generally referred to as the Five-Point Peace Plan for the restoration of peace and human rights in Tibet. I elaborated on the plan in a speech in Strasbourg last year. I believe the plan provides a reasonable and realistic framework for negotiations with the People's Republic of China. So far, however, China's leaders have been unwilling to respond constructively. The brutal suppression of the Chinese democracy movement in June of this year, however, reinforced my view that any settlement of the Tibetan question will only be meaningful if it is supported by adequate international guarantees.

The Five-Point Peace Plan addresses the principal and inter-related issues, which I referred to in the first part of this lecture. It calls for 1) transformation of the whole of Tibet, including the eastern provinces of Kham and Amdo, into a Zone of Ahimsa (nonviolence); 2) abandonment of China's population transfer policy; 3) respect for the Tibetan people's fundamental rights and democratic freedoms; 4) restoration and protection of Tibet's natural environment; and 5) commencement of earnest negotiations on the future status of Tibet and of relations between the Tibetan and Chinese people. In the Strasbourg address I proposed that Tibet become a fully self-governing democratic political entity.

I would like to take this opportunity to explain the Zone of Ahimsa or peace sanctuary concept, which is the central element of the Five-Point Peace Plan. I am convinced that it is of great importance not only for Tibet but also for peace and stability in Asia.

It is my dream that the entire Tibetan plateau should become a free refuge where humanity and nature can live in peace and in harmonious balance. It would be a place where people from all over the world could come to seek the true meaning of peace within themselves, away from the tensions and pressures of much of the rest of the world. Tibet could indeed become a creative center for the promotion and development of peace.

The following are key elements of the proposed Zone of Ahimsa:

- the entire Tibetan plateau would be demilitarized;
- the manufacture, testing, and stockpiling of nuclear weapons and other armaments on the Tibetan plateau would be prohibited;
- the Tibetan plateau would be transformed into the world's largest natural park or biosphere. Strict laws would be enforced to protect wildlife and plant life; the exploitation of natural resources would be carefully regulated so as not to damage relevant ecosystems; and a policy of sustainable development would be adopted in populated areas;
- the manufacture and use of nuclear power and other technologies that produce hazardous waste would be prohibited;

• national resources and policy would be directed toward the active promotion of peace and environmental protection. Organizations dedicated to the furtherance of peace and to the protection of all forms of life would find a hospitable home in Tibet;

• the establishment of international and regional organizations for the promotion and protection of human rights would be encouraged in Tibet.

Tibet's height and size (the size of the European Community), as well as its unique history and profound spiritual heritage, make it ideally suited to fulfill the role of a sanctuary of peace in the strategic heart of Asia. It would also be in keeping with Tibet's historical role as a peaceful Buddhist nation and buffer region separating the Asian continent's great and often rival powers.

In order to reduce existing tensions in Asia, the President of the Soviet Union, Mr. Gorbachev, proposed the demilitarization of Soviet–Chinese borders and their transformation into "a frontier of peace and good-neighborliness." The Nepal government had earlier proposed that the Himalayan country of Nepal, bordering on Tibet, should become a zone of peace, although that proposal did not include demilitarization of the country.

For the stability and peace of Asia, it is essential to create peace zones to separate the continent's biggest powers and potential adversaries. President Gorbachev's proposal, which also included a complete Soviet troop withdrawal from Mongolia, would help to reduce tension and the potential for confrontation between the Soviet Union and China. A true peace zone must, clearly, also be created to separate the world's two most populous states, China and India.

The establishment of the Zone of Ahimsa would require the withdrawal of troops and military installations from Tibet, which would enable India and Nepal also to withdraw troops and military installations from the Himalayan regions bordering Tibet. This would have to be achieved by international agreements. It would be in the best interest of all states in Asia, particularly China and India, as it would enhance their security, while reducing the economic burden of maintaining high troop concentrations in remote areas.

Tibet would not be the first strategic area to be demilitarized. Parts of the Sinai peninsula, the Egyptian territory separating Israel and Egypt, have been demilitarized for some time. Of course, Costa Rica is the best example of an entirely demilitarized country. Tibet would also not be the first area to be turned into a natural preserve or biosphere. Many parks have been created throughout the world. Some very strategic areas have been turned into natural "peace parks." Two examples are the La Amistad Park, on the Costa Rica–Panama border and the Si A Paz project on the Costa Rica–Nicaragua border.

When I visited Costa Rica earlier this year, I saw how a country can develop successfully without an army, to become a stable democracy committed to peace and the protection of the natural environment. This confirmed my belief that my vision of Tibet in the future is a realistic plan, not merely a dream.

Let me end with a personal note of thanks to all of you and our friends who are not here today. The concern and support that you have expressed for the plight of the Tibetans have touched us all greatly, and continue to give us courage to struggle for freedom and justice: not through the use of arms, but with the powerful weapons of truth and determination. I know that I speak on behalf of all the people of Tibet when I thank you and ask you not to forget Tibet at this critical time in our country's history. We too hope to contribute to the development of a more peaceful, more humane, and more beautiful world. A future free Tibet will seek to help those in need throughout the world, to protect nature, and to promote peace. I believe that our Tibetan ability to combine spiritual qualities with a realistic and practical attitude enables us to make a special contribution, in however modest a way. This is my hope and prayer.

In conclusion, let me share with you a short prayer that gives me great inspiration and determination:

For as long as space endures,
And for as long as living beings remain,
Until then may I, too, abide
To dispel the misery of the world.

Thank you.

MARCH 10, 1990

The Nobel Peace Prize, Dedicated to Tibet and to Humanity

TODAY, AS WE contemplate the future of our Tibet, we cannot help but think about the historic events of the past year. In China the popular movement for democracy was crushed last June by unrestrained violence. But I do not believe that the demonstrations were in vain. Rather, the spirit of freedom has been rekindled among the Chinese people, and China cannot escape the impact of this spirit of freedom which is sweeping through many parts of the world. Extraordinary changes are occurring in Eastern Europe: events which have set the pace for social-political change throughout the world. Similarly, Namibia has gained its independence from South Africa and the South African government has taken the first steps toward the dismantling of apartheid. It is encouraging to note that these changes are the result of a genuine people's movement, and basically due to the irrepressible human desire for freedom and justice. What these positive changes indicate is that reason, courage, determination, and the inextinguishable desire for freedom will ultimately win. Therefore, I urge the Chinese leadership not to resist the trend of change, but to consider the problems of the Tibetan and the Chinese people with imagination and broad-mindedness. I believe that repression will never crush the determination of any people to live in freedom and dignity. The Chinese leadership must look at the problems of China itself, and the Tibetan issue, with new eyes and fresh minds. Before it is too late, they must listen to the voice of reason, non-violence, and moderation which is spoken by the Tibetan people and by China's own students.

It is imperative, I believe, for China to learn a lesson from the Soviet Union and, in particular, to follow the example set by President Gorbachev who is seeking to solve similar problems through dialogue and compromise. The government of China needs to realize that the problems it faces in the non-Chinese areas under its rule are not merely economic. At root they are political and, as such, can only be solved by political change. An important event for the Tibetan people has been the award of the Nobel Peace Prize. Though it will not change my status as a simple monk, I am happy for the Tibetan people, for this prize brings well-deserved recognition to the Tibetan people's struggle for freedom and justice. This reaffirms our conviction that armed with truth, courage, and determination, we will succeed in liberating our country.

1989 Triumph of Freedom

During the year just ended, the Dalai Lama had not ceased touring the world. In 1989, he went to East Germany and France in April; to the United States, Costa Rica, and Mexico in June and July; to England and again to the United States in September-October; then, in December, to France, Germany, and finally Norway on the 10th, to receive the Nobel Peace Prize. During these trips, he strove to denounce the imposition of martial law in Lhasa, justified by the Chinese under the guise of "treating a handful of criminals engaged in attacks against people, theft, and banditry."[64] Faced with these barely credible accusations, the Dalai Lama persisted in demanding justice. His travels were widely covered by the media. On April 17, 1989, during a conference at the European Parliament, journalists praised his nonviolent philosophy, in contrast to the Chinese virulence and lies. On April 21 in France, his appearance on *Apostrophes*, a popular television program, set a new audience record. Citing a declaration of Mao Zedong that "political power grows out of the barrel of a gun," the Dalai Lama argued that instead, "the real power is in the mind and heart."

These visits abroad were accompanied by the creation of support groups. Their network allowed the religious leader to meet with parliamentarians in Bonn, Paris, and Copenhagen as well as the United Kingdom, where the House of Lords discussed the Tibetan issue for the first time. So the head of a nonrecognized government in exile was having many summit meetings. Also in Washington, the Tibetan lobby pushed the Senate to pass a resolution against the human rights violations in Tibet. Another resolution granted the Tibetan government in exile a fund of $500,000 for the refugees and about 30 scholarships to Tibetan students. Yet it was the Chinese revolt of June 1989 that gave the greatest visibility to the fight of the Dalai Lama.

These events took place in a context where the spirit of freedom in China, as well as the Soviet Union, resonated with the youth. The Dalai Lama regretted that the leadership in Beijing did not show the same conciliation as Mikhail Gorbachev, who, through dialogue, contributed in 1989 to ending the ideological confrontation between East and West. The Cold War ended in the autumn with the velvet revolutions against the dictatorships of the former Soviet bloc. "The irrepressible human desire for freedom and justice always triumphs," commented the Dalai Lama. A democratization process ran from Hungary to Czechoslovakia, Poland, and the German Democratic Republic. The fall of the Berlin Wall on November 9 symbolized the commitment of the human community to the values of solidarity and fraternal union. The Dalai Lama himself lit a candle at the foot of the wall being demolished, to show his solidarity.

In 1989, the wind of freedom also blew in Africa. At the end of a complex process of decolonization assisted by the United Nations, Namibia was the last country on the continent to embark on the road to independence. In South Africa, with the accession to power of President Frederik de Klerk and under international pressure, Nelson Mandela was released from prison. In Cape Town, negotiations opened between the ANC and the government. The end of apartheid was near.

April 15 to June 4, 1989: The Tiananmen Massacre

The People's Republic was not spared from this wave of freedom. Students and intellectuals, gathered under the banner of democracy, demanded the end of communist dogmatism and the single-party system, calling for the respect for individual liberties guaranteed by the Constitution of 1982. Under their pressure, the power stiffened. The Party totally rejected their claims: "We cannot talk of proletarian or socialist liberalization," said Deng Xiaoping. "Opposing the bourgeois liberalization and strengthening the stability and unity, these are the foundations of our nation."[65] These directives set the tone of the "bourgeois antiliberalization" campaign launched by the government in 1988 against supporters of political pluralism and individual freedom, who identified with Wei Jingsheng. In the Chinese system, such freedoms, although they can be granted by the state, do not constitute the inalienable rights owed to every human being by virtue of his humanity. The Constitution as well as the Penal Code pointed out that the exercise of these freedoms must not question the principles put forward by Deng Xiaoping. On this point, the Party split at that time between the reformers, led by Zhao Ziyang, leader of the Party, and the conservatives led by Li Peng, prime minister. The latter was hostile to abandoning the single-party system for fear of a chaos similar to that of the Cultural Revolution.

Hu Yaobang's death on April 15, 1989, catalyzed the debate. After his dismissal in 1987, he had embodied change. On the 16th and 17th of April, thousands of students waving his portrait gathered in Tiananmen Square to demand his rehabilitation. When they were joined by a crowd of a hundred thousand people at the foot of the monument to the heroes of the people, the police blocked access to the center of Beijing. However, in the following days the popular protest was radicalized and extended throughout the country. In Beijing, but also in Shanghai, Chongqing,[66] and Urumqi,[67] workers joined protesters to denounce the corruption and lack of transparency of the system. To symbolize their aspiration toward democracy, fine arts students erected a statue on the model of "Liberty Enlightening the World." In its American version, the monument represents the emancipation of oppressed peoples and receives, at the foot of New York City skyscrapers, immigrants seeking asylum. In Beijing, its Asian sister raised a torch that, facing the giant portrait of Mao Zedong, challenged the Little Helmsman[68] to return to the youth the freedom that he had confiscated from them.

The foreign press covered the events because it was present for the visit of Mikhail Gorbachev, scheduled on May 15. That's when a thousand students began an unlimited hunger strike. Party leader Zhao Ziyang met with them on May 19 and in a very paternal tone, tried to dissuade them from continuing their movement: "Some of your friends are already very weak: some of your claims can only be resolved through a long process. The situation is complex, it will take us time."[69] The afternoon of the same day, Zhao Ziyang was disowned by Deng Xiaoping, removed by Li Peng, and placed under house arrest. The path of dialogue and negotiation with the students was closed. After seven weeks of protests, loudspeakers announced the establishment of martial law. The 38th Army, responsible for the defense of Beijing, was positioned around the capital while other divisions were called in for reinforcements. When word spread of the imminent arrival of tanks, the crowd raised barricades. Buses were burned to slow down the troops, and students restarted their hunger strike, suspended the day before.

After two weeks of a wait-and-see attitude, on June 3, the army tried to move toward Tiananmen Square, but protesters used their

bodies as a blockade. In the middle of the night, it reached the esplanade where the tents of the hunger strikers were pitched. The soldiers
were ordered to evacuate them before 6 a.m. On behalf of the students,
who had burst into song, "The Internationale," Liu Xiaobo[70] tried to
negotiate a peaceful withdrawal. In vain. Tanks moved in. The soldiers
opened fire with live ammunition on the unarmed crowd. BBC journalists reported seeing tanks crush the demonstrators and block the
roads for the ambulances trying to rescue the wounded. They heard
several desperate students cry, "Fascists, stop the massacre!" while
others called for help, screaming, "Why are you killing us?"[71]

At 5 a.m. on June 4, the day began at Tiananmen Square. Under
the smoke, the wounded were dying; lifeless bodies lay between the
shredded tents and bicycles with twisted wheels. When protesters
tried to enter the premises to rescue their comrades, they were shot
without warning. The soldiers fired into the backs of those who fled.
In the battered city, the shots rang out for several days. The movement
was suppressed with equal brutality throughout the whole country. Li
Peng declared martial law against demonstrators, "criminals, unem-
ployed, thieves, and thugs," whose actions justified, according to
him, the intervention of the army. Official sources have reported 241
dead and 7,000 wounded, of which 5,000 were soldiers. However, in
Tiananmen Square, no deaths would be declared, contrary to reports
of observers present on the scene on the night of June 4. The number
of victims remains controversial to this day. Witnesses reported seeing soldiers carry away the bodies to destroy the evidence of the massacre. Diplomats spoke of carnage. NATO reported 7,000 deaths, the
Chinese Red Cross 2,600, Amnesty International 1,000; and a defec-
tor from the People's Liberation Army cites the figure of an official
circular that recognizes about 3,700.

The Dalai Lama stood informed of the situation hour by hour. The
Indian government had imposed a limit on coverage of events to avoid
offending China. However, reporters from the BBC and CNN, sent to
cover the visit of President Gorbachev, reported the events live. The
demonstrators had written slogans for them, and on their foreheads

encircled with a white cloth had written in English the words "democracy" and "freedom." The crowd, aware of Western sympathy, had surrounded the press to protect them and allow them to testify. Several protesters rushed up shouting: "Tell the world what's happening! The world must know!" But on the evening of June 4, the government interrupted the satellite broadcasts. Journalists, however, continued their reporting by telephone, recording clandestine images. Some were arrested, like a correspondent for the American channel CBS and his cameraman, injured in a fight with soldiers who snatched their mobile phones.

The images of this carnage went around the world. They conveyed a very negative impression of China. Hitherto treated as an ally against the USSR by Nixon and his successors, it suddenly appeared as a threat. George Bush suspended arms sales and canceled various commercial contracts with Beijing. The international condemnation was unanimous.

December 10, 1989:
The Nobel Peace Prize for the Dalai Lama

These events gave credence to the accusations of the Dalai Lama. Martial law, which he had denounced in Lhasa in 1988, seemed to retrospectively prefigure that of Beijing in 1989. When it was known on October 5 that the Nobel Peace Prize was awarded to him, some thought that the bloody suppression of June 4 had pushed the committee to decide in his favor. Perhaps it had indeed made it possible to choose the leader of the Tibetans over other candidates, such as Presidents Gorbachev and Václav Havel. The *New York Times* on October 13, 1989, reported the words of the Oslo sages who declared having tried, by their own choice, to promote democracy and human values in both Tibet and China. Beijing leaders, in turn, did not fail to express their "extreme indignation" and "deep regret" to see this distinction awarded to an "international gangster."[72] They denounced an unacceptable interference in their internal affairs and an encouragement of Tibetan separatism.

The Dalai Lama received the Nobel Peace Prize as well as the post-humous award to Mahatma Gandhi. The committee thus intended to correct its mistake of not honoring in his lifetime the Indian apostle of nonviolence to whom the leader of the Tibetans paid tribute as his "guide" and "source of inspiration."[73] In his acceptance speech, he dedicated his award to his people's struggle for freedom and to the young Chinese who, "educated according to the motto" about the power of the gun, "had nevertheless chosen nonviolence."[74] This distinction earned the Dalai Lama the attention of the world press. His struggle took on an exemplary and universal dimension that he assumed by stating: "The problems we face today, violent conflicts, destruction of nature, poverty, hunger and so on, are human-created problems which can be resolved through human effort, understanding and the development of a sense of brotherhood and sisterhood. We need to cultivate a universal responsibility for one another and the planet we share."[75]

On December 10, 1989, the Dalai Lama of Tibet became the Dalai Lama of the world. Would he succeed in taking front stage in promoting an ethic of nonviolence?

PART THREE
Cultural Genocide in Tibet: The Headlong Rush

1991–2010

*Modern scientific development has, to an extent,
helped in solving mankind's problems. However, in
tackling these global issues there is the need to cultivate
not only the rational mind but also the other remarkable
faculties of the human spirit: the power of love,
compassion, and solidarity.*

THE DALAI LAMA

The Dalai Lama at UN Human Rights Conference in Vienna, June 4, 1993.
© *Vienna Report Agency / Sygma / Corbis*

6

TIBET AND CHINA—
DEADLOCKED DIALOGUE

—▸✦◂—

1991–1994

In 1991, the spiritual leader of Tibet was in the process of becoming the lama of the world. During this fourth decade of exile, he continued to win supporters from all the countries who united with him under the banner of justice and truth, while proclaiming: "Tibet for the world, the world for Tibet!" During this same period, Dharamsala experienced an unprecedented boom. Nehru thought he had isolated the Dalai Lama in 1959. He had thought inaccessible the small town where he had confined him—without imagining that, although distant from the world, the leader of the Tibetans would attract the world all the way to him. Thirty years later, the discomfort of the steep roads did not stop the crowds of visitors. In jeeps and buses, they climbed the chain of mountains where golden victory banners and stupas in ocher and purple renderings sit on top of monasteries, more and more numerous in the land of exile.

Several hotels were built nearby to accommodate hundreds of Europeans, Australians, and Americans, either committed to the Buddhist path or just curious, as well as Asians from Japan, Korea, Thailand, Vietnam, Malaysia, Singapore, Hong Kong, and Taiwan. Since the early 2000s, with the revival of Lamaism in Mongolia and in the former Soviet republics of Kalmykia, Buryatia, and Tuva, groups from Central Asia also came to pay tribute to the Dalai Lama.

Henceforth, on March 10, among representatives from the whole world and the international press, several Chinese would be in attendance. In 2010, Wong Min,[1] their spokesman, called for the day when, in a finally democratic China, Chinese and Tibetans would be fraternally united. The artist Chen Weiming[2] offered the government in exile a stele (an upright stone slab) entitled "Tibet's Road to Freedom"—the freedom to which the Dalai Lama had dedicated his fight.

MARCH 10, 1991

Toward Freedom in China?

IN TIBET, THE situation remains grim. We especially remember young Lhakpa Tsering, who was tortured to death in prison recently, and others who are reportedly in imminent danger of being executed any day. On the 1st of May 1990, Chinese authorities announced the lifting of martial law in Tibet. However, there is clear evidence to conclude that the lifting of martial law is in name only. The People's Armed Police, which was withdrawn, has been replaced by thousands of plainclothed policemen. If the situation is normal, as the Chinese claim, they should immediately withdraw all the plainclothed policemen and let Lhasa be run by civilian authorities.

In 1990 many positive and far-reaching changes took place in the world. In the Soviet Union, the steps taken by President Gorbachev to introduce a more representative and responsible form of government had significant and widespread impact. In many countries, in Eastern Europe especially, one-party dictatorships were replaced by popularly elected governments. The dismantling of the Berlin Wall and unification of the two Germanies are testimonies to the end of the Cold War and a step toward a world no longer haunted by the prospect of a war between the East and the West. In Mongolia as well, the people went to the polls to elect a new government. I particularly welcome the revival of Buddhism in Mongolia, which had uniquely close cultural and religious ties with Tibet. In our part of the world, I must commend the people of Nepal for their efforts in reviving a multiparty system and His Majesty King Birendra for facilitating the process. Regrettably, in many other countries, such as Burma, although the people speak out loudly for greater freedom, the governments have not responded positively.

With such fundamental shifts taking place in the world, I am confident that China cannot remain isolated and unchanging. The Chinese people will one day see that only through a genuinely democratic form of government will they be able to unleash their creative energies for the good of China, and for peace and progress in the world. Signs of this change are evident. The crushing of the democratic movement, led by students and intellectuals, in June 1989 in Beijing may have been a temporary setback. However, in the long run, this event will give the Chinese people inspiration to continue their struggle for greater freedom and democracy.

A peaceful and politically stable future for China lies not just in the success of the Chinese democratic movement, but in the fulfillment of the wishes of millions of non-Chinese to regain their own freedom from Chinese occupation. For stability and peace to return to Asia as a whole, a new China should join a democratic community of states created for the mutual benefit of all its members. Such a community could include Tibet, East Turkestan, and Inner Mongolia, who seek freedom from Chinese colonialist rule, and could also be extended to include other nations interested in building an Asian community. The idea needs much detailed thought, and I hope other Asian leaders and interested persons will be willing to discuss it with me.

I was very saddened by the recent Gulf War and the loss of so many human lives. I consider this crisis an exception in an otherwise encouraging atmosphere. Too often situations that turn explosive are a result of neglect at the early stages when diplomacy and peaceful methods are not adequately applied. A contributing factor to such hostilities is the "strategies" many nations adopt in an attempt to achieve a balance of power that is supposedly in their interest. The worst contributing factor to conflicts such as the Gulf War is the arms trade which individuals and nations indulge in for financial gain. Such trade seems senseless, irresponsible, and completely lacking in human considerations. If we want to avoid such tragic confrontations, we must change our limited selfish strategies and interests and strive for a greater sense of responsibility beyond one's immediate area.

Ever since I was young, I looked forward to the time when we could devise a political system suited to both our traditions and the demands of the modern world. Since we came into exile, we have tried to build up the elected assembly of representatives, as a key feature of our effort to develop such a system. We are now embarking on changes which will further democratize and strengthen our administration in exile. I hope that these changes will allow the people of Tibet to have a clear say in determining the future of their country. It is therefore a matter of great pride for me, and I am sure for all of you, that last month the Tibetan exiles went to the polls for the eleventh time to elect a new assembly for representatives. This assembly will have many more members and will have a much greater role in determining the executive branch of our administration. Already, since the special congress held last May, the members of the Kashag, the executive head of our administration, are elected officials, no longer appointed by me. I believe that future generations of Tibetans will consider these changes among the most important achievements of our experience in exile. Just as the introduction of Buddhism to Tibet cemented our nation, I am confident that the democratization of our society will add to the vitality of the Tibetan people and enable our decision-making institutions to reflect the heartfelt needs and aspirations of all Tibetans.

Spring of the World

From 1987, when Tibet and then China flared up, the world seemed to hear the call of the Dalai Lama. At least, this is how the Tibetans interpreted the 1989 award of the Nobel Peace Prize to their charismatic leader. Finally the world and the Dalai Lama spoke the same language—the language of nonviolence, freedom, and hope. "World" thus became synonymous with renewal, of spring without borders. Freedom blossomed in Berlin, Prague, Budapest, Sofia, Moscow. It challenged the People's Armed Police to bloom for a few days in Lhasa, a few weeks in Beijing. The Dalai Lama wanted to believe that, although brutally contained under tanks and martial law, it would bloom again soon and that the ephemeral Beijing spring would remain an inspiration for the Chinese people. When, on December 10, 1990, the Nobel Peace Prize was awarded to Mikhail Gorbachev, the hopes of the world seemed promised to all the peoples deprived of their fundamental freedoms. During his state visit to the People's Republic during the Tiananmen protests, did the Russian president not declare that the Great Wall of China was a beautiful work, but that there were too many walls between men? Retrospectively, these words seemed to have announced the fall of the Berlin Wall and the Iron Curtain. The bamboo curtain had not yet fallen. Yet, thanks to an unprecedented increase in trade between China and the rest of the world, had it not opened slightly?

On March 10, 1991, the Dalai Lama welcomed the arrival of democracy at the heart of Asia. In Nepal, King Birendra yielded to popular pressure. A national referendum would decide the future government. The establishment of the multiparty system was a first step toward parliamentary democracy, adopted in 1990. That same year also saw the first free elections in Mongolia, after seventy years of Soviet dictatorship. The country succeeded in a smooth democratic transition by adopting a new constitution. Buddhism was reborn from its ashes. Before the Communist persecution, this religion had spread in its Tibetan form through the kingdom of the steppes, from the confines of Ladakh to the lowlands of the Volga. However, Choibalsan, the Mongolian Stalin, destroyed all the religious heritage of his country, and in 1990, only one place of worship existed in Ulaanbaatar. The monks were less religious practitioners than they were officials, zealous defenders of communism. They were forbidden to study philosophy and dialectic, core subjects of Indo-Tibetan Buddhism.[3] Nevertheless, with the recent liberalization, the ancestral practices resurfaced and the population rebuilt temples and monasteries. They adorned them with sacred ancient artifacts that had escaped the looting and melting down in the Russian armament factories. As in Tibet, by ruse and sacrifice in the worst hours of the Stalinist purges, the inhabitants had preserved some of them, buried in natural hiding places or sealed in walls.

The Dalai Lama made intense efforts to help the rebirth of Buddhism in Mongolia, where he brought back the scriptures that were once banned. Tibetan teachers ordained and taught hundreds of new monks. The Mongolian example showed so many similarities with Tibet. Why not find a source of hope in it?

Utopian, the Dalai Lama?

If the global context brought optimism, there were countries where power continued to victimize the people's aspirations. In Burma, the spirit of freedom in 1988 raised a huge wave of protest. The dictatorship of General Ne Win was overthrown, but the new junta oppressed the people and put Aung San Suu Kyi[4] under house arrest. The nonviolent struggle of the Burmese opposition earned her the Nobel Peace Prize in December 1991. The successive allocation of this prize to the Dalai Lama and then to Mikhail Gorbachev and Aung San Suu Kyi allowed large voices to be heard on the international scene in the name of humanity and democracy. In 1991, all hopes seemed credible. The Tibetan leader considered the creation of a community of Asian states, which, following the example of the European Union, would federate countries that had opposed each other throughout history.

Was the Dalai Lama a utopian visionary? In a speech at Yale University in October, he observed that if his proposal for a demilitarized world once seemed idealistic, it was now on the agenda of Presidents Bush and Gorbachev. They continued the process begun under Ronald Reagan, with an eye to halving their nuclear arsenals. The elimination of nuclear weapons would thus be achieved by the end of the year 2000. With this precedent, the Dalai Lama maintained that his country's struggle fell within the context of an inevitable historical evolution. After more than forty years of stasis under Chinese rule, how could one imagine that the situation in Tibet would stay frozen?

Determined to advance, the religious leader emphasized the democratization of the exile administration. In the Tibetan community, in effect, the democratic process did not result from a claim by the population but from his personal conviction. He thus progressively renounced the temporal authority traditionally attributed to him and requested that a Constitution Redrafting Committee finalize the draft text issued in 1963. On June 14, 1991, the Assembly adopted the Charter of the Tibetans-in-Exile, whose preamble recommends principles of peace and nonviolence. The document expresses in 108 articles the rights and duties of refugees, guaranteeing respect for their individual freedoms while insisting on the need to preserve their threatened cultural identity. The charter also organized a separation of powers among the three organs of government, the judiciary, the legislature, and the executive, the last one remaining entrusted to the Dalai Lama. Yet, according to his wishes, the constitutional jurisdiction of the People's Assembly was expanded. For the first time, it elected ministers, or Kalon,[5] whom he used to appoint. Further progress: the legislative authority was reinforced with 46 congressmen[6] in the Assembly, instead of the former 12, to represent the full range of opinions. That same year, a Supreme Justice Commission was established as an independent judicial body, responsible for managing civil disputes. Yet if these generalized developments of democracy brought hope that the utopia of yesterday was becoming today's reality, from Tibet, alarming news was constantly being received.

The International Year of Tibet

Lhakpa Tsering's case, cited by the Dalai Lama on March 10, 1991, is exemplary. Born in Lhasa in 1970, he was only nineteen years old when the Chinese Public Security Bureau ordered his arrest on November 4, 1989. Accused of separatist activities within the "Snow Lion Youth Organization" because he had pasted up proindependence posters and reproduced the Tibetan flag, he was sentenced to two years in prison. Beaten with a spiked chain and tortured with electric batons, he endured without denying his nationalist commitment. He also refused to comply when, in early December 1990, in anticipation of the visit of Amnesty International, the guards ordered prisoners to declare that Tibet was part of China. In retaliation, he suffered further torture. When his mutilated body was returned to his family, his father demanded an investigation but received no answer. Suspicions were reinforced by the unusual generosity of the prison, which gave for the funeral food, butter, and 300 yuan—the equivalent of two months' salary. Amnesty International and Asia Watch requested in vain the release of the autopsy report, then appealed to the Chinese prime minister. On April 6, 1991, the official government agency communicated the statement of the President of the Tibet Autonomous Region that Lhakpa Tsering reportedly died of peritonitis.

If at the time of Mao nothing leaked out, in accordance with the Chinese proverb, "You close your door before beating your dog," the situation had changed considerably since. In 1991, the observers appointed by the UN to certify human rights violations had to be taken into account. Several resolutions had been made since 1989 by the U.S. Congress, demanding the opening of the country to foreign journalists, visits of humanitarian delegates to prisons, and the lifting of martial law. However, it was only on May 1, 1990, four hundred days after they came into force, that China decreed the implementation of these measures. The Dalai Lama expressed his reservations about this, dictated by international pressure, which his office in New Delhi described as a "public relations exercise." In a press release, for his part, the President of the

United States lamented a total lack of clarity. Based on the reports of Amnesty International, he said he was disappointed with a too modest change. The first time a delegation of human rights observers visited Tibet after the lifting of martial law in July 1991, its findings agreed with the Dalai Lama's remarks. The police had retained significant prerogatives and still proceeded with arrests and arbitrary executions.

Under pressure from their own public opinion, more and more sensitive to the Tibetan cause, the Western governments considered sanctions against China. In the United States, an amendment passed unanimously by Congress established that the economic benefits granted to the People's Republic had to depend on the abrogation of repression, the discharge of political prisoners, and the opening of negotiations with the Dalai Lama.[7] Simultaneously, the mobilization for Tibet became widespread, and March 10, 1991, inaugurated the International Year of Tibet, celebrated across thirty-six countries and with more than seven thousand events. The Dalai Lama's visit to New York, welcomed by huge popular fervor, was the highlight.

If, in 1991, the leader of the Tibetans did not make the Chinese government bend, he won the hearts of the people. Despite the formidable propaganda machine of the Interior Ministry, supported by its network of embassies, China lost the battle for public opinion. Did this loss mean a step toward freedom? The Dalai Lama wanted to believe it, in the name of his people and the ever more numerous crowds who came to listen to him. He would embody from now on the hope for a more humane world.

MARCH 10, 1992

Optimism

A S WE COMMEMORATE today the thirty-third anniversary of the March 10 Uprising in 1959, I am more optimistic than ever before about the future of Tibet. I feel certain that within the next five to ten years some major changes will take place in China. The collapse of totalitarian regimes in different parts of the world, the breakup of the Soviet empire and reemergence of sovereign, independent nations reinforce our belief in the ultimate triumph of truth, justice, and the human spirit. The bloody October Revolution of 1917, which controlled the fate of the Soviet Union for seven decades, came to an end in the bloodless, nonviolent August Revolution of 1991. The present Chinese leadership today has two choices. The first one is to start an enlightened political process for a smooth transition toward a fully democratic society and allow the countries they have forcibly annexed and occupied to become free and equal partners in a new world order. The second choice is to push the country to the brink of bloody political struggles, which in a country populated by a quarter of humanity would be a great tragedy.

There has been growing world concern and support for our cause. I was very encouraged by the genuine interest and sympathy shown by political leaders I met during my travels in 1991. We consider these favorable changes in the attitude of governments not to be anti-Chinese, but pro-justice and truth. The indomitable courage and determination of our people of Tibet has been the strength of our movement. The unique feature of our struggle has been its non-violent nature. While we continue to strive for our legitimate rights, we must not deviate from the path of nonviolence. I have no doubt that one day our people, as well as the peoples of Inner Mongolia and East Turkestan, will be reunited in full freedom in their respective countries.

Meanwhile, in exile, we are preparing the ground for a fully democratic Tibet in the future. An official document to this effect has been brought out recently, entitled, "Guidelines for Future Tibet's Polity and the Basic Features of Its Constitution." This document states that the present Tibetan Administration will be dissolved the moment we return to Tibet, and that I will hand over all my traditional political power to an interim government. The interim government, it explains, will be responsible for drawing up a democratic constitution under which the new government of Tibet will be elected by the people. It assures that there will be no political recrimination against those Tibetans who have worked in the Chinese administration. In fact, because of their experience, the Tibetan officials of the existing administration in Tibet should shoulder the main responsibility.

The future Tibet will be an oasis of peace in the heartland of Asia where man and nature will live in perfect harmony, not only benefiting Tibet and Tibetans but also helping to create the basis for a more cordial relationship between India and China. When a genuinely cordial relationship is established between Tibetans and Chinese, it will not only enable us to resolve the disputes between our two nations in this century, but will also enable the Tibetans to make a significant contribution through our rich cultural tradition for mental peace among the millions of young Chinese.

Relaunch of Talks with China?

What were the events on which the Dalai Lama based his optimism on March 10, 1992? His speech did not mention human rights violations, which he normally assessed at each state commemoration. It was not that no abuse had been committed, but the leader of the Tibetans had identified his cause with that of liberty throughout the world. "Our weapons are courage, justice, and truth," he said at the beginning of his exile. Henceforth, he would give this statement a universal impact that he extended to humanity. Speaking as a visionary, he announced the ultimate victory of truth, justice, and the human spirit. In the enthusiasm of the post-1989 years, military force seemed to yield to the power of the mind. Such assertiveness was based on the recent history and the irrepressible aspiration of the peoples to democratic freedom. In 1992, the global geopolitical balance was smoothly redefined. The dismantling of the Eastern bloc continued in a nonviolent manner. Its example opened the door to hope for a democratic transition in Asia, where the Dalai Lama continued to call for a federation of states.

His strength of conviction came not solely from the truths he stated, but from his capacity to embody them. In October 1991, he declared it would be logical "to feel nothing but hatred for the Chinese authorities. After being designated as our enemies, it would be legitimate to condemn their brutality and regard them as unworthy of consideration. But this is not the Buddhist way. Nor the way to achieve peace and harmony."[8] Whoever cultivates the Buddha's wisdom strives to develop a degree of tolerance allowing him to recognize in any offense the possibility of transforming anger and hatred. This attitude invites one to feel gratitude toward the aggressor, for he allows one to evolve spiritually, and practice compassion, given the suffering that his evil action holds for him.

Of such an elevation of the soul, the Dalai Lama and the Tibetans had given many examples in the past fifty years. In Chinese jails and under torture, great resisters had put into practice the heart of these teachings, like Ani Patchen, former princess of eastern Kham, who had become a warrior in the fight against the invaders, then been captured, chained, immured, and imprisoned for twenty years. At the age of seventeen, she who had vowed to overcome her limited ego, "to attain the rainbow body of the world of pure light," learned to sublimate the sufferings of torture into unconditional love: "My face and my body were covered with bruises. The blows made my anger rise and I tried to transform it into prayer: 'May I take upon myself the suffering of all those who undergo the same treatment! May I carry their pain!'"[9]

Lopon-la, Namgyal,[10] a monk, also imprisoned in the worst conditions, was inspired by the same spirit of love and entrusted to the Dalai Lama that during his years in prison, "only one thing terrified him: the possibility of losing his compassion for the persecutors who atrociously tortured and mutilated him."[11] Another great figure, Tenzin Choedrak, former personal physician of the Dalai Lama and his family, was imprisoned shortly after the uprising of March 10, 1959.

He survived thirty years of abuse and torture, thanks to the plants of which he knew the secrets. He secretly picked them during forced labor in quarries and also made his companions partake of them. He owed his release to a Chinese officer whom he cured of cancer.[12]

Driven by the same humanity, the Dalai Lama refused to let himself be won by a hatred that would lower him to the same level as the persecutors. Despite the affronts and insults, he remained committed to a personal dialogue with the Chinese leadership. According to him, relations between peoples and nations would be facilitated by a greater understanding at the level of the heads of state. In this spirit, in 1954, he had agreed to go to Beijing to meet Mao Zedong and Zhou Enlai, who were also human beings. Likewise at Yale, on October 9, 1991, he proposed to go to Tibet with two objectives: to review the situation and to persuade his compatriots to continue the path of nonviolence, the only acceptable form of fighting, restraining the younger ones who were tempted to resort to terrorism in order to attract global attention. Acclaimed by the public at Yale and hailed by the media as a gesture of exceptional tolerance, this proposal was rejected with sarcasm by the Chinese. The Ministry of Foreign Affairs in Beijing demanded that the Dalai Lama cease "his activities aimed at splitting China and breaking the unity of nationalities."

The Yale speech was not enough to restart the talks, so the Dalai Lama made another attempt in December 1991, during the visit to New Delhi of the Chinese Prime Minister Li Peng. India had just lost its main ally with the collapse of the USSR and sought strategic support in the Kashmir problem. It therefore approached the People's Republic to counter the efforts of Pakistan, which was seeking the support of the UN against India. For its part, China wanted to end the internationalization of the Tibetan crisis. The two countries shared the desire to deal with such conflicts without any interference from abroad. So there was a community of interest between Li Peng and his Indian counterpart, Narasimha Rao. For that matter, the Prime Minister of the Indian Union seemed to want to reassure him about this by repressing, with unusual severity, a demonstration of Tibetans gathered in his path.

The Dalai Lama's demand for a private meeting with Li Peng was rejected, and the visit of the Chinese statesman in Delhi concluded with an agreement on the Sino-Indian border. The Chinese tactics had worked: by linking the issues of Kashmir and Tibet, it had obtained a renewed strictness of the Indian authorities toward Tibetan refugees who qualified as separatists—just as formerly, Zhou Enlai had exchanged his agreement on the partition of Pakistan for Nehru's neutrality. "Rao learnt about diplomacy at the feet of Nehru," commented a politician. "We, Indians, have never been very good at the art of negotiation."[13]

International Support for the Cause of Tibet

In this context of Chinese rebuffs and Indian stiffening, the Dalai Lama kept the focus on the democratization of the exiled administration, which according to him was an essential measure for the future of his country. He made public on February 26, 1992, his *Guidelines for Future Tibet's Polity and Basic Features of Its Constitution*. This document outlined the need for a multiparty parliamentary system. Radically innovative in relation to a community that gave him blind faith, the religious leader said he was in favor of separating the spiritual power and the state. He had in mind a secular democracy, where monks would not take political positions and would not go to the polls. He himself stated unambiguously that he would not participate in government, once his country was liberated, and that the next leader should be elected by universal suffrage. The text listed the different stages of the organization of power, from the announcement of the withdrawal of Chinese troops to the formation of an interim government to ensure the transition before the election of the new head of state and the National Assembly, consisting of two chambers. The policy of future Tibet would have a social orientation, remain faithful to the principle of nonviolence, and give great importance to environmental protection. The document reaffirmed, as in Washington in 1987 and Strasbourg in 1988, that Free Tibet would be an oasis of peace for the world.

In this post-1989 period when all utopias seemed possible, this idealism met with the enthusiasm of other governing bodies. Before the popular mobilization, for the first time, on April 16, 1991, a U.S. president received the Dalai Lama at the White House. For half an hour, George H. W. Bush spoke with him about the violation of human rights in his country, of the threatened Tibetan culture and his efforts for negotiations with China. Two days later, the Dalai Lama was given a long ovation after he addressed the members of Congress to ask for their support in his attempts to engage in dialogue with Beijing. Following this hearing, on May 21, 1991, Congress passed a resolution stating that Tibet was a country that had been occupied illegally and was lawfully represented by the administration of Dharamsala. Its "distinct and sovereign identity on the national, cultural and religious level"[14] was established in the Chinese records and in the chronicles of the first Tibetan dynasties. Other evidence of its independence was its neutrality during the Second World War, recognized by the U.S. government, and its diplomatic exchanges with the United States, Mongolia, Bhutan, Sikkim, Nepal, India, Japan, the United Kingdom, and Russia, which had dealt with it directly without mentioning it to the Chinese government.[15] Furthermore, the Senate confirmed that "Congress and the people of the United States approved the march of the Tibetan People for freedom."[16] The term "freedom" denoted a novel support for the political aspirations of the Tibetans, the previous resolutions having been limited to the defense of their human rights.

Yet how can one ignore the fact that resolutions of Congress are in no way decisive? They express the legislature's recommendations without engaging the executive. When in July 1992, the Senate held a hearing with a spokesman of the State Department on Tibet, he reaffirmed the U.S. government's official position adopted thirty years before: "Like all the other governments of the world, we consider that Tibet is part of China, where it has the status of an autonomous region. No country recognizes Tibet as being independent from China. The United States has never accepted that Tibet is an independent country and the Dalai Lama has not been recognized as the leader of a government in exile. Although favorable to the self-determination of Tibet, we do not think that it implies its independence."[17]

Although on September 22, 1992, Congress had approved a resolution linking trade with China to the improvement of democratic reforms and human rights in Tibet, President Bush took no account of it. He used his veto power, while declaring in a letter to the House of Representatives that he fully approved of the objectives of his legislature. The split between the reason of the state and the congressional representation was obvious. The intense activity of the Dalai Lama in favor of humanism in politics had won him general esteem. Under pressure from public opinion, he was now received by heads of state and government. Yet, would the almost unanimous indignation about the repression in Tibet and in China bend the intransigence of the great powers, forcing them to adopt binding resolutions against China? The People's Republic knew how to manipulate the functioning of international bodies. When in 1990 and 1992 the conclusions of the Subcommittee for the Protection of Minorities came before the Commission on Human Rights at the UN, it managed to denounce them, arguing technicalities and procedures, with the help of Pakistan. It did the same in 1994 and 1996, thanks to the unconditional support of that country and by arranging the support also of India and Russia.

While peoples and parliaments heard the call of the Dalai Lama, governments persisted in their indulgence toward the Chinese state, in the name of the best interests of their nations. The dictatorship in Tibet was strengthened under the leadership of the strongmen of Beijing. Hu Jintao, the "Butcher of Lhasa," appointed Chen Kuiyuan in 1992 as Secretary of the Communist Party of the Autonomous Region, foreshadowing a tightening power. Also known as "the butcher," Chen Kuiyuan had to his credit the crushing of the Mongolian rebellion. Jiang Zemin, noted for having subdued the revolt of Shanghai in 1989, would become President of the People's Republic in 1993. Finally, Li Peng, prime minister, had ordered the massacre in Tiananmen Square. These leaders of the People's Republic of China who soon courted their hosts in Western capitals all had blood on their hands—hands that in iron fists hindered the fate of Tibet.

Yet, in 1992, the Dalai Lama still wanted to believe in the victory of humanism, in the triumph of ethics over market logic. His optimism and hope for the world drew the crowds. However, rather than creating the basis for a dialogue, his peace proposals exacerbated the tension with China, causing an increase in repression. Would international disapproval, in the long term, bring the regime to change its policies, as he hoped?

MARCH 10, 1993

China Interrupts the Dialogue

MILLIONS WHO LIVE under the repressive yoke of communism and other forms of dictatorship are now free and democratic aspirations are on the rise in all the continents. The Tibetan people continue to resist subjugation and colonization with courage and determination. No amount of repression and propaganda has lessened their yearning for a life of freedom, peace, and dignity. As we adjust to the changing global scene, we need to focus our efforts on four fronts. Firstly, we must continue to engage the Chinese government in a dialogue that is mutually beneficial and will eventually lead to earnest negotiations to peacefully resolve the question of Tibet. Secondly, we need to intensify our effort to further educate the world community of the problems of Tibet. International concern and pressure are conducive to bringing about a change in the Chinese government's position on negotiation and respect for human rights. Thirdly, because the new economic policies in Tibet will have a profound impact on the very survival of the cultural identity of the Tibetan nation, we must carefully study and monitor these developments. Fourthly, the democratization of the Tibetan administration in exile and the implementation of democracy at the grassroots level must be further encouraged.

For centuries Tibet and China have lived as neighbors, and I am convinced that we can find a way to live in peace and friendship in the future too. In this spirit I have, over the years, personally met with Chinese brothers and sisters throughout the world. I have encouraged my fellow Tibetans to engage in friendly discussions with members of the Chinese communities abroad. I am also greatly pleased with the increasing contacts and friendly dialogue between the exiled Tibetans and the members of the Chinese democracy movement. As a result, there is a growing understanding of the just aspirations of the Tibetan people, and therefore a sympathy and support for Tibet among our Chinese brothers and sisters.

Throughout human history, dictators and totalitarian governments have learned that there is nothing more powerful than a people's yearning for freedom and dignity. While bodies may be enslaved or imprisoned, the human spirit can never be subjugated or defeated. As long as we uphold this human spirit and determination, our inspirations and beliefs have the power to ultimately prevail. The sweeping global changes in recent years reaffirm my beliefs, and I am more optimistic than ever before that freedom and peace for the Tibetan people is now within our reach.

The Chinese Members of the Movement for Democracy

The dialogue between the Dalai Lama and Chinese dissidents was part of the evolution of the Chinese democracy movement, heavily repressed on June 4, 1989, in Tiananmen Square. Contrary to the expectations of Western countries, who believed that China would collapse, Deng Xiaoping restored his *manu militari* authority.

All liberal reforms in progress were swept away, with the exception of the ultraliberal economic reforms. True to its millenary imperial authoritarianism, the People's Republic of China persisted in banning independence of the spirit. A large number of students and intellectuals who had expressed themselves for democracy were arrested, and union leaders who had joined them were summarily executed. Shocked by this brutality, the U.S. government proceeded to an exfiltration operation for six months after the events. Thanks to agents stationed in Hong Kong and Macao, the main organizers of the protest and hundreds of dissidents were expatriated. They later founded most of the Chinese pro-democracy organizations in the world, benefiting from the sympathy of Westerners who, in the United States, formed the China Support Network. In Paris, the Chinese Federation for Democracy initiated on October 12, 1989, a dialogue with a delegation of the Dalai Lama. Freed from the shackles of the official propaganda in their European or American exile, the democratic leaders had discovered the reality of the Chinese occupation of Tibet. Striving to conceive the foundations of a new regime, they developed a draft constitution in the context of a future Federal Republic of China offering Tibet as well as Inner Mongolia, Xinjiang, and Taiwan the status of autonomous state. However, at the Conference on Sino-Tibetan Dialogue in Washington in October 1992, the Tibetan spokesman criticized the outline of this project. It in fact perpetuated the Chinese supervision, even though the Lhasa riots had made heard the popular aspiration for independence. He also criticized the authors for only considering the Autonomous Region, to the exclusion of other areas with Tibetan populations.[18]

The Dalai Lama, however, encouraged the continuation of dialogue and set the example himself. In 1992, he had met in the United States the dissident Harry Wu, who had made known to the world a reality ignored: that of the *laogai*, Chinese "reform through labor" camps, where Wu had been interned from 1960 to 1979. Once released, he campaigned for the word *laogai* to be entered in the international vocabulary, like "gulag," and to appear in the dictionaries of all the languages of the world. The *laogai* system dated from the early 1950s. These concentration camps were tools of the repression, created to smother dissent. Between forty and fifty million people were deported to about a thousand *laogai*, built across China and in Tibet. From the 1980s, the labor force of prisoners was put to the service of the country's economic boom. The revenues generated by the goods thus produced were no less than US$100 million in annual exports. A singular incident in 1993 supported the accusations of Harry Wu.

From the bottom of a *laogai* "abyss of suffering," in his own words, a certain Chen Pokong[19] took the risk of appealing to the UN. Defying censorship, his letter arrived at its destination, it is unclear by what improbable means. A prisoner wrote it by hand, begging the international organization to assume its responsibilities and enforce human rights in China. Chen included the labels that prisoners had to staple onto artificial flowers. The price was indicated in dollars, he discreetly learned. The decorations that he manufactured by night, after twelve hours of relentless work in a quarry, would reach the U.S. market via an import-export company based in Hong Kong. He knew what fate awaited him: "After the publication of my letter, I will be persecuted even more cruelly. I might even be executed. But I have no choice!"[20]

This moving testimony of direct contact with the horror of concentration camps was sent to Harry Wu, who alerted the government of the United States. With supporting evidence, the former political prisoner who had become founding president of the Laogai Museum confirmed that Christmas garlands, shoes, toys, and other consumer goods were being manufactured under the same conditions as the flowers that passed through Chen's hands. America prohibited the importation of these products of forced labor, but Harry Wu denounced the government's laxity. As for Europe, it had no legislation on the subject. So Chen Pokong continued to languish in the *laogai*. And Western consumers continued to buy goods *made in China*. Low-priced, they thought . . . as long as they did not evaluate the cost of pain and tears that these "good deals" required.

Chinese prisoners and Tibetan prisoners, their stories merged. All had experienced what the Dalai Lama evoked on March 10, 1993: "If the body can be enslaved or imprisoned, never will the human mind allow itself to be submitted or defeated." As before with Alexander Solzhenitsyn or Primo Levi, Harry Wu and the *laogai* survivors subjected their torturers to the gaze of intelligence. Their stories illuminated the inhumanity of the jails of the People's Republic. All witness statements reported the same abuses: water and food deprivation; forced destitution; rape in the mouth, vagina, or anus with electric batons (originally manufactured in the Netherlands, to lead cattle to the slaughterhouse); punches, kicks, blows with rifle butts, sticks, or metal rods; exposure to dog attacks; cigarette burns; prolonged barefoot standing on ice; suspension in the air by the thumbs, ankles, or shoulders.[21] A refugee from eastern Tibet, a member of the Public Security Bureau, passed abroad a Party manual for internal use. These tortures were listed among thirty others.[22]

International Pressure on the People's Republic of China

The testimonies increased, contradicting the allegations of Chinese authorities that they had ensured compliance with the Convention Against Torture, signed in December 1986 and ratified in 1988. International support continued to grow, and 1993 saw an unprecedented mobilization of the American political class. In January, during a speech to the Senate, Secretary of State Warren Christopher stressed the need for binding pressures on China, given its continued violations of human rights. Then, in May, President Bill Clinton announced that the renewal of "most favored nation" status would be granted to China only if it respected human rights and was committed to protecting the religious and cultural heritage of Tibet. He demanded access to detention centers for humanitarian agencies and publication of the files on political prisoners. In August 1993, at the instigation of the Massachusetts Senator Edward Kennedy, thirty-four senators signed a call for the immediate release of several Tibetan prisoners of conscience.

At the same time, many governments called on China to enter into dialogue and negotiation with the Dalai Lama. In January 1993, the UK's Foreign Office urged Beijing to hold talks with Dharamsala. Then on May 26, it published a report on Tibet, urging the Chinese authorities to consider a more complete autonomy for the Himalayan region and a meeting with the Dalai Lama, without preconditions. Finally, on June 1, 1993, following a diplomatic mission in Tibet, the European Community and its Member States made public in Copenhagen a statement urging the authorities to negotiate with the Dalai Lama.

On the Chinese side, the tactic consisted in keeping the issue on the political field. The Beijing government had noted that since the beginning of the invasion in 1950, no foreign government had recognized the independence of Tibet. Besides, the Strasbourg Proposal favored its strategy, as the leader of the Tibetans no longer claimed independence and accepted the principle of autonomy. The international criticism was therefore mainly focused on human rights, and Beijing responded by denouncing this as unacceptable interference. The regime accused the West of instrumentalizing the question of human rights. It reiterated its adherence to all international conventions, maintaining that human rights are not universal and should be addressed in the national context. In China, in terms of both the traditional community and the Marxist ideology, individual liberties were subordinated to the dictatorship of the proletariat. Minorities should therefore, like the Chinese majority, accept the common law to enjoy the rights guaranteed to all, and contesting it was punishable by law. This cultural relativism[23] became the shield of repression. The modern mandarins were inflexible, while they were getting ready to implement in the Himalayan region an unprecedented project of economic development. Tibetans would therefore have no choice but integration or marginalization. Indeed, what weight did the ethical and humanistic considerations of the Dalai Lama have before the growth targets that propelled China to the rank of the first global economic power?

MARCH 10, 1994

Disenchantment

I MUST NOW RECOGNIZE that my approach has failed to produce any progress. Moreover, I am conscious of the fact that a growing number of Tibetans, both inside as well as outside Tibet, have been disheartened by my conciliatory stand not to demand complete independence for Tibet. Because of my statements, some Tibetans have come to believe that there is no hope at all of the Tibetan people regaining their basic rights and freedoms. This and the lack of any concrete results from my conciliatory approach toward the Chinese government over the past 14 years have caused disillusionment and undermined the resolve of some Tibetans. Internationally, my initiatives and proposals have been endorsed as realistic and reasonable by many governments, parliaments, and nongovernmental organizations. But despite the growing support of the international community, the Chinese government has not responded constructively.

I continue to remain committed to finding a peaceful and negotiated resolution to the issue of Tibet with the Chinese government directly, but the Chinese are merely paying lip service to this approach. It is evident that only increased international political and economic pressure can bring a sense of urgency to bear on the Chinese leadership not merely to pay lip service but to resolve the problem of Tibet peacefully and amicably. The tragedy of Tibet can be relieved through the determined and concerted efforts of various governments and NGOs championing human rights, liberty, and democracy the world over.

Our cause is gathering momentum. For example, a long letter written on October 5, 1992, by the well-known Chinese dissident Wei

Jingsheng, to Deng Xiaoping, speaking out against his government's unjust claims over Tibet and their misguided policies there, has just become public. These expressions are the manifestations of genuine human respect for truth and justice. Fearful of these developments, China has now formulated policies to undermine our administration in exile as well as to create discord and division in our community. Therefore, every one of us must be alert and renew our commitment to the just cause of our country. I firmly believe that the day is close when our beloved Land of Snow will no longer be politically subjugated, culturally ravaged, and economically and environmentally exploited and devastated. Our dedication, sacrifice, and hard work will lead our captive nation to freedom and peace in dignity. However, it is important that our struggle must be based on nonviolence.

Still Reasons to Hope?

In 1994, the tone was no longer optimistic. The door to negotiations had been closed, and the tightening Chinese policy turned the Dalai Lama toward caution. His confidence was reserved. After 1989, once the Cold War confrontation of the world ended, it was thought the page of long deadlocks and UN compromises had been turned. The global context was favorable to Tibet, as evidenced by the unprecedented support of public opinion. But the conclusions of an internal Communist Party conference, held in Beijing in March 1993, show the fears aroused by the implosion of the Soviet Union. Chinese leaders feared a balkanization of their country under the pressure of nationalism. If the collapse of the USSR was celebrated by the Dalai Lama and all supporters of freedom around the world, it made the Politburo shudder and was used as an argument by the hard-liners of the Party. In the name of national unity, this faction took Tibet as a target, where it strengthened the troops of the People's Armed Police.[24]

The Chinese counteroffensive also took the form of an attempt to destabilize the Tibetan government in exile and the refugee community. It was accompanied by virulent propaganda against the "Dalai clique," whose willingness to negotiate was described as a "smoke-screen to mislead public opinion."[25] The position of the Dalai Lama could certainly look strong, for he had won over to his cause Western public opinion, a "vast market in perpetual growth."[26] However, this enthusiasm would fall quickly once the Party had let everyone know that "prosperity, freedom of religion and belief, democratic rights, peace, and joy reigned in Tibet."[27] Chinese embassies should relay this message to all countries and systematically protest against any invitation of the Dalai Lama around the world.

This is how, on June 14, 1993, the Chinese lightning struck the orga-nizers of the World Conference on Human Rights, the first of the post-Cold War era, held in Vienna by the UN. The Austrian government had invited the Dalai Lama to the inaugural session, but before Chinese pressure, it finally prohibited him access. In an act of solidarity, the oth-er Nobel Prize winners decided to boycott the opening ceremony, and the Austrian Ministry of the Interior found itself compelled to allow the Dalai Lama to speak in the tent of Amnesty International. The head of the Chinese delegation retorted in an open letter, accusing the Dalai Lama of wanting to undermine the unity of China to restore servitude in his country. The Chinese rhetoric accused the spiritual leader of acting against the human rights that the Chinese claimed to defend.[28] Nobody was fooled by these allegations, but they made the Austrian government give in.

When the Market Dictates Its Law . . .

The Chinese methods were even more effective after the events of Tiananmen, when China had entered the most rapid growth period in its history. In 1993, the U.S. Congress had linked verification of China's respect for human rights to its inclusion in the category of most favored nation for trade. This humanitarian bias was short-lived. On May 26, 1994, in disregard of such commitments, President Clinton decided to grant China what it wanted.[29] In fact, repression had intensified in Tibet, and in China itself, the leaders did not listen to the dissidents' demands. Nevertheless, Bill Clinton's pragmatism took into account the reality of the Chinese market, supposed guarantor of two hundred thousand jobs in the United States. If most favored nation status was not renewed, goods *made in China* would have been subject to higher customs duties, causing an increase in the prices for a range of popular products, from Nike shoes to Barbie dolls. The U.S. executive gave in, so as not to incur the wrath of consumers. Commenting on his decision, President Clinton affirmed that human rights and democracy were important to the United States, but that he could not sacrifice trade with China for them.

This decision did not bode well for the determination of Western democracies to defend their great principles. Who to turn to then? The Dalai Lama drew on the letter on Tibet written by Wei Jingsheng to the attention of Deng Xiaoping. From his concentration camp in Qinghai, the Chinese dissident criticized a regime that behaved as the owner of Tibet and its people. To maintain that Tibet belongs to China is as grotesque, he said ironically, as to characterize Canada and Australia as English territories under the pretext of past ties of allegiance. "History will judge you and condemn you," Wei assured the most powerful man in China, who had sworn that as long as Wei lived he would not get out of prison.

What if the weakest in appearance was in fact the strongest? In such dissidence, even suffocated, even persecuted, the Dalai Lama saw "a moral force more powerful than governments and their armies."[30] He exalted "the spectacular popular movement in favor of human rights and democratic freedoms in the world,"[31] which he saw as the spearhead of his nonviolent fight. However, if in 1994 the people of the world supported Tibet through a network that continued to grow, their leaders gave priority to the imperatives of economic growth. The market dictates its law to politicians. What counter-power would the Dalai Lama be able to oppose to them?

7

CONFLICT OF CIVILIZATIONS

———◀┼▶———

1995-2002

MARCH 10, 1995

Drowned in a Sea of Chinese

THE CHINESE GOVERNMENT has intensified its repression in Tibet. Recent Chinese policies demonstrate more clearly than ever their intention to resolve the question of Tibet through force and population transfer. The Chinese authorities have lately adopted a series of new measures to tighten political control in Tibet. Under a program of "investigation and scrutiny," tighter security measures were imposed and a new crackdown on advocates of human rights and independence has been launched. Victims of this new political persecution include Tibetans who work for the preservation of Tibetan culture, which includes teaching the Tibetan language and opening private schools. Tibetan cadres and members of the Chinese Communist Party are made to undergo political reeducation, reminiscent of the days of the Cultural Revolution. Those suspected of harboring religious and national feelings are being purged. Monasteries have been raided by the People's Armed Police and the chain of political arrests has been extended to rural areas. The rebuilding and construction of new monasteries have been prohibited and the admission of new monks and nuns stopped. Tibetan travel agents and tourist guides have been dismissed in order to control the flow of information, and Tibetan children are no longer permitted to study abroad. Those who are presently studying abroad have been ordered to return.

At a high-level meeting in Beijing last July these policies were sanctioned and sixty-two new "economic development projects" in Tibet announced. As in the past, these projects are designed primarily to increase the immigration of Chinese into Tibet to ultimately drown the Tibetans in a sea of Chinese. Similarly, China's proclaimed intention to build a railroad to Central Tibet is particularly alarming. Under the present circumstances this will enable a dramatic acceleration of China's population transfer policy. We only need to look at the large influx of Chinese who are arriving by train every week in different parts of Eastern Turkestan to understand the impact such a railway will have on the survival of the Tibetan people with their unique cultural heritage.

With the occupation of Tibet, Tibetan Buddhism has been robbed of its cradle and homeland, not only violating the Tibetan people's right to freedom of religion but also endangering the very survival of our spiritual and cultural tradition. This is particularly true of China's policy of cutting Tibet up into many separate administrative units, most of which have been incorporated into neighboring Chinese provinces. Historically, the contribution of Tibetans from these areas to Tibet's cultural and spiritual heritage has been immense. But as tiny minorities in Chinese provinces it will be very difficult for these Tibetans to preserve their Buddhist culture and distinct identity in the long run. The Tibetan entities outside the so-called Tibet Autonomous Region (TAR) comprise a larger portion of the Tibetan area and roughly four of the six million Tibetans. A solution to the question of Tibet cannot be found without all these parts of Tibet being incorporated into one Tibetan entity. This is essential to the survival of Tibetan culture.

A Society Under Surveillance

In 1995, the effort at forced sinicization was stronger than ever, and President Jiang Zemin stressed the need to "marry the beautiful traditional Tibetan culture to the fruits of modern culture."[32] Measures to achieve this were detailed in the document *A Golden Bridge Leading to a New Era*, edited by the Party. The text recommended forcing the reshaping of Tibetan society, deemed "backward due to lack of mental programming of the people."[33] The recommended methods were always the same: cultural assimilation, migration of a Chinese workforce, and the imposition of a market economy. Beijing strategists did not innovate. They were exemplifying the remarks, still valid today, of the eminent sinologist Simon Leys, who in 1989 observed: "The historian of contemporary China who retrospectively considers the events from three years ago, from ten years ago, from twenty years ago, feels dizzy. It's always the same story—the scenario is identical, you only need to change the names of a few actors. The sinister carousel goes nowhere, it goes around in circles, more and more squeaky and dilapidated: its bloody machine is satisfied with ever more brutally crushing a population that is more and more thirsty for freedom."[34]

In this system doomed to repetition, as in the days of Deng Xiaoping, the growth index was the only mark of success. The new mandarins knew that the influx of Chinese workers caused the anger that ignited Lhasa between 1987 and 1989. They did not, however, consider another solution to the Tibetan problem. In order to facilitate their arrival, the government deployed new transportation routes, including the Beijing-Lhasa railway. "Drown the Tibetans in a sea of Chinese." This demographic submersion was based on the principle that for every Tibetan, two Chinese must be living in Tibet, both in the name of economic development and because the Tibetans are lazy compared to the Chinese, who work hard. However, this policy brought into question the region's autonomy, keystone of the relationship between the central power and the minorities. Also, at the Third Work Forum on Tibet, held in Beijing in July 1994 under President

Jiang Zemin and Prime Minister Li Peng, the very word "autonomy" was banished. It was no longer politically correct, and the leadership preferred to speak of "special characteristics." The message was clear: Tibet was no longer entitled to any exceptions.

The Dalai Lama was thus identified as the main enemy of this strategy of sinicization and the instigator of Tibetan separatism. A defamatory campaign presented him as the "head of the snake," from the proverb: "To kill a snake, you must cut off its head."

The Third Work Forum on Tibet had further recommended zero tolerance toward the religious, identified as his most inveterate partisans. "The monasteries, which are on the side of the secessionists and continue to cause problems, must be reorganized. If necessary, their doors will be closed. In the future, to build a new monastery, one must receive permission from the Office of Religious Affairs of the Autonomous Region."[35] The Buddhist institutions were therefore compelled to comply with the requirement of "stability" that President Jiang had imposed upon Tibetan society.

Certain regulations, under the pretext of the fight against religion, actually had another significance. This was, for example, the case with the restrictions on the funeral custom of "sky burial." Tibetans continued to value this tradition,[36] but when it was the dead bodies of prisoners, it often happened that the priests uncovered serious damage to internal organs, caused by torture—in contradiction to the declarations of the prison authorities, who in general attributed the deaths to disease. New rules were therefore promulgated to "raise the quality and morality of priests responsible for sky burials." They were henceforth required to be approved by the Ministry of Civil Affairs and take lessons of indoctrination.[37]

This limitation of religious freedom accompanied the launch of the "Investigation and Surveillance" campaign aimed at establishing a daily police framework. The monitoring of all activities, professional and private, was assured by the multiplication of the supervisory bodies in places of work, leisure, and worship. From the early 1960s, the authorities had established "neighborhood committees" to ensure the implementation of reforms. Their leaders held regular meetings to which every household was required to send one of its members; otherwise they were prohibited from buying food at subsidized prices. The frequency of these meetings increased from 1995 with the "Seven don'ts" campaign—"Don't look," "Don't participate," "Don't support," "Don't repeat rumors," "Don't believe the rumors," "Don't be in solidarity," and "Don't dissimulate." A network of Tibetan and Chinese civilians tracked the behavior of everyone, and informal security units patrolled at night, encouraged to make reports to the police. Their members were recruited, for a fee or under threat. If they did not cooperate with zeal, they risked detention of their family members or themselves.

"Investigation and Surveillance" was radicalized even more with the creation of the "Committee for Stabilization of the Situation." Its mission was to train a thousand observers to find the discontented and recalcitrants. This network of the population would force them to adopt the ideology of the Party, in reality the basis of the sinicization process. The relay bodies of this security framework, supported by the police and the courts, operated as government agencies in a strategy of systematic eradication of dissidence. Such measures were the subject of numerous reports of the Commission on Human Rights at the United Nations. It had gathered enough evidence and proof against the People's Republic, but the Permanent Representative of China in the UN denied the accusations. China was a multiethnic state, and the Maoist Republic strove to peacefully transform "backward" Tibet into a modern state, guarantor of individual freedoms. It was necessary to dismiss the reports by labeling them the fantasies of separatist propaganda that provided the "false information" with which the UN reports were supposedly stuffed. To finish, the diplomat expressed his indignation before so many "disgraceful falsehoods." These denials did not prevent an international conference of thirty eminent jurists from examining for four days the case of Tibet, before concluding that "since the military aggression of 1949–1950, the country came under foreign domination of the Peoples' Republic, who have administered it through an oppressive colonial regime."[38] The right to self-determination was thus formally recognized as due to the Tibetan people by the 51st session of the UN Commission on Human Rights, held in Geneva in early 1995.

However, the same year, the masters of Beijing were going to try to strike down Tibetan Buddhism at its heart, with a terrible blow to the man who for forty-five years had opposed them only with the forces of peace, forgiveness, and love.

MARCH 10, 1996

The Youngest Political Prisoner in the World

A S WE COMMEMORATE today the thirty-seventh anniversary of the Tibetan People's uprising, we are witnessing a general hardening of Chinese government policy. This is reflected in an increasingly aggressive posture toward the peoples of Taiwan and Hong Kong and in intensified repression in Tibet. We also see rising fear and suspicion throughout the Asia-Pacific region and a worsening of relations between China and much of the rest of the world.

Within the context of this tense political atmosphere, Beijing has once again sought to impose its will on the Tibetan people by appointing a rival Panchen Lama. In doing so, it has chosen a course of total disregard both for the sentiments of the Tibetans in general and for Tibetan spiritual tradition in particular, despite my every effort to reach for some form of understanding and cooperation with the Chinese government. Significantly, the official Chinese media compares the present political climate in Tibet with that in Poland during the Solidarity years of the 1980s. This demonstrates a growing sense of insecurity on the part of the Chinese leadership as a result of which, through a continuing campaign of coercion and intimidation, Beijing has greatly reinforced its repression throughout Tibet. I am therefore saddened to have to report that the situation of our people in Tibet continues to deteriorate.

Nevertheless, it remains my strong conviction that change for the better is coming. China is at a critical juncture: its society is undergoing profound changes and the country's leadership is facing the transition to a new generation. It is obvious too that the Tiananmen Massacre has failed to silence the call for freedom, democracy, and human rights in China. Moreover, the impressive democratization in process across the Taiwan Strait must further invigorate the democratic aspirations of the Chinese people. Indeed, Taiwan's historic first direct presidential elections later this month are certain to have an immense political and psychological impact on their minds. A transformation from the current totalitarian regime in Beijing into one which is more open, free, and democratic is thus inevitable. The only outstanding question is how and when and whether the transition will be a smooth one.

As a human being, it is my sincere desire that our Chinese brothers and sisters enjoy freedom, democracy, prosperity, and stability. As a Buddhist monk, I am of course concerned about a country which is home to almost a quarter of the world's entire population and which is on the brink of an epic change. As a Tibetan, I recognize that the future of our country and our people depends to a great extent on what happens in China during the years ahead. Whether the coming change in China brings new life and new hope for Tibet and whether China herself emerges as a reliable, peaceful, and constructive member of the international community depends to a large degree on the extent to which the international community itself adopts responsible policies toward China. I have always drawn attention to the need to bring Beijing into the mainstream of world democracy and have spoken against any ideas of isolating and containing China. I would like to take this opportunity to thank the numerous individuals, also the members of governments, of parliaments, of nongovernmental organizations, and of religious orders, who have supported my appeal for the safety and freedom of the young Panchen Lama, Gendhun Choekyi Nyima. I am grateful for their continued intervention and efforts on behalf of this child who must be the world's youngest political prisoner.

The Living Buddha of the Chinese Communist Party

The life of spiritual lineage holders does not begin at their birth. It does not end with their death. The Dalai Lamas are the emanations on earth of Avalokiteshvara, the buddha of compassion. The Panchen Lamas are emanations of Amitabha, the buddha of infinite light. Deep soul ties unite forever the heads of these supreme lineages of Tibet. The First Dalai Lama built in Shigatse in 1447 the great Tashilhunpo[39] Monastery, which the Fifth Dalai Lama offered in 1642 to his spiritual master, after having conferred upon him the honorary title of Panchen Lama or "Great Master Scholar." Historically, the Dalai Lamas and Panchen Lamas have by custom confirmed each other's reincarnation. Two years after the death of the tenth Panchen Lama, on March 21, 1991, the Dalai Lama sent a message to the Chinese government that he would supervise the search for the new Panchen Lama. He proposed to send a religious delegation to Lhamoi Lhatso. On the waters of this sacred lake, near Lhasa, prophetic visions had revealed the location of many incarnations, including his own, in 1937. However, after three months, the Chinese authorities informed him that they had entrusted the search for the eleventh Panchen Lama to the abbot of Tashilhunpo, Chadrel Rinpoche. Exiled Tibetans and foreigners were not allowed to interfere in the investigation.

In August of the same year, the Beijing authorities made public their plan for the search for the Panchen Lama using the traditional method of consulting mystical signs and past memory tests, but introduced as well the ceremony of the "golden urn." This rite dates from the Manchu dynasty of the eighteenth century, an epoch when the Emperor Qianlong was a devoted disciple of the sixth Panchen Lama. Intervening to restore order in Tibet, which was weakened by internal divisions, he had promulgated an edict in 1793 for the reincarnation of great lamas. The text provided for the selection of young boys showing certain favorable signs, of whom the name and date of birth were to be written on a tablet and then placed in a golden urn. After a random draw, the elected child would be designated as the official reincarnation. However, the process of the golden urn was actually used only three times, with the aim of undermining the influence of Mongol clans. Apart from these exceptions, the Seventh Dalai Lama recognized the sixth Panchen Lama, who, in turn, recognized the eighth golden throne holder of Lhasa, who confirmed the seventh Panchen Lama . . . thus perpetuating the lineages over time. The recognition of the eleventh Panchen Lama by the Fourteenth Dalai Lama was therefore faithful to the tradition. However, the objective of the Politburo in Beijing was clear: to arrogate to themselves power over the predestined of Tibet. Indeed, they thought that, as the Dalai Lama and Panchen Lama enthroned each other reciprocally, a Panchen Lama appointed by the Communist Party augured a future Dalai Lama at his command.

The leader of the Tibetans could not tolerate such a manipulation of the reincarnation process. He therefore discreetly made contact with Chadrel Rinpoche and was kept informed, during the summer of 1993, of the oracle signs gathered on the banks of Lhamoi Lhatso. After propitiatory rituals to the spirits who open the doors of embodied time, the waters boiled. Rainbows were reflected on their surface and, like mirages, radiant symbols and letters appeared. The lake had spoken.

Chadrel Rinpoche decrypted the secret. In February 1994, he sent anonymous research teams northeast of Tashilhunpo. A group of twenty-eight children was selected, and a year later, the monks gathered once again on the shores of the lake. Other signs allowed them to eliminate twenty candidates. Eight remained, among them Gendhun Choekyi Nyima, aged six. During previous memory tests, the boy had recognized without hesitation the personal belongings of his predecessor. His parents reported that when he was little he used to say, "I must return to my monastery of Tashilhunpo." In secret, emissaries of the government in exile gathered this information. On May 14, 1995, the day of Sagadawa,[40] the Dalai Lama officially proclaimed that Gendhun Choekyi Nyima, born on April 25, 1989, in the region of Lhari, was the eleventh Panchen Lama.[41]

The news of this recognition irritated the Chinese government. Yet would it go as far as rejecting the choice of the Dalai Lama? It could maintain that the child had no power without its approval and then proceed to his official enthronement. It would derive great benefit from having under its influence a dignitary accepted by the population.

There was, along with this, the previous case of the seventeenth Karmapa. The third religious dignitary of Tibet, whose title means "Master of Awakened Action," had been discovered in 1992, following the traditional method. His disciples, led by Tai Situ Rinpoche, a lama in exile, had identified the child born in the Chamdo region, in a family of simple nomads. Tai Situ Rinpoche had obtained the agreement of both the Dalai Lama and the Chinese authorities to enthrone the new Karmapa at the seat of his lineage, Tsurphu Monastery, northwest of Lhasa. However, once installed, the Karmapa was forbidden to go to Sikkim to receive religious education in accordance with his rank. The protests of Tai Situ Rinpoche had no effect. The Chinese government intended to use the Karmapa's spiritual authority to influence the population, who showed him immense devotion.

In the case of the Panchen Lama, the situation was different. Beijing could not tolerate that the Dalai Lama had disregarded any obligation of requiring its approval. He had challenged the Chinese sovereigns who, although avowed materialists, now also intended to work in the spiritual realm. It is true that the red mandarins appropriated this mystical process for the appointment of senior officials: "The search and confirmation of the reincarnation of the Panchen," confirmed Radio Lhasa, "has never been a strictly religious and ritual matter. Politically, it is a matter subject to the central government and is under its authority."[42] The boy chosen by the Dalai Lama was thus rejected on the grounds that his appointment was contrary to Buddhist doctrine and threatened the sovereignty of the state.

Three days after the proclamation of the Dalai Lama, on May 17, 1995, Gendhun Choekyi Nyima disappeared. He was taken away to prevent the Tibetan people from paying tribute to him, as is the custom in the announcement of the reincarnation of a great master. The Tibetan Communist Party executives denounced the Dalai Lama's proclamation as the illegal intervention of a "religious reactionary and renegade whose degenerate practices betray the Buddhist faith."[43] Chadrel Rinpoche, accused of complicity, was imprisoned with his entourage of monks. A work team of fifty people from the Office of Public Safety moved within the confines of Tashilhunpo, with a mission of purging the monastery surrounded by the army. The monks were ordered to accuse the Dalai Lama of counterrevolutionary activity. Most refused to comply and underwent sessions of reeducation and then torture.

A few months later, on November 29, 1995, the ceremony of the golden urn took place at night in Lhasa, where an impressive security presence had been deployed. The superintendents of the Council of State had made the trip from Beijing. Gathered in secret in the Jokhang Temple, at the foot of the Potala, they sat alongside the Chinese and Tibetan officials of the Communist Party, in the presence of some religious persons in ceremonial costumes and the parents of three children selected by their process. In the golden urn on the altar before the statue of Buddha were three golden silk pockets, each containing an ivory tablet. At its end, according to the ritual dating from the Qianlong Emperor, a label was stuck bearing the name of one of the candidates. The lama responsible for the "Democratic Management Committee" of Tashilhunpo prostrated himself before the urn and then took it in his hands, recommending prayer for the good outcome of the ceremony. The president of the Tibetan branch of the Buddhist Association of China[44] was then called to "draw lots" for the name of the future Panchen Lama. The designated child was called Gyantsen Norbu. Born in Lhari, the same area as the choice of the Dalai Lama, he was, opportunely, the son of Party members. The tablet passed from hand to hand among the officials, who read his name aloud, thus confirming the authenticity of his appointment. All applauded the young

Gyantsen Norbu, who appeared, wearing a sumptuous brocade cos-
tume, after having been hidden, it seems in advance, behind a curtain.
He walked up to the statue of Buddha, and as he had been instructed,
prostrated himself three times. Monks and lamas then offered him ceremonial scarves before bowing to receive his blessing. At the end of this
parody of recognition orchestrated by the Party, Beijing made public
the appointment of its eleventh Panchen Lama.

On December 8, the enthronement took place at Tashilhunpo
Monastery. The date had been kept secret until the last moment. A
curfew was even imposed in Shigatse, Lhasa, and Chamdo, the three
major cities of the Autonomous Region. The "Chinese Panchen,"
as the people called him, arrived at the monastery on November
30, escorted by the army. Senior lamas, dignitaries, and monks of
Tashilhunpo had only heard the news the night before. Their presence was required, and they were threatened with the worst abuses
if they pretended to be sick in order to avoid it. The ceremony took
place without the fervor of the crowd, which normally acclaimed with
overflows of joy a great spiritual teacher returning to the world to fulfill his sacred mission. The head of the Religious Affairs Bureau had
come from Beijing especially for the occasion. Five hundred soldiers,
outnumbering the religious, guarded the entrance to the monastery,
armed with guns, sifting through the guests of a ritual that insulted
the soul of Tibet and hid a crime committed against two children:
Gyantsen Norbu, elevated on a throne for which he was not destined,
and Gendhun Choekyi Nyima, secretly held in a Chinese jail.

"Ridiculous crime, but still a crime, to so crudely mix politics and
religion," said the foreign press,[45] indignant. Politicians around the
world protested. On November 8, 1995, a statement from the U.S.
State Department indicated "discouragement and discontent of
Washington before these intrigues carried out in these recent weeks."
Beijing's attitude gave rise to "serious questions about how the Chinese government was keeping its commitment to respect the beliefs
and religious practices of Tibetan Buddhism."[46] On December 14,
1995, the U.S. Senate unanimously adopted a resolution demanding

respect for the candidate selected by the Dalai Lama. The Australian Senate and the European Parliament insistently asked for the release of the eleventh Panchen Lama. In France, two hundred deputies and senators gathered in the Tibet Study Group of the National Assembly and the parliamentary Friendship Association for Tibet of the Senate, denouncing the "stranglehold of the Republic of China on Tibet." Considering that Gendhun Choekyi Nyima had become de facto the youngest political prisoner in the world, they decided to foster him. His case was examined by the UN Committee on the Rights of the Child, which called upon China to explain itself. It took a year for some news to finally filter out. China's ambassador to the United Nations in Geneva admitted that his government had made the boy disappear to "protect him from a risk of abduction by dangerous Tibetan separatists." While this same government had hitherto pretended to be completely unaware of his fate, the diplomat stated that he was now in safe custody at the request of his parents. When the UN Committee demanded the right to visit, it was turned down completely. A global Amber Alert (America's Missing: Broadcast Emergency Response) was launched by the Tashilhunpo Monastery rebuilt in exile, promising a reward to anyone who would bring it into contact with the eleventh Panchen Lama.

China's policy had as a target the spiritual power of the Dalai Lama. This was not without contradiction. On the one hand, the Communist Party fought religion, poison of the people; on the other, it arrogated to itself the right to recognize in Tibet the reincarnation of a lama, "a living buddha." However, a longer-term strategy was in sight.

Only Time Will Conquer Tibet

The sixtieth birthday of the Dalai Lama, on July 6, 1995, was an opportunity for the officials of the Communist Party to remind him that time was in their favor. After the death of the religious leader, the Tibetan resistance movement would be doomed to extinction. Mao

Zedong himself had said that only time would overcome the Tibetans. In time, it would suffice to designate a Fifteenth Dalai Lama who would be as manipulable as the new Panchen Lama. At the heart of their modern empire, the mandarins of the Forbidden City thought they had the spiritual masters of Tibet at their mercy. The seventeenth Karmapa was under house arrest in his monastery of Tsurphu. The eleventh Panchen Lama was held in secrecy while a puppet Panchen Lama grew up under socialist authority. They did not doubt that the next Dalai Lama would also be under their orders. Already in 1996, the Xinhua News Agency said: "The Buddhist believers know that the Dalai Lama is no longer a religious leader."[47] The Party launched against him a campaign of denigration that was supposed to last for five years, as part of "a struggle whose nature was not a question of believing or not in a religion, but to defend the motherland and to oppose secessionism."[48] The power always used the same processes: move the Tibet issue to the person of its spiritual guide and break the people's faith, the foundation of his identity.

Nevertheless, the Dalai Lama persisted in wanting dialogue with the Chinese authorities, in the name of his three life commitments. First, as a *human being*, he considered the Chinese his "brothers and sisters." Second, as a *Buddhist monk*, he wanted to avoid suffering and cultivate nonviolence until his last breath. Thirdly, as a *Tibetan*, he felt that the future of his country depended on the changes that inevitably would occur in China. With the rise of a new generation of leaders, the democratization of the People's Republic was inevitable. The question was not whether democracy would be established, but *when* and *how*.

These three life commitments of the Dalai Lama are essential to understand his political struggle.[49] Presented in his speech of March 10, 1996, they had been publicly stated for the first time in his speech on accepting the Nobel Peace Prize. On December 10, 1989, in Oslo, as on March 10, 1996, in Dharamsala, the Dalai Lama reminded us of our duty to be humane, bruised and degraded by our inability to overcome violence and hatred.

The Chinese Version of the Clash of Civilizations

Despite this conciliatory attitude, the People's Republic of China demonstrated a renewed aggressiveness. Just as the authorities had not been afraid to attack the Dalai Lama head-on about the succession of the Panchen Lama, they adopted a provocative attitude before the international criticism. In jargon worthy of the Cold War, the Office of Propaganda in Beijing noted that, living in exile for thirty-six years, the Dalai Lama had taken over the malicious designs of the anti-Chinese forces. The West had "bribed the Dalai clique and tried to use the Tibetan issue as a spearhead to weaken, destabilize and divide China."[50] In the Mao era, already, Tibet was considered the "back door" through which the imperialists tried to introduce themselves into the motherland. Going back over the theme of the clash of civilizations by Samuel Huntington,[51] which was much commented on in the Chinese press, the leading thinkers in Beijing believed that the confrontation between East and West had "to happen sooner or later."[52] Huntington's thesis was being used, according to them, to rally the Westerners in an anticommunist crusade aimed at breaking the spectacular growth of their country.

If the succession of the Panchen Lama is placed in this context, one can understand why the leadership of the Party neglected the political gain that the popularity of the Panchen Lama chosen by the Dalai Lama could have represented. It is reasonable to ask whether the Chinese government had not deliberately engaged in an open confrontation with him.[53] In China's efforts to win its competition with the West, the Tibetan issue had become inseparable from the Chinese claim on Taiwan and Hong Kong. In 1996, China made a demonstration of strength, testing missiles and deploying warships off the coast of Taiwan. To this the United States responded by sending two aircraft carriers and air patrols, in their largest military operation in Asia since the Vietnam War. However, the Chinese expansionism aimed for the whole of Asia and the Pacific. The world had seen the intervention in Burma, territorial disputes around the Spratly Islands, installation of a naval spy base in the Indian Ocean, and nuclear tests in East Turkestan (violating agreements on nuclear nonproliferation).[54] Chinese aggressiveness was at its height. Before the Chinese threat, how not to hear the warnings of the Dalai Lama?

MARCH 10, 1997

"Curtain of Mental Bamboo"

IN THE CLOSING years of the twentieth century, it is evident that the human community has reached a crucial juncture in its history. The world is becoming smaller and increasingly interdependent. One nation's problem can no longer be solved by itself. Without a sense of universal responsibility, our very future is in danger. Today's problems of militarization, development, ecology, population, and the constant search for new sources of energy and raw materials require more than piecemeal actions and short-term problem solving. Modern scientific development has, to an extent, helped in solving mankind's problems. However, in tackling these global issues there is the need to cultivate not only the rational mind but also the other remarkable faculties of the human spirit: the power of love, compassion, and solidarity.

A new way of thinking has become the necessary condition for responsible living and acting. If we maintain obsolete values and beliefs, a fragmented consciousness and a self-centered spirit, we will continue to hold to outdated goals and behaviors. Such an attitude by a large number of people would block the entire transition to an interdependent yet peaceful and cooperative global society.

We must draw lessons from the experience we gained. If we look back at the development in the twentieth century, the most devastating cause of human suffering, of deprivation of human dignity, freedom, and peace, has been the culture of violence in resolving differences and conflicts. In some ways, the twentieth century can be called the century of war and bloodshed. The challenge before us, therefore, is to make the next century a century of dialogue and of peaceful coexistence. The promotion of a culture of dialogue and nonviolence for the future of mankind is thus an important task of the international community. It is not enough for governments to endorse the principle of nonviolence or hold it high without any appropriate action to promote it.

Under the "Strike Hard" campaign launched by the Chinese authorities in April last year, Tibetans are subjected to increased torture and imprisonment for peacefully expressing their political aspirations. Political reeducation conducted by the authorities in monasteries and nunneries throughout Tibet have resulted in mass expulsions, imprisonment, and death. Last year China dropped all pretense of respecting the ancient religious and cultural heritage of Tibet by launching a large-scale reform of its religious policy. The new policy states that "Buddhism must conform to socialism and not socialism to Buddhism." Under the pretext that religion would have a negative influence on Tibet's economic development, the new policy aims to systematically undermine and destroy the distinct cultural and national identity of the Tibetan people.

New measures to curtail the use of Tibetan language in education were introduced. The Tibet University in Lhasa has been compelled to teach even Tibetan history in the Chinese language at the Tibetan Language Department. Experimental Tibetan language middle schools, established in the 1980s with the active encouragement and support of the late Panchen Lama, are being closed down. These schools were very successful and highly appreciated by Tibetans.

These new measures in the fields of culture, religion, and education, coupled with the unabated influx of Chinese immigrants to Tibet, which has the effect of overwhelming Tibet's distinct cultural and religious identity and reducing the Tibetans to an insignificant minority in their own country, amount to a policy of cultural genocide.

MARCH 10, 1998

THE POST–DENG XIAOPING leadership in China seems to have become more flexible in its international policy. One indication of this is China's greater participation in international forums and cooperation with international organizations and agencies. A remarkable development and achievement has been the smooth transfer of Hong Kong to Chinese sovereignty last year and Beijing's subsequent pragmatic and flexible handling of issues concerning Hong Kong. Also, recent statements from Beijing on restarting cross-strait negotiations with Taiwan reflect apparent flexibility and softening of its stance. In short, there is no doubt that China today is a better place to live in compared to 15 to 20 years ago. These are historic changes that are commendable.

In stark contrast to these positive aspects of the development in China proper, the situation in Tibet has sadly worsened in recent years. Of late, it has become apparent that Beijing is carrying out what amounts to a deliberate policy of cultural genocide in Tibet. The infamous "Strike Hard" campaign against Tibetan religion and nationalism has intensified with each passing year. This campaign of repression—initially confined to the monasteries and nunneries—has now been extended to cover all parts of the Tibetan society. We are witnessing the return of an atmosphere of intimidation, coercion, and fear, reminiscent of the days of the Cultural Revolution.

MARCH 10, 1999

IN TERMS OF history, culture, religion, way of life, and geographical conditions, there are stark differences between Tibet and China. These differences result in grave clashes of values, dissent, and distrust. At the sight of the slightest dissent, the Chinese authorities react with force and repression, resulting in widespread and serious violations of human rights in Tibet. These abuses of rights have a distinct character, and are aimed at preventing Tibetans as a people from asserting their own identity and culture, and their wish to preserve them. Thus, human rights violations in Tibet are often the result of policies of racial and cultural discrimination and are only the symptoms and consequences of a deeper problem. The Chinese authorities identify the distinct culture and religion of Tibet as the root cause of Tibetan resentment and dissent. Hence their policies are aimed at decimating this integral core of the Tibetan civilization and identity. To continue along this path does nothing to alleviate the suffering of the Tibetan people, nor does it bring stability and unity to China or help in enhancing China's international image and standing.

I firmly believe that it is possible to find a political solution that ensures the basic rights and freedoms of the Tibetan people within the framework of the People's Republic of China. My primary concern is the survival and preservation of Tibet's unique spiritual heritage, which is based on compassion and nonviolence. And, I believe it is worthwhile and beneficial to preserve this heritage since it continues to remain relevant in our present-day world. What is required is the political will, courage, and vision to tackle the root cause of the problem and resolve it once and for all to the satisfaction and benefit of the concerned people.

I feel that the Chinese leadership is sometimes hindered by its own suspicions so that it is unable to appreciate sincere initiatives from my side, either on the overall solution to the Tibetan problem or on any other matter. A case in point is my consistent and long-standing call for the need to respect the environment situation in Tibet. I have long warned of the consequences of wanton exploitation of the fragile environment on the Tibet Plateau. I did not do this from selfish concern for Tibet. Rather, it has been acutely clear that any ecological imbalance in Tibet would affect not just Tibet, but all the adjacent areas in China and even its neighboring countries.

It is sad and unfortunate that it took last year's devastating floods for the Chinese leadership to realize the need for environment protection. I welcome the moratorium that has been placed on the denudation of forests in Tibetan areas and hope that such measures, belated though they may be, will be followed by more steps to keep Tibet's fragile ecosystem intact.

On my part, I remain committed to the process of dialogue as the means to resolve the Tibetan problem. I do not seek independence for Tibet. I sincerely believe that my "Middle Way Approach" will contribute to stability and unity of the People's Republic of China and secure the right for the Tibetan people to live in freedom, peace, and dignity.

Independence and Autonomy: The Misunderstanding

From 1997 to 1999, the twentieth century closed. In the wake of the millennium, a "mental bamboo curtain" closed on Tibet. It had at one point been partly opened. At least we had believed so in December 1978, when Deng Xiaoping declared that the Dalai Lama had the right to return to Tibet, even if it was "only as a Chinese citizen." Dialogue seemed possible, subject to the condition not to assert any claim for independence. On the day of Deng's death, February 19, 1997, the Dalai Lama regretted that during his lifetime, no compromise had been reached. Yet his Middle Way policy complied with the requirement of Deng by suggesting that Tibet be associated with China, without being independent, but granted significant autonomy. This *middle* policy, in the sense of "moderate," would safeguard, according to the Dalai Lama, the vital interests of China by guaranteeing its long-term stability in respect of its territorial integrity. In return, Tibet would become free to decide its socioeconomic development and preserve its culture, religion, and national identity.

In contrast to the beliefs of the Dalai Lama, in Beijing, "everything but independence" was never understood as the search for a mutually beneficial solution. It only implied that Tibetans had to admit Chinese sovereignty. Deng's opening policy did not ratify the reforms of Hu Yaobang, considered as being too radical. No real progress toward a Sino-Tibetan dialogue was ever made, even if, in response to international pressure, some statements gave that illusion. President Jiang Zemin clearly stated, in October 1997, his government's position, unchanged since Deng Xiaoping: "Our policy towards the Fourteenth Dalai Lama is clear. He must publicly acknowledge that Tibet is an inalienable part of the PRC, renounce Tibetan independence, and cease all activities aimed at splitting the motherland."[55]

The Dalai Lama had agreed to waive the independence of his country before the European Parliament in Strasbourg, in order to initiate negotiations with Beijing. He was, however, not as ready to rewrite history. To assert that Tibet had always been part of China was an untruth he could not claim. We can measure in retrospect the extent of the misunderstanding that had settled around the slogan "everything except independence." On the question of Tibet, China had in reality no escape. Open negotiations amounted to de facto recognizing the illegitimacy of its invasion of 1950 and the ensuing crimes, not to mention the contradiction between a colonial policy on the roof of the world and Communist ideology. Wei Jingsheng's letter on Tibet, addressed to Deng Xiaoping in 1992, was irrevocable: "You have always supported anticolonialism and national independence. Yet you do not understand what these terms really correspond to. You've only used them to maneuver without sincerely believing in it."[56]

The Tibetan problem actually turned out to be more thorny than the retrocession of Hong Kong or the annexation of Taiwan. For in those cases, the People's Republic could not be accused of imperialism against a non-Chinese people. One therefore understands the inflexibility of Deng and the intransigence of the new generation of leaders. Unable to negotiate a compromise, they turned down flat each proposal of the Dalai Lama and reinforced their ideological rigidity in response to Western pressure. Nationalism had become the spearhead of the Party and the location of its legitimacy, once socialism had been abandoned for a form of market economy. Finally, the takeover by force of the succession of the Panchen Lama had given the masters of the Forbidden City the idea that they could do without the support of the Dalai Lama, even in the religious sphere.

The concept of regional autonomy for Tibet was the subject of another misunderstanding. According to communist ideology, individuals are less Tibetan, Mongolian, or Chinese than feudals, landowners, intellectuals, or proletarians. Nationalism declines after the class struggle. It is supposed to gradually disappear, along with the demand for autonomy, as the Party educates the political consciousness of citizens, called to blend harmoniously into a classless society. Autonomy is therefore just a step in the fusion process in the "socialist paradise." However, the resurgence of nationalism in Tibet in the 1980s convinced the Politburo that Tibetan autonomy threatened the national sovereignty of China and that the only solution was forced sinicization. The assimilation process was then implemented, not with the cooperation of the Tibetans, as Mao had expected, but against their will. Under demographic and economic pressure of Chinese people, respect for Tibetan autonomy was replaced by an alienating policy of assimilation. Obviously, this Chinese-style "autonomy" did not meet the expectations of the Dalai Lama.

When he requested autonomy from the international tribunes, he understood this as the guarantee of fundamental freedoms and the preservation of the cultural heritage of his people, whose legitimacy was recognized by the three resolutions of the UN General Assembly on Tibet. Autonomy, recommended in the first resolution of October 21, 1959, was interpreted in a contradictory way: for the Chinese, it was only a step. It differed completely from the idea that the UN experts had. According to international conventions, autonomy means the right of a people to self-determination and independence, if the majority decides so. The dismantling of the Soviet Union is an example. It was on the grounds of their right to self-determination that about thirty peoples, subjected to decades of forced integration in the USSR, regained their independence. These precedents provide a substantial foundation for the Tibetan claims, especially as the collapse of the USSR in the late 1980s put an end to the claims of communism that it was the advent of a new heaven and a new man. All these factors contribute to undermining the political foundation of the Chinese Communists, for whom the right to self-determination within the motherland is nonexistent.

Yet the Tibetans' right to self-determination is legitimized by their uniqueness as a people. If the former Soviet Union and China have argued that only a *nation* can claim self-determination, the international community supports that it is enough to be a *people*. Tibetans meet all criteria for qualification as a people. From this point of view, the Dalai Lama's insistence on autonomy encompassing the three provinces of historical Tibet is perfectly justified. Amdo, Kham, and Ü-Tsang correspond to the area of the sociocultural expanse of the Tibetan people, whose indivisible geographical entity inhabits the plateau known as the roof of the world. Conscious of these objective realities, the People's Republic has attempted to distort the situation by annexing the two eastern provinces to various Chinese regions, whose lowland areas are mainly inhabited by Chinese.

To prevent Tibet from claiming self-determination, a right that international jurisprudence had recognized from the very beginning of the Chinese occupation, the Beijing regime attempted to erase as much as possible all traces of Tibetan history, beliefs, and language. Then, after the riots in Lhasa in the late 1980s, the Party decided that the persistence of the Tibetan identity still conveyed nationalist aspirations, though it could not acknowledge its paradoxically singular character, fundamentally distinct. So, without examining the core of the issue, the central government in Beijing argued for an imperative of "cultural safety," considering that the disappearance of ethnic differences in the areas of national minorities was a priority. The past became the target of reinterpretation with the creation of Tibetology institutes, intended to support the official doctrine of Chinese sovereignty over the Himalayan kingdom. In the religious field, the intervention in the succession of the Panchen Lama showed to what extremes the power was ready to go to use popular beliefs to their own advantage. As for Tibetan, it had to pass to the rank of "second language" in education, after Mandarin as the main language—in disregard of the Chinese Constitution and the laws of autonomy emphasizing the importance of preserving the mother tongues of ethnic minorities.

"Eradicating the influence of the Dalai separatist forces"

It was in this context that in January 1997, the Dalai Lama expressed his wish to make a pilgrimage to Mount Wutai. This sacred place of Chinese Buddhism is worshiped as the earthly abode of Manjushri, the buddha of wisdom. The Thirteenth Dalai Lama had gone there, and his successor would not fail to show his willingness to reconcile with his "Chinese brothers and sisters." However, his request was rejected by Beijing, under the pretext that his visit posed a "great risk of instability."[57] It would inevitably lead to an uncontrollable wave of popular fervor in Tibet and probably also in Inner Mongolia. Furthermore, the authorities feared that Chinese Buddhists and human rights defenders would later turn the place of pilgrimage into a rallying point.

At the turn of the millennium, the Dalai Lama, a simple monk, as he liked to present himself, worried China. Yet if his quiet strength made the masters of the Forbidden City tremble, it did not make them give in. Their counteroffensive unfolded across three campaigns launched in Tibet, titled "Patriotic Education," "Spiritual Civilization," and "Strike Hard," intended to "eliminate the influence of the Dalai separatist forces."[58] On July 23, when he addressed a crowd of Tibetans in Lhasa at the launch of the "Spiritual Civilization" campaign, Chen Kuiyuan, Communist Party Secretary for the Autonomous Region, declared: "An important task consists in eliminating the influence of the Dalai in the spiritual field."[59] Monasteries and convents were indeed still the strongholds claimed to be "the soil and the home of the separatist activities of the Dalai clique in Tibet."[60] In order to control them, the government decreed that the religious should henceforth be officially accredited and given a special identity card, without which they would be expelled from their monasteries. To achieve this, one had to denounce the Dalai Lama and pledge allegiance to the Communist Party. Many preferred to leave the religious life rather than apostatize their faith.[61]

The campaign for "Patriotic Education" had borne fruit, since in March 1998, Raidi, Vice-Secretary of the Party for the Autonomous Region, could congratulate himself on "thirty-five thousand monks and nuns, accounting for more than seven hundred religious institutions, having been brought back on the right path."[62] Ironically, at the moment of the mass destruction of religious life in Tibet, the China News Agency boasted of a golden age of Tibetan religion, with more monasteries in Tibet than before the arrival of the People's Liberation Army![63] In reality, they were far fewer and deserted monasteries. At Ganden, one of the largest religious facilities in the valley of Lhasa, six hundred monks had chosen to flee rather than deny the Dalai Lama. Not far away, in Sera, three times a week, seventy reeducators organized four-hour indoctrination sessions. Attendance records were required, and the absent were punished. Instructors repeated the instructions of the Party, brandishing threats of dismissal or imprisonment. At night, they searched the cells and subjected recalcitrants to individual reeducation sessions. In secret, the religious made fun of the officials: "After a year of their courses, we will finally be ready to replace Deng Xiaoping!"[64] However, most hoped to join the religious community in exile in India.

From 1997, the "Patriotic Education" campaign extended the measures of indoctrination to all sectors of society, including government officials, deemed too susceptible to the religious discourses of the Dalai Lama. Schools, colleges, and universities must ensure the graduation of ten thousand zealous young patriots, eager to promote socialism: "Our schools must produce replacements of the separatist forces," declared Chen Kuiyuan during the fifth Congress of the Communist Party of the Autonomous Region. He denounced the students who attended school wearing a red scarf around their neck as a sign of membership in the Communist Youth League but in the evening made offerings of butter lamps. It was also useful to ensure that literature and the arts did not propagate "spiritual garbage."[65]

The application of these measures collided with strong resistance. Yet the repression was without mercy. Some cited cases of people who died under torture rather than denounce the Dalai Lama.[66] Deeply saddened when he was told about these tragedies, the Dalai Lama invited his people to deny him. The abuses of the Cultural Revolution had been repudiated, but the Beijing regime continued its mission of destruction. "Religion cannot be abolished at one stroke," reported the authorities of the Party. "To weaken its influence will require a patient, meticulous and repeated education."[67] Six million unarmed Tibetans were hostages of the Chinese state machine and its People's Armed Police, while the flow of Chinese immigrants effected an inexorable transformation of lifestyles. Yet, far from crushing the protests, the oppression tightened the ranks of the Tibetans. However, it also fueled despair. Acts of sabotage and some explosions in Lhasa raised the fear of the possible radicalization of the conflict. Simultaneously, revolt also rumbled in Xinjiang,[68] where, since 1996, the arrests of people identified as separatists, terrorists, and criminals had multiplied.

Cultural Genocide in Tibet

Taking note of the repeated attacks, in 1997, the Dalai Lama described the repression that raged in his country as "cultural genocide." Robert Badinter was the first to use this term in 1989 because it seemed "just to describe China's policy toward the Tibetan people."[69] He used it again twenty years later,[70] considering that "if 'cultural genocide' was not registered in positive law, it did nonetheless possess a major political resonance."[71] In 1933, the inventor of the word "genocide," Raphael Lemkin, had also argued that genocide could be either physical or cultural. History gave several examples of cultural genocide with the elimination of Mayan or Inca cultures by the conquistadores, the political unification of the Soviets in Central Asia, and colonialism in general. However, on December 9, 1948, the signatory countries of the Convention on the Prevention and Repression of the Crime of Genocide[72] ignored the cultural component of this crime. They decided to stick to acts of physical liquidation of a group, refusing to characterize as genocide attacks on a community in terms of identity and culture. Since then, the concept of "cultural genocide" has remained absent from the discourse on genocide, this term being reserved, so as not to relativize the horror, for the mass murder of people, for example Armenians and Jews in the twentieth century.

"Why should this be surprising?" asks Robert Badinter. "Between colonial states and the USSR who signed the 1948 Convention, it is understandable that the suspicion was great. An international recognition of cultural genocide might be a source of cultural recovery for native peoples. Just because cultural genocide is not yet listed in international conventions does not mean that the concept cannot be used. It does not justify a lawsuit, but it does authorize a moral condemnation. In the case of Tibet, it serves to raise awareness of the eradication of a culture which deprives a people of its identity. I campaign for the moral recognition of cultural genocide in Tibet."[73]

In 1997, the facts justifying the accusations by the Dalai Lama were documented by the International Commission of Jurists. This organization, which in 1959 and 1964 had already denounced physical genocide in Tibet, published a new report.[74] The planned extermination of the Tibetan civilization by a policy of racial and cultural discrimination was certified by the campaigns "Patriotic Education," "Spiritual Civilization," and "Strike Hard." In a picturesque manner, a lama in exile evoked with desperate humor the alarming state of his country, among the three fish on the Chinese menu: Tibet is "grilled and served on the table, already half devoured, with its tongue, its religion, its culture and its inhabitants which are melting faster than its glaciers; Hong Kong wriggles, but it is captive in the Chinese aquarium; and if Taiwan swims freely in the ocean, it is under close supervision."[75]

Nevertheless, in this context, on May 20, 1997, Bill Clinton renewed again the most favored nation status of China, though not without arousing the opposition of the American political class, which intended to link respect for human rights and economic sanctions. A voice then rose to defend this decision—the voice of the Dalai Lama. His followers were disconcerted. How to understand him? His position was extraordinary, and it had not changed: he did not want to ostracize China, hoping to bring it back into the community of nations by persuasion. While denouncing cultural genocide committed by the Chinese government, he continued to advocate nonviolence and called on his followers not to give in to hatred. For he wanted to believe in the forces of goodness, love, and forgiveness. At the dawn of the third millennium, the challenge of the Dalai Lama to the world was the challenge of peace.

MARCH 10, 2000

For a Political Culture of Dialogue

IT IS TRUE that the root cause of the Tibetan resistance and freedom struggle lies in Tibet's long history, its distinct and ancient culture, and its unique identity. The Tibetan issue is much more complex and deeper than the simple official version Beijing upholds. Because of lack of understanding, appreciation, and respect for Tibet's distinct culture, history, and identity, China's Tibet policies have been consistently misguided. In occupied Tibet there is little room for truth. The use of force and coercion as the principal means to rule and administer Tibet compels Tibetans to lie out of fear, and local officials to hide the truth and create false facts in order to suit and to please Beijing and its stewards in Tibet. As a result, China's treatment of Tibet continues to evade the realities in Tibet. This approach is shortsighted and counterproductive. These policies are narrow-minded and reveal the ugly face of racial and cultural arrogance and a deep sense of political insecurity. The development concerning the flights of Arjia Rinpoche, the Abbot of Kumbum Monastery, and more recently Karmapa Rinpoche are cases in point. However, the time has passed when in the name of national sovereignty and integrity a state can continue to apply such ruthless policies with impunity and escape international condemnation. Moreover, the Chinese people themselves will deeply regret the destruction of Tibet's ancient and rich cultural heritage. I sincerely believe that our rich culture and spirituality not only can benefit millions of Chinese but can also enrich China itself.

MARCH 10, 2001

THE CHINESE GOVERNMENT continues to whitewash the sad situation in Tibet through propaganda. If conditions inside Tibet are as the Chinese authorities portray them to be, why do they not have the courage to allow visitors into Tibet without any restrictions? Instead of attempting to hide things as "state secrets," why do they not have the courage to show the truth to the outside world? And why are there so many security forces and prisons in Tibet? I have always said that if the majority of Tibetans in Tibet were truly satisfied with the state of affairs in Tibet, I would have no reason, no justification, and no desire to raise my voice against the situation in Tibet.

Successive leaders of the People's Republic of China, from Mao Zedong and Zhou Enlai to Deng Xiaoping and Hu Yaobang, have repeatedly acknowledged the "unique nature" and "special case" of Tibet's status. The 17-Point Agreement of 1951 between the Tibetans and the Chinese, embodying the original spirit and concept of "one country and two systems,"[76] is the best proof of this recognition. No other province or part of the People's Republic of China has any such agreement with Beijing. The Chinese government promised to respect the "unique nature" of Tibet. What is actually "unique" today about Tibet is that it is the poorest and most oppressed area where policies implemented by ultraleftist elements are still active, even though their influences have long been diminishing in China proper.

MARCH 10, 2002

THE WORLD IS greatly concerned with the problem of terrorism as a consequence of September 11th. Internationally, the majority of the governments are in agreement that there is an urgent need for joint efforts to combat terrorism, and a series of measures have been adopted. Unfortunately, the present measures lack a long-term and comprehensive approach to deal with the root causes of terrorism. What is required is a well-thought-out, long-term strategy to promote globally a political culture of nonviolence and dialogue. The international community must assume a responsibility to give strong and effective support to nonviolent movements committed to peaceful changes. Otherwise, it will be seen as hypocrisy to condemn and combat those who have risen in anger and despair but to continue to ignore those who have consistently espoused restraint and dialogue as a constructive alternative to violence.

It is my sincere hope that the Chinese leadership will find the courage, wisdom, and vision to solve the Tibetan issue through negotiations. Not only would it be helpful in creating a political atmosphere conducive to the smooth transition of China into a new era but also China's image throughout the world would be greatly enhanced. It would have a strong, positive impact on the people in Taiwan and will also do much to improve Sino-Indian relations by inspiring genuine trust and confidence. Times of changes are also times of opportunities. I remain committed to the process of dialogue. As soon as there is a positive signal from Beijing, my designated representatives stand ready to meet with officials of the Chinese government anywhere, anytime.

In exile we continue with the democratization of the Tibetan polity. Last March, I informed the elected representatives of the Assembly of Tibetan People's Deputies that the Tibetan exiles must directly elect the next Kalon Tripa[77] (Chairman of the Tibetan Cabinet). Consequently, last August, for the first time in Tibet's history, the Tibetan exiles directly elected Samdhong Rinpoche as the new

Kalon Tripa by a margin of over 84 percent of the total votes cast. This is a big step forward in the continuing growth and maturity of democracy in our exiled Tibetan community. It is my hope that in the future Tibet can also enjoy an elected democratic government.

The Commitment to Nonviolence

In a troubled world after the attacks of September 11, 2001, in New York, the Dalai Lama presented the Tibetan current situation as a model of nonviolence from which he learned lessons of peace. Mahatma Gandhi had made this recommendation: "Be the change you wish to see in the world!" The Dalai Lama *was* the peace that he encouraged. Severely tested by the sufferings inflicted on his people, from Mao Zedong to Jiang Zemin, he never deviated from a fraternal attitude toward the Chinese. From this experience, he learned a definition of peace that he interpreted as more than the absence of conflict: the fruit of compassion, true peace matures in the human heart and shines on the world. He sometimes referred to the biblical image of turning swords into plowshares: "I love this image of a weapon turned into a tool, at the service of fundamental human needs. It symbolizes an attitude of inner and outer disarmament."[78]

In a world of which he repeatedly stressed the growing interdependence, the Dalai Lama invited us to think in terms of *us* rather than *I* and to achieve the supreme disarmament of altruism. Applying compassion to the political field, he renewed his call to the global community to develop and teach the spirit of nonviolence. He invited it to invest for this purpose sums comparable to those assigned by states for their defense programs. While the September 11th attacks shook world opinion, he regretted the direction taken by the fight against terrorism. In China in particular, the tragedy of the World Trade Center was used to legitimize the repression of Tibetans and Uighurs struggling for their independence. More generally, the major flaw of the measures adopted by the major powers was due to the absence of a thorough analysis of the causes of the event. For the

September 11th attacks showed that "modern technology and human intelligence guided by hatred can lead to immense destruction."[79] To uproot the core of this hatred, it would therefore be best to favor a cultural policy of dialogue on a global scale.

An icon of nonviolence, the Dalai Lama still saw the doors close on his participation in the global Summit of the Millennium for peace. He was the most noticeably absent among the thousand religious leaders of the world gathered from August 28–31, 2000, in New York. All expected him, but the Secretary-General of the UN, Kofi Annan, gave in to the pressure from China and justified the exclusion of the spiritual leader. His argument? The UN headquarters is "the house of Member States" whose sensitivities must be respected. Such is the diplomatic language used to cover the retreat of nations when cowardice gives way to moral ambiguity. They condemn the terrorists but ignore those who oppose them peacefully. This dilemma is not new. Ten years earlier, in 1991, during a trip to the United States and Great Britain, the Dalai Lama had called out to the governments involved in the Gulf War against Iraq's invasion of Kuwait. On behalf of what interests, he asked, would Tibetans have less of a right than the Kuwaitis to possess a national territory? "China is no less colonialist than Iraq and Tibetans want the same treatment as the people of Kuwait. If it is refused to us, is it because starting with me, we have always negotiated peacefully and excluded violence?"[80] While this religious leader never demanded that the international community fight a war for the liberation of Tibet, he exhorted it to enforce its resolutions and to push Beijing to the negotiating table. "Governments may be cynical about the suffering of the people," observed the Dalai Lama. "They put forward their strategic and commercial interests above all else. However, they must take into account their public opinion. That's why I feel very encouraged by the growing support of the global community."[81] To the work of the pro-Tibetan association network, determined not to close their eyes to the cultural genocide that he denounced, were added the pressures of the European Parliament and the U.S. Congress on the Chinese authorities. In the early 2000s, important resolutions were passed to recognize the right of Tibetans to self-determination. Congress forced the government's diplomacy into the appointment of a special coordinator for Tibetan affairs at the State Department. In France, the Tibet support group of the Senate and the National Assembly became the largest in the world. It was mobilized in an exemplary way by sponsoring the young detained Panchen Lama and other political prisoners.

Tibet's Spiritual Breeze: A Good Thing for China

In China itself, the gap between government and public opinion became more evident, and in civil society, support for the head of the Tibetans multiplied. The Dalai Lama continued to express his gratitude for his Chinese brothers and sisters who fought in the name of freedom and democracy. In 1992, Wei Jingsheng was the first involved in the struggle for democracy in China to open a dialogue with the Tibetan leader. He was followed by Liu Xiaobo, who in early October 1997 signed a manifesto with Wang Xizhe[82] affirming the fundamental right of peoples to self-determination and calling for negotiations with the Dalai Lama.[83] Both were arrested a few days later, on October 8. Their example showed that despite the repression, democracy remained an ideal for many Chinese. This was the solution recommended by the Dalai Lama for Tibet, insofar as a democratic government in China would give its people free choice of independence, autonomy, or federalism.

The formation of a united front between Chinese democrats and Tibetans was something to "worry the old men of Beijing," according to lawyer Michael van Walt van Praag. Personalities among Chinese exiles, such as the astrophysicist Fang Lizhi and the university professor Xue Haipei,[84] also spoke out in favor of the right of the Tibetans to self-determination. "We must respect the choice of the Tibetan people," stated Xue Haipei. "As I often say, half in jest, half in seriousness, I hope that Tibet remains as a part of China, because then the spiritual breeze blowing from the high plateaus will be a good thing for China. We need the kindness and moral value of the Dalai Lama."[85]

The leader of the Tibetans knew that historically, it was always the scholars or intellectuals in China who brought change. This was true for Zhou Enlai and Deng Xiaoping, who studied in France before participating in the revolution in their country. In the early 2000s, nearly one hundred thousand Chinese students were enrolled in Western universities. They represented, in the eyes of the Tibetan leaders, a force of change to lean upon. In each of his trips abroad, the Dalai Lama met them in the American, European, or Australian Chinatowns. When he could finally go to Taiwan in March 1997 at the invitation of President Li Teng-hui and thousands of Buddhists, the religious leader explained in these terms the issue of his visit: "As a Tibetan, the opportunity to interact with the Chinese people, in China or abroad, is dear to my heart. It is crucial that the Tibetan and Chinese peoples develop greater mutual understanding. We must coexist, it is an inescapable fact."[86] This trip, which irritated Beijing, was a success and represented an important step of the Sino-Tibetan rapprochement, while Taiwan had just adopted a democratic regime.

The Ideological War

The intransigence of the leadership in Beijing could have suggested that it did not give any importance to public opinion, whether Chinese or international. Yet the arrest of dissidents, and protests made through diplomatic channels during each of the Dalai Lama's visits abroad, showed that this was not the case. This was also very explicitly attested in the report of a conference organized by the Department of Propaganda and the State Council in June 2000 in Beijing.

For the first time, leading experts on Tibetan culture came together to develop strategies of persuasion toward writers, journalists, and historians in the West, India, and Asia.[87] "Tibetology" had become the weapon of choice against the "Dalai clique" and the foreign forces hostile to the motherland. Strategists in Beijing condemned the emergence of a new culture of intervention, illustrated by U.S. involvement in Yugoslavia in the name of religion and ethnicity. They denounced the support of the United States for the Dalai Lama and his presence at international conferences, accusing him of promoting the cause of Tibetan independence. His influence, beyond Europe and the United States, now also extended to South America, Asia, Africa, and the UN lobbies. The "Dalai clique" was suspected of wanting to create an anti-Chinese force, rallying the Chinese democracy movement, the members of the independence movements of Taiwan and Xinjiang, as well as the followers of Falun Gong.[88]

For the ideologists in Beijing, the Dalai Lama's speeches on love, compassion, peace, and nonviolence were only masked propaganda, of an undeniable effectiveness and popularity: "The media in the world are monopolized by Westerners. The Dalai clique has conquered them for a long time with his misleading propaganda and use of modern means of communication such as the Internet, cinema, and television. Our fight to win international public opinion looks more difficult than ever."[89] The text then enumerated the strategy of a vast campaign supporting the idea that Tibet was historically Chinese and that the generous policy of the Party had considerably enriched and modernized it. The members of the Tibetology institutes and of the Buddhist Association of China were invited to defend this thesis in international conferences and publications in foreign languages. This followed an impressive list of film projects and works destined to flood Western countries during performances and exhibitions by Chinese artists. Forty countries were targeted on all continents, for an audience of one million people and two thousand journalists.

To intensify the efforts to bring to light one great day the crimes of the "Dalai clique," a thousand Tibetologists would be charged with the mission to "produce arguments that would win the public's heart" in a context qualified as hostile. It was necessary to counter nine hundred publications on Tibet as well as the Dalai Lama's books, global best-sellers and vectors of anti-Chinese ideas. Such directives were an admission of defeat. If the President of the People's Republic was himself committed in this crusade, it was because the balance of forces was not in his favor. The number one enemy of the Chinese power was a stateless monk, spokesman for a devastated country. The People's Republic of China was mobilized against him for a battle with an uncertain outcome. This inferiority was difficult to accept, to a man who had no weapons other than courage, justice, and truth.

In 2001, a true war was launched—a war of words, pictures, and ideas. While propaganda was unleashed, the repression worsened. President Jiang Zemin continued to target the religious institution: "We must actively guide religion to fit the socialist society and serve the general interest of the nation."[90] A revealing example of this policy: the expulsion by the army of thousands of religious, Chinese as well as Tibetans, from the Serthar Institute of Buddhist Studies in eastern Tibet.[91] This establishment had received academic certification from the authorities and gathered nearly nine thousand students, of whom at least seven hundred originated from mainland China. Accused of intellectual deviance, from June 1999, the facility was closed and largely destroyed. In this context, the flight into India of Arjia Rinpoche in November 1998, followed by the Karmapa in December 1999, was a setback for the Party, deprived of two "patriot" eminent lamas it thought it could count on. The Abbot of Kumbum,[92] Arjia Rinpoche had refused to obey the dictates of Beijing, who asked him to make the faithful accept their so-called Panchen Lama. As for the Karmapa, despite his socialist education, he remained loyal to the Dalai Lama. Faced with these defections that belied its propaganda on the freedom of religion in Tibet, the Chinese government, embarrassed, chose to keep a low profile. Jiang Zemin, then the Secretary of the Communist Party, even wrote verses of homage to Arjia Rinpoche, encouraging him to return. In response to the international emotion caused by the flight of the seventeenth Karmapa, the Chinese state media demonstrated their imagination: the fourteen-year-old monk had left Tibet to recover the black crown,[93] symbol of his lineage, which remained at Rumtek Monastery,[94] where his predecessor had lived in exile.

In 2002, the masters of Beijing continued to believe that time was on their side. However, as the Dalai Lama pointed out, no Chinese leader at the time of Mao could have imagined that in 2000 the Tibet issue would still arise. If time was enough to make it disappear, it would have meant that time could erase the voice of justice and truth. Yet the reality was different. Repression did not have the final say. The Tibetan resistance persisted after more than fifty years of occupation. Internalized resistance, gagged resistance, did not attract the attention of the international media through terrorist attacks. However, like its charismatic leader, it deeply moved the conscience.

8

"TIBET IS DYING"

—◆—

2003–2010

MARCH 10, 2003

Toward Negotiations?

A PRAGMATIC AND FLEXIBLE approach has been lacking when it comes to upholding the basic civil and political rights and freedoms of its citizens, especially with regard to those of the so-called minorities within the People's Republic of China. We were encouraged by the release of several Tibetan and Chinese political prisoners of conscience in 2002. I was pleased that the Chinese government made it possible for my envoys to visit Beijing to reestablish direct contact with the Chinese leadership and to also visit Tibet to interact with the leading local Tibetan officials. The visit of my envoys last September to Beijing provided the opportunities to explain to the Chinese leadership our views on the issue of Tibet. I was encouraged that the exchanges of views were friendly and meaningful.

MARCH 10, 2004

MY HOPE IS that this year may see a significant breakthrough in our relations with the Chinese Government. As in 1954, so also today, I am determined to leave no stone unturned for seeking a mutually beneficial solution that will address Chinese concerns as well as achieve for the Tibetan people a life in freedom, peace, and dignity. Despite the decades of separation, the Tibetan people continue to place tremendous trust and hope in me. I feel a great sense of responsibility to act as their free spokesman. In this regard, the fact that President Hu Jintao has personal knowledge about the situation and problems in Tibet can be a positive factor in resolving the Tibetan issue. I am therefore willing to meet with today's leaders of the People's Republic of China in the effort to secure a mutually acceptable solution to the Tibetan issue.

My envoys have established direct contact with the Chinese government on two trips to China, in September 2002 and in May/June 2003. This is a positive and welcome development, which was initiated during the presidency of Jiang Zemin.

China is undergoing a process of deep change. In order to effect this change smoothly and without chaos and violence, I believe it is essential that there be more openness and greater freedom of information and proper awareness among the general public. We should seek truth from facts—facts that are not falsified. Without this, China cannot hope to achieve genuine stability. How can there be stability if things must be hidden and people are not able to speak out their true feelings?

China's emergence as a regional and global power is also accompanied by concerns, suspicion, and fears about her power. Hosting the Olympic Games and World Exposition[95] will not help to dispel these concerns. Unless Beijing addresses the lack of basic civil and political rights and freedoms of its citizens, especially with regard to minorities, China will continue to face difficulties in reassuring the world.

MARCH 10, 2005

URING THESE MORE than four decades, great changes have taken place in Tibet. There has been a great deal of economic progress along with development in infrastructure. The Golmud-Lhasa railway link that is being built is a case in point. However, during the same period much has been written by independent journalists and travelers to Tibet about the real situation in Tibet and not what they have been shown. Most of them portray a very different picture than what the Chinese government claims, clearly criticizing China about the lack of human rights, religious freedom, and self-rule in Tibet. What has actually happened and is still happening is that since the establishment of the Tibet Autonomous Region the real authority has been solely held by Chinese leaders. As for the Tibetan people, they have been facing suspicions and growing restrictions. The lack of true ethnic equality and harmony based on trust, and the absence of genuine stability in Tibet clearly shows that things are not well in Tibet and that basically there is a problem.

The world in general, of which China is a part, is changing for the better. In recent times there is definitely a greater awareness and appreciation for peace, nonviolence, democracy, justice, and environmental protection. The recent unprecedented response from governments and individuals across the world to the tsunami disaster victims reaffirms that the world is truly interdependent, and the importance of universal responsibility.

Tibet and China—The Resumption of Dialogue?

On September 9, 2002, a delegation of four Tibetans flew to Beijing, led by Lodi Gyari.[96] China had set its conditions. It did not agree to receive "emissaries" of the Dalai Lama. The delegates were therefore described as "simple overseas Chinese" on a private visit. On the Tibetan side, it was a question of reestablishing the contact broken off since 1993 and clearing up the misunderstanding of the Dalai Lama's Middle Way Approach. This meeting represented the culmination of ten years of efforts by the Dalai Lama. His call for dialogue had been heard in the West. In the United States, since his accession to power in 2001, President George W. Bush had considered him an ideal partner to achieve the goal of regional and national stability for the Chinese government. He therefore urged Beijing to engage in negotiations in the interest of China as well as Tibet.[97] In January 2001, an interparliamentary conference on Tibet gathered in Berne with representatives from a dozen countries, the Minister of International Relations of the Tibetan government in exile, and those responsible for the Offices of Tibet across Europe, as well as Michael van Walt van Praag. The goal was to develop a unified strategy for the parliamentary support groups in Tibet, in anticipation of the UN session on Human Rights expected in Geneva in April 2002.

Since 1992, indeed, a draft resolution on Tibet had been filed each year, but never adopted. China consistently proposed a "no-action motion" with the support of its friendly countries. To oppose this tactic, parliamentarians thus committed themselves in January 2001 to ratify in their respective countries the Brussels resolution of July 6, 2000, stipulating that the EU institutions would formally recognize the Tibetan government in exile if no serious negotiations on Tibet were initiated during the next three years. Under pressure and before the mobilization of public opinion, the Chinese finally accepted the principle of dialogue. After the meeting of September 9, 2002, new talks were held in Beijing in May 2003.

The Dalai Lama warned that it would take time, patience, and determination for these meetings to bear fruit. He was also aware of the general skepticism about China's real will to initiate a genuine process of rapprochement. It was true that one month after the visit of the Tibetan delegation in May 2003, the Indian prime minister was received in Beijing. The discussions focused on the reopening of the trade route between Tibet and India through Sikkim. An agreement recognized Indian sovereignty over this region, subject to Chinese territorial claims. In return, India admitted once again that the Tibet Autonomous Region was part of Chinese territory and promised that its government would not allow Tibetan refugees to engage in pro-independence activities. Members of the Tibetan Youth Congress[98] condemned this as a treacherous trading strategy using Sikkim, a result of Indian complacency. The Dalai Lama said, on the contrary, he was encouraged by the improving relations between the two countries. He hoped it will result in a favorable political context for Sino-Tibetan understanding. Samdhong Rinpoche, then prime minister of the Tibetan government in exile, agreed with this analysis: "If, between China and India, there was a mutual trust, the issue of Tibet could be resolved. For the moment, India cannot take sides in favor of Tibet, because it would fuel even more suspicions from the People's Republic."[99] Would this optimism prove well founded?

The "Go West" Policy

In Tibet, the Beijing regime alternated repression, human rights violations, and massive transfers of population, amplifying its policy of destruction of Tibetan society under the guise of modernization. The Fourth Work Forum on Tibet, held in Beijing in June 2001, adopted an ambitious plan, with 117 development projects for the Himalayan region. The program to transform the "Wild West" had as its first objective to shift economic activities from the coastal areas inland to reduce the growth gap, while relieving demographic pressure on the megacities of the east. It was also necessary to meet the growing demand for raw materials, minerals, and energy from Chinese industrialists.

This "Go West" policy represented the culmination of half a century of concerted strategy of the People's Republic in Tibet. At the beginning of the invasion, the Soviet Union had helped China to build factories on the high plateau. Then in the 1960s, Mao Zedong introduced heavy industry. From 1980, Deng Xiaoping's market economy reform focused on the east, asking the west to be patient. In 2000, Jiang Zemin proclaimed the "opportunity of the millennium" by laying the groundwork for the development of the western regions. Hu Jintao, his successor, a former state engineer who built roads and bridges in the Gobi Desert, since he became president in 2003 had dreamed of building a new China. It must therefore attract foreign investment in Tibet, known in Chinese as the "Western Treasure House."

Of these "treasures," a large-scale geological survey undertook an inventory. Over a thousand engineers and technicians located 600 sites of mineral wealth: several billion tons of iron, 30 million tons of copper, 40 million tons of lead and zinc. The study only covered half of the plateau, the extreme cold and altitude having obstructed the exploration of the other half. Inestimable reserves of gold, uranium, lithium, and chromite, whose deposits were not made public, also provoked the greed of the leadership in Beijing. A prospection of oil and gas fields was also launched, for the coastal provinces had an urgent need and these resources were of great interest, given soaring world prices.[100]

However, the "Go West" policy was part of a vision of long-term growth. The first phase, until 2010, provided for the creation of infrastructure, such as the Golmud-Lhasa railway. The second, from 2010 to 2030, promised to be a period of acceleration, characterized by rapid industrialization and urbanization. In a Tibet that was 80 percent rural, this represented a real revolution, planned as part of the state management of the central government. Finally, the third phase, from 2030 to 2050, should bring to perfection the modernization of the country, transformed into California in Chinese style. . . . A senior official of the Party had anticipated these developments in 1994, during the Third Work Forum on Tibet. He had at the time compared the conquest of the American far west to the transfer of population onto the plateau: "We need immigrants of the new world to develop the population of the ancient one."[101] During the Fourth Forum, seven years later, these words were more relevant than ever and evidenced by *Tibet's March Toward Modernization,* a white paper issued by the State Council on November 8, 2001, to mark 50 years of Chinese occupation of Tibet. Indeed, this paper presents modernization as, "the most important task of all ethnic groups of China, including Tibetans."[102] According to impressive statistics, liberated Tibet was considerably enriched, and the dramatic decline in the number of poor was praised. Half a million in the early 1990s, today it seemed to have declined to less than 70,000. A study by the World Bank provided an explanation for the miracle: officials in Beijing had moved the poverty line from 365 to 76 dollars per year![103]

"As if the Chinese took away the ground from beneath our feet . . ."

The exile administration responded to the Chinese white paper with an analysis of the secret agenda of Beijing in Tibet:[104] "After the occupation by Communist China, it is the greatest catastrophe that has been faced by the Tibetan people. Where brute force and military repression without mercy failed, China tries, through a new form of colonization, to destroy the only possibility for Tibet to survive."[105] China's "Go West" strategy represented a flagrant violation of the right to development, which recognizes peoples' right to the "exercise of their inalienable sovereignty over all their natural resources."[106] In contrast to these recommendations, Beijing subordinated the development of Tibet to China's overall growth, without taking into account any form of local self-sufficiency or the fight against instability. In the Chinese exploitation of its wealth, Tibet was itself graced with the arrival of "educated" settlers, which helped to open the Tibetan market to Chinese manufactured goods.

From 2002 to 2005, in his speeches of March 10, the Dalai Lama nevertheless showed great restraint, probably so as not to close the door to dialogue. He did not condemn the progress that, as he had said many times, contributed to well-being. He also admitted that the Golmud-Lhasa railway would allow him to make the trip of more than a thousand miles from his home province to the capital of Tibet in just a few days, but as a child, he had needed three months, in his gold palanquin, to cover this distance. But the modernization imposed by Beijing was particularly aimed at strengthening the Chinese economy, exacerbating the social and economic marginalization of the Tibetans. A nomad, today a refugee in India, thus summed up the feeling of total dispossession of the population, even in his physical connection with the land: "It's as if the Chinese took away the ground from beneath our feet."[107] Tibetans were reduced to the status of stateless persons in their own country. Foreigners at home, with body and soul sapped in a race for progress from which they benefited so little and that destroyed their identity. How could this policy avoid adding tension to the talks with the representatives of the Dalai Lama? When in September 2004, after a third meeting, the Tibetan delegation returned to Dharamsala, it could only admit "major differences of position on several major points, some of which are fundamental."[108] For three years, the discussions did not progress.

The dictatorship of Beijing exacerbated Tibetan nationalism, which was not compensated by the release of some prisoners about whom international opinion had been mobilized for years. Ngawang Sangdrol is an exemplary case. Emblematic figure of the Tibetan resistance, she was only ten years old when in 1987, she participated in a peaceful demonstration and was arrested and then detained for fifteen days. Just released, she did it again and, at fifteen, was sentenced to three years in prison, subjected to torture and ill treatment. Since she refused to capitulate, her sentence was extended. At seventeen, Ngawang Sangdrol was sentenced to twenty-one years of detention. Her executioners put her in complete isolation in a rough concrete cell without lighting, where she could neither lie down nor stand up. If her fortitude was intact, her health deteriorated rapidly. In a state of exhaustion and fearing for her life, she was finally released in 2002. After several months of hospitalization in the United States, barely recovered, she began to testify.[109]

Her release did not augur the end of the repression, which was worsening because of the still very strong link between religion and Tibetan identity. Buddhism remained the target of the authorities because they perceived it as a threat to the cohesion and stability of the state, to the extent of bringing up to date an aphorism of the Cultural Revolution: "Just as there cannot be two suns in the sky, Buddhism and Socialism are incompatible." However, didn't this policy specifically go against the priorities of a lasting stability, unity, and prosperity shown by the government? As questioned by the Dalai Lama for so many years, is it logical to pursue these development goals without associating them with the democratization of society? On March 10, 2005, he reiterated yet again his confidence, citing the example of the December 2004 tsunami. After the tragedy, the planet had been mobilized. Everyone felt solidarity. How could China, still for so long, be an exception and not assume its responsibility as a major power? When Beijing applied for the Olympic Games, the leader of the Tibetans supported it, against a part of his community and his supporters. Even if the talks were not moving forward, the door of dialogue had to remain open. However, as time passed, doubts arose.

MARCH 10, 2006

Harmony and Dictatorship: A Paradox?

IN THE FIFTH round of talks held in January 2006, the two sides were able to clearly identify the areas of major differences and the reasons thereof. They were also able to get a sense of the conditions necessary for resolving the differences. In addition, my envoys reiterated my wish to visit China on a pilgrimage. As a country with a long history of Buddhism, China has many sacred pilgrim sites. As well as visiting the pilgrim sites, I hope to be able to see for myself the changes and developments in the People's Republic of China. Over the past decades, China has seen spectacular economic and social development. This is commendable. The Tibetan areas have likewise seen some infrastructural development, which I have always considered positive.

Today, President Hu Jintao's theory of "Three Harmonies" envisages peaceful coexistence and harmony within China, as well as with her neighbors and the international community. And today China is emerging as one of the major powers in the world, which she deserves, considering her long history and huge population. However, the fundamental issue that must be addressed is that in tandem with the political power and economic development, China must also follow the modern trend in terms of developing a more open society, free press, and policy transparency. This, as every sensible person can see, is the foundation of genuine peace, harmony, and stability.

Tibetans—as one of the larger groups of China's fifty-five minority nationalities—are distinct in terms of their land, history, language, culture, religion, customs, and traditions. This distinctiveness is not only clear to the world, but was also recognized by a number of senior Chinese leaders in the past. I have only one demand: self-rule and genuine autonomy for all Tibetans, i.e., the Tibetan nationality in its entirety. This demand is in keeping with the provisions of the Chinese constitution, which means it can be met. It is a legitimate, just, and reasonable demand that reflects the aspirations of Tibetans, both in and outside Tibet. This demand is based on the logic of seeing the future as more important than the past; it is based on the ground realities of the present and the interests of the future.

The long history of the past does not lend itself to a simple black-and-white interpretation. As such, it is not easy to derive a solution from past history. This being the case, I have stated time and again that I do not wish to seek Tibet's separation from China, but that I will seek its future within the framework of the Chinese constitution. Anyone who has heard this statement would realize, unless his or her view of reality is clouded by suspicion, that my demand for genuine self-rule does not amount to a demand for separation. If China sees benefit in sincerely pursuing dialogue through the present contact, it must make a clear gesture to this effect. A positive atmosphere cannot be created by one side alone. As an ancient Tibetan saying goes, one hand is not enough to create the sound of a clap.

MARCH 10, 2007

I N 2006, THE hard-line position was intensified with a campaign of vilification against us, and more disquietingly, heightened political restriction and repression in Tibet. In China itself, we saw some improvement with regard to the freedom of expression. In particular, there is a growing feeling among Chinese intellectuals that material development alone is not sufficient and that there is a need to create a more meaningful society based on spiritual values. Views that the present system is inadequate to create such a society are gaining ground, as a result of which belief in religion in general, and particularly interest in Tibetan Buddhism and culture, is growing. Moreover, there are many who express their wish that I make a pilgrimage to China and give teachings there. President Hu Jintao's continued call for a harmonious society is laudable. The basis for the realization of such a society is to foster trust among the people, which can take place when there is freedom of expression, truth, justice, and equality. Therefore, it is important that officials at all levels not only take heed but also implement these principles. It is true that the Chinese constitution guarantees national regional autonomy to minority nationalities. The problem is that it is not implemented fully, and thus fails to serve its express purpose of preserving and protecting the distinct identity, culture, and language of the minority nationalities. What happens on the ground is that large populations from the majority nationalities have spread in these minority regions. Therefore, the minority nationalities, instead of being able to preserve their own identity, culture, and language, have no choice but to depend on the language and customs of the majority nationality in their day-to-day lives. Consequently, there is a danger of the languages and rich traditions of the minority nationalities becoming gradually extinct.

Hexie, "Harmony," from Confucius to Hu Jintao

Hexie, "harmony" (pronounced *he-shiey*), became in 2005 the new slogan of the Chinese Communist Party. This term, laden with history, represented a social ideal advocated by ancient philosophers and adopted as a political model by the humanist emperors of the past. The Chinese associated it with the aura of Confucius, the greatest of their sages. It was in reference to this prestigious tradition that in February 2005, two years after his accession to power, President Hu presented his political program. Stemming from the fourth generation of Communist leaders, he proclaimed his wish "to promote harmony between man and nature" and to "strengthen social harmony in a harmonious and stable political environment." The theory of the "Three Harmonies," *Heping, Hejie,* and *Hexie,* or "Peace, Unity, Harmony," marked a break with the Maoist policy, founded on contradiction and struggle. "A harmonious society is characterized by democracy, rule of law, equity, justice, sincerity, benevolence, and vitality," declared the president.[110] It carried the ambition for peace for the world, reconciliation with Taiwan, and inner balance.

In a troubled social climate, where the number of demonstrations of those forgotten by growth reached seventy-five thousand a year,[111] the strongman of Beijing considered it appropriate to adopt a populist stance. The launch of the Three Harmonies was accompanied by slogans directly taken from Confucius: "Priority to the People," "The Administration at the Service of the People," and "For Harmony in Diversity." Grants were also allocated to disadvantaged social groups for the redeployment of redundant workers and the improvement of safety conditions at work, particularly in the coal mines. Three Harmonies did not mean, however, the liberalization of political life. They introduced instead a neo-Confucian authoritarianism, which excluded the participation of the masses and prohibited trade unions and associations not controlled by the Party. However, asked the Dalai Lama, how could the society of the Three Harmonies form, if the party did not loosen its grip?

For, far from democratizing public life, President Hu preferred to follow the example of Deng Xiaoping. The People's Liberation Army, the People's Armed Police, and the Ministry of Public Security remained the three ramparts of social stability. By relying on them, he consolidated his power, without meeting the expectations of the Chinese intelligentsia, who demanded the return of moderate dissidents exiled after the Tiananmen events. President Hu therefore interpreted harmony as the obedience of society under the leadership of the Party. Freedom of the press and political transparency, bases of peace, harmony, and stability according to the Dalai Lama, were not on the agenda.

As if, in the People's Republic, the policy of smiling could only be accompanied by the crushing of human rights and freedoms, the "Three Harmonies" coincided with increased repression in Tibet. In 2006, to escape persecution, nearly two thousand five hundred Tibetans had no other alternative but to flee. Half were under the age of eighteen. The older ones were religious in search of spiritual education, and nomads uprooted from their lands by mining companies or the construction of infrastructure projects such as the Golmud-Lhasa railway line.

The terrible conditions of the clandestine border passage were revealed by the tragedy of September 30, 2006. On that day, a Chinese patrol fired without warning on a row of disarmed refugees. There were 75 refugees trying to reach Nepal by the Nangpa pass at 5,700 meters of altitude. Kelsang Namtso, a 17-year-old Tibetan nun, collapsed. In fear of being arrested, her companions fled without taking her body riddled with bullets. The next day, soldiers threw her into a crevice, under the eyes of Danish climbers. During the shooting, a young man of 20, Kunsang Namgyal, was wounded and taken prisoner with 30 of his companions. None gave signs of life despite the pressing demands of international organizations. The special rapporteur of the UN on executions asked China to publicly explain the circumstances of the shooting, and it ignored his request.

The incident had witnesses. From the base camp of Mount Cho Oyu,[112] mountaineers of all nationalities filmed the soldiers shooting, then chasing and arresting fugitives. The images were posted on the Internet: "I am seven years old, my name is Dekyi Paltso." Before the cameras, a girl with a sharp look recounted her journey. Two days by truck from eastern Tibet to Lhasa. Then twenty days of walking up to the pass of Nangpa. The People's Armed Police suddenly appeared. Cries. Crazy race. Bullets whistled. All children were arrested and taken away. Only Dekyi Paltso escaped.

The border crossing was more and more risky for the Tibetans since the Chinese government put pressure on Nepal to return prospective emigrants. In the area of Nangpa, tourists were able to save some of them. Their freedom and their lives were negotiated with border guards for about twenty dollars, clothing, a carton of cigarettes, or Coca-Cola cans. In Nepal under Chinese influence, refugees were threatened with losing their right to asylum, which was, however, guaranteed by international convention. If the shooting at Nangpala moved the world, it only radicalized the Chinese surveillance at the border. In December 2006 a video conference brought together representatives from all offices of Public Security of the Autonomous Region. It decreed drastic measures during the first half of 2007. These children, these men and women fleeing were the living witnesses of the Himalayan genocide. The Chinese government intended to prohibit them from testifying.

The Party Is the True Buddha!

In October 2006, the plenary assembly of the Party of the Autonomous Region decreed the elimination of the members of the "independence movement, until the final victory." The decision was taken after massive demonstrations of loyalty and devotion of the Tibetans to their spiritual guide. A few months earlier, on January 6, while he was giving the Kalachakra[113] initiation in Amaravati in South India, the Dalai Lama had called for a boycott of the fur of endangered wild animals. His compatriots liked to decorate their ceremonial costumes with tiger, leopard, lynx, or otter skins. They were proud of them, but did not hesitate to sacrifice them. From February 2006, fires were lit all over the country to destroy tons of fur transported by trucks, of an estimated value of 60 million euros. These manifestations of unconditional allegiance to their religious leader disappointed the authorities, who had been struggling for years to persuade the people to abandon their traditional clothing. Then the Party responded, imposing a counterboycott. Tibetans were henceforth prohibited from gathering together to burn animal skins. Presenters of the channel Qinghai TV, whose audience was mostly Tibetan, were ordered to wear fur while on the air.

A few months later, in July, renewed uncontrollable popular fervor. Following a rumor that spread through the grasslands of Amdo, nearly one hundred thousand nomads crowded around Kumbum Monastery. Intimidation and beatings had no effect. The crowd continued to grow. The authorities, caught up short, finally understood the reason for this gathering: rumors of the imminent arrival of the Dalai Lama in this holy place, near his hometown. Deeply annoyed, a leader denounced the Tibetans who "suck the teats of the motherland but take the Dalai Lama for their mother."[114]

The ineffectiveness of denigration campaigns against the religious leader was flagrant. However, the authorities decided to intensify them. They hardened the patriotic education sessions in monasteries, "hotbeds of dissidence." From 2006, a wave of terror swept back over the Autonomous Region, driven by the slogan "Love your country, love your religion." The monastic institutions and spiritual masters had to align themselves with the Party's ideology. The mysteries of faith were regulated by articles of law with the promulgation of measures for "the management of the reincarnation of living buddhas." This decree required lamas to request from the authorities a permit for their future incarnations. The Chinese media considered these guidelines "an important step to institutionalize the process of reincarnation." This was actually another maneuver intended to undermine the religious hierarchy and the authority of lineage leaders. Indeed, the Party's authority replaced the traditional methods of recognition of spiritual masters. The mission of religion was denatured, reduced to senseless rites.

In February 2007, the appointment as the head of the Party of the Autonomous Region of Zhang Qingli, a protégé of President Hu Jintao, announced a strengthening of the surveillance in Tibet. The new strongman of Lhasa inaugurated his leadership by stating that the Communist Party was the true Buddha. The officials of the Autonomous Region were called upon to engage in a "class struggle to life or death" against the Dalai Lama. New laws indicated a return of the war on the "Four Olds" advocated under the Cultural Revolution. In 2007, the army destroyed worshiped statues in monasteries "noncompliant with the regulations of the Office of Religious Affairs." The Dharamsala administration condemned this escalation, which was a fatal blow to the soul of Tibet.

Terror for the Minorities

The Chinese writer Ma Jian declared that he always felt in his travels in Tibet that the country was "a vast open-air prison where coercion and contempt prevailed." Extending his reflection to the whole of the People's Republic, the author of *Beijing Coma*[115] added: "China aims to become the largest prison in the world, since it is the only way the Party finds a sense of security. However, in the Chinese prison, there are secondary freedoms. If I am a shopkeeper and do not like to get too worked up, China is for me the freest country in the world—until I commit a mistake or my son, unbeknown to me, starts to think."[116]

Although he implied relaxation and even conciliation in his speeches, Hu Jintao did not diverge from his hard-line policy toward minorities. The Tibetan spiritual leader denounced the persistence of "Han chauvinism," once fought by Mao Zedong. In 1953, the Great Helmsman invited self-criticism by the Party executives suspected of maintaining bourgeois ideas about Chinese supremacy. For all that, he did not respect the regional autonomy he had given to the Tibetans and Uighurs. His calls did not diminish the views of Chinese nationalism based on ethnocentricity.

For the first time in a March 10 speech, in 2007, the Dalai Lama mentioned the entirety of minorities, victims of this form of racism. The policy of ethnic cleansing had become widespread, with reinforced measures of sinicization (demographic submersion, generalized teaching of Chinese), plundering of natural resources, and destruction of cultural heritage in Tibet, as in Inner Mongolia and East Turkestan. Peoples, their lands, and their cultures were absorbed into the "spiritual Communist civilization." Some regions, called autonomous, become Chinese provinces, such as Inner Mongolia, where the settlers were now seven times more numerous than the Mongols.

The Uighurs were also outnumbered by the Han in Xinjiang,[117] economic exploitation leading to the requisition of their land without compensation or consideration. Since 2001, under the pretext of antiterrorism efforts, Koranic schools had been prohibited and individual freedoms restricted drastically. The Movement for the Independence of East Turkestan,[118] a pacifist organization for democracy, was presented as a terrorist organization; its members faced arrests, detentions, and arbitrary sentences. The Chinese authorities did not hesitate to pressure neighboring countries for their extradition.

A reign of terror was also in force in Inner Mongolia where, since 2000, the exploitation of energy resources had become a priority in Beijing. Simultaneously the economic and social rights as well as the freedom of expression of the Mongols were violated. The defense of cultural, linguistic, and religious identity of this population was, as in Tibet, described as "separatist activism" and liable to heavy sentences.

Before this policy, most European governments were outraged. They especially reminded the People's Republic that it had committed itself to opening a constructive dialogue with the Tibetan government in exile. On February 15, 2007, the European Parliament adopted in Strasbourg a new resolution in favor of meetings without preconditions with the Dalai Lama. The writers of the text believed that acceptable solutions could be found to the extent that were respected, on the one hand, the legitimate aspirations of the Tibetan people and on the other hand, Chinese territorial integrity—the Dalai Lama had stopped asking for separation from China more than twenty years earlier. The two parties were called to act with pragmatism, considering the future rather than the past, something the Dalai Lama had fully accepted. From March 10, 2006, he maintained that "the future is more important than the past" and that the future of Tibet fell "within the constitutional framework of the People's Republic and not in separation." Without giving way to skepticism or becoming discouraged, he only called for a sign from Beijing.

This sign did not come. Furthermore, the awarding of the U.S. Congressional Gold Medal triggered a renewed terror. On October 17, 2007, under the Capitol rotunda in Washington, President Bush welcomed the leader of the Tibetans by quoting Thomas Jefferson, for whom "the freedom to believe was one of the greatest blessings of America." According to the head of the White House, this freedom is not the prerogative of a nation but of the world. To defend it, his country would resort to force. At the head of the most powerful nation in the world, he advocated a peace based on the balance of terror. Instead, the Dalai Lama was committed to following a path of peace toward the goal of peace. For that matter, the medal engraved with his portrait sums up the essence of his struggle: "World peace must be born from inner peace. Peace is not the absence of violence but the manifestation of human compassion."

However, in Tibet, the People's Armed Police were ordered to smash up the protesters who celebrated the event. At Drepung in the Lhasa Valley, three thousand heavily armed soldiers began a blockade of the monastery. Accused of having expressed their joy by painting their walls white, the monks no longer had the right to go out, even to get food. Eight laypeople were imprisoned for having offered incense, hung prayer flags, and detonated firecrackers. However, the escalation of terror, the insecurity, and the discrimination measures created the conditions for a revolt that the communist dictatorship tried to prevent, but in vain.

MARCH 10, 2008

Wildfire

F OR NEARLY SIX decades, Tibetans have had to live in a state of constant fear, intimidation, and suspicion. Nevertheless, in addition to maintaining their religious faith, a sense of nationalism, and their unique culture, the Tibetan people have been able to keep alive their basic aspiration for freedom. I have great admiration for the Tibetan people and am proud of their indomitable courage.

In Tibet, repression continues to increase with numerous, unimaginable, and gross violations of human rights, denial of religious freedom, and the politicization of religious issues. All these take place as a result of the Chinese government's lack of respect for the Tibetan people. These are major obstacles the Chinese government deliberately puts in the way of its policy of unifying nationalities, which discriminate between the Tibetan and Chinese peoples. Therefore, I urge the Chinese government to bring an immediate halt to such policies.

Although the areas inhabited by Tibetan people are referred to by such different names as autonomous region, autonomous prefectures, and autonomous counties, they are autonomous in name only. Instead, they are governed by people who are oblivious of the regional situation, and driven by what Mao Zedong called "Han chauvinism." As a result, this so-called autonomy has not brought the concerned nationalities any tangible benefit. Disingenuous policies that are not in tune with reality are causing enormous harm not only to the respective nationalities but also to the unity and stability of the Chinese nation.

The Chinese government severely criticizes me when I raise questions about the welfare of the Tibetan people before the international community. Until we reach a mutually beneficial solution, I have a historical and moral responsibility to continue to speak out freely on their behalf. The world is eagerly waiting to see how the present Chinese leadership will put into effect its avowed concepts of "harmonious society" and "peaceful rise." For the realization of these concepts, economic progress alone will not suffice. There must be improvements in observance of the rule of law, transparency, and right to information, as well as freedom of speech. Since China is a country of many nationalities, they must all be given equality and freedom to protect their respective unique identities if the country is to remain stable. On the 6th of March 2008, President Hu Jintao stated: "The stability in Tibet concerns the stability of the country, and the safety in Tibet concerns the safety of the country." He added that the Chinese leadership must ensure the well-being of Tibetans, improve the work related to religions and ethnic groups, and maintain social harmony and stability. President Hu's statement conforms to reality, and we look forward to its implementation.

This year, the Chinese people are proudly and eagerly awaiting the opening of the Olympic Games. I have, from the very beginning, supported the idea that China should be granted the opportunity to host the Olympic Games. Since such international sporting events, and especially the Olympics, uphold the principles of freedom of speech, freedom of expression, equality, and friendship, China should prove herself a good host by providing these freedoms. Therefore, besides sending their athletes, the international community should remind the Chinese government of these issues. I have come to know that many parliaments, individuals, and nongovernmental organizations around the globe are undertaking a number of activities in view of the opportunity that exists for China to make a positive change. I would like to state emphatically that it will be very important to observe the period following the conclusion of the Games. The Olympic Games no doubt will greatly impact the minds of the Chinese people. The world should, therefore, explore ways of investing their collective energies in producing a continuous positive change inside China even after the Olympics have come to an end.

March 2008: The Rebellion

On Monday, March 10, 2008, in Dharamsala, India, the Dalai Lama commemorated the uprising of 1959. On the other side of the Himalayas, the Tibetan Lhasa woke up earlier than the Chinese Lhasa. The Eternal City awakened at the foot of the Potala Palace, which still houses the relics of the past Dalai Lamas. Today confined to the historic district of the Barkor, its lanes bypass the holy places and still rustle with devotion in the morning mist. Before dawn, the faithful complete, by prostrating themselves, the circumambulation of the Jokhang. They recite the sacred mantras and burn juniper branches as a sign of purification. Among them, wandering silhouettes, strapped in green uniforms with a red star, a cap pulled down over the forehead, with arms in hand or at the waist. Others who are not pilgrims observe, supervise, spy. Threatening presence, sly presence. Internalizing their gaze, the faithful ignore them.

Nearby, Chinese Lhasa has built itself along the broad avenues laid out in straight lines, at the location of old houses razed by bulldozers. It lives in modern times and wakes up when cars and buses begin to circulate. Both Lhasas coexist without interacting. An invisible dividing wall separates two worlds. Two eras. Two cultures. However, the memory of the past has not deserted the city, despite the sinicization of the urban landscape dominated by ideograms, despite the bars and the places of entertainment of this garrison town, where twenty thousand soldiers are stationed. The Potala is today reflected on the glass façades of Chinese skyscrapers, and on a foreign modernity, it prints the seal of the ancient Tibet. The soul of Tibet is nonetheless not just a distorted image that varies along the walls of the city. On this March 10, 2008, it cried its pain to the world, carried by the voice of a new generation that defied dictatorship. Armed with courage and determination, as formerly in 1959.

An incident disturbed the routine of the Lhasapas that morning. A procession of more than three hundred monks of the great monastery of Drepung tried to reach the city center. The security forces were mobilized. To great fanfare of sirens, armored cars, and armed men, a roadblock rapidly stopped the progress of the demonstrators. They demanded the release of monks detained in October 2007 for having celebrated the Congressional Gold Medal. Joined by laypeople, they sat for several hours in a sit-in that lasted until dusk. Then other religious people, joined by students, gathered in the Barkor neighborhood. The police intervened and proceeded to make seventy arrests.

The next day, Tuesday, March 11, those arrests triggered mass protests. The five hundred monks of Drepung were joined by those of Sera, the second largest monastery in the valley of Lhasa.[119] Supported by passersby, they faced in the late morning the People's Armed Police, which dispersed them using tear gas. Some were beaten and injured. That same day, the wave of protests spread well beyond the capital. Incidents broke out in several monasteries in the Autonomous Region and also remotely in Kham[120] and Amdo.[121] During peaceful marches, demonstrators waved pictures of their religious leaders in exile or banners that called for the return of the Dalai Lama and the respect of their fundamental rights. Never had such a stir spread into the mountainous borders since the uprising of 1959.

Wednesday, March 12, the movement was amplified, stirred up by rumors. Two monks from Drepung had committed suicide by slashing their veins. Two others had been severely beaten by the police for having started a hunger strike. In a country where religious people are still revered as living treasures, the fury of the crowd went wild. A deployment of policemen and paramilitary units blocked off the streets and went on the attack. A spokesman for the Chinese Ministry of Foreign Affairs denounced the "illegal demonstrations threatening social stability." However, the next day, authorities said calm had returned. As proof of their assertiveness, they did not dispel foreigners from the capital. A newspaper correspondent was even allowed to go there to get coverage. It was a serious mistake. A major confrontation had just burst out.

One could not reproach President Hu Jintao for unpreparedness. He oversaw a vast plan of security measures in anticipation of the sensitive date of March 10. The Office of State Security intensified its interference with the radio station Voice of America[122] and proceeded to insert proclamations to warn of the riots. The counterinsurgency measures in case of a turbulent situation in Tibet were well established, with a special war strategy[123] that enabled rapid retaliation by means of light armored vehicles. The government wanted to avoid at all costs reproducing a scenario of heavy repression, recalling the battle tanks launched against civilians in Tiananmen Square. To prepare for Tibetan guerrillas, "Snow Leopard" units, created in the People's Liberation Army, had been trained in Russia in tactics inspired by the commando operations in Chechnya.[124] In March 2008, the Chinese government was therefore ready, but it misjudged the gravity of the Tibetan uprising.

Friday, March 14, while the police and armed forces patrolled the town, the historic heart of Lhasa was agitated. By late morning, trouble broke out when two monks were again mistreated by security guards around the temple of Ramoche.[125] A crowd of laypeople mobilized. In the afternoon, it converged on the main street, Beijing Avenue. Very quickly, the demonstration was radicalized. Five hundred people screamed their resentment and threw cobblestones toward an alley where about fifty policemen were sheltering behind their shields. Young people, eager for battle, rushed against the security forces and chased after them when they abandoned their position. An old Chinese citizen who tried to block the way with his rickshaw was violently thrown to the ground. The riot spread through the streets. Prey to a destructive rage, the demonstrators attacked the symbols of the occupation of their country, the shops run by Hans and Huis.[126] Quickly, their stores were ransacked. Tibetan shops were spared, indicated by white scarves hung hurriedly in the front window. There was no looting. The rioters gathered the goods in the street and burned them in fires using gas cylinders. Between two explosions, screams resounded: "Long live the Dalai Lama!" and "Long live free Tibet!" Taxis, in Lhasa driven mostly by Hans, were burned and their drivers manhandled. Thirteen people,[127] including a young Tibetan girl, perished, trapped in their burning shops. The riot did not dissolve in the smoky streets, littered with flour, pepper, dried fruit, drugstore articles, clothes, and toys. At no point did the police intervene. The field was left open to the demonstrators. Western witnesses reported the assault on Chinese pedestrians, stoned or pursued by rebels armed with swords, sticks, and iron bars. Covered by antiriot squadrons, at nightfall, fire trucks came to extinguish the fires.

Saturday, March 15, when the sun rose, units of the People's Armed Police surrounded the Tibetan quarter. The helmeted soldiers gathered on the Jokhang square but avoided the streets, while the rioters continued to vandalize Han shops well beyond the Tibetan area. They tried to burn the main mosque in Lhasa and smashed the windows of the building of the *Tibet Daily*, the Party newspaper. The first shots and tear gas explosions resounded at the end of the day. The paramilitary police charged, moving on the rooftops, from house to house, in order to better target the insurgents. In the evening, calm had returned.

On the morning of Sunday, March 16, the army patrolled in deserted Lhasa. Witnesses recounted scenes of a besieged city. A Western student saw the police search a house and then drag out six young people. Soldiers threw them to the ground, striking them with kicks and their clubs before bringing them together on a bus that took off rapidly. In the streets, the troop covered the bloodstains with sawdust. The people hid in their homes. Military convoys reinforced each other and the rows of trucks were parked on the esplanade of the Potala. Troops armed with bayonets were deployed along the major arteries leading to the great monasteries. The monks had hardly participated in the riots of March 14 and 15, but to prevent further movement, a blockade was imposed on them at Drepung, Sera, Ganden, and Ramoche. Water and electricity were cut and restocking supplies was prohibited. Without martial law having been declared officially, the army surrounded the Tibetan quarter and applied the same measures as in 1988.

However, Beijing emitted cautious press releases, citing "special restrictions on circulation" and "inviting" foreigners to move away to hotels on the outskirts of Lhasa. The commentators noted a restraint on the part of the authorities, who feared media coverage of a massive repression on this eve of the Olympics. However, historical Tibet came into rebellion beyond the Autonomous Region, even in areas incorporated into the Chinese provinces. The map of the insurrection in March 2008 corresponded to the traditional boundaries of the country. Unlike the interethnic clashes in Lhasa, in the provinces, protesters attacked the state symbols and the official buildings. This extension and the magnitude of the revolt concerned the authorities. They need to restore order and a semblance of normal life as quickly as possible: the Olympic flame must pass the Tibetan side of Everest and reach Lhasa on June 20.

"What Human Rights Do We Have Over Our Bodies?"

The repression was ruthless. In early April, hundreds of soldiers invaded the monasteries of the Lhasa Valley, under blockade. The raids took place in the early morning for several days in a row. Monks, deprived of water and food for weeks, were beaten, their cells searched. On April 25, six hundred were arrested at Drepung Monastery, then deported, hoods over their heads, into the "Chinese Guantanamo,"[128] right in the Gobi Desert. Their brothers of the Sera and Ganden communities quickly joined them. Tibetan teachers of the "Tibet" University and of the Academy of Medicine were also transferred *manu militari* to teach civic education to the thousands of incarcerated religious.

On April 29, the Tibetan exile administration announced 203 killed, over 1,000 wounded, and 5,715 imprisoned. Because the police lacked handcuffs, they tied up the detainees with electric cables. The figures were in all probability below reality, based on the reports sent by Tibetans from inside to their exiled compatriots. Yet soon these voices were silent. Telephone lines and Internet connections were cut. Calling abroad became a crime against state security.

Tibetan TV presenter, writer, and singer Jamyang Kyi was arrested on April 1, 2008, by the Public Security Office of Xining, capital of Qinghai, for having sent from her phone messages about the riots. During several weeks of interrogation, she was handcuffed to a metal chair. Thanks to her reputation, she obtained her release by paying a hefty fine. However, one of her relatives, Norzin Wangmo, was sentenced to five years in prison for e-mails and phone calls sent abroad at the time of the riots. Jamyang Kyi, defying censorship, wrote on her blog a nostalgic letter to this friend: "It's been seven months of imprisonment and repeated torture inflicted on you. You are in your thirties, the prime of life. . . . You and many heroes like you have had to separate yourselves from your parents and your relatives to walk alone, leaving your children. Five years represent one thousand eight hundred twenty-five days. Forty three thousand eight hundred hours. Whatever you may take from the pride of the sacrifice and courage that you have shown, you are also aware that behind this courage lies an ocean of unspeakable suffering."[129]

In the Himalayan region, closed to journalists and foreigners, police violence knew no bounds. The counterattack organization was like the crushing of the democratic movement in Tiananmen in 1989. By whole truckloads and trains, soldiers arrived from Sichuan. Roundups, arrests, police raids. Search notices were stuck up on the walls of Lhasa and other major cities. The army mauled the passersby at the slightest incident. Terror reigned in all the Tibetan settlements, yet failed to silence the opponents. For protests continued, about one hundred and fifty throughout the whole country. Slogans had been banned, so silent crowds gathered. They marched through the main cities of eastern Tibet. The soldiers were initially surprised before these quiet and determined groups; then they charged.

At Charo, in Amdo, Paltsal Kyab, a nomadic father, was beaten to death. He had decided to show his indignation because the UN and foreign media did not listen to the truth about Tibet. When the police returned his body, he was unrecognizable, covered with bruises, burns, and blood clots. His sky burial took place in the presence of two police officers responsible for ensuring that no one took pictures. However, the priests observed serious injuries to the internal organs, evidence of the violence of the abuse.

Having become a martyr, Paltsal Kyab inspired a Tibetan writer who hid behind the pseudonym "The Wild One from Sichuan" to write an essay entitled "What Human Rights Do We Have Over Our Bodies?" "That Paltsal was beaten until death ensued, is it not a crime we would never have had to witness in our time?" he asked. "For his children, the murder of their father leaves an impression they will never forget in their lifetime. We wish to see the day when the younger generation will not have scores to settle."[130] Defying censorship, the author put this text online. Other artists and writers testified on their blogs about the cruelty of the repression, in the hope that the world might know.

It was with the same courage than on March 28, in Lhasa, a group of monks interrupted the tightly controlled coverage of foreign journalists at the Jokhang. The temple was reopening its doors after being closed for seventeen days. Novices burst in, screaming: "Do not listen to their lies!" "We are not free!" "The Dalai Lama is innocent. He did not ask us to demonstrate." A young monk burst into tears, crying his loyalty to the Dalai Lama. These images went around the world. Relayed through the Internet, they contradicted the official propaganda. The Tibetans were living neither free nor happy. The Dalai Lama had not organized the March 14 riots in Lhasa. "In a few seconds," wrote Tsering Woeser, "the authorities could no longer hide their intentions behind their masquerade." These shocking outbursts lasted for about fifteen minutes. I clearly remember the indescribable pain I felt that night while watching a short segment on the Internet. The pain reminded me of the words of Anna Akhmatova: "My heart has drained of blood."[131] Yet the monks confronting the forbidden and the fear were young novices, recently admitted to the Jokhang, where they benefited from very comfortable living conditions. In one of the most visited holy places in Tibet, they were treated as officials.

It was the same scene ten days later at Labrang in the Chinese province of Gansu, when on April 9, some twenty Chinese and foreign journalists entered the courtyard of the monastery. Fifteen monks rushed out. They complained that they had no human rights and demanded the return of the Dalai Lama. In tears, trembling, some waving Tibetan flags they had drawn on sheets of paper. Everyone knew the price of this act of bravery. In December 1988, the People's Armed Police had killed at close range two Tibetans who had exhibited the national emblem. Some monks from Labrang managed to escape and then join the exile community. Most were arrested, tortured, and deported.

But on June 3, in front of reporters from Hong Kong and Taiwan, the government brought in one of the protesting monks from the Jokhang. Supposedly repentant, he confessed: "My name is Logya. I was abused by false rumors, when on March 27 I spoke before the press. I regret my words." The journalists noted the young man's discomfort. As if a terrible threat overwhelmed him, he spoke with his head down throughout the whole interview. Later, in an article in the *Guardian* published on October 1, the head of the Office of Religious Affairs for the Autonomous Region asserted that nothing had happened in the Jokhang. He was unaware of the incident: "The monks are very happy. They appreciate the benefits granted to them by the government."[132]

The Conspiracy Theory

Manipulation and blocking of information were the responses from Beijing to the Tibetan crisis. The day after the March 14 riot in Lhasa, Zhang Qingli[133] stated in the *Tibet Daily*: "The Dalai is a wolf in a frock, a monster with a human face but the heart of a beast. We are engaged in an intense struggle of fire and blood with the Dalai clique, a struggle to the death between us and him."[134] The Party had no other explanation for the burning of Tibet than a plot devised by the Dalai Lama, supported by Western anti-Chinese forces. Wu Heping, spokesman of the Ministry of Public Security, accused a network called "Tibetan People's Uprising Movement." This organization had tried to destabilize the government by acts of sabotage. The Lhasa police claimed to have arrested one of the leaders, accused of plotting the March 14 riot, following the instructions of the Dalai Lama. Yet there was no evidence to support these allegations.

The conspiracy theory was accompanied by a manipulation of information. Presenters and Internet users insisted on the violence of March 14, submitting images of stoned Chinese, wounded soldiers, and scenes of vandalism. This bias of victimization on the Chinese side hid the fundamental question. "They were discussing the riots and ignoring the demonstrations," aptly summarized an analyst.[135] The focus on violence legitimated the repression, under the pretext of preventing repeat offenses by Tibetan nationalists and their foreign allies. The rioters were accused of "striking-breaking-looting-burning," like the Red Guards, who remained in history as "strikers-breakers-looters." The choice of these words refers to the trauma of the Cultural Revolution, very present in the collective unconscious. While the protesters, many in the People's Republic gathered together as those left behind by growth, were categorized as "troublemakers" or "outlaws,"[136] these less freighted terms were not selected by the Chinese media to refer to the Tibetan rebels of March 2008. They privileged an ideologically loaded vocabulary, stigmatizing violence, and several weeks of nonviolent demonstrations were reduced to the extremes of the single day of March 14.

The Dalai Lama responded to the accusations addressed to him from Dharamsala on March 18: "I demand an investigation by independent bodies. This delegation must be able to travel to Tibet, but also here in India for investigations with the administration in exile."[137] He confirmed what he had said twenty years before, after the events of 1987: "If the majority of Tibetans in Tibet used violence in their struggle for freedom, I would have no other option but to resign my position as spokesman for the Tibetan people."[138] Difficult to imagine that the Tibetan government in exile could have coordinated more than one hundred protests in the Autonomous Region and the neighboring Chinese provinces. Assuming it had the capacity, would his countrymen have revolted if they were satisfied with their living conditions?

Chinese Paranoia

The conspiracy theory was certainly absurd, but no less revealing. It showed that in Beijing, the leadership had strayed into a security paranoia, because it was disconnected from the reality on the ground and from human reality. This phenomenon was not new. Nearly thirty years before, Deng Xiaoping had opened the doors of Tibet to observation missions of the government in exile, convinced of the progress made on the high plateau. He then realized his mistake, based on falsified reports given to him about the supposed contentment of the Tibetans. In 2008, the same causes produced the same effects.

Certainly, the parameters differed. The development of Tibet was spectacular. Double-digit growth of the GDP of the Autonomous Region for the previous fourteen years, through development targeting infrastructure and huge capital input. Ninety percent of expenditures were subsidized by the richest cities and provinces of the People's Republic, which were required to transfer a portion of their tax revenues to finance the growth of Tibet. In the context of such prosperity, why did the population engage in a revolt? Specialists agreed to speak of "boomerang aid" in these funding strategies. For the grants were given in the form of profit-generating investments that systematically returned to their sender. Intended solely to exploit the natural resources without transforming the industrial infrastructure, these funds did not allow for the creation or accumulation of wealth on site. In addition, the Chinese support in Tibet led to "significant cultural, linguistic and political distortions, such as the use of the Chinese language, working habits of the Chinese and the business networks in mainland China."[139]

Following the simplistic reasoning of power that does not cease to associate prosperity and popular satisfaction, the authorities had tried to buy the loyalty of Tibetans. This error had been encouraged by the officials of the Autonomous Region who, as at the time of Deng Xiaoping, practiced systematic misinformation. According to them, the loyalty of Tibetans to the regime was secured. Most had lost interest in the Dalai Lama and the separatist claims. The central government turned a blind eye to these complacent reports. If it had not institutionalized the misinformation, it could have predicted the crisis. However, this would have undermined the profession of faith of the Beijing leaders, who should have been self-critical and recognized that economic development does not guarantee social order or political allegiance. The harmony valued by President Hu Jintao did not only result from GDP performance, imposed by force in the context of violations of fundamental rights and freedoms. For harmony cannot be decreed. The Dalai Lama warned: "If harmony could have occurred under the threat of arms, it would already have been there for sixty years."[140]

The conspiracy theory was nevertheless not without interest. It saved the careers of senior officials, who at the head of the state had implemented the development strategy in Tibet. "The society of lies," denounced by the writer Ma Jian, can only be frozen. Power was a victim of its anachronism for, under the control of a global economic giant, it persisted in perpetuating a politically backward dictatorship. The obsession with growth obscured the political dimension, the government's only legitimacy being the spectacular growth of the economy. To keep society under control, it found in the events of March 2008 the beginning of an ideological relaunch. Employing well-developed methods used by the Party leaders since Mao Zedong, it strengthened the nationalist fiber by appointing new scapegoats for public prosecution. Starting in 2008, the enemies of the people were more than ever the Dalai Lama and the Tibetan separatists, with their supporters, the Western countries, and the traitors from within, reformers like Liu Xiaobo, or the lawyers who defended them. This demonization of the West and the personality of the Dalai Lama had, however, shown its limits. It led to a policy of making things worse, where only the violence of despair could be a bulwark against forced assimilation.

The crisis in Tibet has often been described as an explosion, literally and figuratively. The Tibetans inside Tibet and in exile saw the manifestation of resentment built up by years of the denial of their fundamental freedoms. In his speech of March 10, 2008, the Dalai Lama had spoken with unusual vehemence, which contrasted with his usually more conciliatory tone. Yet the year 2007 saw an increase in arbitrary arrests and hardening of the patriotic education campaign, widespread in all sectors of society. To this was added the exasperation of a population held hostage by an alienating development model and demographic policy. The exacerbation of the tensions inspired these lines from the "The Wild One from Sichuan":

The smoke that filled the sky above Lhasa on March 14, was the smoke of fifty years of suffering patiently endured. It was the smoke that people had kept inside themselves continuously for fifty years. The smoke we keep inside for exactly fifty years, is it not bound to escape? Our country is overwhelmed by a burden of grief, abuse and injustice in each of our towns and villages, with endless examples of brutality, years of lies after lies and punishment of innocents. Our people, without shelter or protector, without strength or allies, stood up with the energy of despair for the cause of human rights.[141]

The Next Upheaval Will Be Even More Serious

The blindness of power persisted after March 2008. In a denial of the current crisis, the Communist Party mobilized its arsenal of repressive techniques. Its priority was to isolate the "counterrevolutionary elements" and "engage in a struggle for life and death" by taking control of historical Tibet with tens of thousands of soldiers. Total closure of the Autonomous Region; lockup of Tibetan settlements in Sichuan, Gansu, and Yunnan; xenophobic and racist propaganda calling for racist attacks. All of this five months before the opening of the Olympics. About this treatment of the crisis, the Chinese public was divided. The strategy of intransigence catalyzed the fascist temptation of a community of "angry young people," the *fenqing*. For these neoconservative nationalists, the conspiracy theory was credible. They created an anti-CNN website on March 18, denouncing the anti-Chinese deviance in the media in the United States and Europe, accused of trying to slow down Chinese economic growth by instrumentalizing the Tibetan revolt.

However, other voices were raised. Two discordant voices criticized the management of the crisis and the politico-ideological stiffening of the regime. Li Datong, opposition journalist, wrote on the website Open Democracy: "A country ruled by law should guarantee its citizens the right to protest. If, in these circumstances, citizens break the law, you have to stop them without hesitation. However China did things the wrong way round. Legitimate right to protest has been denied to certain monks and then, when the turmoil started, the army did not intervene for fear of international opinion. This is what allowed the rioters to escape control and caused damage to people and property."[142] The Party's legitimacy was in question. It had proven its inability to ensure equal treatment to all, and committed gross strategic errors by ignoring regional specificities. The administrative mechanisms that prevented the power from anticipating the crisis in Tibet were reproduced after the fact, again falsifying reality. That was how five inspection teams were dispatched to the places of the most radical revolts. However, no official took the risk to report that the excitement was due to the government's policy, not the "plot" of the Dalai Lama. When in March 2009, senior Tibetan leaders could finally express their views, they suggested the need to identify the "policies that had failed rather than the scheme, for not everyone is separatist." Yet Beijing's leaders did not listen to them.[143]

The writer and thinker Wang Lixiong[144] warned the government: "It is time to make an assessment, to admit that the economic strategy has not worked in Tibet and to try something else. The old problem persists, and it is certain that it will continue and maybe spread among the

Uighurs, if a more intelligent solution is not adopted."[145] Wang Lixiong accused the bureaucrats of having transformed the events of March 2008 into an ethnic conflict, catalyzing the racial hatred of the so-called "Han" Chinese. With other intellectuals such as Liu Xiaobo, already convicted for his commitment to Tibet in 1996, the Christian writer Yu Jie[146] on March 22 wrote a petition entitled "Twelve Suggestions for Dealing with the Tibetan Situation." This text requested evidence of the alleged conspiracy organized by the Dalai Lama and appealed to the Beijing government to soften its policy toward Tibetans.

From spring 2008, Chinese lawyers initiated a historical reflection in order to propose an alternative to the repression. A nongovernmental organization, the *Gongmeng*, "Open Constitution Initiative," published an essay on "Social and Economic Causes of the 14 March Incident." Based on a survey conducted in Gansu and in Lhasa, it denounced the lack of real autonomy in Tibet, but also in Xinjiang and Mongolia. The authors criticized the government for its failure to respect the rights of minorities enshrined in the Constitution. According to Zhang Boshu, professor at the Academy of Social Sciences in Beijing, who summarized the findings of the Gongmeng investigation, the violation of human rights in Tibet was an effect, not a cause. The cause was a dictatorial system with an irrational way of functioning.

These statements showed an unprecedented mobilization against government policy in the Himalayan region. At risk of losing their licenses, twenty-one lawyers committed themselves to defending the Tibetans who came before the courts. The case of Li Fangping is quoted, who obtained the release of a lama, Phurbu Rinpoche, unjustly accused of terrorism. This trial was a first. Until then, no Chinese lawyer had ever rescued a Tibetan.[147] The gap between the intellectuals and the government in China about Tibet continued to widen. Wang Lixiong called for negotiations with the Dalai Lama. He concluded an essay published in 2000 by claiming that the religious leader was the key to the problem in Tibet: "But the police did not discuss with me at the time. Its responsibility has become limited to suppressing agitation, without analyzing its causes. However, I predict again. The next time there is unrest in Tibet, it will be worse than in the spring 2008."[148]

MARCH 10, 2009

Nobel Prize to a Dissident, Worldwide Condemnation of the Chinese Regime

QUITE APART FROM the current process of Sino-Tibetan dialogue having achieved no concrete results, there has been a brutal crackdown on the Tibetan protests that have shaken the whole of Tibet since March last year. Therefore, in order to solicit public opinion as to what future course of action should be taken, a Special Meeting of Tibetan exiles was convened in November 2008. Efforts were made to collect suggestions, as far as possible, from the Tibetans in Tibet as well. The outcome of this whole process was that a majority of Tibetans strongly supported the continuation of the Middle Way policy. Therefore, we are now pursuing this policy with greater confidence and will continue our efforts toward achieving a meaningful national regional autonomy for all Tibetans.

Since the occupation of Tibet, Communist China has been publishing distorted propaganda about Tibet and its people. Consequently, there are, among the Chinese populace, not many who have a true understanding about Tibet. It is, in fact, very difficult for them to find the truth. There are also ultraleftist Chinese leaders who have, since last March, been undertaking a huge propaganda effort with the intention of setting the Tibetan and Chinese peoples apart and creating animosity between them. Sadly, as a result, a negative impression of Tibetans has arisen in the minds of some of our Chinese brothers and sisters. Therefore, as I have repeatedly appealed before, I would like once again to urge our Chinese brothers and sisters not to be swayed by such propaganda, but instead to try to discover the facts about Tibet impartially, so as to prevent divisions among us. Tibetans should also continue to work for friendship with the Chinese people.

MARCH 10, 2010

SINCE THE DEMONSTRATIONS in Tibet in 2008, Chinese intellectuals inside and outside China have written more than 800 unbiased articles on the Tibetan issue. During my visits abroad, wherever I go, when I meet Chinese in general, particularly the intellectuals and students, they offer their genuine sympathy and support. Since the Sino-Tibetan problem ultimately has to be resolved by the two peoples themselves, I try to reach out to the Chinese people whenever I can to create a mutual understanding between us. Therefore, it is important for Tibetans everywhere to build closer relations with the Chinese people and try to make them aware of the truth of the Tibetan cause and the present situation in Tibet.

Let us also remember the people of East Turkestan, who have experienced great difficulties and increased oppression, and the Chinese intellectuals campaigning for greater freedom who have received severe sentences. I would like to express my solidarity and stand firmly with them. It is also essential that the 1.3 billion Chinese people have free access to information about their own country and elsewhere, as well as freedom of expression and the rule of law. If there were greater transparency inside China, there would be greater trust, which would be the proper basis for promoting harmony, stability, and progress.

As a free spokesperson of the Tibetan people, I have repeatedly spelled out their fundamental aspirations to the leaders of the People's Republic of China. Their lack of a positive response is disappointing. Although the present authorities may cling to their hard-line stand, judging by the political changes taking place on the international stage as well as changes in the perspective of the Chinese people, there will be a time when truth will prevail. Therefore, it is important that everyone be patient and not give up.

We acknowledge the Central Government's new decision taken at the Fifth Tibet Work Forum to implement their policies uniformly in all Tibetan areas to ensure future progress and development, which Premier Wen Jiabao also reiterated at the recent annual session of the National People's Congress. This accords with our repeatedly expressed wish for a single administration for all those Tibetan areas. Similarly, we appreciate the development work that has taken place in Tibetan areas, particularly in the nomadic and farming regions. However, we must be vigilant that such progress does not damage our precious culture and language and the natural environment of the Tibetan plateau, which is linked to the well-being of the whole of Asia.

"A Hell on Earth"

In 2009 and 2010, the repression did not bear the name of martial law but had all its severity. Authorities hastily built new detention centers. Raids, arrests, deportations, summary executions, disappearances of people, and torture continued in the most lawless way. On August 4, 2009, the Dalai Lama called again for an international investigation. He estimated that more than a thousand Tibetans had died since March 2008 and four thousand people had been imprisoned or gone missing.

In Lhasa and other major cities, police and paramilitary units continued to patrol. Terror reigned. The exiled Tibetans still dared not call their family, for fear that their loved ones would be arrested on the grounds of crime against the safety of the state. All lines were monitored, as well as Internet messages. The Tibetans from inside communicated with foreigners from the large Chinese cities, where they were less perceptible. In the monasteries, the living conditions were those of incarceration. Extensive purges had emptied religious communities. Before the invasion of 1959, Drepung, for example, was a monastic city of seven to eight thousand religious people. After the Cultural Revolution, it still housed about a thousand. However, in 2009, in the abandoned places, there were no more than seventy monks. The authorities had decided, after March 14, 2008, to apply to the religious sector the *hukou* system. This "passport" fixes the place of residence of Chinese citizens, who depend on a single village or a single city from birth to death. Migrants can be returned at any time to their place of origin under a simple administrative decision. This measure helped to depopulate the monasteries, where the monks would gather depending on their schools and lineages, regardless of their place of birth. Religious life was thus struck at the heart, with an unprecedented increase in tension. In addition to administrative and police harassment, monks and nuns underwent a mental reprogramming during patriotic reeducation sessions that occupied the greater part of the day. Recalcitrants were expelled and their cells destroyed, because they would not be replaced. The *trulküs*, or reincarnated lamas, were threatened with being removed from their lineage if they attempted to communicate abroad or take part in demonstrations. Buddhist studies were suspended in the institutions that housed dissidents. These measures threaten to extinguish Buddhist practice, more precious than their own lives in the eyes of Tibetans. The survival of their identity was more than ever in danger. "Tibet is dying": it was with these words that the Dalai Lama concluded a visit to France in August 2008.

Before the Tibetan rebellion, the Chinese government did respond with repression, coupled with a wait-and-see attitude based on the belief that time was working on its side. The death of the Dalai Lama would solve the problem. In the absence of the Nobel Peace Prize winner, who traveled the globe and rallied supporters to his cause, Westerners would lose interest in Tibet. As for Tibetans, once they were deprived of their charismatic leader, their resistance would quickly dissolve. This scenario was, however, not assured. For several years, Indian intelligence units had noted the radicalization of refugees, especially the Tibetan Youth Congress. The leaders of this movement, born in exile, were more politicized than their elders. They contested the Middle Way of negotiation with Beijing and called for uprising for the full independence of their country. Wang Lixiong seemed justified in maintaining that, contrary to official attitudes, the disappearance of the Dalai Lama would cause terrible conflicts if the Tibet issue were not resolved: "As long as the Dalai Lama is alive, regardless of the obstacles, the Tibetans maintain hope. However when he will die, this hope will be replaced by despair. Anger will replaced fear. Pain will engender rage. The next upheaval will therefore be extremely brutal."[149] On the Tibetan side, this point of view was shared by Lodi Gyari, who highlighted the exceptional tolerance of the Dalai Lama in accepting that the Communist Party would take responsibility in an autonomous Tibet, whereas in general, the Tibetans did not favor this, due to understandable resentment. "If the Chinese wish to find a solution," he concluded, "it is the time, because they have someone who will listen."[150]

If the Middle Way Does Not Result . . .

Chinese intellectuals mobilized themselves massively to criticize the anti-Tibetan repression. On March 10, 2010, the Dalai Lama quoted "eight hundred unbiased articles" written on the subject since the beginning of the events in March 2008. Journalists, lawyers, and artists had had the courage to defy power. A text of particular interest was the *Charter 08*, so named by its authors as inspired by the *Charter 77*,[151] and its vision of "socialism with a human face." Signed by more than three hundred people, it was put online on December 10, 2008. Two reasons explain the choice of this date. The authors wished first of all to commemorate the thirtieth anniversary of the Wall of Democracy,[152] the epoch of a ephemeral "Beijing Spring" where, in December 1978, Wei Jingsheng proclaimed the democratization of the regime. They also referred to the sixtieth anniversary of the UN Declaration of Human Rights by deploring the denial of fundamental freedoms in China. The drafters of the *Charter 08* asked these questions: "Where is China headed in the twenty-first century? Will it continue its authoritarian modernization, or will it embrace universal values? Will it join the mainstream of civilized nations, and will it build a democratic system?" Nineteen lines of thought were proposed for a new constitution that would introduce the freedoms of expression and association, the independence of the judiciary, and democratic elections at all levels. A federal form of government must ensure a more significant autonomy for Tibet and Taiwan.

Among many personalities, the Dalai Lama saluted the courage of the authors of the *Charter 08*. He qualified as "admirable" their call for political, legal, and constitutional reforms, considering it compatible with the harmonious society proposed by President Hu Jintao.[153] He had already personally met with Hu Jia, one of the main drafters of this text, along with Liu Xiaobo and Wang Lixiong. In July 2009, the Dalai Lama confided in the latter, during a visit to Dharamsala: "I sometimes joke by saying that the Tibetan question has not been made by us, but by hosts that we had not invited. If these hosts became reasonable democrats, we would no longer refuse to receive them. Even if they had not been invited, we could still compose together a large family."[154] Renouncing Tibetan independence in favor of autonomy within the People's Republic was the point of view that envoys of the Dalai Lama tried to articulate once again in the middle of a crisis, by going to Beijing in early July 2008, on the eve of the opening of the Olympics.

On the Chinese side, there was no proof of any willingness to conciliate. Du Qinglin, Vice-President of the People's Political Consultative Conference, expressed himself in the purest Maoist style, formulating "Four Conditions for Nonsupport" for the resumption of dialogue. If the Dalai Lama wanted to "work during the time he has left to live, for the happiness of the Tibetan people," he must make the non-negotiable commitments of not supporting sabotage of the Olympics, not supporting incitement of crime and violence, and finally not supporting Tibetan independence and the separation from the homeland.[155] Thus formulated, these conditions did not bode well for talks, which resembled nothing more than a public relations operation. Two months before the opening of the Games, after a turbulent passage of the Olympic flame through the capitals of the world, international pressure was at its peak. Several heads of state were threatening to boycott the opening ceremony if China continued to refuse dialogue with envoys of the Dalai Lama.

Leaders in Beijing thus accepted talks to defuse the critics. Following these discussions, the seventh since 2002, the Xinhua News Agency announced that a new round of consultations would take place at an unspecified date. The Chinese officials rejected the idea of a joint statement committing both parties. These meetings had become an end in themselves, and the failure of dialogue was confirmed. However, the tactic of the Politburo worked. At the opening ceremony of the Olympics, the prime minister welcomed with great pomp Nicolas Sarkozy, then President of the European Union, and other leaders who had conditioned their visit on the resumption of the Sino-Tibetan dialogue. The repression intensified in a Tibet closed to the press. The alibi of the talks nevertheless allowed the regime to save face, by taking advantage of the bad faith of world leaders. Dictatorship was obliged. . . .

Despite this international disavowal under Chinese pressure, the Tibetan administration in exile was resolved to meet the demand of Du Qinglin, who requested written details on the autonomy, stability, and development of Tibet claimed by the Dalai Lama. The "Memorandum on Genuine Autonomy for the Tibetan People," made public in fall 2008, thus offered a synthesis of these various topics. It affirmed the compatibility between the principle of autonomy under the Chinese Constitution and the legitimate aspirations of the Tibetan people. A significant autonomy must guarantee the right to form a government of Tibet, to elect a legislative assembly, and to establish a separation of powers between state and regional institutions.

The memorandum was presented during the eighth round of talks held in Beijing in early November 2008. The Chinese negotiators rejected it without appeal, on the grounds that the Tibetan design of the autonomy called into question the founding principle of the "Three Memberships"—to the supreme authority of the Party, to socialism, and to the system of national autonomy for minorities. The demand to regulate the flow of migrants to avoid minimizing the Tibetan people on their own soil was denounced as an attempt at ethnic cleansing. The Politburo still accused the Dalai Lama of seeking independence under the guise of autonomy. These accusations brought the talks back to square one. The Dalai Lama admitted failure: "It is difficult to talk to people who do not believe in the truth. My confidence in the Chinese people is intact. However, my confidence in the Chinese government has declined."[156] The Chinese intransigence also strengthened the opposition of many Tibetans to the Middle Way. Pursuant to Article 59 of the Constitution of the government in exile, which authorizes him to convene a special meeting in the event of a crisis, the Dalai Lama asked the ministers, parliamentarians, government officials, NGOs, and Tibetan intellectuals to come together to deliberate about their future.

On November 17, 2008, six hundred representatives of the diaspora met in Dharamsala, in the absence of the Dalai Lama, who preferred not to influence their debates. Over five days, until November 22, they examined the appropriateness of continuing with the Middle Way. The participants took note of the fact that the Chinese government was determined to complete the sinicization of Tibet. The failure of the negotiations reinforced the belief of the supporters of independence. Some, more moderate, defended the right to self-determination and advocated a referendum organized in Tibet under the auspices of the United Nations. At the end of open and passionate discussions, delegates voted to continue the policy of the Middle Way, with one reservation. If China persisted in its intransigence and remained closed to compromise, they would radicalize their position and demand independence. These conclusions were in accordance with the result of the consultation of the Tibetans in Tibet, the vast majority of whom supported the position of the Dalai Lama. The assembly also believed in not resuming talks with China as long as the

Beijing leadership did not show willingness to negotiate. It also unanimously affirmed its loyalty to the principle of nonviolence, whether in the demand for autonomy or, in case of failure, for independence. "What has changed this time," said Tenzin Tsundue, poet and freedom fighter, "is that we adopted the alternative of independence."[157]

Karma Chopel, spokesman of the meeting, concluded the discussion by declaring that a report would be sent to the Chinese authorities, asking them to cease their libelous attacks against the Dalai Lama, which hurt the feelings not only of the Tibetans but also of many Chinese Buddhists in the world. China also had to admit that the 2008 unrest in Tibet had resulted from its inappropriate development policy. In Beijing, the spokesman of the Chinese Ministry of Foreign Affairs replied through the press that the Special Meeting in Dharamsala did not represent the majority of Tibetans and that its separatist attempts would fail. It also accused the Indian government of failing to comply with its commitments, by tolerating activities that threatened the national unity of China.

Certain disenchanted statements of the Dalai Lama before the failure of dialogue with China might have made us believe that he had lost hope. This was not the case. In the press conference following his speech on March 10, 2009, he confided that he had three reasons for hope. The first was the courage and determination of his people. The revolts of 2008 had demonstrated the resistance of the new generation of young Tibetans. Born after 1959, they had not known a free Tibet. Yet despite the indoctrination and dictatorship, they dared to challenge the regime. The other two reasons for hope were internal to China. On the one hand, its economic growth placed it at the head of the superpowers; on the other hand, it could not keep that place without democratizing itself.[158] In the article "Negotiations Without Outcome Have a Role,"[159] Wang Lixiong perceived a benefit in the Sino-Tibetan talks, where many saw only the chronicle of an announced failure. From the point of view of history, it was important, according to him, to have initiated this process, even if the result took so long. In addition, these meetings had demonstrated the autocratic functioning of the regime, shattering any illusion of power. They therefore presented a double benefit: preparing for the future and revealing the reality of the present.

"Final Solution" for Tibet?

The talks returned to the agenda in January 2010, at the end of the Fifth Work Forum on Tibet, held in Beijing in the presence of three hundred senior executives of the Party, government members, and military officials. The news of this forum was leaked to the press only two days after its end, with statements by President Hu Jintao and Prime Minister Wen Jiabao. No substantive change was designed for Tibet: forced sinicization and demographic submersion were more than ever on the agenda. However, observers noted a change in tone. The Dalai Lama was no longer the target of defamatory attacks, and the authors of the report no longer incriminated either his separatist activities or the revolts by the Tibetans. Only some "difficulties" were mentioned, as well as the need to consolidate stability. No action was recommended to eradicate religion. Yet since the repression of 2008, was it still necessary? Buddhism had been bled dry.

Another manifest difference was the inclusion of all cultural Tibet in the economic development plan, forbidden by the Dalai Lama. Priority was given to improving the living conditions of the population. Hu Jintao announced that the income of farmers and nomads by 2020 would be close to the national average, thanks to areas of development that still gave priority to heavy infrastructure and the exploitation of natural resources. The plan also affirmed the need to protect the environment, starting with areas along major rivers, the Brahmaputra, Mekong, Indus, Yellow River, and the Blue River, which flow off the Himalayan peaks.

In reality, these supposedly ecological measures appeared to have been planned with a view to strategic appropriation of freshwater resources in Tibet, the second largest reserve in the world after polar ice. On this blue gold from the roof of the world depend the populations of the lowlands of Asia, as much in China as in India, Pakistan, Bangladesh, Burma, Thailand, Laos, Cambodia, and Vietnam. However, for two decades experts had repeatedly pointed out the risk of water shortage in China in the near future, given its increasing use for agriculture, industry, and consumption by the rising middle class. The Chinese government had thus anticipated solutions with the construction of around one hundred dams and the transfer of water between different basins of Tibetan rivers.[160] These hydraulic works, often built without meeting all the necessary safeguards, sometimes resulted in irreversible damage to the environment. This happened at the Yamdrok Lake,[161] where the tenth Panchen Lama had managed to postpone the construction of a tunnel evacuating the water from the lake, 850 meters below, to power a hydroelectric plant located on the Brahmaputra. The turbine system, which should then propel the water in the opposite direction into the lake, had ceased to function shortly after its start-up in 1995. This will lead to an inevitable drying out of the sacred lake by 2020.[162] This ecological disaster signals the fulfillment of a warning prophecy: when the water of the lake has dried up, Tibet will disappear. . . .

The scale of the hydroengineering work already undertaken throughout the high plateau is illustrated by these figures: from over 40,000 dams listed in the world, half are Chinese.[163] To date, the Indus and the Salween are the only rivers spared.[164] On June 30, 2005, a conference of hydrological experts gathered in Beijing published its findings in a document with the explicit title: "Tibet's Waters Will Save China."[165] This official report recommended a project recently approved by the Fifth Work Forum on Tibet in January 2010: the diversion of the course of the Brahmaputra toward the Yellow River, now dry 250 days a year. The Chinese government had identified the diversion point, in Shuomatan, where the "heavenly river" forms the longest and deepest canyon in the world before entering India. The transfer of its waters, a titanic $50 billion project entitled "Great Western Route," would require the drilling of 56 kilometers of tunnels,[166] including the use of nuclear explosions under the Kunlun mountains, according to a statement of the Xinhua News Agency on November 30, 1997. The Chinese issued denials in response to international criticism, alarmed at the risk of radioactive contamination in the river. Official statements of nonfeasibility and incremental costs would have justified the report *sine die* of the work, or even its abandonment. Were they merely decoys? For, without prior consultation with the countries concerned, on November 15, 2010, the Chinese press announced the start of construction of a 300-meter-high dam on the Brahmaputra in Zhangmu,[167] in order to build the largest hydroelectric plant in the world.[168] This dam was the preliminary setup by the hydrological engineers of Beijing for the diversion of the waters of the Brahmaputra. The first step had therefore been taken in a huge work program whose implementation was spread out until 2030. "The question is not whether China will reroute the Brahmaputra, but when," said Brahma Chellaney, Indian expert in strategic studies. "Once the work is started, the project will be presented as a fait accompli."[169]

The goal was to irrigate desert areas of Xinjiang, Gansu, and Gobi to promote intensive agriculture, and bring the water to the cities of the northeast. However, these undeniable benefits for China would result in the inescapable downstream drying of the Indo-Gangetic plain, a humanitarian and economic catastrophe of incalculable scale. Hundreds of millions of people could be deprived of water resources, and Asia would become the field of "a World War for Water."[170] The sensitive decisions taken during the Fifth Work Forum on Tibet indicate China's resolution to manage the Himalayan water resources for its own advantage. One can thus interpret the displacement and *manu militari* settlement of seven hundred thousand Tibetan nomads, decreed "environmental refugees." For they are traditionally distributed in large numbers around water sources and along the major rivers.[171] However, in a first step, the government decided to turn the region of the sources of the Yellow River, Mekong, and Yangtze into a "no man's land." Downstream, fourteen boomtowns had emerged, since "concentrating habitat" had become the new watchword for "fighting nomadism."

Ten days after this forum, which cemented the outlines of Chinese policy in Tibet for the next decade to come, a ninth round of talks was held in Beijing on January 26, 2010. The Dalai Lama first reminded everyone that Tibetans, Chinese, and Indian peoples were brothers united by history because they had inherited the culture of the Buddha's enlightenment. To coexist was for them the only choice; dialogue, the only way. The world was convinced of it and had announced it through the voice of the Secretary-General of the United Nations, Ban Ki-Moon, calling on China to resume talks. Even within India, in March 2008, Foreign Minister Pranab Mukherjee had insisted on a resolution of the conflict through negotiation. On March 11, 2009, the House of Representatives in the United States passed a resolution deploring the plight of the Tibetan people, committing to supporting a multilateral effort to bring a lasting and peaceful solution to the Tibet issue. Finally, on March 13, 2009, the European Parliament asked Beijing to reestablish dialogue on genuine autonomy in Tibet, asking the People's Republic of China to consider the "Memorandum on Genuine Autonomy for the Tibetan People" as a basis for discussion.

The meeting in January 2010 lasted four days. The fact that it took place was in itself a success. At least that was how the Tibetan envoys wanted to understand it. Upon their return, they declared to the press, in very diplomatic language, that they saw no reason not to reach an agreement with their Chinese counterparts. . . . However, in Beijing, the tone rose very quickly because a meeting was in sight between the Dalai Lama and President Barack Obama in Washington, on February 17, 2010. Zhu Weiqun, one of the Chinese negotiators, declared in a press conference that no compromise on the sovereignty of Tibet was conceivable. The Tibetan and Chinese positions remained irreconcileable. Also, the old stereotypes resurfaced: the genuine autonomy required by the Dalai Lama was only a disguised independence; only the Autonomous

Region, to the exclusion of other Tibetan settlements, was the concern of the negotiations.

The Emancipation Day of the "Serfs"

The mandarins of modern times didn't want to end either the fiction of the liberation of Tibet or the demonization of its charismatic leader. Also, March 28 was declared a national holiday dedicated to the emancipation of the "serfs." It was on March 28, 1959, indeed, that the People's Republic proclaimed the dissolution of the spiritual and temporal government of the Dalai Lama and replaced it with the dictatorship of the proletariat. To celebrate the fiftieth anniversary of the event, in 2009, President Hu Jintao, accompanied by the learned assembly in power, inaugurated an exhibition that boasted a half-century of democratic reforms in Tibet. The official media described with deference the torments of servitude, opposing it to the modernization of society conducted under the aegis of the Party. This exhibition, a pure exercise of denial, toured the country, accompanied by a vast campaign of misinformation. Mao Zedong was compared to Abraham Lincoln, the author of the "Emancipation Proclamation" that, on January 1, 1863, abolished slavery in the United States. The propaganda services of the People's Republic of China emphasized that, like Lincoln, Mao emancipated a million Tibetan slaves in a feudal system described as a dictatorship. Irony of history! When state lies become the official truth of the People's Republic of China, it seems that nothing can stop the verbal escalation and imagination.[172] If evidence indeed showed that most Tibetans were bound by written documents to the land on which they lived and to the lord who possessed it,[173] many historians dispute the technical pertinence of the word "serf" to refer to those whom they prefer to call "subjects" or "poor farmers" because they could repay a portion of their debt and change residence.[174] Furthermore, the propaganda associated this alleged serfdom with bad treatment that it exaggerated, in order to be consistent with the Marxist ideology and to legitimizing the "liberation" of the oppressed. The question of the social history of Tibet was thus highly politicized in the name of an inadmissible argument: the current abuses of the regime would be less than those of the theocracy half a century ago.

Questioned on this version of the past, the Dalai Lama straightforwardly admitted that feudal Tibet was backward and unequal. However, his predecessor had abolished the death penalty, and no historical or biographical paper, apart from those provided by the Chinese authorities, provided evidence that "the serfs were working under the whip of intendants" or that "many lords had built prisons and maintained dungeons in their domain."[175] It was therefore easy to bring nuances to the picture that Mao's followers blackened. The feudal Tibetan society was much more compassionate and less unjust than Chinese or Indian societies of the same time. If we compare the Tibet of the past with that of today, the figures speak for themselves. A single prison in the basement of the Potala against the thousands currently existing and the new ones under construction, not to mention the hundreds of reeducation labor camps, the *laogai*, where prison conditions are such that they are compared to Nazi internment camps and Stalinist gulags.[176]

The skillfully orchestrated charade of the "emancipation of the serfs" thus attempted to conceal the scale of an oppression that the international organizations and the international press had repeatedly denounced. Tsering Woeser described, in sensitive language, the pain of her crucified country, the lack of freedom and the resistance, silent but persistent. Sometimes the Tibetan codes were not identified as such by the occupier: "Wednesday is the most precious day of the week. All Tibetans say Gyalwa Rinpoche[177] was born on a Wednesday. Every Wednesday, the smoke of juniper leaves that are burned as an offering is very dense in the city and the prayers are more intense. I had not imagined that after March 14, 2008, many Tibetans would come out to light lamp offerings to the one whom they deeply miss, while in the streets, soldiers are massively deployed."[178]

Avatar Against *Confucius*

Faced with the Tibetan tragedy written in the blood of four generations, Chinese power continued to stiffen, based on its obsession with
security and colonialist expansion. However, the fortress was trembling. The revolt had spread to the icy solitudes of Qinghai. In July
2009, the Uighurs, like the Tibetans, shouted their revolt. The repression was without mercy in Urumqi, as it had been in Lhasa a year
earlier. In his speech of March 10, 2010, the Dalai Lama expressed
his solidarity with the victims of these riots. As in Tibet, the regime
responded with a political scapegoat whose perverse effect was to con-
flate ethnic minorities with terrorists, unleashing Chinese nationalism
against them. Certainly, in the short term, power was an advantage.
The population did not dispute the use of force and censorship. But it
was a major challenge for the team of Hu Jintao. The power had to be
based on a military structure of martial law to keep under control two-
thirds of its territory. Urumqi and Xinjiang, where the Han already
accounted for nearly half of the population, were easier to control
than Lhasa and Tibet. The sandy oases of the Gobi Desert, accessible to armored cars and tanks, were better suited to the construction of highways and airports allowing the rapid movement of troops.
Difficult, however, for the Politburo to fight on two fronts. The rebellions in Tibet and Xinjiang weakened them. They feared a contagion
effect among minorities and chose to settle the Uighur problem first
by finalizing the sinicization process. They would then attack in Tibet,
where economic development had so far failed to silence demands for
independence. Especially as the security response, with thousands of
prisoners of conscience and tortured or disappeared people, alienated
every day a little more of the population, voiding a political settlement that could only be brought about by negotiations. However, for
fifty years, the Chinese government had refused the outstretched hand
of the Dalai Lama. Meeting the demand for autonomy and freedom
of the Tibetan people would involve the commitment of the People's
Republic to the democratic process. The Chinese themselves, however,

were increasingly numerous in claiming it. Would the power eventually hear their voice?

This would require that the masters of the Forbidden City be realistic. Ironically, the China of the red dictators is comparable to the buddhocratic Tibet of yesteryear. The Himalayan kingdom ignored the contemporary world. And this negligence of the reality of the twentieth century was, according to the Dalai Lama, responsible for the Tibetan tragedy. With the pendulum swing of history, in 2010, it was China that appeared as an anachronistic regime. The former leader of the roof of the world gave Mao's sons lessons on democracy! He also wanted to see encouraging signs in some recent remarks by the Chinese leadership. The word "democracy" had repeatedly returned in the inaugural speech of Hu Jintao at the Seventeenth Party Congress, and Vice President Xi Jinping had pleaded for the adoption of democratic behavior, while defending the organization of elections at the base level of the Party.[179] Wen Jiabao, the prime minister, also spoke in favor of political reform. Nevertheless, it had to be remembered that, in the jargon of the Party, "reform" usually meant "careful reorganization." Other statements by Wen were surprising, such as his tribute to Hu Yaobang in April 2010 and in October about the need for democratization of political life. Perhaps it was only a communication operation, according to the sinologist Marie Holzman, who cited dissidents maintaining that "Wen Jiabao could win the award for best actor in China."[180] In the same satirical vein, with the pamphlet *Wen Jiabao, the King of Comedy*,[181] Yu Jie demystified the behavior of the prime minister, human joker of the regime, staged and orchestrated by other members of the Politburo. How to believe in these soothing words, even though the leadership seemed to have found the response to the lessons of democracy given regularly by his dissidents, the Westerners and the Dalai Lama?

The Chinese had used great resources to tell the world in 2010 that they did not feel compelled to become democrats, unlike the commonly accepted American idea that a market economy presupposes the adoption of a rule of law. The challenge for the leaders of Beijing was to maintain China as the second largest economic power while turning its back on democracy. How to find an ideology adapted to this unique situation among the richest countries in the world, without undermining the old dogmas of the Party? The answer was developed in universities, thanks to research programs funded for several years at the cost of millions of yuan.[182] This resulted in an authentic cultural counterrevolution: Confucius became the philosopher of the mandarins in the twenty-first century. Mao had proscribed him and, from 1966, the Red Guards broke up the last vestiges of Confucian society. However, in 2010, the sage was elected by the team of Hu Jintao in order to assign to each citizen his place in a hierarchical society, where equality was banned. The advent of this Neo-Confucian modernity was celebrated in Beijing by the launch of a big-budget movie, sponsored by the government.

Confucius: The Life of the Chinese Sage, according to its director, Hu Mei, marked the return to favor of the mentor of an entire country on the occasion of his 2,560th birthday. The public was invited to reclaim a millenary intellectual legacy by adopting his maxims on harmony and social respect. His biography, adapted to the screen, was a production costing more than three million euros, favoring a visual script meant to be very realistic. The film was accompanied by the opening of Confucian schools where kindergarten students dressed in period costumes repeated precepts that they could not understand.[183] After thirty years of unbridled economic development, Chinese society seemed attracted by this return to traditional values, good morals, and a philosophy advocating obedience to authority.

According to international criticism, *Confucius*, presented as the film event of 2010, was unlikely to become a cinema classic. Without doubt the ideological offensive was too subtle, and in competition with *Avatar*, which was preferred by the public in China itself. This proved that Hollywood still knew how to make a dream, while magic was not part of the *made in China* blockbuster. To the extent that in the country of censorship, the authorities ordered the removal of the film from cinemas. This decision not only was based on box office criteria but also took into account the controversy surrounding the American film, which neither James Cameron nor the Propaganda Ministry had anticipated. However, the scenario of *Avatar*, by evoking the forced uprooting of a population, rekindled a sensitive issue: the consecutive forced evictions for the realization of industrial or real estate mega-projects, in both China and Tibet. How, indeed, to avoid a parallel between the Naavis of the film and the Tibetans, exploited to allow their invaders to steal the Western Treasure House? In the Himalayan region, the film took on a particular depth, with images reminiscent of and even mistaken for the spectacular landscapes of the roof of the world. The human settlers who moved the "natives" to exploit a valuable deposit could only draw attention to some of the incidents briefly reported by the media but present in everyone's mind, like in May 2010, the protest of Tibetans in the Shigatse region against a mining company responsible for an ecological disaster. The protesters were crushed by a troop of a thousand soldiers during bloody confrontations. Journalists were ironic about a regime that had "emancipated" the serfs only to put them down the next day by depriving them of their sources of livelihood.[184]

Avatar against *Confucius*: in China the fight was uneven. After having caused some turmoil, the first was thrown out and the country made a triumph of the second one. The social phenomenon created by this blockbuster was even amplified by issuing lottery tickets bearing the image of the new guru of contemporary China, the publication of manuals of Confucian thought to reform the convicts in prisons, and the creation of a network of two hundred and fifty "Confucius Institutes" around the world to teach Mandarin.

Liu Xiaobo, Nobel Peace Prize Winner After the Dalai Lama, or the People's Republic of China Condemned a Second Time

Outside China, however, a global disavowal was coming. Even though the dictatorship could adorn itself with the clothes of an eminent sage, it was a small illusion. How not to see that in the country of Confucius, "punishment begets strength, strength begets power, power begets submission, submission begets virtue?"[185] Indeed, in 2010, the UN seemed unable to enforce international law, and governments bowed to the Chinese giant whose trade volume reached 1,000 billion euros. However, voices spoke up in the name of conscience and human dignity, defending dissidents who had the courage to challenge the regime. Thus on January 23, 2010, the Dalai Lama, President Vaclav Havel, and Archbishop Desmond Tutu nominated Liu Xiaobo for the Nobel Peace Prize. The democrat and humanist activist had been sentenced in 2009 to eleven years in prison for inciting "subversion of state power," since that was how judges characterized his participation in the drafting of the *Charter 08*. Those who thus drew attention to him considered him equal to Martin Luther King, Lech Walesa, or Aung San Suu Kyi, icons of peace and democracy.[186] However, on October 8, 2010, the Nobel Committee confirmed the award to a man who had said at Tiananmen Square on June 2, 1989, that he was "without an enemy and hatred" and confirmed this on December 23, 2009, at his trial: "none of the police who supervised, arrested, or questioned me, none of the prosecutors who prosecuted me, none of the judges who condemned me are my enemies . . . for as hate corrodes the wisdom and consciousness of a person, in the same way, the feeling of enmity can poison a nation's spirit and block its progress towards democracy and freedom."[187]

These words from the mouth of a Chinese dissident could have been pronounced by the Dalai Lama. The latter welcomed the award to Liu Xiaobo as "a recognition by the international community of all those voices that rise among the Chinese people to push China towards political, legal and constitutional reforms."[188] The day would come unavoidably, according to the spiritual leader, of a democratization of the People's Republic. Justice would then be given to Liu Xiaobo and to the Tibetans. Most would call this idealism. Would the Dalai Lama, who said to preach realism, sin by being unrealistic? He had often said that as a Buddhist, he was not a political leader like the others. No head of state would probably be inclined to ask such a question: "What if it was spirituality that overthrew Chinese communism?"[189] How should this be understood?

Spirituality is the transformation of the mind, which cultivates the basic human values of love, compassion, tolerance, and forgiveness. "The spiritual revolution that I advocate," says the Dalai Lama, "is not a religious revolution. It corresponds to an ethical reorientation of our attitude, since it is a question of learning to take the aspirations of others into account as much as our own."[190] Such a revolution allows all of our human potential to come out and opens the way to changing oneself in order to transform the world. It is a commitment on behalf of humanity, one and interdependent. The awareness that everything is linked is expressed through compassion at the individual level, and through universal responsibility at the collective level. The position of the Dalai Lama on ethics, human rights, and ecology has advanced these concepts on the international stage. They are present in several UN declarations, written to inspire people around the world with a new sense of interdependence and shared responsibility for the well-being of humanity.[191]

This revolution gives full meaning to the nonviolent struggle of the Tibetan leader. The practice of nonviolence turns the enemy into a friend or brother and an opponent into an ally. The Dalai Lama always addresses the Chinese as "brothers and sisters," urging them to build bonds of friendship and cooperation with his people. His struggle for more than half a century with the weapons of courage, justice, and truth has not yet given him victory in the political sense. Yet the charismatic leader of Tibet calls for another form of victory. He defines himself as a leader different from the others because he has dedicated his fight to universal human values. He also keeps reminding his followers: "You are not the defenders of Tibet. You are the defenders of truth and justice." Tibetans also have, according to him, a particular mission to assume in the world. He expressed this publicly in a speech given at the Children's Village in Dharamsala in November 2008, at the height of the repression. He passed on in these words the essence of his commitment to the younger generation:

"The survival of the Tibetan national identity is very different from that of any nation or people of this planet. If the Tibetan national identity is preserved, its value system—based on Buddhist principles of compassion and tolerance—has the innate quality to benefit the world. This is why our fight for truth is not only dedicated to the welfare of six million Tibetans. It is also closely linked to our ability to also provide welfare for the whole world."[192]

By its roots in a culture that is based on interdependence and compassion, the Tibetan people's vocation is to promote basic human values. Tibetans defend Tibet on behalf of humanity, and the Dalai Lama calls us to make together at the roof of the world a sanctuary, dedicated to peace on earth. The human being is at the heart of this struggle. The Dalai Lama does not predict the future. He formulates two hypotheses. The first: "If, in the future, we succeed in our fight for the truth, it will certainly help millions of people, including those in China, to discover new ways to live a healthier and more meaningful life, allowing happiness, both mental and physical."[193]

The second hypothesis corresponds to what the Dalai Lama called the "final solution"[194] for Tibet, in 1987, before Congress in Washington. In history, the "final solution" is the Nazi euphemism referring to the measures taken for the systematic execution of six million European Jews. Although mist and fog from concentration camps seem to have migrated to the roof of the world, the spiritual leader does not encourage jumbled similarities. He meant by this formula the eradication of the identity and memory of his people through forced sinicization and demographic submersion. The persecutors exterminate the soul of Tibet in what the Chinese dissident Harry Wu calls "the mental gas chambers"[195] of a cultural genocide. Even though this undertaking is related to the worst cruelties of human history, far from succeeding, it looks more and more like a headlong rush. Neither the Cultural Revolution, from 1966 to 1976, nor the repression of the late 1980s, nor campaigns against ethnic groups, which have increased since 1996, have brought to an end the Tibetan irredentism. Despite the escalation of terror and intimidation, the Chinese regime endures one failure after another. Denial is continuous, yet the spirit of resistance is transmitted from generation to generation.

Thus, from October 19–28, 2010, four thousand children from age seven to sixteen took to the streets of major cities in eastern Tibet, in Malho, Tsolho, and Golog. Schoolchildren and college students protested against the distribution of Mandarin textbooks and demonstrated to defend the right to study in their mother tongue. They also expressed their exasperation about the new set of measures entitled "Schools Consolidation Program." Since the events of March 2008, these guidelines were aimed at transforming their schools into residential establishments, which they were allowed to leave only once a month to return to their families. They were thus deprived of the transmission of their culture of origin from their parents, which reinforced the assimilation process. The Dalai Lama therefore admitted the risk that, by 2020, his people will be completely sinicized. Tibet would thus be transformed into "a society that would only pursue material benefit, due to the complete obliteration by China of its religion and culture, based on compassion." This scenario would lead not only the Tibetans but also the Chinese to ruin. For, assures the Dalai Lama, "our struggle is actually beneficial to all."[196]

The outcome of this battle depends on us. And on our answer depends the future of the world that we want to pass on to our children. Will we support the resistance of Tibetans and Chinese who, at the cost of their lives, defy a dictatorship that is in the process of becoming the world's largest economy? Will we hear the call of the Dalai Lama? He fights in the name of justice and truth to safeguard fundamental human values and prevent the ecological disaster that the pursuit of profit and industrialization pose not only in Tibet but also on our planet. No other political gesture will ever have served thus as an exemplary commitment to the cause of nonviolence and peace. Neither has history ever allowed before that, throughout such a long period and with such consistency, one single man calls out to the world.

MARCH 10, 2011[197]

The Sun Will Rise Again in Tibet

TODAY MARKS THE 52nd anniversary of the Tibetan people's peaceful uprising of 1959 against Communist China's repression in the Tibetan capital Lhasa, and the third anniversary of the nonviolent demonstrations that took place across Tibet in 2008. On this occasion, I would like to pay tribute to and pray for those brave men and women who sacrificed their lives for the just cause of Tibet. I express my solidarity with those who continue to suffer repression and pray for the well-being of all sentient beings.

For more than sixty years, Tibetans, despite being deprived of freedom and living in fear and insecurity, have been able to maintain their unique Tibetan identity and cultural values. More consequentially, successive new generations, who have no experience of free Tibet, have courageously taken responsibility in advancing the cause of Tibet. This is admirable, for they exemplify the strength of Tibetan resilience.

This Earth belongs to humanity, and the People's Republic of China (PRC) belongs to its 1.3 billion citizens, who have the right to know the truth about the state of affairs in their country and the world at large. If citizens are fully informed, they have the ability to distinguish right from wrong. Censorship and the restriction of information violate basic human decency. For instance, China's leaders consider the communist ideology and its policies to be correct. If this were so, these policies should be made public with confidence and open to scrutiny.

China, with the world's largest population, is an emerging world power, and I admire the economic development it has made. It also has huge potential to contribute to human progress and world peace. But to do that, China must earn the international community's respect and trust. In order to earn such respect, China's leaders must develop greater transparency, their actions corresponding to their words. To ensure this, freedom of expression and freedom of the press are essential. Similarly, transparency in governance can help check corruption. In recent years, China has seen an increasing number of intellectuals calling for political reform and greater openness. Premier Wen Jiabao has also expressed support for these concerns. These are significant indications, and I welcome them.

The PRC is a country comprising many nationalities, enriched by a diversity of languages and cultures. Protection of the language and culture of each nationality is a policy of the PRC, which is clearly spelled out in its constitution. Tibetan is the only language to preserve the entire range of the Buddha's teachings, including the texts on logic and theories of knowledge (epistemology), which we inherited from India's Nalanda University. This is a system of knowledge governed by reason and logic that has the potential to contribute to the peace and happiness of all beings. Therefore, the policy of undermining such a culture, instead of protecting and developing it, will in the long run amount to the destruction of humanity's common heritage.

The Chinese government frequently states that stability and development in Tibet are the foundation for its long-term well-being. However, the authorities still station large numbers of troops all across Tibet, increasing restrictions on the Tibetan people. Tibetans live in constant fear and anxiety. More recently, many Tibetan intellectuals, public figures, and environmentalists have been punished for articulating the Tibetan people's basic aspirations. They have been imprisoned allegedly for "subverting state power" when actually they have been giving voice to the Tibetan identity and cultural heritage. Such repressive measures undermine unity and stability. Likewise, in China, lawyers defending people's rights, independent writers, and human rights activists have been arrested. I strongly urge the Chinese leaders to review these developments and release these prisoners of conscience forthwith.

The Chinese government claims there is no problem in Tibet other than the personal privileges and status of the Dalai Lama. The reality is that the ongoing oppression of the Tibetan people has provoked widespread, deep resentment against current official policies. People from all walks of life frequently express their discontentment. That there is a problem in Tibet is reflected in the Chinese authorities' failure to trust Tibetans or win their loyalty. Instead, the Tibetan people live under constant suspicion and surveillance. Chinese and foreign visitors to Tibet corroborate this grim reality.

Therefore, just as we were able to send fact-finding delegations to Tibet in the late 1970s and early 1980s from among Tibetans in exile, we propose similar visits again. At the same time we would encourage the sending of representatives of independent international bodies, including parliamentarians. If they were to find that Tibetans in Tibet are happy, we would readily accept it.

The spirit of realism that prevailed under Mao's leadership in the early 1950s led China to sign the Seventeen-Point Agreement with Tibet. A similar spirit of realism prevailed once more during Hu Yaobang's time in the early 1980s. If there had been a continuation of such realism, the Tibetan issue, as well as several other problems, could easily have been solved. Unfortunately, conservative views derailed these policies. The result is that after more than six decades, the problem has become more intractable.

The Tibetan Plateau is the source of the major rivers of Asia. Because it has the largest concentration of glaciers apart from the two poles, it is considered to be the Third Pole. Environmental degradation in Tibet will have a detrimental impact on large parts of Asia, particularly on China and the Indian subcontinent. Both the central and local governments, as well as the Chinese public, should realize the degradation of the Tibetan environment and develop sustainable measures to safeguard it. I appeal to China to take into account the survival of people affected by what happens environmentally on the Tibetan Plateau.

In our efforts to solve the issue of Tibet, we have consistently pursued the mutually beneficial Middle Way Approach, which seeks genuine autonomy for the Tibetan people within the PRC. In our talks with officials of the Chinese government's United Front Work Department, we have clearly explained in detail the Tibetan people's hopes and aspirations. The lack of any positive response to our reasonable proposals makes us wonder whether these were fully and accurately conveyed to the higher authorities.

Since ancient times, Tibetan and Chinese peoples have lived as neighbors. It would be a mistake if our unresolved differences were to affect this age-old friendship. Special efforts are being made to promote good relations between Tibetans and Chinese living abroad, and I am happy that this has contributed to better understanding and friendship between us. Tibetans inside Tibet should also cultivate good relations with our Chinese brothers and sisters.

In recent weeks we have witnessed remarkable nonviolent struggles for freedom and democracy in various parts of North Africa and elsewhere. I am a firm believer in nonviolence and people power, and these events have shown once again that determined nonviolent action can indeed bring about positive change. We must all hope that these inspiring changes lead to genuine freedom, happiness, and prosperity for the peoples in these countries.

One of the aspirations I have cherished since childhood is the reform of Tibet's political and social structure, and in the few years when I held effective power in Tibet, I managed to make some fundamental changes. Although I was unable to take this further in Tibet, I have made every effort to do so since we came into exile. Today, within the framework of the Charter of the Tibetans-in-Exile, the Kalon Tripa, the political leadership, and the people's representatives are directly elected by the people. We have been able to implement democracy in exile that is in keeping with the standards of an open society.

As early as the 1960s, I have repeatedly stressed that Tibetans need a leader, elected freely by the Tibetan people, to whom I can devolve power. Now, we have clearly reached the time to put this into effect. During the forthcoming eleventh session of the fourteenth Tibetan Parliament in Exile, which begins on 14th March, I will formally propose that the necessary amendments be made to the Charter of Tibetans-in-Exile, reflecting my decision to devolve my formal authority to the elected leader.

Since I made my intention clear, I have received repeated and earnest requests from both within Tibet and outside, to continue to provide political leadership. My desire to devolve authority has nothing to do with a wish to shirk responsibility. It is to benefit Tibetans in the long run. It is not because I feel disheartened. Tibetans have placed such faith and trust in me that as one among them I am committed to playing my part in the just cause of Tibet. I trust that gradually people will come to understand my intention, will support my decision and accordingly let it take effect.

I would like to take this opportunity to remember the kindness of the leaders of various nations that cherish justice, members of parliaments, intellectuals, and Tibet support groups, who have been steadfast in their support for the Tibetan people. In particular, we will always remember the kindness and consistent support of the people and Government of India and State Governments for generously helping Tibetans preserve and promote their religion and culture and ensuring the welfare of Tibetans in exile. To all of them I offer my heartfelt gratitude.

With my prayers for the welfare and happiness of all sentient beings.

The End of the Political Authority of the Dalai Lamas

On that Thursday, March 10, 2011, the Dalai Lama spoke in the presence of the prime minister, Samdhong Rinpoche, and members of his government. He solemnly read the text of his speech, a copy of which was distributed to the audience that had been assembled since dawn. The speech was short, barely eighteen minutes. Eighteen minutes that have radically changed nearly four hundred years of Tibetan history.

Indeed, in 1642, the Great Fifth Dalai Lama received the temporal and spiritual responsibility for Tibet, ruling from the Golden Throne of Lhasa. First in his reincarnation lineage to exercise political authority, he had set up his capital in Lhasa and unified his country, ranging from Dartsedo, at the gates of China, to the borders of Ladakh, as in the great era of imperial Tibet. On the former palace of the religious sovereign Songtsen Gampo[198] he had built the Potala, the symbol of his domination and seat of a centralized administration. His reign marked the golden age of the Dalai Lamas, venerated as supreme by their people as much as by the khans of Mongolia and the emperors of China.

The Tibetan Buddhist institution of monastic governance, unique in the world, was entitled Ganden Phodrang, after the name of the residence of the Dalai Lamas established in the monastic city of Drepung until their transfer to the Potala. This clerical and secular diarchy allied religious and political authority, the one supporting the other, according to these verses full of imagery from the Tengyur:[199]

> The sovereign is the tree whose root is the monk.
> Ministers are the branches and the people, the leaves.
> If the root is protected, the tree does not perish.
> The monk must thus be well protected.[200]

The Ganden Phodrang defended the integrity of the Tibetan nation for centuries among the great powers of Central Asia, and the Thirteenth Dalai Lama proclaimed the independence of his country in 1913, signing treaties of alliance with its Mongolian and British neighbors. This sovereignty persisted until the Maoist invasion, and the Ganden Phodrang government then had to adapt itself to the conditions of exile.

The Ganden Phodrang ended in 2011 with the last March 10 commemorative speech given by the Fourteenth Dalai Lama. Temporal and spiritual powers would henceforth be separated. Secular political responsibility was devolved to the prime minister and the representatives of the people. The democratic process, initiated in the early days of exile, was thus finalized with the initiative of the Dalai Lama. He was pleased with this outcome, for he had, already at a young age, observed the inconveniences of concentrating all the power in his hands. That is why, despite popular reluctance, he had decreed a first

Parliament in 1960, written a future Constitution of Tibet in 1963, passed a Charter of Tibetans-in-Exile in 1991, and in 2001, arranged for the election of the prime minister by popular vote.

On March 10, 2011, by assigning what remained of his executive power, the Dalai Lama fully democratized the Tibetan institutions. In doing so, he preserved the outcome of the struggle for independence of his people, in case of vacancy of the supreme authority. Before the National Assembly of the Tibetan people in exile gathered in special session a few days later, on March 19, he declared:

Given that the line of Dalai Lamas has provided political leadership for nearly four centuries, it might be difficult for Tibetans generally and especially those in Tibet to envisage and accept a political system that is not led by the Dalai Lama. Therefore, over the past 50 years I have tried in various ways to raise people's political awareness and encourage their participation in our democratic process. I want to acknowledge here that many of my fellow Tibetans, inside and outside Tibet, have earnestly requested me to continue to give political leadership at this critical time. If we have to remain in exile for several more decades, a time will inevitably come when I will no longer be able to provide leadership. Therefore, it is necessary that we establish a sound system of governance while I remain able and healthy, in order that the exiled Tibetan administration can become self-reliant rather than being dependent on the Dalai Lama. If we are able to implement such a system from this time onward, I will still be able to help resolve problems if called upon to do so. But, if the implementation of such a system is delayed and a day comes when my leadership is suddenly unavailable, the consequent uncertainty might present an overwhelming challenge. Therefore, it is the duty of all Tibetans to make every effort to prevent such an eventuality.[201]

On that March 19, the Dalai Lama also explained that, at the request of his countrymen, he would remain as their spiritual leader and spokesperson. He would continue to demand from the international tribunes that China respect the human rights and freedoms of the Tibetan people by granting them the autonomy guaranteed to minorities under the Chinese constitution. Yet he went even further in his will to adapt to the modern world the institution of the Dalai Lama and the destiny of Tibet from which it is inseparable. Six months later, on September 24, 2011, he issued a landmark statement that made a second revolution at the heart of Tibetan Buddhism.

Tenzin Gyatso, Last of the Dalai Lamas?

Tibetan buddhocracy is unique in history, with the enthronement of reincarnated children in the line of the Dalai Lamas. Tenzin Gyatso, the current title holder, recounted the unusual circumstances of his recognition at the age of two and a half, preceded by divination and oracular signs. He affirmed that his predecessor, the Great Thirteenth, voluntarily left his body at a premature date. Whereas prophecies unanimously predicted he would live a very long life, to about eighty, he died in Lhasa on December 17, 1933, aged only fifty-seven.

The Thirteenth Dalai Lama left behind a text that history remembers as his "Testament." About twenty years earlier, in this premonitory writing he announced the invasion of Tibet and the destruction of the traditional society in blood and tears: "Very soon in this land with a harmonious blend of religion and politics, if we do not dare to protect our territory, our spiritual personalities including the Victorious Father and Son[202] may be exterminated without trace, the property and authority of our monasteries may be taken away. Moreover, our political system, developed by the Three Great Dharma Kings, will vanish without anything remaining. The property of all people, high and low, will be seized and the people forced to become slaves. All living beings will have to endure endless days of suffering and will be stricken with fear. Such a time will come."[203]

The premature death of the Great Thirteenth was, according to the current Dalai Lama, a final attempt to save Tibet. Considered progressive by historians, the sovereign had abolished the death penalty in 1898, rectified the abuses of the monastic system, and organized a small army on the British model. His efforts to propel Tibet into the international scene and his reforms to modernize the feudalistic society were, however, met by skepticism and determined opposition from the aristocracy. Realizing that he would not reach his goals, he took a radical decision to reincarnate earlier and thus confront in adulthood the foreseen events: "He mystically stepped aside and passed away, making way for the new reincarnation. As a consequence, when the Chinese Communists eventually invaded, they were forced to deal with a young energetic Dalai Lama, rather than with an old man."[204]

Like his predecessor, the current Dalai Lama is faced with the question of his succession amid the speculations of the Chinese power about his age. In a political context threatening the survival and identity of his people, he has publicly stated that the Fifteenth Dalai Lama will be born outside Tibet as long as the country is occupied by the People's Republic of China. On May 27, 1997, during a meeting with the Tibetan diaspora in New York, the spiritual leader had already affirmed: "That reincarnation will definitely not come under Chinese control, it will be born outside, in the free world."

The situation of Tibet under the Chinese iron rule, as well as societal changes, motivated the Dalai Lama to shake up the religious tradition with the same democratic conviction that he showed on the political level. Indeed, he called his people to decide on the recognition of a fifteenth holder of the golden throne of Lhasa: "In fact, as far back as 1969, I made clear that concerned people should decide whether the Dalai Lama's reincarnations should continue in the future."[205] He reiterated this statement, almost word for word, forty-two years later, on September 24, 2011, six months after his retirement from the political scene. Whether the Fourteenth Dalai Lama is the last one or not now depends on the Tibetans, who will vote in a referendum. In his speech the current Dalai Lama gave precise instructions on how to identify him if they confirm their choice of a successor.[206]

Unlike the Thirteenth, who cut short his life to save Tibet, the Fourteenth plans to live long to try to solve the Tibetan issue before his death. The debate on the subject of his succession should therefore only be opened around 2025, when he will be ninety years old. In this area, he also innovates. In his speech of September 24, 2011, following a consultation with the hierarchs of the different schools of Tibetan Buddhism, the Dalai Lama argued that the enthronement of a young reincarnation might not be wise. It would mean many years of training to maturity, while the situation in Tibet and the world will probably require that the new spiritual leader act and speak at his inauguration.

Rather than having a divine child rising onto the golden throne of Lhasa, several options are thus proposed by the Dalai Lama. He strives to preserve the essence of the reincarnation process, which consists in identifying a single stream of consciousness perpetuating from one life to another. In the past, young boys were recognized as the "reincarnations" of the previous Potala master who died. However, what is changing is that the current Dalai Lama plans to designate even before his death the Fifteenth Dalai Lama, who would be an *emanation* of his own mind rather than a *reincarnation*. His successor would thus be fully legitimized, and this would invalidate any Chinese attempts to enthrone a Tibetan spiritual leader under the orders of Beijing.

"Why would my successor not be a woman?" the Dalai Lama often asks. Reincarnated women are so rarely represented in Tibetan monasticism that his intermediaries generally burst out laughing when he voices the question. Yet he precisely tries to change this fact by observing that the patriarchal model is in decline and that women, because they give life, are biologically more apt to express and radiate the qualities of compassion.

The Sun Will Rise Again in Tibet and the World

Since February 2009, human torches have been lit on the roof of the world. In Tunisia, a single self-immolation was enough to set off the Jasmine Revolution that overthrew the government in power. More than a hundred immolations have failed to significantly revive the cause of the Tibetan *satyagraha*[207] in the international media. A journalist reported in March 2012 that terrifying rumor circulating on the highlands: "When two thousand Tibetans will have immolated themselves, the sacrifice will be such that, by a sort of divine miracle, Tibet will finally become free."[208]

While the official Chinese propaganda tries to make believe that the self-immolated are simple-minded people who are manipulated by instigators at the service of the Dalai Lama, women, men, and even children, the youngest aged only fifteen and sixteen,[209] make the choice of an agonizing death. The agony of a body that burns is slow and painful. One remains conscious until the end, and until the end, the self-immolated make this vow, whispering in a last breath: "The sun will rise again in Tibet." This sun beyond the sun is the Dalai Lama, a sun of love and compassion. From his homeland he will light up Tibet and the world.

This is a Tibetan singularity. This people have historically chosen to be guided by this embodied compassion. Despite sixty years of indoctrination and repression, Tibetans continue to want the reestablishment of the supreme authority of compassion at the head of their nation. When Tibet left isolation with the Chinese invasion, followed by the forced exile of thousands of people since 1959, the Dalai Lama immediately made a new language heard on the international stage. His speeches in favor of a peaceful resolution of the Sino-Tibetan conflict soon won a wide audience, way beyond the political sphere. He naturally emerged as the one who teaches the world about the secular ethics of inner peace, compassion, and universal responsibility. At a time of uncertainty and fear of the future due to the rapid degradation of the environment, when paradigms that were believed to be immortal have collapsed, his message brings hope. The Dalai Lama reminds us that what unites us is stronger than what too often divides us. By engaging us to reconcile with our deeply altruistic and benevolent reality, he invites us to rehumanize the world.

The Dalai Lama devolves his political authority to a democratically elected leader. March 10, 2011, Dharamsala, India. © *Office of His Holiness the Dalai Lama*

EPILOGUE

It Would Be a March 10 . . .

It would be a March 10 . . .

That morning, a day long hoped for breaks. Women, men, and sometimes children had dreamed of it in the pain of endless days as prisoners of the Chinese concentration camp system.

It would be a March 10 . . .

On the esplanade of the Potala, the crowd gathers before dawn. Dense, compact, cheerful. All eyes gaze at the giant screens arrayed up to the foot of the ancient lamasery. It is no longer topped with the five-star red flag of the People's Republic of China, but with the Tibetan banner of the snow lions and the blue flag of the UN. They flutter in the wind, along with banners reproducing in all languages of the world the slogan: "Tibet, sanctuary of peace."

On the platform, standing in front of the purple and white façade of the Potala, thirty-three winners of the Nobel Peace Prize, from every corner of the world, are seated in a semicircle. The leader of the Tibetans had repeatedly expressed a desire to bring together an ethics committee, composed of peacemakers, to reflect on the problems of humanity. His idealism had made us smile. . . . Today, his wish has come true.

It would be a March 10 . . .

Before the tribune, the Dalai Lama and Liu Xiaobo join for a fraternal hug. The crowd applauds them, and Aung San Suu Kyi speaks. The former opponent, now winner over the Burmese military junta and Secretary-General of the United Nations, proclaims on that March 10 the first World Day of Universal Responsibility, dedicated to altruism and solidarity among all living beings. It pays tribute to the supreme leader of Tibet, who has taught these values, sources of compassion and peace for the world.

It would be a March 10 . . .

The Dalai Lama and Liu Xiaobo declare that justice and truth are weapons that defeat all weapons. Their lives testify it: with bare hands they made a dictatorship bend and won a victory of peace. From the esplanade of the Potala, the world listens to the message of two men without hatred and enemies. Tibetan and Chinese, with one voice, they speak on behalf of mankind.

H. H. the Dalai Lama XIV, 1935–
McLeod Ganj, India, March 10, 2009—observing two
minutes of silence, in honor of the 50th Anniversary of
the Tibetan Uprising of 1959. *(Reuters / Corbis)*

MAPS

TIBETAN CULTURAL AREA

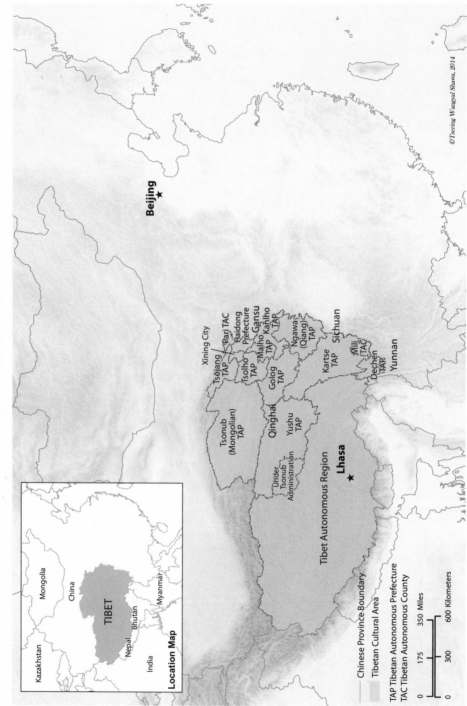

Location Map

Kazakhstan
Mongolia
China
Nepal Bhutan
TIBET
India
Myanmar

Beijing ★

Xining City
Tsojang TAP
Pari TAC
Haidong Prefecture
Tsolho TAP
Malho TAP
Gansu
Kanlho TAP
Ngawa (Qiang) TAP
Sichuan
Tsonub (Mongolian) TAP
Qinghai
Golog TAP
Yushu TAP
Kartse TAP
Mili TAC
Under Tsonub Administration
Dechen TAP
Yunnan
Lhasa ★
Tibet Autonomous Region

©Tsering Wangyal Shawa, 2014

— Chinese Province Boundary

Tibetan Cultural Area

TAP Tibetan Autonomous Prefecture
TAC Tibetan Autonomous County

0   175   350 Miles
0   300   600 Kilometers

TIBET IN CHINA AND IN ASIA

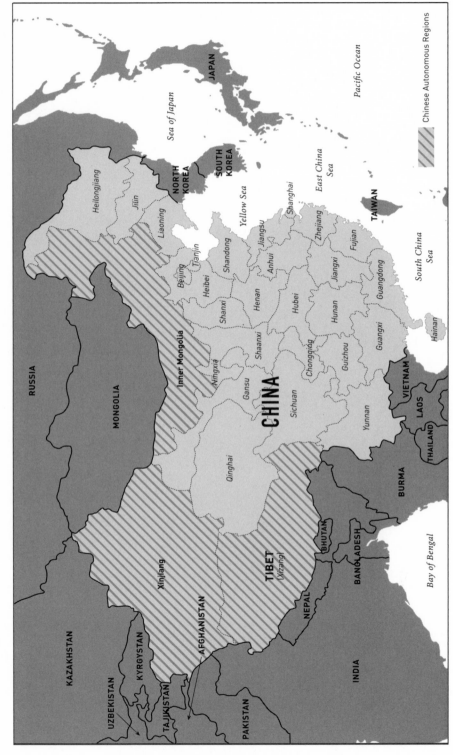

Chinese Autonomous Regions

TIBET UNDER CHINESE OCCUPATION

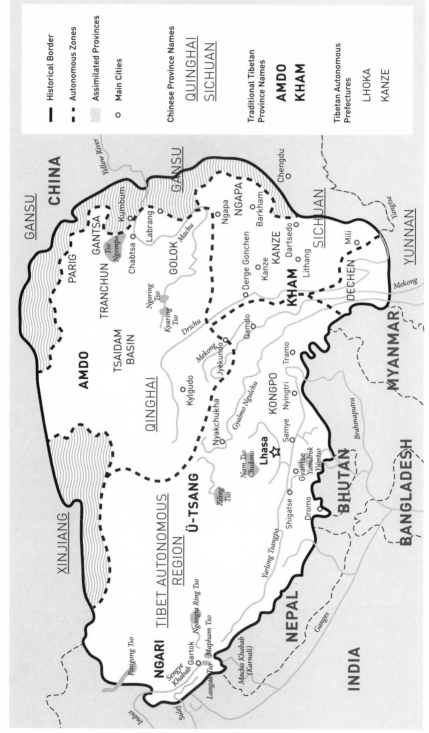

Legend:

— Historical Border

- - - Autonomous Zones

░ Assimilated Provinces

○ Main Cities

Chinese Province Names
QUINGHAI
SICHUAN

Traditional Tibetan Province Names
AMDO
KHAM

Tibetan Autonomous Prefectures
LHOKA
KANZE

RESOURCES, NUCLEAR BASES, AND COMMUNICATION ROUTES

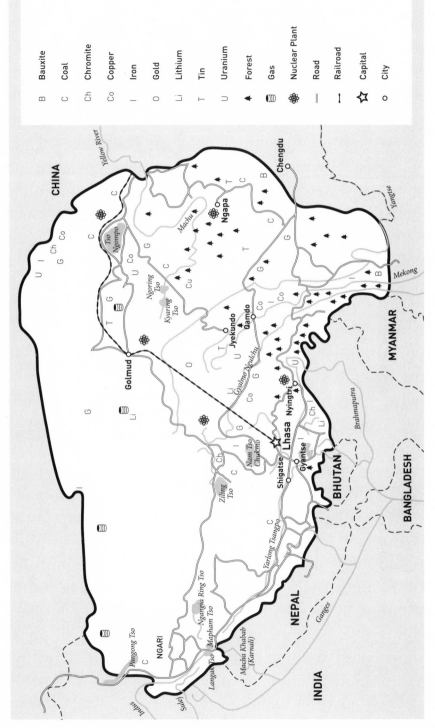

B	Bauxite
C	Coal
Ch	Chromite
Co	Copper
I	Iron
O	Gold
Li	Lithium
T	Tin
U	Uranium
◄	Forest
▥	Gas
⚛	Nuclear Plant
—	Road
⊢	Railroad
☆	Capital
○	City

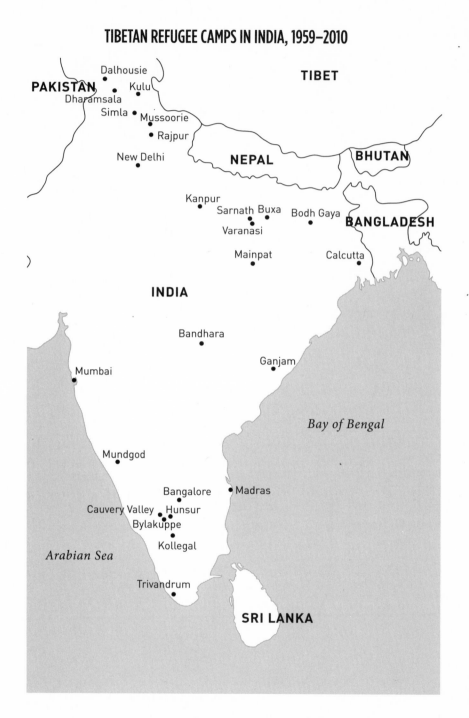

TIBETAN REFUGEE CAMPS IN INDIA, 1959–2010

PAKISTAN

TIBET

Dalhousie

Kulu

Dharamsala

Simla

Mussoorie

Rajpur

New Delhi

NEPAL

BHUTAN

Kanpur

Sarnath Buxa

Varanasi

Bodh Gaya

BANGLADESH

Mainpat

Calcutta

INDIA

Bandhara

Ganjam

Mumbai

Bay of Bengal

Mundgod

Bangalore

Madras

Cauvery Valley

Hunsur

Bylakuppe

Kollegal

Arabian Sea

Trivandrum

SRI LANKA

NOTES

INTRODUCTION: IN THE NAME OF HUMANITY

1. Middle mountain station in Uttarakhand state in northern India.
2. Border area between Assam and Tibet, formerly called NEFA (North East Frontier Agency), now called Arunachal Pradesh.
3. Hindi translation of "Long live the Dalai Lama!," "Long life to the Dalai Lama!"
4. Siliguri, Benares, and Lucknow.
5. The Dalai Lama, *My Spiritual Journey*, collected by S. Stril-Rever, trans. Charlotte Mandell (New York: HarperOne, 2010), 180.
6. Tibetan Buddhism, derived from Nalanda University-style Buddhism, sometimes called "Vajrayana" because it retains unique resources of esoteric Mahayana Buddhism.
7. Mayank Chhaya, *Dalai Lama: The Revealing Life Story and His Struggle for Tibet* (New York: Doubleday, 2007), 5.
8. "Long live Papa Nehru!" in Hindi.
9. See *Universal-International Newsreels* of April 30, 1959, available under the title *The Dalai Lama Greeted by Nehru*, on the website of the French edition of this book: www.appelaumondedudalailama.com.
10. In South African prisons, Gandhi, classified as a "negro," had to wear this cap, which in the early days of the Republic of India politicians adopted in his honor.
11. Sarvepalli Gopal, *Jawaharlal Nehru: A Biography* (London: J. Cape, 1984), 90.
12. Gopal, *Jawaharlal Nehru*, 90.
13. Gopal, *Jawaharlal Nehru*, 90.
14. In Arunachal Pradesh.
15. CIA, *Teletyped Information Report*, E79–0129, April 23, 1959.

16. On October 7, 1950, 40,000 soldiers of the 16th and 18th Chinese armies had crossed the Sino-Tibetan border in Kham. 8,500 Tibetans, equipped in an archaic manner, tried to resist but failed to prevent them from reaching Lhasa. Faced with this invasion, the 16-year-old Dalai Lama unsuccessfully appealed to the United Nations. The Korean War had broken out on June 25, 1950, riveting the attention of the world on the 38th parallel. In addition, as Mao Zedong had just sent reinforcement troops to North Korea, he had the unconditional support of the USSR. The Tibetan government then decided to make a final attempt at reconciliation, sending four senior officials to Beijing on January 7, 1951. After five months of negotiations and under the pressure of an ultimatum threatening to demolish Lhasa, they had no other alternative but to go beyond the limits of their mission by placing the fake seals of the Dalai Lama at the bottom of the "Agreement for the Peaceful Liberation of Tibet," commonly known as the Seventeen-Point Agreement. Under this treaty, Tibet became an autonomous province attached to mainland China; the Dalai Lama retained his spiritual and temporal power. The Chinese government committed not to interfere in the internal affairs of Tibet; only foreign policy and defense came under the control of Beijing. Politically isolated, having refused to emigrate to the United States as part of his entourage had encouraged him to do, and at the urging of Nehru, on October 24, 1951, the Dalai Lama could only ratify the Seventeen-Point Agreement.

17. Warren Smith, *Tibetan Nation: A History of Tibetan Nationalism and Tibetan Sino-Relations* (New Delhi: Rupa, 2009), 461.

18. City of Northern Assam, on the banks of the Brahmaputra.

19. New China News Agency, "Commentary on the so-called Statement of the Dalai Lama," April 20, 1959, in Smith, *Tibetan Nation*, 379.

20. Foreign Office document, cited in Tsering Shakya, *The Dragon in the Land of Snows* (London: Pimlico, 1999), 219.

21. Shakya, *The Dragon in the Land of Snows*, 220.

22. Subimal Dutt, *With Nehru in the Foreign Office* (Calcutta: Minerva Publications, 1977), 152.

23. Dutt, *With Nehru in the Foreign Office*, 152.

24. The Lower House of the parliament of the Indian Union.

25. Excerpt from the article "Deputies to the Second National People's Congress Condemn the Imperialists and Indian Expansionists" in *Concerning the Question of Tibet* (Beijing: Beijing Foreign Languages Press, 1960), 88.

26. Nehru's speech in Lok Sabha on April 27, 1959, in *Prime Minister on Sino-Indian Relations* (New Delhi: Ministry of External Affairs, 1959), 1:39.

27. The Laogai Research Foundation (www.laogai.org) contradicts the Chinese allegations on the number of prisons and prisoners, as officials only use the term "prisoner" to designate a person convicted of a crime and sentenced by a court. All places where people are interned but not judged are therefore considered "nonprisons," and include reeducation through labor camps and various centers of detention, accommodation,

and survey, and even military prisons. See interview with Marie Holzman on www
.appelaumondedudalailama.com.

28. President of the Constitutional Council, former Minister of Justice.

29. Speech given by Robert Badinter at the Bercy sports stadium on June 7, 2009, as an introduction to the conference held by the Dalai Lama, "Ethics and Society."

30. Nongovernmental organization in consultative status with the Economic and Social Council—ECOSOC—of the United Nations, created in 1952 in Berlin to enforce the respect of the rights of people around the world.

31. Sixteen nonautonomous territories are listed to date: Anguilla, Bermuda, Gibraltar, Guam, the Cayman Islands, the Falkland Islands, the Turks and Caicos Islands, the U.S. and British Virgin Islands, Montserrat, New Caledonia, Pitcairn, Saint Helena, Western Sahara, American Samoa, and Tokelau. The Administering Powers are the United States, France, New Zealand, and the United Kingdom.

32. Report on the situation in Tibet corresponding to Resolution 1991/10 of the Security Council of the UN.

33. A former Tibetan political prisoner, he spent thirty-three years in the Chinese re-education through labor camps. His autobiography, *Fire Under the Snow*, translated by Tibetan historian Tsering Shakya (New York: Grove Press, 1998), is a worldwide best-seller that has been adapted for the screen.

34. See interview posted on www.appelaumondedudalailama.com.

35. Statement made in Nantes in August 2008.

36. Interview of September 29, 2010.

PART 1. THE STRUGGLE FOR INDEPENDENCE, 1961–1979

1. Northwestern state of India.

2. The bungalow has today been converted into a mountaineering training base for the Indian army units responsible for supervising the northwestern border.

3. Extract from the speech; see Introduction, p. 12.

4. *The Question of Tibet and the Rule of Law*, Geneva, 1959; *International Commission of Jurists Report on Tibet*, Geneva, 1960; English versions at www.tibet.com.

5. Resolution 1353 of the United Nations General Assembly, October 21, 1959.

6. Resolution 1515 of the United Nations General Assembly, December 15, 1960.

7. Cited by Claude Arpi in *The Fate of Tibet* (New Delhi: Har-Anand Publications, 1999), 99.

8. In accordance with the Convention on the Prevention and Punishment of the Crime of Genocide, adopted by the United Nations General Assembly on December 9, 1948, according to Article 2, the crime corresponds to the "intent to destroy, in whole or in part, a national, ethnical, racial or religious group." In Tibet in 1961, China was already guilty for four of five acts stated by the UN as qualifying a crime as genocide: "killing members of the group; causing serious bodily or mental harm to members of the group; deliberately inflicting on the group conditions of life calculated to bring

about its physical destruction in whole or in part; forcibly transferring children of the group to another group." It would soon be guilty of the fifth act, "imposing measures intended to prevent births within the group."

9. Speech given at Lokh Sabha, September 1959.

10. Sardar K. M. Panikkar, *In Two Chinas: Memoirs of a Diplomat* (London: Allen & Unwin, 1955), 106.

11. Resolution 1353 of the UN General Assembly.

12. Economic policy designed and applied by Mao Zedong from 1958 to 1960, to stimulate industrial and agricultural production through the development of infrastructure, gigantic public works, and collectivization in rural areas. The entire population was mobilized under duress, but this unrealistic program led to the collapse of the economy, resulting in three years of famine, at least 30 million deaths, and practices of cannibalism in the countryside. The dissident Wei Jingsheng evokes a time when "parents crazed by hunger surrendered to others the flesh of their flesh to appease their hunger, receiving the flesh of the flesh of other parents to soothe their own hunger." Excerpt from *La Cinquième Modernization et autres écrits du Printemps de Pékin* (Paris: Christian Bourgois, 1997).

13. See the article "Tibet: Starvation Diet," *Time Magazine*, January 27, 1961.

14. Or mantra of compassion.

15. Tsering Woeser, *Memoire interdite*, trans. Li Zhang-Bourrit and Bernard Bourrit (Paris: Gallimard, 2010), 127. See his photo archives at www.appelaumondedudalailama.com.

16. Figures from the report "Tibet: Proving Truth from Facts" (Dharamsala: Department of Information and International Relations, Tibetan Government in Exile, 1993).

17. Self-determination is the right of a people to determine its own form of government. Article 1 of the UN Charter, signed in 1945, states "respect for the principle of equal rights and self-determination of peoples."

18. Buddha of compassion.

19. Referring to the invasion of the northeastern territories and of the Aksai Chin by the PLA in 1962.

20. Tubten Khétsun, *Memories of Life in Lhasa Under Chinese Rule* (New York: Columbia University Press, 2008).

21. Palden Gyatso, *Le Feu sous la neige*, trans. Christian Dumais-Lvowski and Sabine Boulongne (Arles: Actes Sud, "Babel," 1997), 127.

22. See map, page 322.

23. See *A Poisoned Arrow: The Secret Report of the 10th Panchen Lama*, trans. R. Barnett, Tibet Information Network (TIN), 1997.

24. The name of the plenipotentiary negotiator who, in 1914, had separated the Tibetan territory from the possessions of the British Raj in India.

25. Territory at the junction of Tibet, Pakistan, and India, claimed by Delhi as part of the State of Jammu and Kashmir, but strategically significant because it connects Tibet and Xinjiang by the Chinese highway 219.

26. George Ginsburg and Michael Mathos, *Communist China and Tibet* (The Hague: Martinus Nijhoff, 1964).

27. Or Cabinet of Ministers.

28. See in this regard the analysis of Jane Ardley, *The Tibetan Independence Movement: Political, Religious and Gandhian Perspectives* (London: Routledge, 2002), 44.

29. Speech of April 1993, delivered in Washington.

30. See the Declaration of Independence for colonized countries and peoples adopted by the UN in 1960.

31. Resolution 1723 of the UN General Assembly, December 20, 1961.

32. Between 1956 and 1977.

33. See in this regard Lu Ting'en and Peng Kunyuan, *General History of Africa: Modern Times* (Shanghai: Huadong Normal University Press, 1995).

34. Mao Zedong, "Statement Supporting the Afro-Americans in Their Struggle Against Racial Discrimination by U.S. Imperialism," August 8, 1963, www.marxistleninist.worldpress.com.

35. Translation of Panchen Lama.

36. Statement at the International Conference that brought together sixty-eight communist parties of the world in Moscow in 1957. See "Heroes and Killers of the 20th century," www.moreorless.au.com, and Jung Chang and Jon Halliday, *Mao, the Unknown Story* (London: Jonathan Cape, 2005).

37. Jaime Torres Bodet, Mexican writer (1902–1974), General Director of UNESCO (1949–1952).

38. Archives of the Charles de Gaulle foundation, press conference of January 31, 1964, the Élysée Palace. Two years earlier, in 1962, General de Gaulle had, however, brought to France twenty young Tibetan refugees. These ten boys and ten girls were entrusted to host institutions, but it was the French government that until their adulthood provided for their material needs and education. They had been administratively classified as "pupils of the state, stateless refugees of undetermined origin."

39. Or Sun Tzu, author of the oldest book on military strategy, *The Art of War.* One of its maxims, "All warfare is based on deception," characterizes contemporary Chinese diplomacy and propaganda.

40. Doctor by profession trained in Hawaii, Sun Yat-sen (1866–1925) became the "father of modern China" by overthrowing Pu Yi, the last emperor of the Qing dynasty. Founder of the Kuomintang, he became the first president of the Republic of China in 1912 and tried between 1917 and 1925 to reunify the country dominated by warlords. His political philosophy is known as the "Three Principles of the People": nationalism, democracy, and livelihood.

41. Sunni Muslim people related to the Uzbeks living in Xinjiang, the former East Turkestan. Their language is Uighur.

42. Mao Zedong, "Contradictions Among the People" statement of February 27, 1957, quoted in Robert R. Bowie and John K. Fairbank, *Communist China 1955–1959* (Cambridge, Mass.: Harvard University Press, 1962), 273.

43. See *Livre blanc sur l'autonomie régionale ethnique au Tibet*, published in May 2004 by the Chinese embassy in Paris.

44. Resolution 2079 of the UN General Assembly on December 18, 1965, adopted by a majority of 43 votes in favor, with 26 against and 22 abstentions.

45. He had informed the Dalai Lama in January 1966 that India was ready to recognize the Tibetan government in exile, but died prematurely before endorsing this decision. See "The Dalai Lama and Indian PMs," posted August 22, 2010, on the blog of Claude Arpi, claudearpi.blogspot.com.

46. See the discussion of this point by Alain Pellet, "Inutile Assemblée générale?" *Pouvoirs* 109 (2003).

47. Tibet was divided into three provinces: Ü-Tsang in the center; Kham and Amdo in the east. It was divided into five administrative regions: 1) the TAR (Tibet Autonomous Region) or central Tibet; 2) Western Sichuan and 3) Yunnan in the north, which includes the former province of Kham; 4) Gansu in the southwest; and 5) Qinghai, which includes the former province of Amdo. See map, page 322 and www.appelaumondedudalailama.com.

48. Ngabo Ngawang Jigmé, head of the delegation who signed the Seventeen-Point Agreement, appointed Chairman of the TAR in 1965. He died on December 23, 2009.

49. Avalokiteshvara, the bodhisattva of compassion, with eleven heads and a thousand arms in certain representations.

50. See the report *Tibet, 1950–1967* of the Union Research Institute of Hong Kong, 1997, cited in Tsering Shakya, *The Dragon in the Land of Snows* (London: Pimlico, 1999).

51. Heather Stoddard, professor at the National Institute of Oriental Languages and Civilizations (Inalco), thinks that the green color refers to the mold on cheese and butter.

52. See Kenneth Lieberthal, *Governing China* (New York: Norton, 1995), 195.

53. Among other cases cited in Woeser, *Mémoire interdite*, 313.

54. Testimony by Woeser, *Mémoire interdite*, 17.

55. Ibid.

56. Ancestral funeral ritual practiced by the *ragyapa* or "body cutters" caste of specialized priests, who dismember the deceased on a rocky ledge, then grind its bones and mix them with barley flour, tea, and yak milk, preparing dumplings offered to the vultures.

57. *Kyichu* in Tibetan, a tributary of the Brahmaputra.

58. Reported by Khétsun, *Memories of Life in Lhasa Under Chinese Rule*, 174, and Woeser, *Mémoire interdite*, 314.

59. Testimony by Woeser, *Mémoire interdite,* 140.

60. Reproducing the characters *Hong Weibing*, which in Mandarin means "Red Guards."

61. Extract from the online magazine *The Revolutionary Worker* 752 (April 1994).

62. Quoted in *China: The Roots of Madness*, film by Theodore White, 1967.

63. *Les Massacres de la Révolution culturelle,* texts compiled by Sang Yangyi (Paris: Buchet/Chastel, 2008).

64. Woeser, *Mémoire interdite*, 90.
65. Ibid., 395.
66. Han, native of Sichuan, former president of the association of Tibetan antique collectors, now transferred to the Chinese Center for Tibetan Studies in Beijing.
67. Woeser, *Mémoire interdite*, 226–228.
68. Speech given at Dharamsala, May 1960, quoted in Sofia Stril-Rever, *Enfants du Tibet* (Paris: Desclée de Brouwer, 2000).
69. See map, page 324.
70. Winner of the Outlook-Picador Award for Non-Fiction in 2001; author of *Kora. Combat pour le Tibet* (Paris: L'Harmattan, 2006).
71. See the full poem in Stril-Rever, *Enfants du Tibet,* 128.
72. Founded by Tsongkhapa, 40 kilometers east of Lhasa. One of the three monastic universities of the Lhasa Valley, with Sera and Drepung.
73. Woeser, *Mémoire interdite*, 93.
74. Norbu Aten, *Un cavalier dans la neige* (Paris: Maisonneuve, 1981), 100.
75. Woeser, *Mémoire interdite,* 289.
76. Ibid., 222.
77. Remarks made at the Gesar Festival in 2001, quoted in Woeser, *Mémoire interdite,* 302.
78. Khetsun, *Memories of Life in Lhasa Under Chinese Rule.*
79. In the TAR, out of 2,711 existing monasteries in 1958, there remained only 370 in 1960, and the number of monks went from 114,000 to 18,104. See the study by Zhang Tianlu, *Population Change in Tibet* (Beijing: Tibetan Studies Publishing House of China, 1989), 28.
80. Or "House of the Lord," the first temple in Lhasa, built in the seventh century by King Songtsen Gampo to house Tibet's most revered Buddha statue.
81. Figures provided by Tsering Shakya, *The Dragon in the Land of Snows*, 512.
82. Ngari Rinpoche interviewed in *Dalai Lama, une vie après l'autre,* a film by Franck Sanson, written by Sofia Stril-Rever (Arte, 2008).
83. See Thubten Ngodup, *Nechung, l'oracle du Dalaï-lama*, autobiography with Françoise Bottereau-Gardey and Laurent Deshayes (Paris: Presses de la Renaissance, 2009), 40.
84. Ibid., 39.
85. At the request of Songtsen Gampo, king of the Yarlung Dynasty (617–650).
86. Marshall Lin Biao was then Vice-President of the Central Committee of the Communist Party.
87. Reported by Woeser, *Mémoire interdite,* 137.
88. Ibid., 182.
89. Better known by its English acronym, TIPA (Tibetan Institute of Performing Arts).
90. Or TCV, Tibetan Children's Villages, a nonprofit organization based in Dharamsala and responsible for the care and education of 12,000 young Tibetans in India.
91. County and city located 100 kilometers west of Lhasa.

92. Kham city whose name means "confluence," as it is located at the confluence of two rivers.

93. In the north of Lhasa.

94. The collectivization, begun in 1966, was interrupted by the Cultural Revolution.

95. At the administrative level, the municipality corresponded to the territorial subdivision of a canton. Farmers work their fields together grouped into a single entity, under the authority of a brigade, earning a meager salary, barely enough to cover their basic expenses.

96. Extract from the article "People's Communes Set Up," *Beijing Review*, July 19, 1974, 9.

97. Extract from the article "Tibet on Its Way Towards Socialism," *Beijing Review*, September 19, 1975.

98. Figures from Warren Smith, *Tibetan Nation: A History of Tibetan Nationalism and Sino-Tibetan Relations* (New Delhi: Rupa & Co., 2009), 552.

99. Located in Xinjiang on the advice of Soviet experts, this is the largest nuclear site in the world, where China has carried out all its nuclear tests without warning people of the radioactive risks incurred. According to the Uighur opponents, it has resulted in twenty thousand deaths.

100. The construction of these shelters has caused irreversible cracks in the lamasery, whose repair seems to cause insoluble technical problems.

101. *Les Dits du Bouddha. Le Dhammapada* (Paris: Albin Michel, 2004), verse 5.

102. Ibid., Verse 201.

103. Ibid., Verse 103.

104. See *U.S. News and World Report* LXV, no. 12 (September 16, 1968).

105. "We were convinced," recalled Kissinger in his memoirs, "that an increase of U.S. foreign policy options, far from harming the Soviet position, would ease it." Henry Kissinger, *Diplomatie* (Paris: Fayard, 1996), 654.

106. See the developed analysis on the subject by Chen Jian, *Mao's China and the Cold War* (Durham: University of Northern Carolina Press, 2000).

107. Kissinger, *Diplomatie*, 654.

108. Legendary king who lived from 374 to 493. A book of Buddha's teachings and ritual objects descended from the sky into his palace.

109. Songtsen Gampo (609–650), thirty-third king; Trisong Detsen (704–797), twenty-seventh king; and Tri Ralpachen (806–838), fortieth king.

110. Tzvetan Todorov, *Les Abus de la mémoire* (Paris: Arléa, 2004).

111. An approximately 3,000-km-long river with its source at Mount Kailash that crosses three countries, in which it has three different names: Yarlung Zangpo in Tibet, southeast of Lhasa; Brahmaputra in northeastern India, in Assam; and Jamuna in Bangladesh, where it joins the Ganges delta and flows into the Bay of Bengal.

112. See the article by historian Helga Uebach in Anne-Marie Blondeau and Katia Buffetrille, eds., *Le Tibet est-il chinois?* (Paris: Albin Michel, 2002).

113. Or *Choesi-sungdrel* in Tibetan, which literally means "spiritual-temporal" and refers to the inseparable union of religion and politics.

114. Interview by Sylvaine Pasquier, *L'Express*, October 14, 1993

115. Laurent Deshayes, *Histoire du Tibet* (Paris: Fayard, 1997), 73.

116. This system, originally retained for the Karmapa succession, has replaced the traditional succession from uncle to nephew.

117. Conclusions of Michael van Walt van Praag, Dutch professor of international law and legal adviser of the Dalai Lama since 1984. See his reference book, *The Status of Tibet: History, Rights and Prospects in International Law* (Boulder: Westview Press, 1987).

118. Hierarch of the Sakya school (1182–1251). Accomplished spiritual master, he became in 1247 an adviser of Prince Godan and concluded an alliance with the Mongol power.

119. Melvyn C. Goldstein, *A History of Modern Tibet*, 2 vols. (Berkeley: University of California Press, 1989), 60.

120. The Dalai Lama, *Mon pays et mon peuple*, trans. Alain Rodari (Geneva: Olizane, 1993), 63.

121. Smith, *Tibetan Nation*, 555.

122. Palden Gyatso, *Le Feu sous la neige*, 224–225.

123. Ibid.

124. Proceedings of the exhibition *La Colère des serfs, une série de sculptures* in the magazine *Beijing Review*, September 19, 1975.

125. Or ghost villages, which Potemkin, a Russian government minister, erected in Crimea to hide the reality of the misery of the people during the visit of Catherine II in 1787.

126. See Anna Louise Strong, *When Serfs Stood up in Tibet* (1960; reprint, Beijing: Red Sun, 2009), Stuart and Roma Gelder, *The Timely Rain: Travels in New Tibet* (London: Hutchinson, 1964); Israel Epstein, *Tibet Transformed* (Beijing: Foreign Languages Press, 1983).

127. Han Suyin, *Lhasa, étoile fleur* (Paris: Stock, 1976).

128. Simon Leys, *Ombres chinoises* (Paris: UGE, 1974), and Patrick French, *Tibet, Tibet, une histoire personnelle d'un pays perdu* (Paris: Albin Michel, 2005), 83 and 294.

129. Khetsun, *Memories of Life in Lhasa Under Chinese Rule*, 198.

130. See Tsering Shakya, *The Dragon in the Land of Snows*, 357.

131. Among the first participants in the Tibetan Studies program, Westerners such as Glenn Mullin, B. Alan Wallace, Stephen Batchelor, Alexander Berzin, Jon Landau, Ruth Sonam, and Brian Beresford have each published more than a dozen works on Tibetan Buddhism.

132. During this first journey, the Dalai Lama did not visit France, where a visa was refused to spare China's sensibilities.

133. Nagarjuna, *Traité du Milieu*, trans. Yonten Gyatso and Georges Driessense (Paris: Seuil, 1998).

134. The "law" or the Buddha's teaching in Sanskrit.

135. Overseen by the central administration of Chinese broadcasting, this station broadcasts controlled information to China and abroad; its journalists must also prepare reports on sensitive issues for the Party executives.

136. Expression of Henry Kissinger, who notes about Mao in his memoirs: "I've never met anyone, except maybe Charles de Gaulle, who exuded such determination, solid as concrete. He was fascinated by the almost tangible feeling that emanated from his thirst for domination." Henry Kissinger, *À la Maison Blanche* (Paris: Fayard, 1979).

137. Remarks of the Chinese dissident Wei Jingsheng, *La Cinquième Modernization et autres écrits du Printemps de Pékin,* trans. Huang San and Angel Pino (Paris: Christian Bourgois, 1997).

138. Palden Gyatso, *Le Feu sous la neige,* 242.

139. Quoted in Margaret Nowak, *Tibetan Refugees: Youth and the New Generation* (New Brunswick, N.J.: Rutgers University Press, 1984), 147.

140. See "Week-end 'chinois' à Montargis," *Le Monde,* May 26, 2005.

141. National Security Advisor to President Jimmy Carter.

142. The Dalai Lama, *Au loin la liberté: mémoires,* trans. Eric Diacon (Paris: Fayard, 1990), 332–333.

143. Wei Jingsheng, "Qingchen: A Twentieth-Century Bastille," *Exploration* (March 1979).

144. A Tibetan born in 1922 in eastern Tibet, he founded the Tibetan Communist Party when he was seventeen. Accused of nationalism, in 1960, he was placed in solitary confinement in Beijing for eighteen years. Rehabilitated later, he is the author of *Witness to Tibet's History* (New Delhi: Paljor, 2007).

PART 2. THE MIDDLE PATH, OR THE CHALLENGE OF PEACE, 1980–1990

1. Avalokiteshvara in Sanskrit, Chenrezi in Tibetan.

2. Traditional chasuble dress.

3. See Sofia Stril-Rever, *Kalachakra, un mandala pour la paix*, photos by Matthieu Ricard (Paris: La Martinière, 2008).

4. Interview by Sofia Stril-Rever in Jetsun Pema and Sofia Stril-Rever, *Enfants du Tibet* (Paris, Desclée de Brouwer, 2000), 204.

5. Or "Island of the Mahayana Teaching."

6. Hypothesis of Juchen Namgyal, former prime minister of the government in exile and head of the Tibetan delegation. Cf. Claude Arpi, "Interview with Kasur Thubten Namgyal Juchen," March 15, 1997, www.claudearpi.net.

7. Originally designed to house the relics of the Buddha, *stupa*s have become the main monuments of Tibetan Buddhism, now containing the relics of spiritual masters as well as texts and sacred objects.

8. Arpi, "Interview with Kasur Thubten Juchen Namgyal."

9. Tubten Khétsun, *Memories of Life in Lhasa Under Chinese Rule* (New York: Columbia University Press, 2008), 286.

10. Arpi, "Interview with Kasur Thubten Juchen Namgyal."

11. In front of the Jokhang, where public teachings, theological debates, and religious ceremonies had once taken place.

12. Arpi, "Interview with Kasur Thubten Juchen Namgyal."

13. See Jing Jun, "Socioeconomic Changes and Riots in Lhasa," report cited in Warren Smith, *Tibetan Nation: A History of Tibetan Nationalism and Sino-Tibetan Relations* (New Delhi: Rupa & Co., 2009), 568.

14. Quoted in Robert Barnett and Shirin Akiner, *Resistance and Reform in Tibet* (Bloomington: Indiana University Press, 1994), 288.

15. Arpi, "Interview with Kasur Thubten Juchen Namgyal."

16. Approximately 60 meters wide by 45 high.

17. Jetsun Pema, *Tibet, mon histoire*, interviewed by Gilles Van Grasdorff (Paris: Ramsay, 1996), 173.

18. Ibid., 188.

19. Ibid., 179.

20. Ibid., 192.

21. Ibid., 188.

22. Letter made public by the Dalai Lama in September 1993. See full version in *Tibetan Review* XXVIII, no. 10 (1993): 9–14.

23. Tsering Shakya, *The Dragon in the Land of Snows: A History of Modern Tibet Since 1947* (New York: Columbia University Press, 1999), 388.

24. See the report of the International Campaign for Tibet, "Forbidden Freedom," 1990, 48.

25. Prime minister and project manager of the economic policies of Deng Xiaoping.

26. Wang Xiaoqiang and Bai Nanfeng, *The Poverty of Plenty* (Basingstoke: Macmillan, 1991), 146.

27. Excerpt from the article "Tibet Changes in a Quarter Century," *Beijing Review*, April 9, 1984.

28. The highest number of deaths in an ethnic conflict, after that of Sudan, which caused 1.9 million deaths. The number of deaths is distributed as follows: 173,221 in prisons and labor camps; 156,758 by execution; 342,970 of famine; 432,705 in fights and insurrections; 92,731 under torture, and 9,002 by suicide—count published in the report "Tibet: The Facts," submitted to the UN Commission on Human Rights in 1990. This estimate cannot be verified due to lack of access to the archives of the People's Liberation Army.

29. See Tom Grunfeld, *The Making of Modern Tibet* (Armonk, N.Y.: M. E. Sharpe, 1987), and Barry Sautman, *Contemporary Tibet* (Armonk, N.Y.: M. E. Sharpe, 2006).

30. Figures from the report "New Majority: Chinese Population Transfer into Tibet," published by Tibet Support Group UK, 1995. According to the 1982 census, the Han accounted for 14 percent of the population of Lhasa, but this percentage does not include the migrant workers or the Chinese military.

31. In *Le Quotidien du peuple*, November 22, 1952.

32. See Embassy of the People's Republic of China in New Delhi, "Movement Westward," February 4, 1985.

33. See Reuters news agency dispatch, Beijing, June 30, 1987.

34. "Great Prayer Festival," instituted by Tsongkhapa, held from the third to the twenty-fifth day of the first lunar month.

35. Fayard, 1973.

36. In *Le Matin*, August 1, 1985. A. Robbe-Grillet is one of the most translated foreign novelists in China.

37. *Le Nouvel Observateur*, January 19, 1985.

38. *La Vie* 2107 (January 16–22, 1986).

39. Palden Gyatso, *Fire Under the Snow: Testimony of a Tibetan Prisoner*, trans. Tsering Shakya (New York: Grove Press, 1998), 290.

40. *Government Resolutions and International Documents on Tibet*, published by the Office of Information and International Relations of the Central Tibetan Secretariat in Dharamsala, 1989, 23.

41. Ibid., 25.

42. See "China Objects to Two U.S. Amendments," *Beijing Review*, July 6, 1987, p. 7.

43. See "Tibet population Develops," *Beijing Review*, August 17, 1987, p. 21.

44. See the discussion of this point in Smith, *Tibetan Nation*, 600.

45. Writer, activist for human rights, feminist, and ecologist, she organized in Bonn the first conference on human rights violations in Tibet in 1989, bringing together forty experts and six hundred participants. Follower of nonviolence, which she defined as a way of life and not a philosophy, she was murdered on October 1, 1992, under conditions that are unclear to this day. The Dalai Lama praised "her compassion for the oppressed, the weak and the persecuted."

46. On this point see the analysis developed by Olivier Masseret, "Une diplomatie parlementaire pour le Tibet?" *Revue d'histoire diplomatique* 4 (2001): 351–374.

47. See *State Department Bulletin* 87, no. 212 A (December 1987).

48. See *Beijing Review*, October 5, 1987.

49. The largest monastery of the Geluk order of the Dalai Lamas, northwest of Lhasa, founded in 1416 by a disciple of Tsongkhapa.

50. Pilgrimage street encircling the Jokhang that became the rallying point for independence demonstrations in the 1980s.

51. Palden Gyatso, *Fire Under the Snow*, 290.

52. See *Beijing Review*, October 12, 1987, and the analysis of Smith, *Tibetan Nation*, 604.

53. See Blake Kerr, *Sky Burial: an Eyewitness Account of China's Brutal Crackdown in Tibet* (Ithaca, N.Y.: Snow Lion, 1993), which describes the conditions of this investigation; "Women's Rights: Violation in Tibet," summary document published by the Tibetan Centre for Human Rights and Democracy, November 2000.

54. Speech of the Panchen Lama on January 23, 1989. In the presence of Hu Jintao, he deplored the communist dogmatism that caused the destruction of religious Tibet and threatened the survival of the country. Five days later, on January 28, he died of a heart attack. Many Tibetans believe that his frankness and courage cost him his life and that he was poisoned at the behest of Chinese authorities. The Dalai Lama asked permission to send a delegation to dedicate a religious Kalachakra ceremony in his memory, which was refused.

55. Because he feared for his life after having released sensitive information to students.

56. Information published in *The Observer* (London), August 13, 1990.

57. A graduate of the highly selective Qinghua University, the Chinese MIT, one of the most gifted politicians of his generation. His appointment to Tibet signaled that the Party leadership wanted to bring an end to the instability in the region.

58. Also called "Middle Way," in reference to the wisdom that avoids extremes and that the Buddha presented in his first sermon as the true path to enlightenment.

59. AFP, dispatch dated July 28, 1988.

60. Statement from the *Daily Telegraph,* June 23, 1988.

61. Embassy of the People's Republic in New Delhi, press release, September 28, 1988.

62. One of the founders of the Unrepresented Nations and Peoples Organization (UNPO), of which he was general secretary from 1991 to 1998 (www.unpo.org).

63. See *Politique de la Voie médiane*, a publication of the Department of Information and International Relations of the Tibetan government in exile, 2007. This information is contradicted by Tsering Shakya's description of the shock of the Strasbourg Proposal (*The Dragon in the Land of Snows*, 423).

64. Embassy of the People's Republic in New Delhi, press release, May 17, 1989.

65. Circular of the PCC Central Committee, dated January 28, 1987, in *Chinese Law and Government* 21, no. 1 (1988): 23.

66. One of the largest and most populated cities of southwestern China.

67. Capital of Xinjiang, in northwest China; its name in Uighur means "Beautiful Pasture."

68. Nickname of Deng Xiaoping.

69. Extract from the speech of Zhao Ziyang to the students on May 19, 1989, posted on www.lautrefraternite.com.

70. Future Nobel Peace Prize winner, then literature professor at Beijing University.

71. Charlie Cole report for the BBC.

72. See the front page of the *Quotidien du peuple*, October 11, 1989.

73. The Dalai Lama, *La verité est la seule arme dont nous disposons*, trans. Lise Medini (Paris: Points, 2009), 47.

74. Ibid., 45.

75. The Dalai Lama, *My Spiritual Journey*, with Sofia Stril-Rever, trans. Charlotte Mandell (New York: HarperOne, 2010), 20.

PART 3. CULTURAL GENOCIDE IN TIBET: THE HEADLONG RUSH, 1991–2010

1. President of the Alliance for a Democratic China, an association based in the United States.

2. Born in Hangzhou, China; sculptor and publisher, permanent resident of the United States and citizen of New Zealand, where he emigrated in 1998.

3. Tibetan Buddhism took root in Mongolia in the thirteenth century.

4. Leader of the National League for Democracy, which in 1990 won the legislative elections with more than 80 percent of the vote. Wife of the British Tibetologist Michael Aris.

5. Seven in number: Prime Minister and Ministers of Information and International Relations, Education, Religion and Culture, Security, Finance, and Health.

6. Ten representatives for the three traditional provinces of Tibet, two for each of the four schools of Buddhism and Bön, two for the diaspora in Europe, one for the diaspora in North America, one to three for culture, science, or community service.

7. H.R. 63, May 16, 1989.

8. Speech given at Yale University, October 9, 1991.

9. Ani Patchen, *Et que rien ne te fasse peur!*, trans. Carisse Busquet (Paris: Nile, 2000), 215.

10. Private monastery of the Dalai Lamas.

11. His Holiness the Dalai Lama, *Sagesse anciene, monde moderne,* trans. Eric Diacon (Paris: Fayard, 1999), 127.

12. Tenzin Choedrak, *Le Palais des arcs-en-ciel*, interviewed by Gilles Van Grasdorff (Paris: Albin Michel, 1998).

13. Claude Arpi, *Dharamsala and Beijing, the Negotiations That Never Were* (New Delhi: Lancer Publishers, 2009), 147.

14. See *Foreign Relations Authorization Act*, House of Representatives Conference Report 102–238, October 3, 1991.

15. See the full report of these different points in Warren Smith, *Tibetan Nation: A History of Tibetan Nationalism and Sino-Tibetan Relations* (New Delhi: Rupa & Co., 2009), 623.

16. S. Res. 107, April 18, 1991, in *Congressional Record*, vol. 137, no. 57.

17. See "U.S. and China, Policies Toward Occupied Tibet," U.S. Senate, July 28, 1992, 5, cited in Smith, *Tibetan Nation*, 623.

18. See "Draft Constitution for a Federal China," *Tibet Press Watch* 7 (February 1994).

19. Economics professor at Zhongshan University in Guangzhou, deported for his involvement in the democratic movement in 1989, released in 1992, and arrested again in 1993.

20. Harry Wu, *Laogai: The Machinery of Repression in China* (New York: Umbrage Books, 2009), 66.

21. See the filmed testimonies and portraits on www.appelaumondedudalailama.com.

22. "To control others, first control yourself," *TAR Internal Party Study Document* 2 (September 1989): 21 ff.

23. See the analysis of Jean-Marie Domenach, *Approches de la modernité* (Paris: Ellipse, 1986).

24. The PAP includes two million men.

25. See China's Public Relations Strategy on Tibet in "Classified Documents from the Beijing Propaganda Conference," International Campaign for Tibet, 1993, 23.

26. Ibid., 33.

27. Ibid., 40.

28. Open letter, June 22, 1993, signed by the deputy head of the Chinese delegation, Jin Yongjian.

29. The United States guaranteed through this clause that no Chinese goods would be taxed a duty exceeding the tariffs on exports from other nations.

30. Vienna Conference, 1993.

31. Ibid.

32. Speech published by the Xinhua News Agency, July 26, 1994.

33. Quotations extracted from the *Quotidien du Tibet*, Lhasa, July 4, 1994.

34. Simon Leys, *Les Habits neufs du président Mao. Chroniques de la Révolution culturelle* (1971; reprint, Paris: Gérard Lebovici, 1989), extract from the preface to the new edition.

35. See Human Rights Watch, "Cutting Off the Serpent's Head: Tightening Control in Tibet," 1996, 155.

36. See Part 1, note 56.

37. See "Funérailles sous surveillance," *Actualités tibétaines* 2 (2nd Quarter 1996): 7.

38. See "London Statement on Tibet," Report of the Conference of International Lawyers on Issues Relating to Self-Determination and Independence for Tibet, London, January 6–10, 1993.

39. This Tibetan name means "all fortune and happiness gathered here."

40. The biggest festival of the Buddhist calendar that celebrates the birth, enlightenment, and passing into supreme nirvana of the Buddha on the full moon of the fourth lunar month.

41. Reconstruction based on Smith, *Tibetan Nation*, and Gilles Van Grasdorff, *Panchen Lama, otage de Pékin* (Paris: Ramsay, 1998).

42. Program of November 5, 1995, quoted by Smith, *Tibetan Nation*, 651.

43. Declaration of the Fifth Congress of the Communist Party, August 30, 1995.

44. The Patriotic Buddhist Association of China was founded in 1953 in Beijing in order to "unify all Buddhists in the country in accordance with the standards of the socialist state."

45. See the November 27, 1995, edition of the *Times International*.

46. Quoted in *Actualités tibétaines* 1 (December 1995): 27.

47. Words of Gyaincain (Gyantsen) Norbu, President of the Autonomous Region, March 10, 1996.

48. Agence France-Presse, news release, May 3, 1996.

49. See *My Spiritual Journey*, with Sofia Stril-Rever, trans. Charlotte Mandell (New York: HarperOne, 2010).

50. "How the Dalai Clique Has Sabotaged the Work About the Reincarnation of the Tenth Panchen Lama," Radio Lhasa, November 3, 1995.

51. Samuel P. Huntington, "The Clash of Civilizations?" *Foreign Affairs* (Summer 1993): 22–49 (trans. from: "Le choc des civilizations," *Commentary* 66 [Summer 1994]: 238–252), whose thesis was developed in the book *Le choc des civilizations* (Paris: Odile Jacob, 2000).

52. "How the Dalai Clique Has Sabotaged the Work About the Reincarnation of the Tenth Panchen Lama."

53. Thesis defended by Smith, *Tibetan Nation*, 653.

54. The Treaty on the Non-Proliferation of Nuclear Weapons (NPT) was concluded in 1968 and ratified by China when it became a member of the Security Council of the UN. It aims to reduce the nuclear arms race by limiting the application of nuclear energy for civilian purposes. The Chinese tests were against the resolution of May 11, 1995, of the UN, urging the countries possessing nuclear weapons not to use them against the signatory countries of the NPT who were not equipped.

55. Statement at Harvard University, October 1997.

56. *Actualités tibétaines* 6 (2nd Quarter 1997): 8.

57. *Tibet Times*, August 31, 1999, quoted in *Actualités tibétaines* 20 (September 2000).

58. According to the editorial of *Tibet Daily*, April 5, 1996.

59. *Actualités tibétaines* 21 (1st Quarter 2001): 30.

60. Public discourse on January 1, 1998, cited in *Tibet Information Network News Review* 27 (1999).

61. The Tibetan Centre for Human Rights and Democracy in Dharamsala took a census on March 1997 of the expulsion of over 2,800 monks and nuns, 165 arrests, and 9 deaths from mistreatment. In 1998, the Centre counted 7,156 expulsions and 327 arrests.

62. *Tibet Information Network News Review* 27 (1999): 30.

63. Press release dated August 5, 1997.

64. Confidence collected by the delegates of the Tibet Information Network in August 1998.

65. See the AFP wire quoted in *Actualités tibétaines* 5 (1st Quarter 1997): 7.

66. See the *Tibet Info* report quoted in *Actualités tibétaines* 13 (1st Quarter 1999): 4.

67. *Questions and Answers About China's National Minorities* (Beijing: New World Press, 1985), 165.

68. Former East Turkestan was attached to China in 1949.

69. December 2, 2010, interview with S. Stril-Rever.

70. See Introduction, note 29.

71. Interview, December 2, 2010.

72. Signed in Paris, at the Palais de Chaillot, by the fifty-eight Member States of the UN General Assembly, on the eve of the adoption of the Universal Declaration of Human Rights. R. Lemkin was the chief editor and creative writer of the text.

73. Interview December 2, 2010.

74. Entitled "Tibet: Human Rights and the Rule of Law."

75. Arjia Rinpoche, *Surviving the Dragon: A Tibetan Lama's Account of 40 Years Under Chinese Rule* (Emmaus, Penn.: Rodale, 2010), vii.

76. Method adopted for the retrocession of Hong Kong and considered for the annexation of Taiwan, but that the Chinese government refuses to implement in Tibet.

77. Head of the Tibetan government in exile.

78. Speech given at the Earth Summit in Rio de Janeiro, June 6, 1992.

79. Speech January 14, 2003.

80. Speech of the Dalai Lama at the Royal Institute of International Affairs, London, May 19, 1991, in *Actualités tibétaines* 3 (3rd Quarter 1996): 40.

81. Ibid.

82. Wang Xizhe, writer and democrat, was in 1974 the coauthor of a political manifesto stuck on the walls of Canton, entitled "On Socialist Democracy and Legal System." He was arrested in 1981 and again in 1996 for commemorating the seventh anniversary of Tiananmen.

83. See the text of the manifesto in *Perspectives chinoises* 37 (1996).

84. Director of the Independent Federation of Chinese Students and Scholars based in Washington.

85. See *Actualités tibétaines* 6 (2nd Quarter 1997): 18.

86. See the full text in ibid., 7.

87. "Ninth Annual Conference on External Propaganda on Tibet," June 12, 2000. Report posted on the website www.freetibet.org.

88. Chinese spiritual movement founded in 1992, with nearly ninety million practitioners. Declared illegal by the Party since 1999, it is subject to severe persecutions against its members.

89. See note 87.

90. Declaration made at the Consultative Conference of the National Committee of the Chinese people and taken by the Xinhua News Agency, March 4, 1999.

91. Founded in Kham in the late 1970s by the ecumenical religious leader Khenpo Jigme Phuntsok.

92. Main Gelug monastery of the Amdo region, it was founded in 1560 on the birthplace of Tsongkhapa, then enlarged by the Third Dalai Lama.

93. Symbol of authority of the Karmapas, this cap is woven with the hairs of dakinis, female deities of enlightenment.

94. To the east of Sikkim.

95. Expected respectively in Beijing in August 2008 and in Shanghai in June 2010.

96. Politician born in Nyarong in eastern Tibet in 1949 and exiled in India in 1959; Special Representative of the Dalai Lama to the United States, responsible for the dialogue with China.

97. See the report on the negotiations between Dharamsala and Beijing on the website www.cecc.gov.

98. Tibetan nongovernmental organization founded in Dharamsala, October 7, 1970, in the presence of the Dalai Lama, which brings together more than seventy thousand Tibetans in exile across the world. Very active in defending the cause of Tibet, it is committed to the principle of nonviolence. The congress has seventy-seven regional branches located in India, Nepal, Bhutan, Norway, Canada, France, Japan, Taiwan, Australia, United States, and Switzerland.

99. "Interview with Prof. Samdhong Rinpoche," Olivier Masseret, *Actualités tibétaines* 19–20 (3rd Quarter 2000): 48.

100. See map, p. 323.

101. *Tibet Press Watch* (May 1994): 16.

102. Quoted in Arpi, *Dharamsala and Beijing, the Negotiations That Never Were*, 179.

103. Another body, the Steering Group for Poverty Reduction, observed that these statistics artificially regrouped the population in administrative bodies to further minimize the number of poor in Tibet.

104. *Height of Darkness: Chinese Colonialism on the World's Roof*, Dharamsala, Department of Information and International Relations (DIIR), 2001.

105. Ibid., 1.

106. UN, Article 1 of the Declaration on the Right to Development, December 4, 1986.

107. "Tracking the Steel Dragon," Report of the International Campaign for Tibet, 2008, 9, www.savetibet.org/documents/reports/tracking-steeldragon.

108. Arpi, *Dharamsala and Beijing, the Negotiations That Never Were*, 189.

109. See Philippe Broussard and Danielle Laeng, *La Prisonnière de Lhassa. Ngawang Sangdrol, religieuse et résistante* (Paris: Stock, 2001), and the documentary *Ngawang Sangdrol, une prisonnière au Tibet*, directed by Marie Louville, France 2, 2005.

110. See Thomas Kuhn, "Hu Jintao Philosophical Policies," March 13, 2010, www.esnips. com.

111. Constantly increasing, they reached ninety thousand in 2009, according to official statistics.

112. Culminating at 8,201 meters, the sixth highest mountain in the world situated in the Himalayas 20 kilometers from Everest. To the west lies the Nangpa-la Pass, where the Nepal-Tibet border passes, at 5,716 meters.

113. Or "Wheel of Time." Teaching system considered as supreme in Tibetan Buddhism, which describes the integration of humans and the cosmos.

114. The incident is reported by Ursula Gautier in *Le Nouvel Observateur*, January 17, 2008.

115. Paris: Flammarion, 2008.

116. "La Chine, machine à laver les cerveaux," interview by Ma Jian Ursula Gauthier, *Le Nouvel Observateur*, January 17, 2008.

117. Or East Turkestan. Area located in northern China.

118. Or East Turkestan Independence Movement (Etim), placed by the United States on the list of international terrorist organizations.

119. Geluk monastery of the order of the Dalai Lamas, founded in 1419 by a disciple of Tsongkhapa.

120. In the monasteries of Lutsa and Ditsa, in a Tibetan settlement area integrated into the Chinese province of Qinghai.

121. At the Labrang and Ngaba monasteries, in a Tibetan settlement area integrated into the Chinese provinces of Gansu and Sichuan.

122. International broadcasting service of the U.S. government, with radio and television broadcasts in Tibetan.

123. Finalized by General Dong Guishan, specialist in altitude combat and in cons-sub-version, commander-in-chief of Chinese forces in Tibet since 2004. He was respon-

sible for the Chengdu Military Region, which coordinates the military command in Tibet.

124. Narrated by Roger Faligot, *Les Services secrets chinois, de Mao aux JO* (Paris: Nouveau Monde Editions, 2008).

125. Built by King Songtsen Gampo in the seventh century.

126. Muslims, who own most of the butcher shops in the capital.

127. Official figures, reported by James Miles, in *The Economist*, March 20, 2008. Miles was the only Western news correspondent witnessing the week of violence in Lhasa.

128. Expression of Tsering Woeser.

129. Posted on the website www.highpeakspureearth.com, November 16, 2008.

130. *Like Gold That Fears No Fire*, a collection of essays by Tibetan writers, published by International Campaign for Tibet, October 2009, 51.

131. Ibid., 54.

132. Ibid., 62.

133. Secretary of the Party and captain of the Armed Police in the Autonomous Region.

134. Quoted in Pascale Nivelle, "La jeune garde tibétaine soured à la moderation du Dalai Lama," *Libération*, March 20, 2008.

135. Robert Barnett, "Les manifestations au Tibet du printemps 2008," *Perspectives chinoises* 3 (2009).

136. See Michel Bonnin, "La gestion de la crise tibétaine de 2008 par les autorités chinoises," *Perpectives chinoises* 3 (2009): 75.

137. *Actualités tibétaines* 38 (June 2008): 4.

138. Interview with Jonathan Mirsky, *The Observer*, 1987.

139. Andrew Fischer, "The Political Economy of Boomerang Aid in the Tibet Autonomous Region," *Perspectives chinoises* 3 (2009): 42.

140. Statement of the Dalai Lama to James Blitz for the *Financial Times*, May 24, 2008.

141. *Like Gold That Fears No Fire*, 41.

142. http://www.opendemocracy.net/author/li-datong, May 19, 2008.

143. Barnett, "Les manifestations du Tibet du printemps 2008," 23.

144. Born in 1953 in Manchuria, he wrote *Sky Burial: The Fate of Tibet* (Picquier, 2005), after several trips to Tibet between 1995 and 1998. In 1999, he was arrested in Urumqi for his contacts with Uighur opponents and published in 2001 *Xinjiang zhuiji (Memories of Xinjiang)*. He has repeatedly met with the Dalai Lama and reported the interviews in the book *Unlocking Tibet* (Association France-Tibet), 2005. He is married to the Tibetan poet and analyst Tsering Woeser.

145. *Like Gold That Fears No Fire*, 138.

146. Yu Jie, born in 1973, based in Beijing, is the founder of the Chinese branch of the PEN Club, considered a clandestine organization in China. Banned from publishing in his country, he is the author of essays on the human rights movement and the contemporary history of the People's Republic.

147. Marie Holzman, "Comment les intellectuels parlent-ils du Tibet?" *Perspectives chinoises* 3 (2009).

148. *Like Gold That Fears No Fire*, 135.

149. *Like Gold That Fears No Fire*, 135.

150. Lodi Gyari conference, Asia Society, New York, October 8, 2008.

151. This text, which denounced a "decadent totalitarianism," catalyzed the contestation against Soviet communism from 1977 until the Velvet Revolution in Prague in 1989 and the election of President Václav Havel in 1990.

152. Brick wall located along Xidan Street, near Tiananmen Square, where Beijing inhabitants came to read and discuss the *dazibao*, posters with political content written by hand, between November 1978 and December 1979, after the Maoist dictatorship. On December 6, 1979, the Democracy Wall was moved to Chaoyang District, far from the city center, in a closed and paying public park, which allowed the police to easily monitor visits.

153. Press release of the Dalai Lama, Dharamsala, December 12, 2008.

154. *Like Gold That Fears No Fire*, 72.

155. Press release of the Xinhua News Agency, July 6, 2008.

156. Declaration of October 25, 2008, at the Tibetan Children Village.

157. Interview with the author, November 2008.

158. This is the same conclusion reached by the architect of the economic reforms of Deng Xiaoping, Zhao Ziyang: "In reality, it is the Western system of parliamentary democracy which has demonstrated the greatest vitality," he writes in his memoirs. "If we do not take this direction, it will be impossible to manage the consequences of the transition to a market economy in China." However, this judgment contradicts the Chinese leadership, for which the evolution toward the Western political systems is an unthinkable perversion. Zhao Ziyang was under house arrest after Tiananmen until his death in 2005, and wrote his memoirs in secret. Sent abroad surreptitiously, they appeared under the title *Prisoner of State* (New York: Simon & Schuster, 2009)

159. *Like Gold That Fears No Fire*.

160. See International Campaign for Tibet, "Tracking the Steel Dragon," and the film *Meltdown in Tibet* by Michael Buckley, 2009, www.meltdownintibet.com. For this documentary, the director wanted to bring irrefutable evidence by going back to the river sources and by filming the dam works, classified as military-secret, that the Chinese are building.

161. 120 km south of Lhasa; one of the four holy lakes of Tibet; place of pilgrimage dedicated to Padmasambhava.

162. "Diary of Yamdroktso Hydroelectric Project," *Green Tibet Annual Newsletter*, 1995–1996, 30–31.

163. Marie-Line Le Roch, " L'Or bleu tibétain," *Matrices stratégiques*, December 11, 2008.

164. Thirteen dam projects on the Salween had to be postponed due to the demonstrations in Burma provoked by the foreseeable drying up of water resources.

165. Written by hydrologist engineer Li Ling, made public in 2005, and approved by 118 generals and a majority congressman of the National People's Assembly as well as the People's Consultative Conference.

166. "Shuotian Canal" is the name of this huge operation to divert water from the river, by contraction of the toponyms of *Shuo*matan in the Himalayas and *Tian*jing, near Beijing, which it will connect. See map and chart at www.iisc.ernet.in/prasthu/pages/ PP_data/ 98–2.pdf.

167. 325 km east of Lhasa.

168. See *Le Quotidien du peuple,* quoted by Claude Arpi, claudearpi.blogspot.com.

169. Professor at the Centre for Policy Research in New Delhi, he is the author of the study "The Sino-Indian Water Divide," Project Syndicate, 2009, www.project-syndicate.org.

170. See the analysis of Jonathan Watts, correspondent of the *Guardian* in Beijing, *When a Billion Chinese Jump: How China Will Save Mankind—Or Destroy It* (London: Faber & Faber, 2009).

171. See the report "Quarante mille nomades déplacés," *Qinghai News Network*, October 31, 2004.

172. See propaganda films posted on www.cctv.com about March 28.

173. See the analysis of Melvyn Goldstein, *A History of Modern Tibet, 1913–1951* (Berkeley: University of California Press, 1989).

174. See the discussion of this point in A.-M. Blondeau and K. Buffetrille, eds., *Le Tibet est-il chinois?* (Paris: Albin Michel, 2002), 135.

175. Ibid., 356.

176. See the interview with Marie Holzman on the website appelaumondedudalailama. com.

177. Tibetan name of the Dalai Lama, meaning "Precious Victor."

178. *Like Gold That Fears No Fire*, 58.

179. Quoted in an interview with the Dalai Lama published in the journal *Politique internationale* 126 (2010).

180. Interview by Régis Soubrouillard, Monday, October 11, 2010, for the site Marianne2.fr.

181. *Zhongguo Yingdi Wen Jiabao* (Hong Kong, 2010).

182. See François Hauter, *Planète chinoise* (Paris: Carnets Nord, 2008), 96.

183. See the coverage broadcast in the journal *Arte*, "Chine: Confucius au service du régime," March 4, 2010, www.arte.tv/fr.

184. Recent incidents reported on the website www.highpeakspureearth.com.

185. Maxim created in the fourth century B.C. by Shang Yang, minister of one of the seven Warring States, which exhibited masterfully the functioning of the absolute state based on this principle. See *Le Livre de Prince Shang,* presented and translated by Jean Lévi (Paris: Flammarion, 2005).

186. See *Column*, Prague, January 23, 2010.

187. Ibid.

188. Declaration of October 8, 2010.

189. See "A Human Approach to World Peace," www.dalailama.com.

190. *My Spiritual Journey*, 106.

191. See in particular the statements made at the occasion of the launch of the International Decade for the Promotion of a Culture of Non-violence and Peace in 2001.

192. Speech given on the occasion of the forty-eighth anniversary of the Tibetan Children's Village in Dharamsala, October 25, 2008.

193. Ibid.

194. The Dalai Lama informed the press on September 4, 1993, that the "final solution" for Tibet had been put on the agenda of a high-level secret conference of the authorities of the People's Republic of China, held under the code name 512 in Wenjiang, in Sichuan, on May 12, 1993. When I asked whether this was the first occurrence of the expression in the words of Chinese officials, Jigmey Namgyal, secretary of Kalon Tripa Samdhong Rinpoche, prime minister of the Tibetan government in exile, answered: "It is possible that the 'final solution' had already been used by the Chinese authorities, but we only identified it at the conference of 1993" (communication to S. Stril-Rever, December 16, 2010).

195. Harry Wu, interview with S. Stril-Rever, Washington, February 9, 2010.

196. Speech given on the occasion of the forty-eighth anniversary of the Tibetan Children's Village in Dharamsala, October 25, 2008.

197. We have chosen to quote in full the speech of March 10, 2011, as it was the last one delivered by the Dalai Lama as the political leader of the Tibetan government in exile.

198. Songtsen Gampo (609–650) founded Lhasa and unified Tibet, extending his kingdom to the borders that were still his in the early twentieth century.

199. Name meaning translation of the commentaries, collection of 240 works clarifying the Buddha's teachings collected in the Kanjur.

200. Quoted by Nirmal C. Sinha in *Bulletin of Tibetology* 3 (1968): 13–27.

201. Message of His Holiness the Dalai Lama to the Fourteenth Assembly of the Tibetan People's Deputies, March 19, 2011, cf. official website of the Dalai Lama, http://www.dalailama.com/messages/retirement/message-to-14th-assembly.

202. Or the Dalai Lama and the Panchen Lama.

203. Last Testament of the Thirteenth Dalai Lama, cf. the website of Claude Arpi, http://www.claudearpi.net/maintenance/uploaded_pics/testament.pdf.

204. Tenzin Gyatso, Fourteenth Dalai Lama, quoted by Glenn Mullin in *Mystical Verses of a Mad Dalai Lama* (Wheaton, Ill.: Quest Books, 1994).

205. Message of His Holiness the Dalai Lama to the Fourteenth Assembly of the Tibetan People's Deputies; cf. note 5.

206. Ibid.

207. Satyagraha or "the force of truth" is a form of nonviolent protest in the name of truth and justice, as defined by Gandhi, and can go up to the sacrifice of one's life.

208. *Le Nouvel Observateur*, March 29, 2012, report in Tongren (Tibet) by Philippe Grangereau.

209. Dorje Kyab and Dorje Samdup immolated themselves in Ngaba, eastern Tibet, on November 7, 2012.

BIBLIOGRAPHY

BOOKS

BIOGRAPHIES/TESTIMONIES

Agloe, Chukora Tsering. *Song Offerings*. New Delhi: Foundation for Universal Responsibility of HHDL, 2009.

Bagdro. *A Hell on Earth: A Brief Biography of a Tibetan Prisoner*. New Delhi: Ven. Bagdro, 1998.

Dutt, Subimal. *With Nehru in the Foreign Office*. Calcutta: Minerva, 1977.

Gopal, Sarvepalli. *Jawaharlal Nehru: A Biography*. London: Jonathan Cape, 1976.

Gyatso, Palden. *Fire Under the Snow: Testimony of a Tibetan Prisoner*. Trans. Tsering Shakya. New York: Grove Press, 1998.

Holzman, Marie, and Bernard Debord. *Wei Jingsheng, un Chinois inflexible*. Paris: Bleu de Chine, 2005.

Khétsun, Tubten. *Memories of Life in Lhasa Under Chinese Rule*. New York: Columbia University Press, 2008.

Mayank, Chhaya. *Dalai Lama: The Revealing Life Story*. New York: Doubleday, 2007.

Norbu, Thubten. *Tibet Is My Country*. London: Dutton, 1961.

Pachen, Ani. *Sorrow Mountain: The Journey of a Tibetan Warrior Nun*. New York: Kodansha USA, 2002.

Panikkar, Kavalam Madhava. *In Two Chinas: Memoirs of a Diplomat*. London: Allen & Unwin, 1959.

Pema, Jetsun, with Sofia Stril-Rever. *Enfants du Tibet*. Paris: Desclée de Brouwer, 2000.

Rato, Khyongla. *My Life and Lives: The Story of a Tibetan Incarnation*. New York: E. R. Button, 1977.

Shakabpa, Tsultim N. *Dead People Talking*. New Delhi: Paljor, 2008.

Tapongtsang, Adhe. *Ama Adhe, the Voice That Remembers*. Boston: Wisdom, 1997.

Tsundue, Tenzin. *Kora*. Paris: L'Harmattan, 2008.

Wang Lixiong and Woeser. *Unlocking Tibet*. Paris: France-Tibet, 2005.

Wei Jingsheng. *The Courage to Stand Alone: Letters from Prison and Other Writings*. New York: Penguin, 1998.

Woeser, Tsering. *Forbidden Memory*. W-Freedom Books, 2013.

Wu, Harry. *Bitter Winds: A Memoir of My Years in China's Gulag*. New York: Wiley, 1995.

Wu, Hongda Harry. *Laogai: The Chinese Gulag*. Trans. Ted Slingerland. Boulder, Colo.: Westview Press, 1992.

Zhao Ziyang. *Prisoner of the State: The Secret Journal of Premier Zhao Ziyang*. London: Simon & Schuster, 2010.

THE DALAI LAMA

Ethics for the New Millennium. New York: Riverhead, 2001.

Freedom in Exile. New York: Harper One, 2008.

Kindness, Clarity and Insight. With Jeffrey Hopkins. Ithaca, N.Y.: Snow Lion, 1984.

My Land and My People. New York: Grand Central Publishing, 2008.

The Leader's Way. With Laurens van den Muyzenberg. London: N. Brealey, 2009.

A Policy of Kindness. With Sidney Piburn. Delhi: Motilal Banarsidass, 1990.

My Spiritual Journey. With Sofia Stril-Rever. Trans. Charlotte Mandell. New York: Harper-One, 2010.

Towards a True Kinship of Faiths: How the World's Religions Can Come Together. New York: Harmony, 2010.

The Universe in a Single Atom. New York: Harmony, 2006.

HISTORY OF CHINA

Gao, Yuan. *Born Red: A Chronicle of the Cultural Revolution*. Stanford: Stanford University Press, 1987.

Goodman, David. *Deng Xiaoping*. London: Cardinal Books, 1990.

Tuttle, Gray. *Tibetan Buddhists in the Making of Modern China*. New York: Columbia University Press, 2005.

Wu, Harry. *Laogai: The Machinery of Repression in China*. Brooklyn, N.Y.: Umbrage Editions, 2009.

HISTORY OF TIBET

Ardley, Jane. *The Tibetan Independence Movement: Political, Religious and Gandhian Perspectives.* New York: Routledge, 2002.

Arpi, Claude. *Dharamsala and Beijing, the Negotiations That Never Were.* New Delhi: The Lancer, 2010.

Barnett, Robert. *Resistance and Reform in Tibet.* London: Hurst & Company, 1994.

Bultrini, Raimondo. *The Dalai Lama and the King Demon: Tracking a Triple Murder Mystery Through the Mists of Time.* New York: Tibet House US, 2013.

The Dolgyal Shugden Research Society. *Dolgyal Shugden: A History.* New York: Tibet House US, 2014.

Dunham, Mikel. *Buddha's Warriors.* New Delhi: Penguin Books India, 2005.

Goldstein, Melvyn. *A History of Modern Tibet, 1913–1951.* Berkeley: University of California Press, 1989.

Heath, John. *Tibet and China: Nonviolence Versus State Power.* London: Saqi, 2009.

Laird, Thomas. *Une histoire du Tibet.* Trans. Christophe Mercier. Paris: Plon, 2007.

Lelung Tulku Rinpoche XI. *A Drop from the Marvelous Ocean of History.* Trans. Tenzin Dorjee. New York: Tibet House US, 2013.

Rockhill, William W. *The Dalai Lamas of Lhasa and Their Relations with the Manchu Emperors of China.* Dharamsala: Library of Tibetan Works and Archives, 1998.

Smith, Warren. *Tibetan Nation: A History of Tibetan Nationalism and Sino-Tibetan Relations.* New Delhi: Rupa & Co., 2009.

Thurman, Robert. *Why the Dalai Lama Matters: His Act of Truth as the Solution for China, Tibet, and the World.* New York: Atria Books/Beyond Words, 2011.

Van Praag, Michael van Walt. *The Status of Tibet.* Boulder, Colo.: Westview Press, 1985.

Wang Lixiong and Tsering Shakya. *The Struggle for Tibet.* London: Verso, 2009.

Wangyal, Phuntsok, with Melvyn Goldstein. *A Tibetan Revolutionary.* Berkeley: University of California Press, 2004.

SAMDHONG RINPOCHE

Uncompromising Truth in a Compromising World. With Donovan Roebert. Ilford: World Wisdom, 2006.

TIBETAN ART AND CULTURE

Conant, Danny, and Catherine Steinmann. *Vanishing Tibet.* Ed. Thomas F. Yarnall. New York: Tibet House US, 2008.

Dunnington, Jacqueline. *The Tibetan Wheel of Existence.* Ed. Thomas F. Yarnall and Robert A.F. Thurman. New York: Tibet House US, 2000.

Kistler, Brian. *Visions of Tibet: Outer, Inner, Secret*. New York: Tibet House US, 2006.

Leidy, Denise Patry, and Robert A.F. Thurman. *Mandala: The Architecture of Enlightenment*. New York: Tibet House US, 1997.

Rhie, Marylin M., and Robert A.F. Thurman. *A Shrine for Tibet: The Alice S. Kandell Collection*. New York: Tibet House US, 2010.

————. *Wisdom and Compassion: The Sacred Art of Tibet*. New York: Tibet House US, 2000.

————. *Worlds of Transformation: Tibetan Art of Wisdom and Compassion*. New York: Tibet House US, 1991.

TIBETAN BUDDHISM

Āryadeva. *Āryadeva's Lamp That Integrates the Practices (Caryāmelāpakapradīpa): The Gradual Path of Vajrayāna Buddhism According to the Esoteric Noble Tradition*. Trans. Christian K. Wedemeyer. New York: American Institute of Buddhist Studies, 2007.

Cakrasamvara Tantra (Tibetan and Sanskrit Editions). Trans. and ed. David Gray. New York: American Institute of Buddhist Studies, 2012.

The Cakrasamvara Tantra: The Discourse of Śrī Heruka (Śrīherukābhidhāna). Trans. David B. Gray. New York: American Institute of Buddhist Studies, 2007.

Great Treatise on the Stages of Mantra (Sngags rim chen mo) Chapters XI–XII: (The Creation Stage). Trans. Thomas F. Yarnall. New York: American Institute of Buddhist Studies, 2013.

Hackett, Paul G. *A Catalogue of the Comparative Kangyur (bka' 'gyur dpe bsdur ma)*. New York: American Institute of Buddhist Studies, 2012.

Henning, Edward. *Kālacakra and the Tibetan Calendar*. New York: American Institute of Buddhist Studies, 2007.

The Kālacakratantra: The Chapter on the Individual Together with the Vimalaprabhā. Trans. Vesna A. Wallace. New York: American Institute of Buddhist Studies, 2004.

The Kālacakra Tantra: The Chapter on Sādhanā Together with the Vimalaprabhā Commentary. Trans. Vesna A. Wallace. New York: American Institute of Buddhist Studies, 2010.

Losang Chokyi Gyaltsen (The First Panchen Lama). *The Essence of the Ocean of Attainments (dngos grub kyi rgya mtsho'i snying po): Explanation of the Creation Stage of the Glorious Secret Union, King of All Tantras*. Trans. Yael Bentor and Penpa Dorjee. New York: American Institute of Buddhist Studies, 2013.

Maitreya, Vasubandhu. *Maitreya's Distinguishing the Middle from the Extremes (Madhyāntavibhāga): Along with Vasubandhu's Commentary (Madhyāntavibhāga-bhāṣya)*. Trans. Mario D'Amato. New York: American Institute of Buddhist Studies, 2012.

Maitreyanātha/Āryāsaṅga and Vasubandhu. *The Universal Vehicle Discourse Literature (Mahāyānasūtrālaṁkāra): Together with Its Commentary (Bhāṣya)*. Trans. Lozang Jamspal. Ed. Robert A.F. Thurman. New York: American Institute of Buddhist Studies, 2004.

Nāgārjuna, Candrakīrti. *Nāgārjuna's Reason Sixty (Yuktiṣaṣṭikā): With Candrakīrti's Commentary (Yuktiṣaṣṭikāvṛtti)*. Trans. Joseph Loizzo. New York: American Institute of Buddhist Studies, 2007.

The Range of the Bodhisattva (Ārya-bodhisattva-gocara): A Mahāyāṇā Sūtra. Trans. Lozang Jamspal. New York: American Institute of Buddhist Studies, 2010.

The Range of the Bodhisattva, A Mahayana Sutra (Byang Chub Sems Dpa'i Spyod Yul): The Teachings of the Nirgrantha Satyaka. Trans. Lozang Jamspal. New York: American Institute of Buddhist Studies, 2010.

Ratnakīrti's Proof of Momentariness by Positive Correlation (Kṣaṇabhaṅgasiddhi Anvayātmikā). Trans. Joel Feldman and Stephen Phillips. New York: American Institute of Buddhist Studies, 2011.

Tsong Khapa Losang Drakpa. *Brilliant Illumination of the Lamp of the Five Stages (Rim lnga rab tu gsal ba'i sgron me): Practical Instructions in the King of Tantras, The Glorious Esoteric Community.* Trans. Robert A.F. Thurman. New York: American Institute of Buddhist Studies, 2010.

JOURNALS

Actualités tibétaines, 1–41 (1996–2010). Quarterly journal published by the Bureau du Tibet.

Perspectives chinoises, "L'impasse au Tibet," 3 (2009). Journal published by the Centre d'études français sur la Chine contemporaine, CEFC, Hong Kong.

OFFICIAL PUBLICATIONS

"The Communist Party as Living Buddha." International Campaign for Tibet, 2007.

"Dangerous Crossing, Conditions Impacting the Flight of Tibetan Refugees." International Campaign for Tibet, 2008.

"Defying the Dragon: China and Human Rights in Tibet." Tibet Information Network, 1991.

"Discrimination Against Women: The Convention and the Committee." Dharamsala, Tibetan Center for Human Rights and Democracy, 2009.

"Facts About the 17-Point Agreement." Dharamsala, Department of Information and International Relations, Tibetan Government in Exile, 2001.

"A Great Mountain Burnt by Fire." International Campaign for Tibet, 2009.

"His Holiness the XIV Dalai Lama on Environment." Dharamsala, Department of Information and International Relations, Tibetan Government in Exile, 2009.

"Human Rights Situation in Tibet." Dharamsala, Tibetan Center for Human Rights and Democracy, 2009.

Like Gold That Fears No Fire. International Campaign for Tibet, 2010.

"The Mongols and Tibet." Dharamsala, Department of Information and International Relations, Tibetan Government in Exile, 1996.

"Quelle solution politique pour le Tibet?" Documents de travail du Sénat, octobre 2009.

"The Question of Tibet and the Rule of Law." International Commission of Jurists, 1959.

"A 60-Point Commentary." Dharamsala, Department of Information and International Relations, Tibetan Government in Exile, 2008.

"Tibet and the Chinese People's Republic." Investigation Committee of the International Commission of Jurists, 1960.

"Tibet and Manchu." Dharamsala, Department of Information and International Relations, Tibetan Government in Exile, 2001.

"Tibet, un peuple en danger." Paris, Working Papers of the Senate, October 2008.

"Tibet Protests in 2008–2009." Dharamsala, Tibetan Center for Human Rights and Democracy, 2010.

"Tibet: Proving Truth from Facts." Dharamsala: Department of Information and International Relations, Tibetan Government in Exile, 1993.

"Tibet Under Communist China." Dharamsala, Department of Information and International Relations, Tibetan Government in Exile, 2000.

"Tracking the Steel Dragon." International Campaign for Tibet, 2010.

WEBSITES

This book: www.appelaumondedudalailama.com.

Official website of the Dalai Lama: www.dalailama.com.

Tibetan government in exile: www.tibet.com.

Reportage on Tibet in exile: www.tibetnews.com.

Tibetan writers: www.highpeakspureearth.com; www.tibetwrites.org; www.autour-himalaya.over-blog.com; www.universeofpoetry.org/tibet.shtml; www.tenzintsundue.com

International Campaign for Tibet: www.savetibet.org.

Tibet Information Network: www.tibetinfo.net.

Voice of Tibet: www.vot.org.

Radio Free Asia: www.rfa.org.

Laogai Research Foundation: www.laogai.org.

INDEX

policies, 153; fear as foundation of society, 74, 76–77; and "Five Principles of Peaceful Coexistence," 24, 32, 89–90; French approval of leadership, 145–46; Great Leap Forward, 28, 43; and history of Tibet, 87–89, 231, 243; incursion into India (1962), 2, 10, 34, 37–39; international pressure on, 31–32, 154, 178, 203–5, 249, 285–86, 292; international pressure, responses to, 31–32, 34, 44, 154, 178; liberalization under Deng Xiaoping, 106–8; Mao's proclamation of the PRC, 49–50; maps, 321–23; military supremacy as reason for other countries' acceptance of Tibetan occupation, 9, 23; minority groups in, 50, 204, 230, 232, 256, 261–63, 295 (*see also* Inner Mongolia; Xinjiang); "most favored nation" status, 203, 207–8, 235; nuclear weapons (*see* nuclear weapons); and Olympic Games, 254, 265, 270, 278, 286; "one country and two systems" method, 237, 340n76; protests and demonstrations of 1986, 144; Qing dynasty, 88; rapprochement with U.S., 77–80, 89–90, 109; repression in, 141, 166, 172, 175–78, 185, 199–203; Sino-Indian relations, 8–10, 23–24, 26, 249–50; Sino-Soviet tensions, 76–77, 79; Sino-Tibetan dialogue (*see* Sino-Tibetan dialogue); "socialism with Chinese characteristics," 105–7; Soviet support for, 23; Tiananmen Square massacre (1989), 166, 172, 175–78, 185, 199, 200, 215, 299; as UN member, 78–80; water shortage, 289–91. *See also* Chinese occupation of Tibet; Chinese policies on Tibet; dissidents and democrats, Chinese; People's Liberation Army; *specific heads of state*

Chinese occupation of Tibet: as colonial occupation, 14, 21, 41, 43, 77, 139–40, 147, 214; and Cultural Revolution (*see* Cultural Revolution); death toll from, 59, 141, 147–48; development projects (*see* development projects);

and disruption of agriculture, 35–36; dissatisfaction of younger generation of Tibetans, 91, 301–3; and economic development (*see* economic development); and end of buddhocracy, 54, 63, 121–22, 308; establishment of Autonomous Region, 49, 51–52, 54; and exploitation of natural resources, 95–96, 135–36, 139–40, 142, 250–52, 275; foreign observations of conditions, 146, 147, 153–54, 161, 191, 248, 258–59, 269; governance of Autonomous Region, 51–52; hardships, 83–84, 93, 100, 123–24, 167 (*see also* environmental degradation of Tibet; famine; forced labor; genocide; prisons and prisoners; repression; repression, religious; torture); Hu Yaobang's reforms, 123–25, 129–30; and liberalization under Deng Xiaoping, 107–8, 122–23; militarization of Tibet, 25, 29, 38–39, 49, 53, 67; and omens, 101–2; self-delusion of executives and administrators, 116–17, 119, 123, 127, 275–76, 278; and Seventeen-Point Agreement (1951), 6–8, 13, 237, 305, 326n16; and "social paradise" rhetoric, 91–93; UN resolutions ignored, 21, 31–32; violations of promises to respect Tibetan autonomy, 9, 261–62; violations of promises to respect Tibet's unique nature, 237; and violations of the Chinese constitution, 14, 51–52, 232

Chinese policies on Tibet: agriculture policies and resulting famine, 35–37, 95; belief that time is on the side of the Chinese, 221–22, 245, 283; campaigns to eliminate the influence of the Dalai Lama, 232–34 (*see also* propaganda, Chinese); and Chinese fears of balkanization, 206; and Committee for the Stabilization of the Situation, 213; continued religious repression in spite of liberalization (1980s), 132–35; criticism of, from Chinese intellectuals and democrats, 14, 205–6, 208, 229,